Magnitudes: -1 0 1 2 3 4 (5)

○ Open Cluster   □ Nebula

⊙ ○ Variable   ⊕ Globular Cluster   ○ Galaxy

THE PETERSON FIELD GUIDE SERIES®

Edited by Roger Tory Peterson

Part of the Hercules Cluster of galaxies   (National Optical
Astronomy Observatories/Kitt Peak National Observatory)

THE PETERSON FIELD GUIDE SERIES®

A Field Guide

to the

Stars and Planets

THIRD EDITION

JAY M. PASACHOFF
Director, Hopkins Observatory
Williams College

This edition succeeds an earlier book by
DONALD H. MENZEL
Late Director, Harvard College Observatory

With Monthly Star Maps and Atlas Charts by
WIL TIRION

HOUGHTON MIFFLIN COMPANY
Boston • New York

Address correspondence to Field Guides, Houghton Mifflin Co.,
2 Park Street, Boston, Massachusetts 02108

Library of Congress Cataloging in Publication Data

Pasachoff, Jay M.
    A field guide to the stars and planets / Jay M. Pasachoff ; with
monthly star maps and atlas charts by Wil Tirion.
        p.   cm. -- (Peterson field guide series®)
Rev. ed. of: A field guide to the stars and planets / Donald H. Menzel
and Jay M. Pasachoff . 2nd ed. 1983.
    Includes bibliographical references and index.
    ISBN 0-395-53764-9. -- ISBN 0-395-53759-2 (pbk.)
    1. Astronomy--Observers' manuals. II. Title.   III. Series.
QB64.P37   1992
523--dc20   92-17556
                                                                CIP

Printed in the United States of America

HOR 10 9 8 7 6 5

For information about this and other Houghton Mifflin
trade and reference books and multimedia products, visit
The Bookstore at Houghton Mifflin on the World Wide Web
at http://www.hmco.com/trade/.

EDITOR'S NOTE

Although we expect never to publish a guide to the creatures of outer space, it is inevitable that the Field Guide series should include this volume on recognition of the stars and planets.

Among all the inhabitants of the planet earth, we alone have systematically considered the heavenly bodies. We have given names to the constellations and charted their relative positions and movements. Although we formerly believed that we alone were able to navigate by celestial means, now we know that nocturnal bird migrants sometimes take their direction by means of an innate ability to read the night sky and from magnetic fields.

In recent years, in the age of rocket-launched satellites, more people than ever before have become aware of space and want to know what is out there. The tiny dots of light in the night sky may be obscured by city fog, but on clear nights they cannot fail to stir the inquiring mind.

The first step in astronomy, as in zoology, is to put names to things, to identify them. This Field Guide will facilitate the process and is equally usable for the observer depending on the naked eye, the binocular, or a small astronomical telescope. Unlike most of the books in the Field Guide series, which tend to be regional in scope or at least confined to a single continent, it may be used at any point on the earth's surface and on any day of the year. In line with the general policy of the other Field Guides, emphasis has been put on new and simplified techniques of recognition.

Much has happened in the science of astronomy during the decade since the second edition was issued. Also, techniques and equipment used by amateur astronomers to observe the sky have improved greatly. Further, planets move, double stars move around each other, eclipse series continue, and other celestial events listed in tables in the book change so that new information must be and has been provided. This edition also includes many new color plates.

The book should present no problems to beginners interested in finding their way around in the heavens, but at the same time the completeness of its charts and tables should make it a useful tool for serious amateurs and even for professionals.

It is a joy to thumb through the book while relaxing in an armchair, but inasmuch as it is basically a Field Guide, put it to practical use. Use it on clear nights to interpret the free show put on by the heavens.

Roger Tory Peterson

The solar corona appears as a pearly white halo around the moon in the few minutes of totality during a total solar eclipse.
(Jay M. Pasachoff)

ACKNOWLEDGMENTS

It is a pleasure in this third edition to enhance the usefulness and beauty of *A Field Guide to the Stars and Planets*. In the book, I present tours of the stars, the planets, the sun, the moon, and other objects in the heavens. It provides introductory descriptions and figures, graphs, and tables of information in a form useful to novices, while providing this and other information in style and quantity useful for those already quite knowledgeable in astronomy. I am very pleased to have had the complete cooperation of the celestial cartographer Wil Tirion. For the second edition, he not only drew a complete set of Atlas Charts covering the whole sky but also prepared monthly star maps to a new design calculated to make them easier to use than previous styles. He also executed supplemental charts for variable stars and other special objects. For this third edition, he added the position of the major supernova that erupted in 1987, improved the shape of the Large Magellanic Clouds, and made other corrections and improvements.

I appreciate the assistance of Cathryn Baskin for her work on the preparation of descriptive material to accompany the Atlas Charts and on other phases of the previous edition of the book. Robert Murphy of Scientia, Inc., has not only prepared his standard Graphic Timetables showing the positions of the planets but also specially designed Graphic Timetables for this Field Guide to show which of the brightest stars, clusters, variable stars, nebulae, and galaxies are suitable for viewing in various seasons. Robert A. Victor of the Abrams Planetarium of Michigan State University expertly prepared descriptive material to accompany the Graphic Timetables. The fruits of Ewen Whitaker's lengthy study of the moon show in the material he has prepared to accompany the moon maps. Robert Argyle of the Royal Greenwich Observatory and Robert Tanguay have provided updates and new information on double stars. I thank them all.

I appreciate the special cooperation of Leif Robinson, William Shawcross, Robert W. Sinnott, Alan Hirshfeld, Dennis di Cicco, and others at *Sky & Telescope*, and thank them for their permission to reprint some of the tables that they have carefully prepared as part of their *Sky Catalogue 2000.0*.

I thank Dennis di Cicco and Ben Mayer for their helpful advice on many phases of observing, for reading large sections of the text, and for the photographs they provided. I also thank Walter Bennett for his verification, with telescopes, of much of the descriptive material that accompanies the Atlas Charts.

Charles Case and the National Geographic Society were kind enough to allow me to use the special moon maps beautifully prepared in a cooperative effort of the National Geographic Society and the U.S. Geological Survey.

I thank many people who assisted with various phases of the preparation of the book, including Naomi Pasachoff for her work on the history and mythology of the constellations, Janet Akyüz Mattei (American Association of Variable Star Observers) for providing information on variable stars, and Ewen Whitaker (Lunar and Planetary Laboratory, University of Arizona) for providing descriptive information and photographs of the moon. I also thank Brian Marsden and Daniel Green (Harvard-Smithsonian Center for Astrophysics) and John Bortle for comments on minor bodies of the solar system, Peter Millman (Herzberg Institute of Astrophysics, National Research Council of Canada) for material on meteor showers, Robert A. Victor (Abrams Planetarium, Michigan State University) for comments on observing, Robert D. Miller for calculations, Jean Meeus for information about eclipses, and George Lovi for information about mapping.

A Field Guide is obviously based on the work of many people carried out over an extended period of time. Users wanting to go beyond this book to do more observing would naturally refer to such magnificent sources as *Sky & Telescope* and *Astronomy* magazines each month, and Robert Burnham's *Celestial Handbook.* Walter Scott Houston's long runs of columns in back issues of *Sky & Telescope* remain a valuable source. We have consulted all these sources in preparation of this Field Guide. These and other sources are listed in the bibliography.

Liz Stell has worked expertly and diligently with me in bringing this third edition to publication. At Houghton Mifflin, Harry Foster has edited the Field Guide series for some time, and continues to make vital contributions to the success of this and other books in the series. Susan Kunhardt is editor of this third edition, and Anne Chalmers is the designer. I also recall with thanks the contributions to the second edition of Barbara Stratton and Cope Cumpston.

My wife, Naomi, and our children, Eloise and Deborah, continue to inspire me. All of them have also helped read proof.

It is a pleasure for me to be associated with my late professor, Donald H. Menzel, in this Field Guide. He had written the first edition; I only regret that he did not live to participate in the entirely new books that we are calling the second and third editions. I learned so much from him on a series of eclipse expeditions, and so much from his example as a scientist dealing with other aspects of astronomy, that I am forever in his debt. I also thank Florence K. Menzel, who with her husband has been kind and helpful to me since my student days. My entire family continues to value Mrs. Menzel as a friend.

I hope that you all enjoy *A Field Guide to the Stars and Planets.* It would be nice if it were error-free, but no book is. I do hope that you will write me with your comments, to point out errors, or with observing suggestions that are not in this book.

Jay M. Pasachoff
Hopkins Observatory, Williams College
Williamstown, Mass. 01267

CONTENTS

TABLES AND APPENDICES

Tables

Appendices

HOW TO USE THIS BOOK

With this *Field Guide to the Stars and Planets* in hand, we hope it will be pleasant for you to find your way around the sky. We have tried to make it easy for you to identify what you see; at the same time, we will try to demonstrate the excitement of our current understanding of the universe.

General organization. We begin by describing in Chapter 1 a framework for observing the heavens. We describe how to tell stars from planets, how to identify the brightest stars, and how to find a few of the most prominent groupings of stars in the sky. Then, in Chapter 2, we give you a brief tour around the heavens, season by season. This chapter can be used together with the Monthly Sky Maps that follow in Chapter 3. No special knowledge or equipment is needed to use these maps. For observers in the northern hemisphere, a set of four maps appears for each month: two maps—one with constellation outlines and one without—for use when facing north, and a similar pair for use when facing south. For observers in the southern hemisphere, a set of two maps shows stars with constellation outlines.

Next, in Chapter 4, we describe the constellations and the classical myths associated with them. A list of the current constellations (Appendix 1) appears on p. 440.

In Chapter 5, we describe the types of objects that are relatively constant in their places in the sky, including stars, nebulae, and galaxies. We discuss astronomers' current understanding of these objects, including the stages in the life of a star. We also provide information about the times of year when a selection of the most interesting double and variable stars, star clusters, nebulae, and galaxies are visible. In this chapter, we include spectacular photographs of some of the most beautiful objects. The celestial objects that *move* with respect to the stars—the moon, the sun, the planets, comets, meteors, and asteroids—have their own chapters later on.

Two types of objects of special interest to those observing the sky are double and variable stars, so Chapter 6 is devoted to them. This chapter includes charts and tables that will enable you to find many examples of these stars.

Chapter 7 is an Atlas of the entire sky, broken down into 52 charts, drawn by Wil Tirion. All of the brightest stars and constellations are shown, as on the Monthly Sky Maps; however, the Atlas Charts provide a more detailed look at each region of the sky. Although many of the objects on the Atlas Charts can be seen with the naked eye or with binoculars, you will find the charts even more interesting if you have access to a small or medium-sized telescope. Each chart shows not only stars but also nebulae, galaxies, and a wide variety of other celestial objects. Descriptions of these objects and photographs of some of them accompany the Atlas Charts. A list of nonstellar, deep-sky objects, the Messier Catalogue, precedes the charts, along with a table showing the region of sky covered by each chart. A visual key to the Atlas Charts appears on the endpapers of this book.

To use the Atlas, first locate an object of interest, using either the Monthly Sky Maps or the celestial coordinates listed in the Messier Catalogue or in other tables in this guide. Then turn to the Atlas Chart where your object is shown. Alternatively, you may choose to survey the whole area shown on a chart with a telescope.

As part of the introduction to the Atlas Charts, we explain the symbols used on the charts and the names used for stars and other types of astronomical objects. We also briefly explain the system of celestial coordinates—right ascension and declination—used to indicate the locations of objects in the sky. The apparent position of objects in the sky changes slightly over the years because the earth wobbles as it spins; we have compensated for this by drawing the charts and calculating the tables in this book for the year 2000, rather than using the 1950 positions most often shown in earlier books.

Though the positions of distant objects in the universe change only slightly in the sky, the positions of the moon, most of the planets, and the sun change quite drastically in the course of the year. The path the sun follows through the sky in the course of a year is called the *ecliptic;* it is indicated by a dotted line on the Monthly Sky Maps and the Atlas Charts. The moon and the planets never stray far from this line.

Chapter 8 describes the moon and includes 10 maps of its craters and other features of its surface. Chapter 9 explains how to locate the planets in the sky and how to predict when they will be visible. Chapter 10 describes what each planet is like and what you may see if you observe it with binoculars or with a telescope.

Chapter 11 describes comets, with special attention to Halley's Comet and its 1985-86 appearance. Chapter 12 discusses meteors and lists meteor showers that you can see in the sky at different times of the year. Meteors usually flash across the sky and asteroids move too slowly for their motion to be apparent. Lights that appear to move slowly and steadily across the sky are usually airplanes or—particularly in the couple of hours after sunset or before sunrise—artificial satellites in orbit around the earth. Chapter 13 discusses asteroids, the minor planets.

In Chapter 14, we turn from the nighttime sky to the daytime sky and discuss the major object that is visible all day—the sun. We discuss not only the everyday sun and how to observe it, but also how to observe at a total solar eclipse and why a total eclipse is so glorious. We also describe annular eclipses, like the one visible from the southeastern United States on May 10, 1994, and how to observe them.

Finally, in Chapter 15, we discuss technical aspects of the positions of objects in the sky and ways to tell time by the sun and the stars. We also discuss calendars and their history.

At the end of the book, we present some information on telescopes, a glossary, suggestions for additional reading, an extensive set of tables, and an index.

Illustrations. Rendering the sky in a book is a difficult problem because it requires stretching and squashing the curve of the sky onto a flat page. We have solved this problem in a new and improved way in collaboration with our celestial cartographer, Wil Tirion. Our Monthly Sky Maps are presented in a special projection that makes the maps easy to use while distorting the shapes of the constellations as little as possible.

In addition to the 72 Monthly Sky Maps and the 52 Atlas Charts by Wil Tirion, 10 detailed maps of the moon's surface, prepared in a collaborative effort of the National Geographic Society and the U.S. Geological Survey, enhance *A Field Guide to the Stars and Planets.* A number of Graphic Timetables have also been provided to help you determine when stars, planets, and other celestial objects will be visible above the horizon. All photographs in this guide are oriented with north at the top (unless otherwise indicated), to make it easy for you to compare them with the Atlas Charts in Chapter 7.

Some observing hints. Your eyes have to be dark-adapted to see the sky well. This process may take 5 to 15 minutes after you go outside from a lighted room. As you watch the sky during this time, more and more stars will become visible. To maintain your adaptation to darkness, cover the front of your flashlight with red plastic.

Telescopes. The observing suggestions in this guide are designed to help you locate interesting objects in the sky, whether or not you have a telescope. When we mention a "small telescope" in this guide, we are referring to one with a lens less than 4 in. (10 cm) in diameter. (Most telescopes that small have lenses rather than mirrors.) A "medium-sized telescope" has a lens or mirror about 4-10 in. (10-25 cm) in diameter. For those interested in purchasing a telescope, we include a discussion of some telescopes that are popular with amateurs starting on p. 488, along with a list of telescope manufacturers.

How to use this book. If you want to survey the stars and constellations, use Figures 3 and 4 in Chapter 1 and the Monthly Sky Maps in Chapter 3. The seasonal tours in Chapter 2 illustrate how the constellations seem to move across the sky as the earth rotates around the sun. The Graphic Timetable of the Brightest Stars (Fig. 2) in Chapter 1 will show you when the brightest stars visible from mid-northern latitudes will be above the horizon.

If you see a bright object in the sky and want to identify it, the first step is to determine whether it is a star or a planet (see p. 5). Then check the Graphic Timetable of the Brightest Stars in Chapter 1 or the Graphic Timetables of the Planets in Chapter 9, to see which bright stars or planets are visible on your date of observation. Or you can refer to the Monthly Sky Maps in Chapter 3. You can plot the positions of the brightest planets on the Monthly Sky Maps in Chapter

3 (or on the Atlas Charts in Chapter 7) using Appendix 11, which shows the planets' longitudes along the ecliptic.

If you are using binoculars or a telescope and want to look at a variety of interesting objects, such as double and variable stars, star clusters, nebulae, or galaxies, use the Graphic Timetables in Chapter 5 to find out which ones will be visible on your date of observation. Then turn to the Atlas Charts in Chapter 7, where observing notes supplement detailed charts of each region of the sky. Each chart is oriented with north at the top. Remember that binoculars give a right-side-up image, but most telescopes give inverted images compared with the way celestial objects appear to the naked eye.

If you want to observe the planets with a telescope, refer to the information in Chapter 10.

If you want to see a meteor shower, use the table in Chapter 13.

If you want to know how to observe the sun safely, or when and where the next solar eclipse will occur, refer to Chapter 14.

If you want to know how to tell time by the sun and the stars, refer to Chapter 15.

Some comments on photographing the sky with still cameras or with video cameras appear on pp. 21–23.

So, if you work your way through this book, you will have made friends with the sun in the morning and the stars at night.

Younger readers and other novice observers may enjoy my two brief introductory shirt-pocket-size books, *First Guide to Astronomy* and *First Guide to the Solar System.* Both are in the Peterson First Guide series. Readers wanting more thorough treatments of contemporary astronomy may be interested in my textbook, *Astronomy: From the Earth to the Universe,* which is available for purchase through Hopkins Observatory, Williams College, Williamstown, MA 01267. Send a self-addressed, stamped envelope for information.

1

A FIRST LOOK AT THE SKY

We hope you will use this book to become familiar with the sky. Finding your way around the sky is like finding your way around a large city—it is easy if you are familiar with the streets and have navigated there before, but otherwise it takes some time to become familiar with routes and shortcuts. In this first chapter of *A Field Guide to the Stars and Planets,* we will assume that you are new to observing the heavens. We will start from scratch and show you some of the basic ways that you can orient yourself when observing. Our focus here will be on some of the most prominent stars and constellations that you can observe with the naked eye or binoculars.

Before you begin to observe the nighttime sky, you should know which way north, south, east, and west are. If you don't know the compass directions for the place from which you are observing, though, you can find them with the aid of the Big Dipper and the North Star, Polaris (see p. 11).

One of the first things you will notice when you start to study the sky is that stars and other objects are of different brightnesses. Perhaps the easiest way to determine what is what in the sky is to take advantage of this fact. Except for the moon, the brightest objects in the nighttime sky are some of the planets. The planets change their position slightly from night to night with respect to the stars in the background; in Chapter 9 we show you how to locate the planets on any given night.

Three characteristics tell you quickly if an object is a planet.

1. **Brightness.** Some of the planets simply appear too bright to be stars. Venus, the brightest planet, is an example. It can never be very far away from the sun in the sky, so whenever an extremely bright dot of light—the "evening star"—appears ·in the sky toward the west after sunset, or in the morning sky toward the east before sunrise—the "morning star"—it is probably Venus. It is often the first bright object visible, before any stars appear in the sky. Mercury also appears in these areas of the sky around sunrise and sunset, but it never looks as bright as Venus nor gets as far from the sun as Venus does. Mercury appears only during twilight, and Venus never remains visible through the night.

Whenever a very bright yellowish-white point of light appears in the sky in the middle of the night, it is probably Jupiter. Unlike Mercury and Venus, Jupiter is not always near the sun in the sky; it can appear high in the sky at midnight. Mars and Saturn can also appear far from the sun in the sky, rising well after sunset; Mars rarely out-shines Jupiter, though, and the brightness of Saturn never equals that of Jupiter or Venus. Mars can often be distinguished by the fact that it has a slight but distinct reddish tinge. Saturn, on the other hand, appears to be yellowish. The other planets are too faint to be seen with the naked eye.

2. ***Twinkling.*** Planets usually seem to shine steadily, while stars twinkle. Twinkling is an effect of turbulence in the earth's atmosphere: the atmosphere bends the starlight passing through it, and, as small regions of the atmosphere move about, the intensity of a star's light varies slightly but rapidly. Observations with a telescope would also reveal that a star appears to move around slightly. The reason why stars twinkle and planets do not is that stars are so far away that they look like points even when viewed through large telescopes. Planets, though, are close enough to earth that their telescopic images are tiny disks. As the light from each different part of a planet's disk twinkles, it averages out and makes the planet appear relatively steady in both brightness and position.

If the atmosphere is especially turbulent, or if you are looking through an especially large amount of atmosphere (when you are looking at an object low in the sky, for example, making your line of sight pass obliquely through the atmosphere), even planets can seem to twinkle. Under these conditions, the object you are observing may even seem to change in color—when Venus is low in the western sky, it is not uncommon to see it change from greenish to reddish and back again.

3. ***Location.*** All the planets always appear close to an imaginary line across the sky, so objects located far from that line cannot be planets. The line is called the *ecliptic,* and it is followed (more or less) not only by the planets but also by the moon. (The ecliptic is actually the path followed by the sun across the background of stars in the course of the year.) Since the earth is but one of the planets, and since all the planets orbit the sun in approximately the same plane, from our point of view the planets and sun must follow roughly the same line across the sky. The moon orbits the earth at only a slight angle to the plane of the planets, so it too always appears close to the ecliptic. The location of the ecliptic is plotted as a dotted line on the Monthly Sky Maps in Chapter 3, which show how the sky looks to the naked eye at different times.

From northern temperate latitudes, including the continental U.S., Canada, and Europe, the ecliptic crosses the southern part of the sky. This means that any bright objects at the *zenith*—the point directly over your head—or in the northern sky cannot be planets. (There are occasional exceptions to this if you are observing from the southernmost parts of the U.S.)

Now that you know how to tell whether you are looking at a star or a planet, you can look around the sky and identify some of the brightest stars. Some people find it easier to identify a few individual bright stars. Others prefer to locate a few favorite constellations or *asterisms*—a few stars, also roughly in the same direction from us, that are parts of one or more constellations.

Fig. 1-1. The Big Dipper, with an aurora in the sky. Note that the middle star in the handle is double; the fainter star, Alcor, is above the brighter star, Mizar. (Dennis Milon)

Many people can identify one or two specific constellations or asterisms, even though they don't know any other constellations. (This statement holds true for many professional astronomers.) The most prominent asterism in the sky is the Big Dipper, whose seven stars trace out the shape of a dipper in the northern sky (Fig. 1-1). The Big Dipper is an asterism rather than a constellation because it makes up only part of the constellation Ursa Major, the Big Bear (Fig. 2-1, p. 18).

The four stars in the bowl of the Big Dipper make a squarish (actually trapezoidal) shape about 10° across. (Ten degrees is about the width of your fist, if you hold it up at arm's length against the sky.) Curving away from the bowl are the three stars in the handle, which cover another 15°. All the stars in the Big Dipper except the one that connects the handle to the bowl are of about the same brightness, which makes it easy to single out the Dipper in the sky.

Sky observers—including both professional and amateur astronomers—usually express star brightness in magnitudes, the scale of which is described in detail in Chapter 3. The lower the magnitude, the brighter the star. The brightest stars in the sky are magnitude zero (0), or in two cases, magnitudes −0.7 and −1.4, respectively. Figures 1-3 and 1-4 on pp. 12–15 show the brightest stars in the sky; the faintest star shown is magnitude 3.5. The naked eye can see stars about 10 times fainter than this, down to those as dim as 6th magnitude under perfect sky conditions.

One difference between the maps or charts in this guide and the real sky is that all the stars in the sky look like points, even though they have different brightnesses. The charts and maps in this guide represent these different brightnesses (magnitudes) as circles of different sizes.

It is often interesting to begin by identifying the brightest star near the zenith. Table 1 (below) lists the 21 brightest stars in the sky. Opposite that table is a display—a Graphic Timetable—that shows when the brightest stars visible from midnorthern latitudes are passing their highest points in the sky. On any given date, different stars will be overhead at different times of night; the whole sequence changes with the seasons as the earth orbits the sun. The positions of the stars repeat from year to year.

To use the Graphic Timetable of the Brightest Stars (Fig. 1-2), run your finger down the side to find your date of observation, then move across the page to find the time of night when you are observing. You will see the names of the brightest stars that are transiting at about that time. An object *transits* when it passes your *meridian*—the imaginary line passing from the point due north on the horizon through the zenith to the point due south on the horizon.

Table 1: The Brightest Stars in the Sky

Rank	Star	Constellation	Magnitude	r.a. (epoch 2000.0)	dec. (epoch 2000.0)
1	Sirius	Canis Major	−1.46	6^h45^m	−16°43'
2	Canopus*	Carina	−0.72	6^h24^m	−52°42'
3	Rigil Kent*	Centaurus	−0.27 (dbl)	14^h40^m	−60°50'
4	Arcturus	Boötes	−0.04	14^h16^m	+19°11'
5	Vega	Lyra	+0.03	18^h37^m	+38°47'
6	Capella	Auriga	+0.08	5^h17^m	+46°00'
7	Rigel	Orion	+0.12 (dbl)	5^h15^m	−8°12'
8	Procyon	Canis Minor	+0.38	7^h39^m	+5°14'
9	Achernar*	Eridanus	+0.46	1^h38^m	−57°14'
10	Betelgeuse	Orion	+0.50 (var)	5^h55^m	+7°24'
11	Hadar*	Centaurus	+0.61	14^h04^m	−60°20'
12	Altair	Aquila	+0.77	19^h51^m	+8°52'
13	Aldebaran	Taurus	+0.85 (var)	4^h36^m	+16°31'
14	Acrux*	Crux	+0.87 (dbl)	12^h27^m	−63°05'
15	Antares	Scorpius	+0.96 (var)	16^h29^m	−26°26'
16	Spica	Virgo	+0.98	13^h25^m	−11°10'
17	Pollux	Gemini	+1.14	7^h45^m	+28°02'
18	Fomalhaut*	Piscis Austrinus	+1.16	22^h58^m	−29°37'
19	Deneb	Cygnus	+1.25	20^h41^m	+45°17'
20	Mimosa*	Crux	+1.25	12^h47^m	−59°41'
21	Regulus	Leo	+1.35	10^h08^m	+11°58'

Notes: (dbl) = double star; combined magnitude of components given.
(var) = variable star; brightest magnitude given.
r.a. = right ascension, in hours and minutes (see p. 432).
dec. = declination, in degrees and minutes (see p. 433).
* = star not visible from midnorthern latitudes. The Graphic Timetable (opposite) shows when the brightest northern stars can be seen above the horizon from midnorthern latitudes; the maximum altitude each star reaches above the northern or southern horizon (for observers at 40° N latitude) is also given, in parentheses.

THE GRAPHIC TIMETABLE OF THE HEAVENS
THE BRIGHTEST STARS

—— Blue Stars
- - - - Yellow Stars
—— Red Stars

Note: The angle shown (in parentheses) is the maximum altitude each star reaches above the northern or southern horizon, for observers at 40° N latitude. For every degree your latitude is farther south than 40°, the star's maximum altitude will be 1° further toward the north along your meridian—**i.e.** 1° further from the southern horizon.

Fig. 1-2. Graphic Timetable of the Brightest Stars (© 1982 Scientia, Inc.)

Figure 1-2 also shows how high the stars are in the sky, in degrees above the horizon, at their time of transit, for an observer at 40° N latitude. This *altitude* above the horizon is the highest point that each star reaches in the arc it traces across the sky. For example, Sirius, the brightest star in the sky, reaches a maximum of 33° above the southern horizon—slightly more than $1/3$ the altitude of the zenith. Since your fist covers about 10° of sky (when you place your thumb flat on the outside of the fist and hold it at arm's length), you can mark off the altitude above the horizon in 10° segments. You may want to verify first that about nine of your fists indeed cover 90° from horizon to zenith.

In the region near the ecliptic, a bright object could be a star or a planet. When looking in this part of the sky, do make sure you know which planets are up—above the horizon. (The Graphic Timetables in Chapter 9 provide this information.)

Figures 1-3 and 1-4 are pairs of sky maps centered on the north celestial pole and on the south celestial pole, respectively. The *celestial poles* are the imaginary points where the earth's axis, if extended, would meet the celestial sphere. The north and south celestial poles lie above the earth's north and south poles respectively. As the earth rotates, the sky appears to rotate in the opposite direction around the celestial poles. The sky thus seems to rotate once around the celestial poles every 24 hours. Midway between the celestial poles is the *celestial equator*, which lies on the celestial sphere, above the earth's equator. The celestial equator separates the northern and southern halves of the sky.

Figure 1-3 shows the northern half of the celestial sphere, and is spread across two pages with some overlap between. This map is centered on the north celestial pole. Below that pole is the Big Dipper. Since the sky appears to rotate around the north or south celestial pole (depending on which hemisphere you are in), whichever pole you can see always remains at a constant height in the sky. (If you are observing from a latitude of 40° N on earth, the north celestial pole will always be tilted up 40° above due north on the horizon; if you are observing from a latitude of 30° N on earth, the pole will always be tilted up 30°, etc.) Observers at midnorthern latitudes will see the Big Dipper appear to revolve around the north celestial pole every 24 hours. For these observers, the Big Dipper is close enough to the north celestial pole that it will never set, and is thus an example of a *circumpolar* asterism.

Figure 1-4 shows the southern half of the celestial sphere. It includes some stars (near the celestial equator) that midnorthern observers can sometimes see, and some stars that never rise above the horizon at northern latitudes.

The Big Dipper is a particularly handy asterism to know because you can follow lines marked out by its stars and trace them across the sky to other interesting objects. Best known is the line marked by the two stars at the end of the bowl, which are known as *the Pointers*. These two stars point to the north star, Polaris; to find Polaris, follow a straight line from the Pointers upward from the bowl of the Dipper and try to imagine the line curving slightly as it follows the curve of the sky for about 30°. (This is three fists' width, or about five times the distance between the Pointers, which are separated by 5^1/$_2$°.) Polaris is at the end of an asterism known as the Little Dipper. None of the stars in the Little Dipper is as bright as the five brightest stars of the Big Dipper; the back two stars of the bowl and the two stars between the bowl and Polaris may be hard to see with your naked eye.

Polaris is not an especially bright star, but it is bright enough to be visible ordinarily. It is the brightest star in that region of the sky, so it is not easily confused with other stars. Polaris is within 1° of the true north celestial pole, and is thus of help not only to navigators at sea but also to land-based amateurs navigating around the sky. If you face Polaris, you are facing north. Thus it is best to find Polaris in order to orient yourself before you use any of the charts or maps in this guide.

If you continue along the arc from the Pointers through Polaris, you will come to the Great Square of Pegasus. This pathway and others that you can follow from one constellation to another are marked with dotted lines on Figures 1-3 and 1-4. For example, instead of following the Pointers to Polaris, you can follow the curve of the Big Dipper's handle over about 30° (three fists' width, thumb included, as always) of sky to the bright star Arcturus. If you can follow the same arc for another 30° without hitting the horizon, you will come to the bright star Spica. To remember this, think of "arc to Arcturus," and then "spike to Spica."

If, instead of finding Polaris, you follow the Pointers or the two stars that form the rear of the Big Dipper's bowl in the opposite direction, you will come to the constellation Leo, the Lion, about 35° away. Leo contains the bright star Regulus, which is located at the base of the "sickle" in Figure 1-3. You can find other stars and constellations using the pathways marked on Figures 1-3 and 1-4; the angles between some of the stars and constellations are listed below.

Table 2: Angles in the Sky

top stars of bowl of Big Dipper	10°
Pointers of the Big Dipper	5^1/$_2$°
Castor and Pollux (in Gemini)	4^1/$_2$°
Great Square of Pegasus, width	17°
end stars of Orion's belt	3°
Orion's belt to Betelgeuse or Rigel	9°
end of Orion's belt to Sirius	21°

Note: *One fist (thumb included flat on top of the pointer finger) covers about 10° of the sky.*

One other asterism is particularly striking and may grab your attention as you scan the sky. This prominent grouping is the straight line marked by three bright stars separated by a total of only

Fig. 1-3. The brightest stars in the northern half of the sky, with arrows showing some of the pathways that help observers locate and identify them. (Wil Tirion)

Magnitudes:

-1 0 1 2 3 4

13

Fig. 1-4 The brightest stars in the southern half of the sky, with arrows showing some of the pathways that help observers locate and identify them. (Wil Tirion)

CETUS

AQUARIUS

Fomalhaut

CAPRICORNUS

Altair

PHOENIX

GRUS

AQUILA

ERIDANUS
Achernar

TUCANA

INDUS

DORADO

HYDRUS

PAVO

RETICULUM

CORONA
AUSTRALIS

False
Dipper

SAGITTARIUS

SERPENS CAUDA

Canopus

PICTOR

-90°

ARA

-80°

Cross

TRIANGULUM
AUSTRALE

SCORPIUS

CARINA

MUSCA
CIR

False Cross

-70°

Hadar

Rigil Kentaurus

OPHIUCHUS

Acrux

-60°

Antares

VELA

CRUX

Mimosa

LUPUS

-50°

CENTAURUS

-40°

-30°

LIBRA

HYDRA

-20°

SERPENS CAPUT

CORVUS

-10°

Spica

EQUATOR

0°

VIRGO

Magnitudes:

-1 0 1 2 3 4

15

3°; it appears at the extreme right of Figure 1-3 and at the extreme left of Figure 1-4. These stars mark the belt of Orion, the Hunter, and appear in the evening sky in winter. One of the stars lies on the celestial equator, which explains why Orion is well into the southern part of the sky for an observer at a midnorthern latitude.

About 10° to the north of Orion's belt is the bright reddish star Betelgeuse, and almost 10° to the south of Orion's belt is the bright bluish star Rigel. (Many people pronounce Betelgeuse as "Beetlejuice"; others say "beh-tel-jooz." Rigel is pronounced "ry-jel," with the accent on the first syllable.) We shall see in Chapter 5 that the colors of stars reveal their temperatures; Betelgeuse is a cool star and Rigel is a hot one. If you follow the line made by Orion's belt to the east (or left, since you are facing south), you will soon come to the bluish-white star Sirius, the brightest star in the sky.

Those who use this Field Guide extensively will quickly find themselves interested not only in stars and constellations but also in double and variable stars, star clusters, nebulae, and galaxies, which are described in Chapters 5 and 6. (A set of Graphic Timetables, showing when a few of the most prominent examples of these objects are visible above the horizon also appears in that chapter.)

Fig. 1-5 Pegasus, from the star atlas of Bayer; the first edition was published in 1603. (Jay M. Pasachoff)

2

A TOUR OF THE SKY

The sun dominates the daytime sky. Sunlight scatters throughout the atmosphere, making the sky blue. This blue sky is brighter than the stars behind it, so we cannot usually see the stars during the daytime, as we shall discuss later in this chapter. When the sky is clear enough, the moon can often be seen even in the daytime, especially if you know where to look. Chapter 8 discusses the phases of the moon and where to find the moon in the sky.

Shortly before sunset or just after sunrise, the sky becomes dark enough for us to see the brightest planets and stars. Venus is the brightest of these objects and is sometimes bright enough to cast noticeable shadows. If you see an exceedingly bright object in the west at or after sunset—the "evening star"—it is usually Venus. If you see an exceedingly bright object in the east before or at sunrise —the "morning star"—it is also usually Venus. A second bright object in the sky, usually even closer to the sun, may be Mercury.

Jupiter, Mars, and Saturn can also be prominent in the sky, and can be quite far from the sun, so planets visible late at night are from this trio. Mars's reddish tinge is subtle, yet not hard to notice even with the naked eye. Saturn's rings are noticeable with a small telescope but are not visible to the naked eye. Jupiter's moons, belts, and Great Red Spot also require a small telescope to be seen. To tell at a glance which planets are visible in the sky on your night of observation, you can use one of the Graphic Timetables in Chapter 9. The characteristics that will help you distinguish the planets from the bright stars nearby are described in Chapter 1.

Beyond the Solar System

As the sky darkens, the brightest stars become visible. In a city, only a few dozen stars may become visible because the sky remains very bright even at night. But far from the haze of pollution and the competing glimmer of city lights, about 3000 stars may be visible to the naked eye. An equal number of stars are hidden beyond the horizon and most can be viewed by waiting through the night or for a different time of year. The rest of the stars become visible only to observers closer to the equator or in the hemisphere opposite to that from which you are observing. The Atlas Charts and descriptions in Chapter 7 show the entire sky—the stars and constellations that are visible from the southern hemisphere as well as the ones that can be seen from the northern hemisphere. However, since most users of this guide are at midnorthern latitudes, much of the following discussion is designed for them.

The region of the sky near Polaris, the North Star, is visible from midnorthern latitudes all through the year. In this region you can easily see the Big Dipper, the asterism that makes up part of the constellation Ursa Major, the Big Bear. In the autumn evening sky, the bowl of the Big Dipper appears right side up, while in the evening sky in the spring, the bowl appears upside-down. Figure 2-1 shows the Big Bear, including the Big Dipper, from the celestial atlas Johann Bayer published in 1603.

On the front side of the bowl of the Dipper, the Pointers point to Polaris, which lies at the end of the handle of the Little Dipper. To find Polaris, follow a line that extends north from the Pointers for about 30°. Thirty degrees is $^1/_3$ of the distance between the horizon and the zenith. Extend your arm upward from horizontal $^1/_3$ of the way toward the zenith to get an idea of 30°. (Also, 30° is about three widths of your hand at the end of your outstretched arm.) The altitude of Polaris about the horizon is equal to your latitude on the earth. For example, if you are at latitude 90°, at the north pole, Polaris is 90° above the horizon, that is, directly overhead.

Polaris remains at this same location in the sky all year. Because

Fig. 2-1 Ursa Major, the Big Bear, from the star atlas of Bayer (1603). The handle of the Big Dipper is in the Bear's tail, and the bowl is in its back. (Jay M. Pasachoff)

its position is stationary, Polaris is visible throughout the year and appears on all the Monthly Sky Maps for the northern hemisphere in Chapter 3. You can use Polaris in all seasons as a reference point for locating other stars. The Big Bear, the Little Bear, and the other circumpolar constellations near Polaris also remain visible above the horizon all year.

Other groups of stars, as we will see below, are visible only during certain seasons of the year. Each night these stars rise above the eastern horizon, travel above and around Polaris, and then set below the western horizon. As the seasons progress, you can see successive groups of constellations making this journey across the sky.

Distances to the Stars

All the stars are so far away that we measure the distance in terms of how long it takes their light to reach us. Light travels very rapidly— 186,000 miles/sec (300,000 km/sec). This is 1,080,000,000 km/hr, 10 million times faster than a car. Light can travel seven times the distance around the earth in a single second, can travel from the moon to the earth in slightly more than a second, and can travel from the sun in eight minutes. Yet light takes over four years to reach us from the nearest star, Proxima Centauri. We call the distance that light travels in a year *one light-year*, and say that Proxima Centauri is thus four light-years away. Only a few dozen stars are within 20 light-years of our sun (see Appendix 4).

To compare stars, it is useful and important to know how bright they would be if they were all at the same distance from us, so that only their intrinsic differences in brightness—how bright they actually are—and not merely their positions affect the result. The standard distance that astronomers use for this purpose is about 32.6 light-years (see p. 21).

All stars move around in space. Astronomers can measure the speed at which they are approaching us or receding from us by measuring their *Doppler shifts*, the slight shifts in color that result from such motion. (You can hear the Doppler shift for sound waves as a change in pitch as an object passes. Doppler shifts for light waves are similar.) But most stars are too far away for us to detect their motions across the sky. For the nearest stars, though, we can detect the *proper motions*, the motions across the sky. The star with the largest proper motion is Barnard's star. It is six light-years away from us. It moves across the sky sufficiently fast that it covers a distance as great as our moon's diameter in only about 180 years (Fig. 2-2). Using the Doppler shift to measure a star's motion toward us or away from us together with the proper motion for the side-to-side direction gives the star's actual velocity in space.

Measuring distances and angles

Astronomers measure the distance to the nearest stars by a method of triangulation called *trigonometric parallax:* the nearest stars appear to move slightly with respect to the more distant stars. To see

Fig. 2-2 The path of Barnard's Star across the sky. This star appears to move across the sky with respect to more distant stars, as marked with the arrow, covering a distance as great as our moon's diameter in about 180 years. (Wil Tirion)

a similar effect, hold your thumb up with your arm outstretched, and look at it first with one eye closed and then, without moving your head, with the other eye closed. Notice how your thumb seems to move slightly across the background. Now do the same thing with your arm bent so that your thumb is closer to your eye—your thumb will appear to move more. Similarly, the more a star appears to move as the earth orbits the sun, the closer it is.

Astronomers figure out how far away from the earth and the sun they would have to be before the distance between the earth and the sun covered an angle of only 1 arc second (where 1 arc second is $1/60$ of 1 arc minute, 1 arc minute is $1/60$ of one degree [1°], and 1° is $1/360$ of the way around the sky). Thus 1 arc second is a tiny angle, $1/3600$ of a degree of arc. The distance at which the angle between the earth and the sun is only 1 arc second is called 1 *parsec* (from the words "parallax," for the method of measuring distance, and "second," for the actual angle). The value of 1 parsec works out to be 3.262... light-years.

The standard distance astronomers use to determine the inherent brightnesses of stars is 10 parsecs. The brightness a star would have at this distance of about 32.6 light-years from us is called its *abso-lute magnitude.* The absolute magnitude is a measure of the intrinsic brightness of the star, how bright the star actually is. By contrast, a star's apparent brightness, how bright it appears to us as opposed to how bright it is intrinsically, is its *apparent magnitude.* A star's apparent magnitude is affected not only by how bright the star is intrinsically but also by how far the star is away from us. In the following chapter, we discuss practical aspects of the magnitude scale.

At the turn of the century, Ejnar Hertzsprung and Henry Norris Russell plotted many stars on the same graph, removing the effect of distance on brightness by either plotting a group of stars that were all at the same distance or by using the absolute magnitudes. When they plotted the temperature on one axis and the magnitude on the other, they found that the points representing most stars fell on the graph in a narrow band—the *main sequence.* The brighter stars are hotter for the most part, and the fainter stars are cooler.

A few stars are brighter than main-sequence stars of the same temperature. These exceptional stars are thus known as *giants,* and a few even more exceptional stars are brighter still, and are known as *supergiants.* Giants and supergiants turn out to be especially large in addition to being especially bright. A few stars are fainter than main-sequence stars of the same temperature. These exceptionally faint stars are known as *white dwarfs.* They turn out to be extraordinarily small for stars—only the size of the planet earth.

Photographing the Sky

Many people like to photograph the sky and the objects in it. Sometimes sky photographs are taken through telescopes, but quite nice photographs of the sky and celestial phenomena can be made with ordinary cameras and lenses mounted on tripods.

Sensitive color films, known as "fast films," are now commonly available that allow photographs to be taken of the constellations in seconds with an ordinary camera and lens. The "faster," or more sensitive, the film, though, the grainier the image usually appears, so each person must make his own tradeoff between speed and grain. A normal, 50-mm, lens on a 35-mm single-lens reflex camera shows a field of view about 50° across, which shows several constellations. The key to a successful constellation photograph is having a sturdy tripod that does not vibrate. It is also usually best to use a cable release or self-timer that allows you to start the exposure without shaking the camera by touching it. Try a series of exposures, such as 1, 2, 4, and 8 seconds. If the lens is opened to its widest, you may see more distortion in the picture—particularly toward its edges—than if the lens is "closed" somewhat. For example, a lens's widest opening may be labelled $f/2$. Each f-stop—1.4, 2, 2.8, 4, 5.6, 8, 11, 16, 21—represents a change in the lens's opening by a factor of 2. So $f/2.8$ lets

Fig. 2-3 Star trails, with an observatory in the foreground. A meteor trail appears at right. (Dale Cruikshank)

in half the light that $f/2$ does. Further, a lens open to $f/4$ lets in half the light of a lens opened to $f/2.8$, and thus one-fourth the light of a lens opened to $f/2$. But the $f/4$ image may prove better, even though the exposure time must be longer, because it may show less distortion.

Sometimes it is fun to take very long exposures, even some hours long, to show the paths of the stars across the sky. When the north celestial pole is in the photograph these star trails show the circles that the stars make around the pole. To take such a picture, put your camera on a sturdy tripod. You must be as far as possible from artificial lights, which would "fog"—or put a uniform glow—on your film and so limit the length of your exposure. To limit the sky fog, it is often best to take star-trail photographs at about $f/11$. Here again, it is for you to experiment. There is no single correct exposure or exposure time.

The moon can be photographed with an ordinary lens. Contrary to what you might expect, it takes a similar photographic lens opening and exposure time to a sunlighted scene on earth. After all, it is about the same distance from the sun as we are. It takes a telephoto lens to show features on the surface of the moon.

You can also use your video camera to photograph the moon, stars, and planets. One advantage of a video camera is that you can see the results right away. Cameras with the telephoto lenses that zoom to the longest focal lengths can fill the screen with the moon. The sensitivity of the camera to faint light levels is more important for including the planets and stars. These show only as points of light; it takes a telescope to show surface features of planets.

To take photographs like most of those in this book, you must attach your camera to a telescope. In those cases, the telescope acts as a lens, so ordinarily you remove the lens from the camera itself. The telescope is set to track the stars, which requires a simple motor that turns the telescope once a day at the rate of the stars. Such telescopes are commercially available. Quite a different hobby, though also an interesting one, is making your own telescope. If you attach an ordinary camera to a tracking telescope, your photograph will show fainter stars and can show the Milky Way.

The electronic revolution is now allowing both amateur and professional astronomers to make images much more quickly than before. Instead of the light from a telescope falling onto film, it now falls onto a light-sensitive silicon chip known as a charge-coupled device (CCD). Similar CCDs are also in common use in consumer electronics, such as video cameras. CCDs record about 50% of the light that hits them, whereas film records only about 1%, so CCDs are 50 times more sensitive than film. Thus an exposure that took almost an hour with film can be made in a minute with a CCD. The CCD's surface is divided into tiny picture elements, or "pixels." Common chips have 512 picture elements in each direction, and so have a total of about 250,000 pixels. When light hits a pixel, a bit of electronic charge results. A computer controls how the charge is moved along a row of pixels, one pixel at a time (thus the charge is "coupled" with that on the adjacent pixel). A computer must process the image. The price of CCDs has declined drastically; consult *Sky & Telescope* or *Astronomy* for ads and reviews.

Seasonal Tours

As you read each tour, please follow along with the suitable Monthly Sky Map in Chapter 3. Many of the invisible pathways in the sky we will follow are shown in Figures 1-3 and 1-4 in Chapter 1.

The Autumn Sky (Monthly Map #8)

In the darkening sky on an autumn evening, the Pointers in the bowl of the Big Dipper point upward toward Polaris. From Polaris, follow the Little Dipper, which is upside-down. An American Indian legend holds that the autumn colors spill out of the Little Dipper at this time of year, making the trees turn bright colors.

Continue along the arc from the Pointers to Polaris for an equal

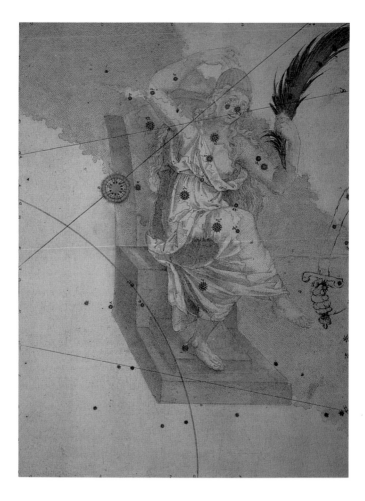

Fig. 2-4 Cassiopeia, from the star atlas of Bayer (1603). The brightest object shown was an exploding star—a supernova—visible only a few decades before the time the chart was drawn. (Mendillo Collection of Astronomical Prints)

distance on the other side of Polaris. You will find a prominent W-shaped constellation, Cassiopeia (Fig. 2-4). This constellation, like most others, was known by the ancient Greeks and was named after a character in Greek mythology. Cassiopeia was married to Cepheus, the King of Ethiopia, who has his own constellation, which is shaped like a house with a peaked roof, lying west of Cassiopeia.

If we continue upward from Cassiopeia, we find the constellation named after Andromeda, who in Greek mythology was Cassiopeia's daughter. In Andromeda, a faint hazy patch of light is sometimes visible to the naked eye. This light actually comes from the center of the Great Galaxy in Andromeda, the nearest galaxy to our own. (A galaxy is an enormous group of billions of stars, plus dust and gas.) The Andromeda Galaxy (M31) is much farther from us than any of the individual stars we see in the sky, so it marks the farthest that we can see with the naked eye. A telescope is necessary to reveal the spiral shape of this galaxy.

Now look high in the sky, in a direction south of Andromeda. You will see four stars marking the corners of a square, known as the Great Square of Pegasus. Pegasus was the flying horse in Greek mythology (Fig. 1-5). It arose from the blood of Medusa after Perseus killed her. One of the stars of the Great Square is actually in the constellation Andromeda.

If it is very dark out, you can also see the Milky Way passing high overhead, directly through Cassiopeia. The Milky Way—a grouping of stars, dust, and gas in our own galaxy—appears as a hazy band across the sky, with ragged edges, dark patches, and rifts (Fig. 2-5). It is actually the gas, dust, and stars of our own galaxy, a disk that we see from a position inside it. Wide-field photographs on fast color film, with your camera mounted on a tripod, will give nice views of the Milky Way.

Moving east from Cassiopeia along the Milky Way, you will come to the constellation Perseus. In Greek mythology, Perseus was a hero who slew the Medusa, flew off on Pegasus (who is conveniently located nearby in the sky), and then from his winged mount saw Andromeda, whom he saved from the sea monster, Cetus (Fig. 2-6). Binoculars or a telescope will show you a pair of *open clusters*, each a group of many stars, close to each other in Perseus. This double cluster is unusual; clusters usually appear by themselves. Thus the double cluster is relatively easy to notice. In general, open clusters, also known as galactic clusters, usually contain a few hundred stars. The stars in open clusters are fairly young by astronomical standards, between 10 million and a billion years old.

Also in Perseus is perhaps the best known of the variable stars, Algol, often called the demon star from its Arabic name. Algol is actually a pair of stars that orbit each other in a way that brings one in front of the other every 2.9 days. During these eclipses, the total brightness we see drops dramatically. We discuss Algol and give a table of its minimum brightness in Chapter 6.

On the opposite side of Cassiopeia, beyond Cepheus along the Milky Way, a cross of bright stars is visible directly overhead. This

Fig. 2-6 The constellation Cetus, the Sea Monster (also sometimes called the Whale), from the sky atlas by Bayer published in 1603. (Jay M. Pasachoff)

prominent grouping of stars, known as the Northern Cross, lies in the constellation Cygnus, the Swan. This swan appears to be flying south, as birds do at this time of year. Deneb is the star at the Swan's tail. Slightly to the west of the Swan, you will see the bright star Vega in the constellation Lyra, the Lyre. Vega is the third brightest star visible from midnorthern latitudes.

Farther westward, beyond Vega, you will come to the constellation Hercules, named for the Greek hero who performed 12 great labors. With binoculars or a small telescope, we can barely see an object that looks like a hazy mothball. This object is a *globular cluster*, a spherical group of thousands of stars. It is labelled M13 (Fig. 2-7), from its place in a catalogue of nonstellar objects—the Messier Catalogue (Table 12, p. 205), compiled in the 18th century by Charles Messier. M13 is the brightest globular cluster that we can see from the northern hemisphere. Globular clusters are interesting because all the stars in them are very old. None is much younger than 10 billion years of age. Further, they are all at the same distance from us, which makes it relatively easy for astronomers to compare their properties without worrying about the effects of distance.

Fig. 2-5 *(Opposite)* The Milky Way, rising almost perpendicularly to the horizon in the summer sky. (Compare, for example, Sky Map 7, p. 89.) It is visible to the naked eye on dark nights if you are far from city lights. (Dennis di Cicco)

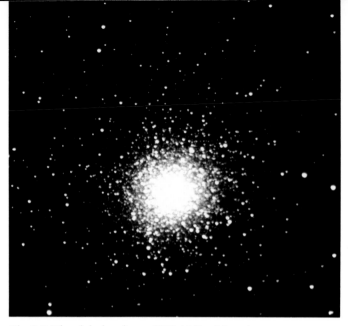

Fig. 2-7 The globular cluster M13. (© Ben Mayer)

The Winter Sky (Monthly Map #11)

At dusk on a winter evening, the Big Dipper is low in the northern sky. The constellations that were easiest to see in the autumn now will appear closer and closer to the western horizon at the same hour on each successive night. By January 1, Cygnus, the Swan, sets in the western sky in the early evening; Cassiopeia is high overhead to our north; Perseus is even higher in the sky.

The Milky Way, the hazy band of gas and dust that gives our galaxy its name, also appears high in the early evening sky at this time of year. Since our home galaxy, the Milky Way Galaxy, is disk-shaped, we see many stars and much dust and gas when we look along the plane of the disk, but few stars and little dust and gas when we look in other directions. The next constellation to the southeast along the Milky Way is Auriga, the Charioteer, with its bright star Capella.

To the south of this part of the Milky Way, you can see a cluster of six or seven stars that are close together in the sky. Though faint, they will catch your eye as your vision sweeps across the sky. These stars are the Pleiades, the Seven Sisters of Greek mythology, the daughters of Atlas. The Pleiades are an open cluster of over a hundred stars; the larger the binoculars or wide-field telescope you use, the more you will see. Figure 7-10 on p. 226, which accompanies Atlas Chart 10, shows the brightest stars of the Pleiades.

Fig. 2-8 The Pleiades, an open cluster of stars known as the Seven Sisters. In Greek mythology, these sisters were pursued by Orion and given refuge in the sky. (© 1985 Royal Observatory Edinburgh/Anglo-Australian Telescope Board)

Look further south, and compare with Sky Map 11, facing south (p. 103). (Turn this book so that its right edge is closest to you.) The most prominent group of stars in the sky in the wintertime is three bright stars in a straight line. They form the belt of Orion, the Hunter (Fig. 2-9). Extending down from Orion's belt (to the right on the photograph) is his sword. On Orion's shoulder (to the left on the photograph) you will see the reddish star Betelgeuse, one of the brightest stars visible from midnorthern latitudes. Symmetrically on the other side of Orion's belt, you will find the bluish star Rigel, marking Orion's heel. In Chapter 4, we will see that the colors of stars tell us their temperatures; reddish stars are relatively cool— about 3000°C—and bluish stars are relatively hot—over 10,000°C.

In the area of Orion's sword (Fig. 2-10) is a hazy region, the Orion Nebula, that is visible with binoculars or small telescopes. A *nebula* is a hazy region of sky that contains clouds of gas or dust (see p. 164). The Orion Nebula (Fig. 2-11) marks the presence of a cloud of gas and dust; in its vicinity new stars are now forming. Many nebulae are really "nurseries" for young stars that have recently been born, and are the site of ongoing stellar birth; we discuss them in more detail in Chapter 5.

The Hubble Space Telescope has been turned to study the Orion Nebula. Computer processing of the image has overcome the limitations of the Space Telescope's mirror. The image in Figure 2-12 shows the region near the Trapezium, a set of bright stars near the center of the visible nebula. The improved resolution shows that the nebula has narrow streamers and jets. Studies of these smaller objects are telling us how stars form in regions such as this.

Fig. 2-9 *(opposite)* A ground-based view of the Orion Nebula, and *(above)* a higher resolution view of part of the nebula with the Hubble Space Telescope (see also Fig. 2-12). North is at top right. Orion is noticeable by the three stars of its belt, with Betelgeuse above and to the left and Rigel below and to the right of the belt. Sirius, in Canis Major, is at lower left. *(above,* Akira Fujii; *opposite,* Space Telescope Science Institute)

Fig. 2-10 *(opposite)* A wide view of Orion, showing his belt, sword, and two nebulae (Atlas Chart 24). The Orion Nebula (M42 and M43) is near the bottom, in the sword. The Horsehead Nebula (IC 434) is below zeta Orionis, the first star (at left) in the belt. (© 1979 Ben Mayer)

Fig. 2-11 *(above)* The Orion Nebula, including M42 (the main nebula) and M43. The breakdown of the nebula into its labelled parts is shown in Atlas Chart 24. (Meade Instruments Corp.)

Fig. 2-12 The central part of the Orion Nebula as observed with the Hubble Space Telescope. The observations are improved in resolution by a factor of at least 5 over the photograph in Fig. 2-11. (Jeff Hester, Image Processing and Analysis Center, California Institute of Technology; and NASA)

Fig. 2-13 The Horsehead Nebula in the constellation Orion. It descends from the star zeta Orionis (Atlas Chart 24), the leftmost star in Orion's belt. (© 1979 Royal Observatory Edinburgh)

The Horsehead Nebula, near the leftmost star in Orion's belt, is difficult to see with a small telescope but is beautiful in photographs. Dark dust absorbs light coming from behind it to silhouette the shape of a horse's head (Fig. 2-13).

Orion (Fig. 2-14) seems to be warding off Taurus, the Bull, a constellation you will find by looking beyond Orion's shield. Between the top of the shield and the Pleiades lies a V-shaped group of stars, the Hyades (Fig. 2-15). The reddish star Aldebaran marks the end of one side of the V. The Hyades outline the face of Taurus; the Pleiades ride on the bull's shoulder. The Hyades and the Pleiades are both *open clusters* of stars (also called *galactic clusters*); these clusters are locations where perhaps 100 or more stars are close together in an irregularly shaped group.

At Orion's heel is his dog, Canis Major. Orion's belt points directly to Sirius, the brightest star in the sky and the brightest star in the photograph of the constellation of Orion (Fig. 2-9). Rising soon after Orion, Sirius appears blue-white and is part of the constellation Canis Major, the Great Dog. To the upper left off the photograph is the yellow-white star Procyon in Canis Minor, the Little Dog. This bright star forms a nearly equilateral triangle with Sirius and Betelgeuse.

Fig. 2-14 Orion, from the star atlas of Bayer (1603). Orion is holding up his shield to ward off Taurus, the Bull. (Mendillo Collection of Astronomical Prints)

Fig. 2-15 The prominent open clusters known as the Pleiades (upper right), and the Hyades (V of bright stars leaning to left near center), both in the constellation Taurus, the Bull. (Dennis W. Dawson, Western Connecticut State University)

The Spring Sky (Monthly Map #2)

As spring approaches, Orion and the V-shaped Hyades move closer to the western horizon each evening, and eventually disappear from our view at sunset. Now you will see a pair of stars, the twins (Castor and Pollux), in the western sky at dusk. Although the two stars are about the same in brightness, Pollux appears slightly reddish, while Castor does not. These stars are in the constellation Gemini, the Twins, which was named after two Roman military gods.

South of the Twins, the bright star Sirius is prominent in the western sky, in the constellation Canis Major, the Great Dog. South of Sirius is the constellation Puppis, the ship's stern. This constellation includes a star, zeta Puppis, that is known to be one of the intrinsically brightest and hottest stars in the sky. Zeta Puppis is so far away, though, that it does not appear prominent when we observe this part of the sky. Puppis and several other constellations in this region and farther south were once considered to form a giant constellation of a ship, Argo Navis (Fig. 2-16).

Fig. 2-16 Argo Navis, the ship, from Bayer's atlas (1603). This former constellation has now been divided into Vela (the sails), Puppis (the stern), Pyxis (the compass), and Carina (the keel). These constellations are not visible from midnorthern latitudes. (Jay M. Pasachoff)

Ursa Major, the Big Bear, appears high in the northern sky on spring evenings, and is tipped so much that any imaginary things in the Big Dipper would spill out. If you follow the Pointers backward, you will see the constellation Leo, the Lion, just to the south of the zenith. To most people, Leo looks more like a backward question mark or sickle than a lion's head. A bright star, Regulus, is at the base of the question mark, at the lion's heart. East of Regulus, a triangle of stars marks the rest of Leo's body. Many people visualize Leo as a lion in the sky with a sickle-shaped head and triangular tail.

On the northern star map, if you follow an arc begun by the stars in the Big Dipper's handle, you will come to a bright reddish star, Arcturus. This star lies in the constellation Boötes, the Herdsman. Farther along the arc from the Big Dipper through Arcturus, you will find another bright star, Spica. This blue-white star rises in the east-southeast in the constellation Virgo, the Virgin.

Look up again toward the northeast, to the lower left of Boötes and Hercules, which rise in the east in the evening. Here in the constellation Lyra (Fig. 2-17) you will see Vega, a star that is brighter than Spica.

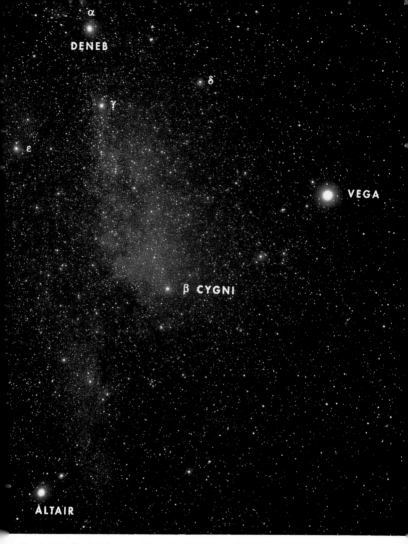

Fig. 2-17 The bright star Vega, in the constellation Lyra, is at right, above center, and is the brightest object on the chart. Cygnus is at upper left; the brightest stars in Cygnus form the Northern Cross (Atlas Chart 18), which lies along the Milky Way. Deneb, α Cygni, is at top left; β Cygni is the reddish star near the center. Perpendicular to them is the Northern Cross's crossbar: ε, γ, and δ Cygni, appearing in a line slanted slightly upward. (Compare Atlas Chart 18.) Altair, α Aquilae (Atlas Chart 31), is the bright star to the lower left of the photograph. North is at top. (Akira Fujii)

The Summer Sky (Monthly Map #5)

On summer evenings at sunset, Vega is the brightest star near the zenith. Arcturus, very slightly brighter than Vega, is the reddish star that is also high in the sky to the west. The constellation Cygnus, which includes the prominent stars that make up the Northern Cross, lies east of Vega along the highest part of the Milky Way. Hercules lies about 10° to the west of Vega.

Continuing north along the Milky Way from Cygnus, you will find the W-shaped constellation, Cassiopeia (Fig. 2-18). To the southeast of Cassiopeia is Andromeda, near the horizon. Andromeda's Great Galaxy in Andromeda, M31 (Fig. 2-19), may be faintly visible to the naked eye as a hazy patch of sky. The spiral galaxy M33 is in the constellation Triangulum, to the side of Andromeda. M31 and M33 are the farthest objects that you can see with your unaided eye, though it is fair to say that the glimpse of haze you can see does not reveal the beauty shown in long-exposure photographs. The Great Square of Pegasus is father south, on the same side of the Milky Way as Andromeda.

Fig. 2-18 The constellation Cassiopeia, the W in the sky. (Cliff Holmes)

Fig. 2-19 The Andromeda Galaxy, the largest and brightest galaxy in the constellation Andromeda. This spiral galaxy is often known as M31, from its place in Messier's catalogue. Near it are two small elliptical galaxies, M32 and NGC 205 (above right). The Andromeda Galaxy is one of the farthest objects you can see with your unaided eye. (© 1959 California Institute of Technology)

The bright star Spica lies toward the southwest, in the constellation Virgo, the Virgin. In the south you will find the bright reddish star Antares in the constellation Scorpius, the Scorpion (Fig. 2-20). (Antares means "compared with Ares," the Greek name for Mars, because Antares is also reddish.) The stars of Scorpius wind a great distance across the sky.

To the east of Scorpius, you will see the constellation Sagittarius, the Archer, in which the center of our galaxy lies. The farther south you are, the higher in the sky Sagittarius rises, and the better you can see the beautiful star clouds in the direction of the center of the Milky Way.

Moving south along the Milky Way, you will come to the star Altair in the constellation Aquila, the Eagle. Altair, Deneb (in the constellation Cygnus), and Vega make up the Summer Triangle.

Every summer around August 12, the Perseid meteor shower occurs (Fig. 2-21). At the height of this shower, as many as one bright meteor per minute may be visible in pre-dawn hours. The meteors streak across the sky like shooting stars or falling stars, though they are only bits of interplanetary dust burning up in the earth's atmosphere. The dates of meteor showers are listed in a table in Chapter 12. To photograph a meteor shower, set up an ordinary camera on a tripod, as you would to take star trails. Use a wide-angle lens to cover an appreciable region of the sky. Then just keep taking photographs of durations at least a few minutes each. There is no telling how soon a meteor will cross in front of your camera. But you must have your camera lens already opened and facing the sky, since you cannot catch up with a meteor trail to take its picture.

Now that you have followed these seasonal tours, you can use the Monthly Sky Maps in the next chapter to find your way around the sky at any time of year.

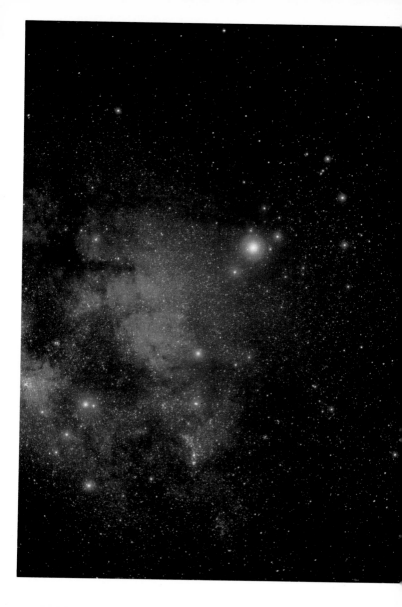

Fig. 2-20 The constellation Scorpius, including the bright reddish star Antares. (Akira Fujii)

Fig. 2-21 A Perseid meteor trail crosses part of the sky while a photograph of star trails is being taken. Though the meteors can be traced back toward Perseus, they are seen in all parts of the sky. (Clyde E. Kirkpatrick)

The Southern Sky (Maps #13-24)

If you are fortunate enough to be able to see the southern sky, you will find some of the prettiest celestial objects in it. Sky Maps 13–24 show what the sky looks like from month to month from southern latitudes.

At any given location, we see stars only within 90° of the point over our head, our zenith. Stars too close to the opposite pole never rise into our view. Thus many of the southern constellations are never seen from midnorthern latitudes. A map of the southern half of the sky contains many constellations whose names are relatively unfamiliar (Fig. 2-22).

Among the most obvious asterisms seen from southern latitudes is the pair of stars in the constellation Centaurus, alpha Centauri and beta Centauri. Alpha Centauri is the nearest star system to us, only about 4.2 light-years away. It is a triple-star system. The nearest

Fig. 2-22 The southern (australis) half of the sky, from the Atlas by Cellarius. (Institute for Advanced Study, Princeton, photo by Jay M. Pasachoff)

of the three, too faint to be easily observed, is the single nearest star to us, and so is known as Proxima Centauri.

The line from alpha to beta, the brighter to the fainter of the pair, leads to Crux, the Southern Cross (Fig. 2-23). Though it is called a cross, it is actually missing a center star, so looks to me more like a kite. Three of its stars are blue and therefore hot, while the fourth is very red and therefore relatively cool. Just to the Centaurus side of the Southern Cross is the Coalsack, a dark region of absorbing dust. The Southern Cross and the Coalsack are quite visible to the unaided eye.

If you look up from a dark spot while you are at southern latitudes, you may seem to see a pair of faint, hazy regions of space. These objects were seen as clouds by the crew of Magellan's ship, and so are known as the Magellanic Clouds. The Large Magellanic Cloud and Small Magellanic Cloud (Fig. 2-24) are really small galaxies that are associated with our own Milky Way Galaxy. We now know, from study of an exciting supernova that went off in it, that the Large Magellanic Cloud is 169,000 light-years away from us. The Magellanic Clouds are best seen in the months around January, which is southern-hemisphere summer (and northern-hemisphere winter).

Fig. 2-23 The constellations Centarus and Crux. Alpha Centauri and beta Centauri point at the Coalsack, beyond which lies Crux, the Southern Cross. These constellations are visible only from southern latitudes. (Akira Fujii)

The Sun

Though many people think of astronomy as the study of the night-time sky, studies of the sun are also part of astronomy. The sun has the advantage, too, that it is up in the daytime, when people are apt to be outside. The sun has the disadvantage, though, that it is too bright to see safely under most circumstances. Only during the brief period of totality during a solar eclipse can one look at the sun without protective filters or without taking other precautions.

The photograph below, taken through a filter that takes out all but about 0.001% of the sunlight, shows the everyday solar surface. Dark sunspots cross it. The number of sunspots waxes and wanes with a cycle that lasts about 11 years (see Chapter 14).

Fig. 2-25 The everyday surface of the sun, photographed through a filter that absorbs all but 0.001% of the incoming sunlight. It is not safe to observe the sun directly without such a special filter. (National Optical Astronomy Observatories/NSO)

Detailed views of sunspots show that they have a dark central region, known as the umbra, and a brighter outer region, known as the penumbra (Fig. 2-26). Sunspots are regions where the sun's magnetic field is extremely high, perhaps three thousand times higher than the average field of the sun or earth, which is about the same as the average field of a toy magnet. With a telescope on earth, one can use a special filter that passes only the reddish hydrogen light from the sun. There is so much hydrogen gas on the sun that this hydrogen light comes from a higher level in the solar atmosphere than the everyday surface from which much of the sunlight comes. Such hydrogen-light images reveal dark filaments snaking their way across the solar surface, and bright prominences, which are what those filaments look like when they are at the edge of the sun silhouetted against space.

Fig. 2-26 A sunspot, showing its dark umbra and lighter penumbra. (W. Livingston, NOAO/NSO)

Fig. 2-27 The sun through an H-alpha filter. Printed over the center of an image showing prominences around the sun's edge is a less-exposed image, which shows dark filaments snaking across the solar disk (and some minor blotches from irregularities in the filter). (© 1983 DayStar Filter Corp.)

Fig. 2-28 A prominence photographed through an H-alpha filter. (R. J. Poole/DayStar Filter Corp.)

Fig. 2-29 Partial phases of a total eclipse, photographed through a dense solar filter. (Jay M. Pasachoff)

The most beautiful and exciting astronomical event that it is possible to view is a total eclipse of the sun (Chapter 14). The partial phases (Fig. 2-29), when the sun is partly covered, are widely visible. But only from a narrow band, thousands of miles long but only one or two hundred miles wide, can the total phase be seen. The everyday sun is completely covered, and only the outermost layers are visible (Fig. 2-30 to Fig. 2-33).

Fig. 2-30 The solar corona, visible from earth for only seconds or minutes at a total solar eclipse. The corona silhouettes the moon, which we see as a dark disk because the sun is lighting the opposite side. (Jay M. Pasachoff)

Fig. 2-31 The view during a total solar eclipse, showing the overexposed corona surrounding the dark, barely visible disk of the moon in the midday sky. The distant horizon is bright because the eclipse is not total there. (Jay M. Pasachoff)

Fig. 2-32 The diamond-ring effect—the last bit of ordinary solar surface shining through a valley on the edge of the moon, is visible at the beginning and end of the total phase of a total solar eclipse. Scattering in the lens adds to the luster of the "diamond."
(Jay M. Pasachoff)

Fig. 2-33 The total solar eclipse of 11 July 1991. (Daniel C. Good)

Fig. 2-34 The green flash, a greenish solar edge appearing at sunset under perfect conditions. (George V. Coyne, S.J., Vatican Observatory)

It is fun to watch the sun under unusual circumstances. If you are watching the sunset with a perfect horizon, usually over water, you may see a greenish edge of the sun detach itself (Fig. 2-34), as explained on p. 422. Sometimes we see the effect of particles that the sun throws off in huge magnetic storms (Fig. 2-35). They cause the aurora.

Fig. 2-35 The aurora borealis, the northern lights, photographed from Massachusetts just after a major solar magnetic storm. (Kevin Reardon, Hopkins Observatory, Williams College)

3

THE MONTHLY SKY MAPS

When we look at the stars at night, we have the feeling that we are underneath a giant bowl. Although the stars are really at many different distances from the earth, which spins underneath them, it is often convenient to picture the sky as the ancients did—as stars attached to a giant sphere rotating overhead. The set of constellations we see appears to rotate $1/12$ of the way around the sky each month, so at the same time of night one month later, we see an additional 30° of constellations in the east and lose sight of 30° of constellations that have set in the west.

It is, of course, very difficult to flatten out a sphere so that it can be reproduced on a flat page. The distortions in the Mercator projection of the earth, in which Greenland is made to look as large as South America merely because it is located much closer to a pole, are familiar to us all.

We have chosen a new way of drawing these star maps to minimize distortions in the regions of the sky that are most often studied. Star maps are made by projecting the positions of the stars onto a flat plane as though their shadows were being cast from a given point. We have chosen this point so that the position approximately halfway up the sky to the zenith (45° in altitude) has minimum distortion. Though the constellations near the boundaries of the maps are expanded, the amount of the expansion is not too great, and constellations near the horizon are not compressed. Also, because of the projection used, when you follow a pathway from one constellation to another using certain pairs of stars, the angles between the paths will be the same on the maps as they are in the sky.

How to Use the Maps

These Monthly Sky Maps are designed to be easy to use. Most of the objects plotted on these maps are of magnitude 4.5 or brighter—bright enough to be seen with the naked eye. Seventy-two maps are included. The first 48 are for northern-hemisphere observers; they are specially marked for latitudes between 10° N and 50° N, and can also be used somewhat outside this range.

The second set of 24 maps is for observers in the southern hemisphere; these maps are specially marked for latitudes between the equator and 40° S latitude, and can also be used somewhat outside this range. The words "Sky Map" and the map number are printed in reverse (black on white, not white on black) on these maps, so you can distinguish the southern-hemisphere maps from the northern-hemisphere ones at a glance.

Across the bottom of each map is a series of curved lines that represent the horizon for observers at different latitudes. In the upper middle portion of each map, the zenith (the point directly overhead) for observers at each latitude is marked with a plus sign. The directions east and west are marked at the edges.

We have provided a considerable amount of extra sky past the zenith on each map, to make it easier to orient yourself. You will soon become used to the locations of the northern and southern horizons and the zenith for your latitude. Some people will find it helpful to cut masks out of opaque paper and use them to hide the stars below the horizons for their latitude.

Each set of maps is valid for specific times on specific days, as shown in Table 6 (pp. 60–61). In particular, Sky Map 1—which is valid in our ordinary system of timekeeping for midnight on January 1—is drawn for *sidereal time* (time by the stars, as described in Chapter 15) of 6^h40^m. Each succeeding map is valid two hours later on the same date or one month later at the same time. Some of the times of night at which the maps are valid are shown to the lower left of the left-hand pages. Arrows near the east and west points show the direction in which the sky rotates through the night.

Each Monthly Sky Map for the northern hemisphere actually consists of two pairs of maps. The first pair has the constellation figures drawn on it; the second pair shows the same stars and omits the outlines of the constellation figures. (For the southern hemisphere, all the maps show constellation outlines.) In each pair of maps, the left-hand page shows what you will see when facing north, and the right-hand page shows what you will see when facing south. When facing north, hold the book with its left edge toward you and look down at the map. In this orientation it will correspond to the sky. When facing south, hold the book with its right edge toward you and look down at the map to have it correspond to the sky.

On the maps, stars of different brightnesses (magnitudes) are shown as dots of different sizes. We describe the magnitude scale of brightness below. The maps in this section include only stars that are bright enough to be visible to the naked eye. In addition, the Milky Way is shown, and a few other objects of special interest. These objects are also shown and described in Chapter 7, where a set of Atlas Charts breaks down the sky into 52 sections. The Atlas Charts (primarily for telescope observers) are more detailed than the Monthly Sky Maps in this chapter; each Monthly Sky Map shows a view of half the sky visible at a given time.

The Magnitude Scale

Astronomers describe the brightness of stars with a scale built on a historical base. In the second century B.C., the Greek astronomer

Hipparchus classified stars by brightness, and by the first century A.D., stars were often divided into six classes of brightness. In about A.D. 140, Ptolemy, perhaps quoting Hipparchus, said that the brightest stars were "of the first magnitude," the next brightest group of stars were "of the second magnitude," and so on. The faintest stars visible to the naked eye were "of the sixth magnitude."

This scale was placed on a mathematical basis in the mid-19th century. Measurements showed that a difference of 5 magnitudes corresponded to a factor of about 100 in brightness; the current magnitude scale is defined so that a factor of 100 corresponds to exactly 5 magnitudes. A few stars are even brighter than first magnitude and have been accommodated by having magnitudes of 0 and then negative numbers on the scale. The brightest star in the sky is Sirius, whose magnitude is –1.4. Canopus, the second brightest star, is not visible north of the southern U.S. and has a magnitude of –0.7. Alpha Centauri, the third brightest star (also not visible from mid-northern latitudes), and Arcturus, the fourth brightest star, are slightly brighter than magnitude 0.0. Another dozen stars are fainter than magnitude 0.0 but brighter than magnitude 1.0. Most stars are much dimmer; the number of stars for each whole unit of magnitude increases rapidly as we go to fainter magnitudes.

The magnitude scale is different from most scales we commonly use in that increasing in brightness by one unit on the magnitude scale corresponds to multiplying by a fixed number (about 2.51) on a scale of brightness given in units of energy. For example, if we consider first a star of 3rd magnitude and then ask how much brighter a star of 2nd magnitude is, we have subtracted 1 on the magnitude scale. The result: the star of 2nd magnitude is about 2.5 times brighter than the star of 3rd magnitude. Thus for each magnitude added or subtracted, stars are about 2.5 times fainter or brighter, respectively. By definition, for each 5 magnitudes added, stars are

Table 3: The Magnitude Scale

differences in magnitudes	factor in brightness	
1 mag	2.512	times
2 mag	6.31	times
3 mag	15.85	times
4 mag	39.81	times
5 mag	100	times
6 mag	251	times
7 mag	631	times
8 mag	1585	times
9 mag	3981	times
10 mag	10,000	times

exactly 100 times fainter. (Thus each magnitude corresponds to the fifth root of 100, or 2.512..., which is about 2.5 times brighter or fainter.) An increase of two magnitudes corresponds to $(2.512)^2$, or a little over 6 times; three magnitudes corresponds to $(2.512)^3$, or a little over 15 times, etc., as shown in Table 3.

Although Sirius, at magnitude −1.4, is the brightest star, the moon and some of the planets are somewhat brighter in the sky. Venus can be as bright as magnitude −4.4. The full moon is magnitude −12.6, and the sun is magnitude −26.8. Note that the smaller the magnitude number (or the more negative it is), the *brighter* the object is.

Going to fainter magnitudes, 6th magnitude is the faintest that the naked eye can see under the best observing conditions. A medium-sized telescope (with a lens or mirror 6–10 inches, 15–25 cm, in diameter) will allow you to see stars of 10th or 12th magnitude. The best ground-based telescopes can observe to about 25th magnitude. The Hubble Space Telescope, launched in 1990, should eventually enable us to observe 28th-magnitude objects.

You don't need a telescope to use the Monthly Sky Maps that follow; they are designed for observations with the naked eye or binoculars. If you want to observe regions of the sky in greater detail, you can use the Atlas Charts in Chapter 7, which are designed primarily for telescope observations.

Table 4: Examples of Magnitudes

−27	Sun
−13	Moon
−5 to −2	Venus
−3 to −1	Jupiter
−2 to +2	Mars
−2 to +3	Mercury (visible range)
−1.4	*Sirius (brightest star)*
0	*Vega*
0 to +1	Saturn
+1.8 to +3.3	*stars in Big Dipper*
+2.0 to +5.0	*stars in Little Dipper*
+6	*faintest naked-eye star*
+6	Uranus
+8	Neptune
+14	Pluto
+25	*faintest ground-based telescope limit*
+28	*Hubble Space Telescope limit*

Note: Solar-system objects are in roman type; farther objects are in *italics*.

Table 5: Which Constellations Are Up At Night?
(Constellations at least 20° above the horizon from 40° N)

See constellation mythology in Chapter 6 and constellation abbreviations in Appendix 1.

Circumpolar (always visible at night): UMi, UMa, Dra, Cep, Cas, Cam

Andromeda: 1N, 7–12N	Lacerta: 6–12N
Aquarius: 7–11S	Leo: 1–6NS, 12NS
Aquila: 5S–10SN	Leo Minor: 1–5NS, 12NS
Aries: 1SN, 8N–12NS	Lepus: 1–2S, 11–12S
Auriga: 1–3NS, 10–12NS	Libra: 4–5S
Boötes: 2–8NS	Lynx: 1–4N, 11–12N
Camelopardalis: all N; highest: 12N	Lyra: 4N, 5–10NS
Cancer: 1–5N, 11–12N	Monoceros: 1–3S, 11–12S
Canes Venatici: 1–7N, 1S, 2S, 6S	Ophiuchus: 4–8S, 4N, 8N
Canis Major: 1–3S, 11–12S	Orion: 1S, 2–3SN, 10–11SN, 12S
Canis Minor: 1–4SN, 11S–12SN	Pegasus: 7–12N, 8–12S
Capricornus: 7–9S	Perseus: 1–2N, 9–12N
Cassiopeia: 1N, 6N–12N	Pisces: 1NS, 8–12NS
Cepheus: 6–12N	Sagitta: 5–10SN
Cetus: 1S, 9–12S	Sagittarius: 6–8S
Coma Berenices: 2–7NS	Scorpius: 5–6S
Corona Borealis: 3–8NS	Serpens Caput: 3–8S
Corvus: 2–5S	Serpens Cauda: 5–8S, 3–9N
Cygnus: 5–11N	Sextans: 1–5S
Delphinus: 5–11NS	Taurus: 1–2SN, 9S–11SN, 12S
Draco: all N; highest: 6N	Triangulum: 1NS, 8–12NS
Equuleus: 6–11SN	Ursa Major: all N; highest: 4N
Eridanus: 1S, 10–12S	Ursa Minor: all N
Gemini: 1–4NS, 11–12NS	Vulpecula: 5–10NS
Hercules: 4–9N	Virgo: 2S–7S, 2N, 6N
Hydra: 1–4S, 12S	

Table 6: Index to Monthly Sky Maps

Standard/D.S.T.	Jan.		Feb.		March		April		May		June	
	1	15	1	15	1	15	1	15	1	15	1	15
6 p.m. /7 p.m. 18 h /19 h	10		11		12		1		2		3	
7 p.m. /8 p.m. 19 h /20 h		11		12		1		2		3		4
8 p.m. /9 p.m. 20 h /21 h	11		12		1		2		3		4	
9 p.m. /10 p.m. 21 h /22 h		12		1		2		3		4		5
10 p.m. /11 p.m. 22 h /23 h	12		1		2		3		4		5	
11 p.m./midnight 23 h /24 h		1		2		3		4		5		6
midnight/1 a.m. 24 h /1 h	1		2		3		4		5		6	
1 a.m. /2 a.m. 1 h /2 h		2		3		4		5		6		7
2 a.m. /3 a.m. 2 h /3 h	2		3		4		5		6		7	
3 a.m. /4 a.m. 3 h /4 h		3		4		5		6		7		8
4 a.m. /5 a.m. 4 h /5 h	3		4		5		6		7		8	
5 a.m. /6 a.m. 5 h /6 h		4		5		6		7		8		9
6 a.m. /7 a.m. 6 h /7 h	4		5		6		7		8		9	

Note: For the southern hemisphere Sky Maps, add 12 to the above Sky Map numbers.

Table 6 (cont.): Index to Monthly Sky Maps

July.		Aug.		Sept.		Oct.		Nov.		Dec.		
1	15	1	15	1	15	1	15	1	15	1	15	**Standard/D.S.T.**
4		5		6		7		8		9		6 p.m. /7 p.m. 18 h /19 h
	5		6		7		8		9		10	7 p.m. /8 p.m. 19 h /20 h
5		6		7		8		9		10		8 p.m. /9 p.m. 20 h /21 h
	6		7		8		9		10		11	9 p.m. /10 p.m. 21 h /22 h
6		7		8		9		10		11		10 p.m. /11 p.m. 22 h /23 h
	7		8		9		10		11		12	11 p.m./midnight 23 h /24 h
7		8		9		10		11		12		midnight/1 a.m. 24 h /1 h
	8		9		10		11		12		1	1 a.m. /2 a.m. 1 h /2 h
8		9		10		11		12		1		2 a.m. /3 a.m. 2 h /3 h
	9		10		11		12		1		2	3 a.m. /4 a.m. 3 h /4 h
9		10		11		12		1		2		4 a.m. /5 a.m. 4 h /5 h
	10		11		12		1		2		3	5 a.m. /6 a.m. 5 h /6 h
10		11		12		1		2		3		6 a.m. /7 a.m. 6 h /7 h

Note: For the southern hemisphere Sky Maps, add 12 to the above Sky Map numbers.

SKY MAP 1
Facing North

Northern Latitudes

	TIME	D.S.T.
January 1	24 h	
January 15	23 h	
February 1	22 h	
February 15	21 h	
March 1	20 h	21 h
etc.		

SKY MAP 1
Facing South

Northern Latitudes

Magnitudes: -1 0 1 2 3 4 (5)

◌ Open Cluster   ☐ Nebula
⊙ Variable   ⊕ Globular Cluster   ○ Galaxy

WIL TIRION

SKY MAP 1
Facing North

Northern Latitudes

WEST

NORTH

EAST

ZENITH 50N
ZENITH 40N
ZENITH 30N
ZENITH 20N
ZENITH 10N

HORIZON 50N
HORIZON 40N
HORIZON 30N
HORIZON 20N
HORIZON 10N

ECLIPTIC

	TIME	D.S.T.
January 1	24 h	
January 15	23 h	
February 1	22 h	
February 15	21 h	
March 1	20 h	21 h
etc..		

EPOCH 2000.0

64

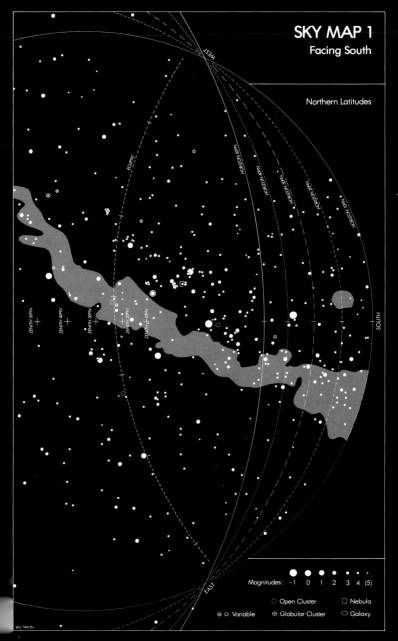

SKY MAP 1
Facing South

Northern Latitudes

Magnitudes: -1 0 1 2 3 4 (5)

☼ Open Cluster ☐ Nebula

⊚ ○ Variable ⊕ Globular Cluster ○ Galaxy

WIL TIRION

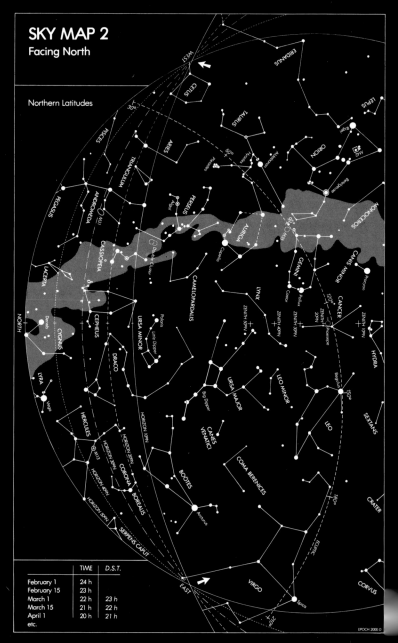

SKY MAP 2
Facing North

Northern Latitudes

	TIME	D.S.T.
February 1	24 h	
February 15	23 h	
March 1	22 h	23 h
March 15	21 h	22 h
April 1	20 h	21 h
etc.		

EPOCH 2000.0

SKY MAP 2
Facing South

Northern Latitudes

Magnitudes: -1 0 1 2 3 4 (5)

⚬ Open Cluster · · · □ Nebula

⊙ ○ Variable · ⊕ Globular Cluster · ○ Galaxy

WIL TIRION

67

SKY MAP 2
Facing North

Northern Latitudes

WEST

NORTH

EAST

ZENITH 50N
ZENITH 40N
ZENITH 30N
ZENITH 20N
ZENITH 10N

HORIZON 10N
HORIZON 20N
HORIZON 30N
HORIZON 40N
HORIZON 50N

ECLIPTIC

	TIME	D.S.T.
February 1	24 h	
February 15	23 h	
March 1	22 h	23 h
March 15	21 h	22 h
April 1	20 h	21 h
etc.		

EPOCH 2000.0

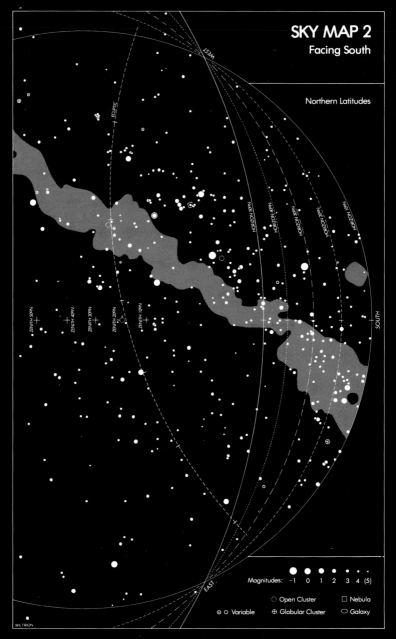

SKY MAP 2
Facing South

Northern Latitudes

WEST

EAST

WEST

SOUTH

ECLIPTIC

HORIZON 50°N
HORIZON 40°N
HORIZON 30°N
HORIZON 20°N
HORIZON 10°N

ZENITH 50°N
ZENITH 40°N
ZENITH 30°N
ZENITH 20°N
ZENITH 10°N

Magnitudes: -1 0 1 2 3 4 (5)

☼ Open Cluster   □ Nebula

⊙ ○ Variable   ⊕ Globular Cluster   ○ Galaxy

WIL TIRION

SKY MAP 3
Facing North

Northern Latitudes

	TIME	D.S.T.
March 1	24 h	01 h
March 15	23 h	24 h
April 1	22 h	23 h
April 15	21 h	22 h
May 1	20 h	21 h
etc.		

EPOCH 2000.0

SKY MAP 3
Facing South

Northern Latitudes

Magnitudes: -1 0 1 2 3 4 (5)

⚬ Open Cluster ☐ Nebula
◉ ○ Variable ⊕ Globular Cluster ⬭ ○ Galaxy

PERSEUS
TAURUS
WEST
Hyades
Aldebaran
ORION
ERIDANUS
AURIGA
ECLIPTIC
LEPUS
COLUMBA
M45
Betelgeuse
Rigel
HORIZON 50°N
HORIZON 40°N
HORIZON 30°N
GEMINI
Castor
Pollux
CANIS MINOR
Procyon
MONOCEROS
Sirius
CANIS MAJOR
PUPPIS
CARINA
PICTOR
Canopus
VOLANS
LYNX
CANCER
Praesepe
120°
HYDRA
PYXIS
VELA
CHAMAELEON
SOUTH
MUSCA
URSA MAJOR
LEO MINOR
LEO
Regulus
150°
SEXTANS
ANTLIA
CENTAURUS
CRUX
Acrux
Mimosa
ZENITH 50°N
ZENITH 40°N
ZENITH 30°N
ZENITH 20°N
ZENITH 10°N
Big Dipper
CANES VENATICI
COMA BERENICES
180°
CRATER
CORVUS
ω
Hadar
Rigil Kentaurus
CIRCINUS
BOOTES
VIRGO
Spica
210°
LIBRA
LUPUS
Arcturus
CORONA BOREALIS
M13
SERPENS CAPUT
M5
240°
270°
SCORPIUS
HERCULES
OPHIUCHUS
EAST
TIRION

71

SKY MAP 3
Facing North

Northern Latitudes

	TIME	D.S.T.
March 1	24 h	01 h
March 15	23 h	24 h
April 1	22 h	23 h
April 15	21 h	22 h
May 1	20 h	21 h
etc.		

EPOCH 2000

72

SKY MAP 4
Facing North

Northern Latitudes

	TIME	D.S.T.
April 1	24 h	01 h
April 15	23 h	24 h
May 1	22 h	23 h
May 15	21 h	22 h
June 1	20 h	21 h

SKY MAP 4
Facing South

Northern Latitudes

Magnitudes: -1 0 1 2 3 4 (5)

◇ Open Cluster   □ Nebula
⊙ ○ Variable   ⊕ Globular Cluster   ○ Galaxy

SKY MAP 4
Facing North

Northern Latitudes

MSTY

ECLIPTIC

ZENITH 60°N
ZENITH 50°N
ZENITH 40°N
ZENITH 30°N
ZENITH 20°N
ZENITH 10°N

NORTH

HORIZON 60°N
HORIZON 50°N
HORIZON 40°N
HORIZON 30°N
HORIZON 20°N
HORIZON 10°N

EAST

	TIME	D.S.T.
April 1	24 h	01 h
April 15	23 h	24 h
May 1	22 h	23 h
May 15	21 h	22 h
June 1	20 h	21 h
etc.		

EPOCH 2000

SKY MAP 4
Facing South

Northern Latitudes

ECLIPTIC

WEST

HORIZON 50°N
HORIZON 40°N
HORIZON 30°N
HORIZON 20°N
HORIZON 10°N

SOUTH

ZENITH 50°N
ZENITH 40°N
ZENITH 30°N
ZENITH 20°N
ZENITH 10°N

EAST

WIL TIRION

Magnitudes: -1 0 1 2 3 4 (5)

⊙ Open Cluster   □ Nebula
⊙ ○ Variable   ⊕ Globular Cluster   ○ Galaxy

SKY MAP 5
Facing North

Northern Latitudes

	TIME	D.S.T.
May 1	24 h	01 h
May 15	23 h	24 h
June 1	22 h	23 h
June 15	21 h	22 h
July 1	20 h	21 h
etc.		

EPOCH 2000

SKY MAP 5
Facing South

Northern Latitudes

Magnitudes: -1 0 1 2 3 4 (5)

☼ ○ Variable   ✧ Open Cluster   ⊕ Globular Cluster   □ Nebula   ○ Galaxy

79

SKY MAP 5
Facing North

Northern Latitudes

	TIME	D.S.T.
May 1	24 h	01 h
May 15	23 h	24 h
June 1	22 h	23 h
June 15	21 h	22 h
July 1	20 h	21 h
etc.		

SKY MAP 5
Facing South

Northern Latitudes

ECLIPTIC

WEST

SOUTH

EAST

HORIZON 50N
HORIZON 40N
HORIZON 30N
HORIZON 20N

ZENITH 50N
ZENITH 40N
ZENITH 30N
ZENITH 20N
ZENITH 10N

Magnitudes: -1 0 1 2 3 4 (5)

☼ Open Cluster   ☐ Nebula

⊙ ○ Variable   ⊕ Globular Cluster   ○ Galaxy

W. TIRION

81

SKY MAP 6
Facing North

Northern Latitudes

	TIME	D.S.T.
June 1	24 h	01 h
June 15	23 h	24 h
July 1	22 h	23 h
July 15	21 h	22 h
August 1	20 h	21 h
etc.		

EPOCH 2000

SKY MAP 6
Facing South

Northern Latitudes

Magnitudes: -1 0 1 2 3 4 (5)

○ Open Cluster □ Nebula

⊕ ○ Variable ⊕ Globular Cluster ○ Galaxy

LEO MINOR

LEO

WEST

ECLIPTIC

URSA MAJOR

CRATER

HYDRA

CANES VENATICI

COMA BERENICES

VIRGO

CORVUS

Big Dipper

BOÖTES

Arcturus

Spica

180°

Antares

210°

CENTAURUS

CRUX

MUSCA

APUS

CORONA BOREALIS

SERPENS CAPUT

M5

LIBRA

SCORPIUS

LUPUS

NORMA

CIRCINUS

TRIANGULUM AUSTRALE

DRACO

ZENITH 50°N

M13

ZENITH 40°N

ZENITH 30°N

ZENITH 20°N

ZENITH 10°N

HERCULES

OPHIUCHUS

240°

ARA

SOUTH

Vega

LYRA

SERPENS CAUDA

SCUTUM

270°

M22

M8

SAGITTARIUS

CORONA AUSTRALIS

TELESCOPIUM

PAVO

VULPECULA

AQUILA

CYGNUS

SAGITTA

Altair

DELPHINUS

300°

CAPRICORNUS

MICROSCOPIUM

INDUS

GRUS

Deneb

LACERTA

EQUULEUS

AQUARIUS

330°

PISCIS AUSTRINUS

PEGASUS

EAST

TIRION

83

SKY MAP 6
Facing North

Northern Latitudes

	TIME	D.S.T.
June 1	24 h	01 h
June 15	23 h	24 h
July 1	22 h	23 h
July 15	21 h	22 h
August 1	20 h	21 h
etc.		

EPOCH 200

SKY MAP 6
Facing South

Northern Latitudes

Magnitudes: -1 0 1 2 3 4 (5)

- ○ Variable
⊕ Globular Cluster

☼ Open Cluster
⊖ Galaxy

□ Nebula

WEST

EAST

SOUTH

ECLIPTIC

HORIZON 50N
HORIZON 40N
HORIZON 30N
HORIZON 20N

ZENITH 50N
ZENITH 40N
ZENITH 30N
ZENITH 20N
ZENITH 10N

TIRION

SKY MAP 7
Facing North

Northern Latitudes

	TIME	D.S.T.
July 1	24 h	01 h
July 15	23 h	24 h
August 1	22 h	23 h
August 15	21 h	22 h
September 1	20 h	21 h
etc.		

SKY MAP 7
Facing South

Northern Latitudes

Magnitudes: -1 0 1 2 3 4 (5)

⬡ Open Cluster ☐ Nebula

⊙ O Variable ⊕ Globular Cluster ○ Galaxy

87

SKY MAP 7
Facing North

Northern Latitudes

	TIME	D.S.T.
July 1	24 h	01 h
July 15	23 h	24 h
August 1	22 h	23 h
August 15	21 h	22 h
September 1	20 h	21 h
etc.		

EPOCH 2000.

SKY MAP 7
Facing South

Northern Latitudes

Magnitudes: -1 0 1 2 3 4 (5)

⊙ ○ Variable   ⊕ Globular Cluster   ○ Galaxy

☼ Open Cluster   □ Nebula

IL TIRION

SKY MAP 8
Facing North

Northern Latitudes

	TIME	D.S.T.
August 1	24 h	01 h
August 15	23 h	24 h
September 1	22 h	23 h
September 15	21 h	22 h
October 1	20 h	21 h
etc.		

EPOCH 2000

SKY MAP 8
Facing South

Northern Latitudes

Magnitudes: -1 0 1 2 3 4 (5)

⋯ Open Cluster   ⬜ Nebula
⊛ ○ Variable   ⊕ Globular Cluster   ○ Galaxy

W. TIRION

91

SKY MAP 8
Facing North

Northern Latitudes

WEST

NORTH

HORIZON 50°N
HORIZON 40°N
HORIZON 30°N
HORIZON 20°N
HORIZON 10°N

30°N
20°N
10°N

ZENITH 50°N
ZENITH 40°N
ZENITH 30°N
ZENITH 20°N
ZENITH 10°N

ECLIPTIC

EAST

	TIME	D.S.T.
August 1	24 h	01 h
August 15	23 h	24 h
September 1	22 h	23 h
September 15	21 h	22 h
October 1	20 h	21 h
etc.		

EPOCH 2000.0

SKY MAP 8
Facing South

Northern Latitudes

Magnitudes: -1 0 1 2 3 4 (5)

◌ Open Cluster   ⬜ Nebula

⊚ ○ Variable   ⊕ Globular Cluster   ◯ Galaxy

WEST

SOUTH

EAST

ECLIPTIC

HORIZON 30°N
HORIZON 40°N
HORIZON 50°N
HORIZON 20°N
HORIZON 10°N

ZENITH 50°N
ZENITH 40°N
ZENITH 30°N
ZENITH 20°N
ZENITH 10°N

WIL TIRION

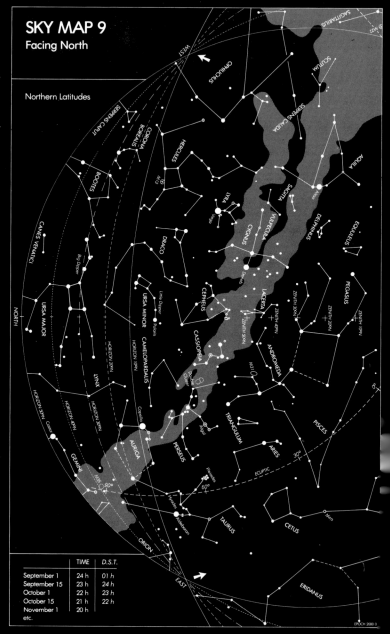

SKY MAP 9
Facing North

Northern Latitudes

	TIME	D.S.T.
September 1	24 h	01 h
September 15	23 h	24 h
October 1	22 h	23 h
October 15	21 h	22 h
November 1	20 h	
etc.		

EPOCH 2000.0

SKY MAP 9
Facing South

Northern Latitudes

Magnitudes: -1 0 1 2 3 4 (5)

◌ Open Cluster   □ Nebula
⊙ ○ Variable   ⊕ Globular Cluster   ○ Galaxy

SKY MAP 9
Facing North

Northern Latitudes

	TIME	D.S.T.
September 1	24 h	01 h
September 15	23 h	24 h
October 1	22 h	23 h
October 15	21 h	22 h
November 1	20 h	
etc.		

ECLIPTIC

EPOCH 2000

WEST

NORTH

EAST

HORIZON 50N
HORIZON 40N
HORIZON 30N
HORIZON 20N
HORIZON 10N

ZENITH 50N
ZENITH 40N
ZENITH 30N
ZENITH 20N
ZENITH 10N

SKY MAP 9
Facing South

Northern Latitudes

Magnitudes: -1 0 1 2 3 4 (5)

○ Open Cluster □ Nebula
⊙ ○ Variable ⊕ Globular Cluster ○ Galaxy

97

SKY MAP 10
Facing North

Northern Latitudes

	TIME	D.S.T.
October 1	24 h	01 h
October 15	23 h	24 h
November 1	22 h	
November 15	21 h	
December 1	20 h	
etc.		

EPOCH 2000

98

SKY MAP 10
Facing South

Northern Latitudes

Magnitudes: -1 0 1 2 3 4 (5)

☼ Open Cluster   ☐ Nebula
⊙ ○ Variable   ⊕ Globular Cluster   ○ Galaxy

WIL TIRION

99

SKY MAP 10
Facing North

Northern Latitudes

	TIME	D.S.T.
October 1	24 h	01 h
October 15	23 h	24 h
November 1	22 h	
November 15	21 h	
December 1	20 h	
etc.		

EPOCH 2000.0

SKY MAP 10
Facing South

Northern Latitudes

WEST

Northern Latitudes

HORIZON 50°N
HORIZON 40°N
HORIZON 30°N
HORIZON 20°N
HORIZON 10°N

ZENITH 50°N
ZENITH 40°N
ZENITH 30°N
ZENITH 20°N
ZENITH 10°N

SOUTH

ECLIPTIC

EAST

Magnitudes: -1 0 1 2 3 4 (5)

⊙ Open Cluster   □ Nebula

⊚ ○ Variable   ⊕ Globular Cluster   ○ Galaxy

WIL TIRION

SKY MAP 11
Facing North

Northern Latitudes

	TIME	D.S.T.
November 1	24 h	
November 15	23 h	
December 1	22 h	
December 15	21 h	
January 1	20 h	
etc.		

EPOCH 2000.0

SKY MAP 11
Facing South

Northern Latitudes

Magnitudes: -1 0 1 2 3 4 (5)

☼ Open Cluster   ☐ Nebula
⊕ ○ Variable   ⊕ Globular Cluster   ○ Galaxy

103

SKY MAP 11
Facing North

Northern Latitudes

WEST

NORTH HORIZON 60°N
HORIZON 40°N
HORIZON 30°N
HORIZON 20°N
HORIZON 10°N

ECLIPTIC

NORTH

HORIZON

ZENITH 50°N
ZENITH 40°N
ZENITH 30°N
ZENITH 20°N
ZENITH 10°N

EAST

	TIME	D.S.T.
November 1	24 h	
November 15	23 h	
December 1	22 h	
December 15	21 h	
January 1	20 h	
etc.		

EPOCH 2000

104

SKY MAP 11
Facing South

Northern Latitudes

Magnitudes: -1 0 1 2 3 4 (5)

○ Open Cluster   □ Nebula
⊙ ○ Variable   ⊕ Globular Cluster   ○ Galaxy

SKY MAP 12
Facing North

Northern Latitudes

	TIME	D.S.T.
December 1	24 h	
December 15	23 h	
January 1	22 h	
January 15	21 h	
February 1	20 h	
etc.		

EPOCH 2000

SKY MAP 12
Facing South

Northern Latitudes

Magnitudes: -1 0 1 2 3 4 (5)

○ Open Cluster   □ Nebula
⊛ ○ Variable   ⊕ Globular Cluster   ○ Galaxy

WIL TIRION

107

SKY MAP 12
Facing North

Northern Latitudes

	TIME	D.S.T.
December 1	24 h	
December 15	23 h	
January 1	22 h	
January 15	21 h	
February 1	20 h	
etc.		

WEST

ECLIPTIC

NORTH

ZENITH 50°N

ZENITH 40°N

ZENITH 30°N

ZENITH 20°N

ZENITH 10°N

HORIZON 50°N

HORIZON 40°N

HORIZON 30°N

HORIZON 20°N

HORIZON 10°N

EAST

EPOCH 2000.0

SKY MAP 12
Facing South

Northern Latitudes

WEST

SOUTH

EAST

HORIZON 50°N
HORIZON 40°N
HORIZON 30°N

ZENITH 50°N
ZENITH 40°N
ZENITH 30°N
ZENITH 20°N
ZENITH 10°N

ECLIPTIC

Magnitudes: -1 0 1 2 3 4 (5)

☼ Open Cluster   □ Nebula

⊕ ○ Variable   ⊕ Globular Cluster   ○ Galaxy

SKY MAP 13
Facing North

Southern Latitudes

	TIME	D.S.T.
January 1	24 h	01 h
January 15	23 h	24 h
February 1	22 h	23 h
February 15	21 h	22 h
March 1	20 h	21 h
etc.		

EPOCH 2000.0

SKY MAP 13
Facing South

Southern Latitudes

Magnitudes: -1 0 1 2 3 4 (5)

Open Cluster   ☐ Nebula
⊕ ○ Variable   ⊕ Globular Cluster   ○ Galaxy

TIRION

111

SKY MAP 14
Facing North

Southern Latitudes

	TIME	D.S.T.
February 1	24 h	01 h
February 15	23 h	24 h
March 1	22 h	23 h
March 15	21 h	22 h
April 1	20 h	
etc.		

EPOCH 2000

Southern Latitudes

Magnitudes: -1 0 1 2 3 4 (5)

◌ Open Cluster   ☐ Nebula
⊙ ○ Variable   ⊕ Globular Cluster   ○ Galaxy

SKY MAP 15
Facing North

Southern Latitudes

	TIME	D.S.T.
March 1	24 h	01 h
March 15	23 h	24 h
April 1	22 h	
April 15	21 h	
May 1	20 h	
etc.		

Southern Latitudes

Magnitudes: -1 0 1 2 3 4 (5)

◇ ○ Open Cluster   □ Nebula

⊙ ○ Variable   ⊕ Globular Cluster   ○ Galaxy

SKY MAP 16
Facing South

Southern Latitudes

Magnitudes: -1 0 1 2 3 4 (5)

☼ ○ Variable   ⊕ Globular Cluster   ○ Galaxy

⊙ ○ Open Cluster   □ Nebula

TIRION

SKY MAP 17
Facing North

Southern Latitudes

	TIME	D.S.T.
May 1	24 h	
May 15	23 h	
June 1	22 h	
June 15	21 h	
July 1	20 h	
etc.		

EPOCH 2000

Southern Latitudes

WEST

EAST

SOUTH

LEO
Regulus
150°
O 31
ECLIPTIC
180°
SEXTANS
VIRGO
Spica
CRATER
CORVUS
HYDRA
210°
ZENITH 10°S
ZENITH 20°S
ZENITH 30°S
ZENITH 40°S
ZENITH 50°S
SERPENS CAPUT
O M5
5h
LIBRA
CENTAURUS
⊕ ω
ANTLIA
PYXIS
PUPPIS
CANIS MAJOR
VELA
Sirius
Canopus
CARINA
PICTOR
DORADO
COLUMBA
CRUX
MUSCA
Mimosa
Acrux
Rigel Kent
Hadar
CHAMAELEON
VOLANS
MENSA
RETICULUM
HOROLOGIUM
ERIDANUS
Achernar
PHOENIX
LUPUS
NORMA
CIRCINUS
ARA
TRIANGULUM
AUSTRALE
APUS
OCTANS
HYDRUS
47 Tuc ⊕
TUCANA
INDUS
PAVO
TELESCOPIUM
GRUS
SCORPIUS
Antares
M4
M6
M7
M8
M20
M22
SAGITTARIUS
CORONA
AUSTRALIS
MICROSCOPIUM
PISCIS
AUSTRINUS
Fomalhaut
OPHIUCHUS
SERPENS CAUDA
SCUTUM
CAPRICORNUS
AQUARIUS
HORIZON 0°
HORIZON 10°S
HORIZON 20°S
HORIZON 30°S
HORIZON 40°S
50°
HERCULES
AQUILA
Altair
DELPHINUS
VULPECULA
SAGITTA

Magnitudes: -1   0   1   2   3 4 (5)

◇ ○ Open Cluster   □ Nebula
⊙ ⊕ Variable   ⊕ Globular Cluster   ○ Galaxy

SKY MAP 18
Facing North

Southern Latitudes

	TIME	D.S.T.
June 1	24 h	
June 15	23 h	
July 1	22 h	
July 15	21 h	
August 1	20 h	
etc.		

SKY MAP 18
Facing South

Southern Latitudes

Magnitudes: -1 0 1 2 3 4 (5)

○ Open Cluster   □ Nebula
⊕ ○ Variable   ⊕ Globular Cluster   ○ Galaxy

WIL TIRION

121

SKY MAP 19
Facing North

Southern Latitudes

	TIME	D.S.T.
July 1	24 h	
July 15	23 h	
August 1	22 h	
August 15	21 h	
September 1	20 h	21 h
etc.		

EPOCH 200

SKY MAP 19
Facing South

Southern Latitudes

Magnitudes: -1 0 1 2 3 4 (5)

☼ Open Cluster   ☐ Nebula
⊙ ○ Variable   ⊕ Globular Cluster   ○ Galaxy

TIRION

123

Southern Latitudes

	TIME	D.S.T.
August 1	24 h	
August 15	23 h	
September 1	22 h	23 h
September 15	21 h	22 h
October 1	20 h	21 h
etc.		

EPOCH 2000

SKY MAP 20
Facing South

Southern Latitudes

Magnitudes: -1 0 1 2 3 4 (5)

☼ Open Cluster   ☐ Nebula
⊙ ○ Variable   ⊕ Globular Cluster   ○ Galaxy

125

SKY MAP 21
Facing North

Southern Latitudes

	TIME	D.S.T.
September 1	24 h	01 h
September 15	23 h	24 h
October 1	22 h	23 h
October 15	21 h	22 h
November 1	20 h	21 h
etc.		

EPOCH 2000

SKY MAP 21

Facing South

Southern Latitudes

Magnitudes: -1 0 1 2 3 4 (5)

☼ Open Cluster   □ Nebula
⊙ O Variable   ⊕ Globular Cluster   ○ Galaxy

SKY MAP 22
Facing North

Southern Latitudes

	TIME	D.S.T.
October 1	24 h	01 h
October 15	23 h	24 h
November 1	22 h	23 h
November 15	21 h	22 h
December 1	20 h	21 h
etc.		

Southern Latitudes

Magnitudes: -1 0 1 2 3 4 (5)

○ Open Cluster   □ Nebula
⊙ ○ Variable   ⊕ Globular Cluster   ○ Galaxy

Il. TIRION

SKY MAP 23
Facing North

Southern Latitudes

	TIME	D.S.T.
November 1	24 h	01 h
November 15	23 h	24 h
December 1	22 h	23 h
December 15	21 h	22 h
January 1	20 h	21 h
etc.		

Southern Latitudes

PEGASUS

EQUULEUS

WEST

AQUILA

AQUARIUS

330°

300°

PISCIS AUSTRINUS

CAPRICORNUS

MICROSCOPIUM

CORONA AUSTRALIS

SAGITTARIUS

Fomalhaut

GRUS

INDUS

TELESCOPIUM

SCORPIUS

PISCES

ECLIPTIC

0°

SCULPTOR

PHOENIX

TUCANA

PAVO

NORMA

CETUS

47 Tuc

ARA

CIRCINUS

LUPUS

ZENITH -10°S

ZENITH -20°S

ZENITH -30°S

ZENITH -40°S

Achernar

HOROLOGIUM

HYDRUS

MENSA

OCTANS

APUS

TRIANGULUM AUSTRALE

SOUTH

FORNAX

RETICULUM

CHAMAELEON

MUSCA

Rigil Kentaurus

TAURUS

ERIDANUS

CAELUM

DORADO

PICTOR

VOLANS

Miaplacidus

Hadar

CRUX

CENTAURUS

LEPUS

COLUMBA

Canopus

CARINA

VELA

ORION

M42

Rigel

CANIS MAJOR

PUPPIS

ANTLIA

Betelgeuse

Sirius

M41

PYXIS

HORIZON 0°

HORIZON 10°S

HORIZON 20°S

HORIZON 30°S

HORIZON 40°S

GEMINI

MONOCEROS

Procyon

CANIS MINOR

EAST

Magnitudes: -1 0 1 2 3 4 (5)

CANCER

HYDRA

☼ Open Cluster

□ Nebula

⊙ ○ Variable

⊕ Globular Cluster

○ Galaxy

IL TIRION

131

SKY MAP 24
Facing North

Southern Latitudes

	TIME	D.S T.
December 1	24 h	01 h
December 15	23 h	24 h
January 1	22 h	23 h
January 15	21 h	22 h
February 1	20 h	21 h
etc.		

EPOCH 2000

132

Southern Latitudes

Magnitudes: -1 0 1 2 3 4 (5)

☼ ○ Variable   ⊙ ○ Open Cluster   □ Nebula
⊕ Globular Cluster   ○ Galaxy

4

THE CONSTELLATIONS

Today we know that the stars in any given constellation do not necessarily have any physical relationship to one another. Some stars within a constellation may be relatively close to earth, while others may be relatively far away. All we know is that the stars are in roughly the same direction as seen from earth. Yet, just as it was convenient for the people of ancient civilizations to divide up the heavens into constellations or groups of seemingly related stars, it remains convenient for us to associate each star with one and only one constellation.

History of the Constellations

Exactly when and where the first system of constellations was devised is not known. Cuneiform texts and artifacts from the civilizations of the Euphrates Valley suggest that the lion, the bull, and the scorpion were already associated with constellations by 4000 B.C. Many scholars have been intrigued by the fact that there is some similarity between the names given to constellations by civilizations separated by vast distances. Perhaps a very ancient common tradition for naming a few groups of stars will ultimately be found. For the most part, however, the constellations of different civilizations appear to have developed independently of one another.

Of the 88 constellations listed by the International Astronomical Union in the definitive compilation of 1930, more than half were known to the ancients. Early records of the Greek constellations are found in the poetry of Homer, from about the 9th century B.C., and of Aratus, from about the 3rd century B.C. Sometime between the lives of these two poets, probably in the mid- to late 5th century B.C., the *ecliptic*—the path the sun appears to follow across the celestial sphere in the course of a year—was identified in Babylon and perhaps in Greece as well. The Babylonians divided the ecliptic into the 12 parts of the *zodiac*—the band of constellations through which the sun, moon, and planets move (as seen from earth) in the course of the year.

During the 2nd century A.D., the astronomer Ptolemy catalogued information about 1022 stars, grouped into 48 constellations. Not surprisingly, Ptolemy's catalogue comprises only stars visible from the latitude of Alexandria, where he lived and wrote.

The *Almagest,* Ptolemy's chief work, remained the last word on the constellations until the 16th century, when European voyages of discovery took navigators into southern latitudes. The first star atlas, published by Johann Bayer in 1603, included 12 new constellations visible in southern-hemisphere skies. In 1624, the German astronomer Jakob Bartsch added three new constellations in the spaces that existed between previously named constellations. Bartsch also listed as a separate constellation the grouping we know as Crux, the Cross, whose four chief stars Ptolemy had noted as part of the constellation Centaurus. (The name Crux also reveals an attempt to depaganize the heavens that was typical of this period.) Earlier in the 17th century, Tycho Brahe likewise elevated to the status of constellation the asterism Coma Berenices, Berenice's Hair, which the ancients had thought of as part of Leo or Virgo.

Seven more constellations visible from midnorthern latitudes were added by the German astronomer Johannes Hevelius in 1687. The visit of Nicolas Louis de Lacaille to the Cape of Good Hope in 1750 resulted in 14 additional southern constellations. There have been other attempts since that time to invent new constellations, but official acceptance has been withheld. However, since the mid-1800s it has become traditional to omit Ptolemy's largest constellation, Argo Navis (Argo the Ship), and to list in its stead three constellations representing the ship's keel (Carina), stern (Puppis), and sails (Vela), in addition to the compass (Pyxis) invented by Lacaille.

The current list of constellations is the one adopted by the International Astronomical Union in 1928, and codified in a list two years later. The IAU defined a constellation as one of 88 regions into which they divided the entire sky; each area of the sky belongs to one and only one of these regions. The boundaries zigzag so that the lines that separate constellations do not wreak havoc with ancient figures. A few stars that had been previously thought of as part of another constellation wound up in a new one—for example, one of the four stars of the Great Square of Pegasus is now officially in Andromeda. But on the whole, the IAU division provided a great simplification.

The lines dividing constellations were originally drawn along lines of right ascension and declination for the year 1875.0. (Astronomers use decimals to indicate parts of a year; 1875.0 means the beginning of the year 1875.) But because of *precession* (the drifting of the direction of the earth's axis among the stars), the lines between constellations have drifted slightly; the Atlas Charts in Chapter 7 show that the lines dividing the constellations are no longer aligned so neatly with lines marking the coordinate scales, which are now drawn for the date 2000.0, the current *epoch.*

Precession has also changed the dates when the sun appears to drift through each constellation of the zodiac, so that the sun is not actually in the sign listed in the newspapers' daily horoscopes. The sun actually passes through 13, not 12, constellations in the course of a year. Further, all or part of 24 constellations are actually in the zodiac, if we define it as the region within about 8° of the ecliptic—

the band in which we find the first eight planets. (If we include Pluto, unknown to the ancients, the band would be wider still.)

The list below divides the constellations into three groups. First come the constellations of the traditional zodiac, listed in order around the sky: Aries, Taurus, Gemini, Cancer, Leo, Virgo, Libra, Scorpius, Sagittarius, Capricornus, Aquarius, and Pisces. Then come, alphabetically, the other constellations catalogued by Ptolemy, arranged here alphabetically. Finally, we list the constellations added since 1600, also alphabetically. Since in many cases more than one mythological story is associated with the same constellation, the list does not aim at providing full coverage of all the myths. For each constellation, we list the numbers of the Atlas Charts on which the constellation is found in Chapter 7. A list of standard abbreviations for the constellations and the genitive form of their names used to make star names (*e.g.* alpha Centauri, in Centaurus) appears in Appendix 1.

The old star atlases of Bayer (1603), Hevelius (1687), and Johann Elert Bode (1801) contain beautiful drawings of some of the constellations. A selection of these drawings appear throughout this guide.

Constellations of the Zodiac

Aries, the Ram. The golden fleece of this ram was the prize ultimately carried off by Jason, leader of the Argonauts. (Atlas Charts 10, 22, and 23)

Taurus, the Bull. Zeus disguised himself as a snow-white bull in order to attract Europa, Princess of Phoenicia. Drawn to the animal by its beauty, she climbed onto its back. Zeus then swam with his passenger to Crete, where he revealed his identity to her and won her. (Atlas Charts 10, 11, 23, and 24)

Gemini, the Twins. These are the two devoted twins and, some say, half-brothers. Gemini is the Roman word for the Dioscuri, who in Greek mythology were the sons of Leda, the wife of Tyndarus, the king of Sparta. Though Castor was the son of Tyndarus, Pollux (Polydeuces in Greek) may have been the son of Zeus, which would have made him immortal. After Castor's death, Pollux was overwhelmed with grief, and wanted to share his immortality with his twin. Finally Zeus reunited them by placing them together in the heavens. (Atlas Charts 12, 24, and 25)

Cancer, the Crab. When Hercules was struggling with Hydra (see p. 141), Juno sent this crab to attack him. The crab did not succeed in its mission, and instead was crushed. But Juno rewarded the crab for its attempt by placing it among the stars. (Atlas Charts 13, 25, and 26)

Leo, the Lion. The thick, tough skin of this, the fiercest lion in the world, became the trademark of Hercules (see p. 141) after the hero succeeded in strangling the lion to death, thus successfully completing his First Labor. (Atlas Charts 13, 14, 26, and 27)

Virgo, the Virgin. Virgo has been identified with a variety of hero-

Fig. 4-1 Taurus, the Bull, from the star atlas of Bayer (1603). (Jay M. Pasachoff)

ines. The association with Ceres, goddess of the harvest, helps explain the name of the brightest star in Virgo, Spica, which means an ear of wheat or corn. (Atlas Charts 27, 28, 39, and 40)

Libra, the Scales. This constellation was probably invented at the time the zodiac was established. The Arabic names of the two brightest stars in Libra mean the southern and the northern claw, confirming that at one time Libra was a part of Scorpius. The constellation was later associated with the scales held by Astraea, goddess of justice. (Atlas Charts 28, 29, and 40)

Scorpius, the Scorpion. According to one account, Apollo, who was concerned about protecting his sister Artemis's virginity, sent the scorpion to kill Orion (see p. 142). Both Orion and Scorpius were placed as far from one another in the heavens as possible, so as to avoid further trouble between them, though Scorpius still pursues Orion around the celestial sphere. (Atlas Charts 29 and 41)

Sagittarius, the Archer. This constellation has been associated with the centaur Chiron, who was known for his marksmanship as well as for his expertise in medicine and music. Others say that Chiron was too civilized a model for Sagittarius; they say that Chiron is associated with the constellation Sagittarius because he identified it in the sky to help guide the Argonauts on their voyage to Thessaly. (Atlas Charts 30, 31, 41–43)

Capricornus, the Sea Goat. The last three constellations of the zodiac are in the region of the sky called the Sea. From early antiquity this constellation has been depicted with the head and body of a goat and with the tail of a fish. According to one interpretation, the goat, an expert climber, represents the sun's climb from its lowest position in the sky, which is in this constellation. The fish's tail may represent the seasonal rains. (Atlas Charts 31, 32, and 43)

Aquarius, the Water Carrier. Early artifacts depict this constellation as a man or boy pouring water from a bucket, also representing the rainy season. (Atlas Charts 21, 31, 32, and 44)

Pisces, the Fish. Venus and Cupid escaped from the monster Typhon (see under Pisces Austrinus, p. 142) by disguising themselves as these fish and jumping into the Euphrates River. (Atlas Charts 9, 21, and 22)

Constellations Catalogued by Ptolemy

Andromeda. Several constellations are associated with the story of Andromeda, the daughter of Cassiopeia and Cepheus. When Cassiopeia boasted that her beauty exceeded that of the sea nymphs, the slighted beauties asked Neptune, the god of the sea, to punish the braggart. Neptune sent the sea monster Cetus to ravage the kingdom of Cepheus. When Cepheus consulted an oracle for advice, he was informed that only the sacrifice of Andromeda to Cetus, the sea monster, would appease the gods. Andromeda was duly chained to a rock by the sea but her fate was averted by the arrival of Perseus (see p. 142), who turned Cetus into stone by flashing the face of Medusa before the monster. (Atlas Charts 9, 10, and 20)

Aquarius, the Water Carrier. Zodiacal; see above.

Aquila, the Eagle. This bird was rewarded with a place in the heavens for having brought from earth the handsome Ganymede to serve as cupbearer of the gods. (Atlas Charts 30 and 31)

Aries. Zodiacal; see above.

Ara, the Altar. The Olympian gods raised this altar to commemorate their victory over the Titans. (Atlas Charts 41 and 51)

Argo Navis, the Ship Argo. This ship carried the Argonauts from Thessaly to Colchis in search of the Golden Fleece. No longer considered a single constellation, this grouping has been subdivided into four constellations: Carina, Puppis, Pyxis, and Vela (see pp. 144–147). See the photograph on p. 38.

Aries, the Ram. Zodiacal; see above.

Auriga, the Charioteer. No story definitively explains the figure that this constellation's stars supposedly define—a charioteer (minus chariot and horse), holding the reins in his right hand, a goat on his left shoulder, and two small kids in his left arm. One myth associates Auriga with Erecthonius, the lame son of Vulcan and Minerva. Erecthonius invented the chariot, which not only enabled him to get around but also won him a place in the heavens. (Atlas Charts 3, 11, and 12)

Boötes, the Herdsman. No single myth is definitively associated with this constellation. According to one story, Boötes was rewarded with a place in the heavens for his invention of the plow. (Atlas Charts 15, 16, 28, and 29)

Cancer, the Crab. Zodiacal; see above.

Canis Major, the Greater Dog. This constellation has been associated with several mythical dogs, including the hound of Actaeon, but it has also been known as the Dog of Orion. Orion loved to hunt wild animals, such as Lepus, the Hare (see p. 141); Canis Major, at Orion's heel in the sky, seems ready to pounce on the Hare. (Atlas Charts 24, 25, and 36)

Canis Minor, the Lesser Dog. Among the dogs with which this constellation has been associated is Helen's favorite, which allowed Paris to abduct her without resistance. (Atlas Chart 25)

Capricornus, the Sea Goat. Zodiacal; see above.

Cassiopeia. See also Andromeda (above). When Cassiopeia objected to the wedding of Perseus and Andromeda, Perseus exhibited the head of Medusa. As a result, his enemies, including Cassiopeia, were turned into stone. Neptune placed Cassiopeia in the heavens, but in order to humiliate her, he arranged it so that at certain times of the year she would appear to be hanging upside down. (Atlas Charts 1, 2, and 9)

Centaurus, the Centaur. This constellation is often identified with Chiron (see under Sagittarius). When Hercules accidentally wounded Chiron with one of his poisoned arrows, Chiron suffered greatly, but, as an immortal, could not find a release in death. He resolved his problem by offering himself as a substitute for Prometheus, a Titan who was suffering because he had stolen fire from heaven for the benefit of humanity. The gods had punished Prometheus by chaining him to a rock, where each day a vulture devoured his liver, which was restored each night. At the request of Hercules, Zeus agreed to release Prometheus if a substitute could be found for him. Chiron offered his immortality to Prometheus and went to Tartarus, where Prometheus had been imprisoned by Zeus. Zeus placed Chiron among the stars. See also Corona Australis (below). (Atlas Charts 38–40, 49, and 50)

Cepheus, a king of Ethiopia. See Andromeda (above). (Atlas Charts 1, 2, and 8)

Cetus, the Whale. A sea monster; see Andromeda. (Atlas Charts 21–23, 33, and 34) See the photograph on p. 27.

Corona Australis, the Southern Crown. Also called Corona Austrina. The Southern Crown is said to represent a crown of laurel or olive, placed on victors in games and on those who perform great service to their peers. According to one story, this constellation symbolizes a laurel wreath ready to be placed on the brow of Chiron in acknowledgment of his service to Prometheus. See Centaurus (above). (Atlas Chart 42)

Corona Borealis, the Northern Crown. This constellation is generally associated with Ariadne, daughter of Minos, king of Crete. Each year, as a tribute to Crete, 14 young people from Athens were fed to the Minotaur, the monster that Minos kept in a labyrinth. When

Theseus arrived from Athens as one of the prospective victims, Ariadne fell in love with him. She offered to help him escape the Minotaur if he promised to take her back to Athens as his bride. Theseus agreed. Ariadne kept her part of the bargain, and after Theseus killed the Minotaur, they sailed off. They stopped on the island of Naxos, where Theseus and the Athenians abandoned the sleeping Ariadne. When she awoke, clamoring for vengeance, she found Dionysus, god of the vine, who married her immediately. As a wedding gift, Dionysus gave her a crown studded with gems. When Ariadne died, Dionysus set the crown among the stars. (Atlas Charts 16, 17)

Corvus, the Raven. According to some, this is the raven that Apollo sent to guard his beloved, Coronis, during his absences. During one of the god's absences, Coronis fell in love with another and was unfaithful to Apollo. When the raven told Apollo what had happened, Apollo rewarded the bird by placing it in the sky. (Atlas Charts 27 and 39)

Crater, the Cup. This constellation, which is supposed to resemble a goblet, has been associated with various gods and heroes, including Apollo, Bacchus, Hercules, and Achilles. (Atlas Charts 27 and 38)

Cygnus, the Swan. According to one legend, this constellation is related to the story of Phaethon, a mortal who learned that his father was Helius, the sun god. Helius rashly promised to let Phaethon drive the chariot of the sun across the sky. Phaethon soon lost control, and his reckless driving threatened to destroy the earth with the sun's heat. Zeus intervened by hurling a thunderbolt at Phaethon, who fell into the Eridanus River (see below). In his grief, Phaethon's devoted friend Cygnus dived into the water in search of the body. Apollo took pity on Cygnus, changed him into a swan, and placed the swan in the sky. (Atlas Charts 7, 8, 18, and 19)

Delphinus, the Dolphin. In one story, the dolphin successfully convinced the sea goddess Amphitrite to marry Poseidon, from whom she had been fleeing. As a reward, Poseidon placed Delphinus among the stars. (Atlas Charts 19 and 31)

Draco, the Dragon. Among the monsters with whom this constellation has been associated is the dragon slain by Cadmus, brother of Europa, on the site of the city that was later to become Thebes. After Cadmus accomplished this feat, Athena instructed him to plant some of the dragon's teeth. Armed men grew up from the soil; when Cadmus threw stones into their midst, they began to fight among themselves. All but five died, and the survivors helped Cadmus build the city of Thebes. (Atlas Charts 4–8)

Equuleus, the Little Horse. This group of stars is associated with Celeris, the brother of Pegasus (see p. 142). Mercury gave Celeris to the hero Castor. (Atlas Chart 32)

Eridanus, the River. The waters of the River Eridanus are said to steam perpetually as a result of Phaethon's fiery fall (see under Cygnus, above). (Atlas Charts 22–24, 34, 35, and 46)

Gemini, the Twins. Zodiacal; see above.

Hercules. The most famous of all the Greek heroes, Hercules was worshiped throughout the Mediterranean world. Best known for his

Twelve Labors, he performed many incredible deeds throughout his life. His death provided an equally dramatic end to his career. After accidentally killing a young man, Hercules decided to go into exile with his wife, Deianira. When they came to a river, Hercules swam on ahead, leaving Deianira in the charge of Nessus, a centaur who offered to carry her across the water on his back. When Nessus tried to rape Deianira, Hercules shot the centaur with a poisoned arrow. Before Nessus died, he suggested to Deianira that she keep his blood as a love charm, should she ever need to revive Hercules's interest in her. Some time later, learning of her husband's interest in another woman, Deinara rubbed the centaur's dried blood on one of Hercules's robes. The hero's body burned as soon as he put the robe on, and when he tried to remove the robe, his skin came off with it. When Deianira learned of the effects of the robe, she hanged herself. Hercules built and mounted a funeral pyre, which only the compassionate Philoctetes had the courage to light. Instantly, a flash of lightning was seen. The pyre burned out completely, leaving no bones behind. It was assumed that Hercules's body had been carried to Olympus. (Atlas Charts 17, 18, 29, and 30)

Hydra, the Water Snake. Successfully eliminating this many-headed monster was Hercules's Second Labor—a difficult task because whenever one head was cut off, two new ones grew in its place. Hercules solved this problem by having his nephew, Iolaus, burn the stump of each head as soon as Hercules cut them off, thus preventing new heads from sprouting. Because Iolaus assisted him in this labor, Hercules was required to substitute another one in its place. Do not confuse this constellation with Hydrus, a southern constellation (p. 145). (Atlas Charts 25, 26, and 37–40)

Leo, the Lion. Zodiacal; see above.

Lepus, the Hare. According to some, the Hare was placed in the heavens to be near its hunter, Orion. (see Canis Major, p. 139; Atlas Charts 24, 35, and 36)

Libra, the Scales. Zodiacal; see above.

Lupus, the Wolf. One story associates this constellation with the impious Lycaon, who doubted Zeus's claim to divinity. In order to test Zeus, Lycaon served the king of the gods the flesh of a child. To punish Lycaon for this impious act, Zeus transformed him into a wolf. (Atlas Charts 40 and 50)

Lyra, the Lyre. This is the instrument given by Apollo to Orpheus, the most famous poet and musician in Greek legend. When his wife Eurydice died, Orpheus was told he could bring her back from the underworld on condition that he not look back at her until she was in the light of the sun. Orpheus led her out, playing on the lyre, but when he reached the light of the sun, he looked back. Because Eurydice had not yet reached the sunlight, he lost her forever. He remained inconsolable and refused the advances of all the women who tried to win his love. One day a group of women whom he had scorned attacked him; drowning out his music, they tore him apart and threw his head and lyre into the Hebrus River. Apollo intervened, however; Orpheus's head was placed in a cave, his limbs were buried at the foot of Mount Parnassus, and his lyre was placed among the stars. (Atlas Chart 18)

Ophiuchus, the Serpent-bearer. This group is generally identified with Asclepius, the first physician and surgeon, who accompanied the Argonauts. He was so successful in curing the ill and wounded that Pluto began worrying about the declining immigration into the underworld. Pluto convinced Zeus to strike Asclepius with a thunderbolt and put him among the constellations. The snake twined around a staff remains the symbol of medicine today, perhaps because of the association of the snake's periodic sloughing off of its skin with the renewal of life. (Atlas Charts 29, 30, and 41)

Orion, the Hunter. When this giant hunter met Artemis, goddess of the hunt and of the moon, her brother Apollo feared for her virginity. Apollo sent Scorpius, the Scorpion (see p. 137), to attack Orion, who leaped into the sea to escape. Apollo then tricked his unsuspecting sister into shooting at a dark spot on the waves—actually Orion. The goddess tried to have Asclepius revive Orion, her hunting companion, but the physician had been killed by Zeus's thunderbolt (see under Ophiuchus, above). Artemis then placed Orion in the heavens, where he would be pursued eternally by the scorpion. (Atlas Charts 11, 12, 23, and 24) See the photograph on p. 31.

Pegasus. This is the winged horse that sprang up from the blood of Medusa after Perseus killed her (see below). Pegasus was tamed by Bellerophon, whose successes against monsters and enemies had gone to his head. When Bellerophon decided to ride Pegasus up to Olympus, the gods were offended, so Zeus sent a gadfly to sting Pegasus. Pegasus reared in pain, causing Bellerophon to topple off. Bellerophon was lamed and blinded, but Pegasus continued to climb Olympus, and earned a place among the stars as a constellation. (Atlas Charts 9, 19–21, and 32)

Perseus. Armed with a polished shield given to him by Athena, Perseus killed Medusa, the only one of the Gorgons who was mortal. The three Gorgons were winged monsters so horrible to behold that all who looked upon them were turned into stone. Athena told Perseus to use the shield as a mirror. He could thus avoid looking directly at the Gorgons. After he cut off Medusa's head, the winged horse Pegasus sprang from her blood. The head of Medusa enabled Perseus to overcome many enemies, as well as to kill the monster Cetus (see under Andromeda, p. 138; Atlas Charts 2, 3, 9–11)

Pisces, the Fish. Zodiacal; see above.

Piscis Austrinus, the Southern Fish. Also known as Piscis Australis, this constellation is linked by some to the story of the monster Typhon. After Zeus and the Olympians overthrew the Titans, sons of Gaea, Gaea gave birth to another son, Typhon. She incited Typhon to attack the Olympians, who assumed various animal forms to evade him—Venus, for example, assumed the form of a fish. (See also under Pisces, p. 138; Atlas Charts 43 and 44)

Sagitta, the Arrow. This constellation has been associated with several different arrows, including the one that Apollo used to slay the three one-eyed giants called Cyclops. (Atlas Charts 18, 19, and 31)

Fig. 4-2 Perseus, from the star atlas of Bode (1804). (Jay M. Pasachoff)

Sagittarius, the Archer. Zodiacal; see above.
Scorpius, the Scorpion. Zodiacal; see above.
Serpens, the Serpent. This constellation is associated with Ophiu-chus (see above). (Serpens Caput, the head, is on Atlas Charts 16 and 29; Serpens Cauda, the tail, is on Atlas Chart 30)
Taurus, the Bull. Zodiacal; see above.
Triangulum, the Triangle. This minor constellation has been asso-ciated with different geographical locations. Not surprisingly, because of its similarity in shape to the Greek letter Δ (delta), it was sometimes called Delta, and thus was associated with Egypt and the Nile, whose delta provided fertile land. It was also associated with the island of Sicily, whose three promontories give it a triangular shape. (Atlas Charts 9 and 10)
Ursa Major, the Great Bear. Zeus fell in love with Callisto, daugh-ter of Lycaon (see under Lupus, p. 141). Together they had a son, Arcas. Callisto was changed into a bear by one of the gods—some say by Artemis, who was angry with Callisto, her formerly chaste companion; some say by Zeus, who was anxious to protect Callisto from the jealousy of his wife, Hera; and some say by Hera. See the photograph on p. 18. (Atlas Charts 4–6, 13–15)
Ursa Minor, the Lesser Bear. When Arcas reached manhood, he was about to shoot a bear, unaware that it was his mother, Callisto. To protect Callisto, Zeus changed Arcas into a bear as well, and car-ried them both off by their tails to the heavens, where they became constellations. Annoyed at this honor, Hera took her revenge by con-vincing Poseidon not to allow the bears to bathe in the sea. For this

reason, Ursa Major and Ursa Minor are circumpolar constellations, never sinking below the horizon. (Atlas Charts 2 and 6)

Virgo, the Virgin. Zodiacal; see above.

Constellations Added Since 1600

Note that the names of constellations reflect the times in which they were named; we find here many names of machines in addition to allusions to classical myths.

Antlia, the Pump. Lacaille called this constellation the Machine Pneumatique, and in Germany it is called the Luftumpe, or air pump. (Atlas Charts 37 and 38)

Apus, the Bird of Paradise. The bird for which this constellation was named was originally found in Papua New Guinea. (Atlas Charts 50 and 51)

Caelum, the Chisel. Lacaille formed this constellation from stars between Columba and Eridanus. (Atlas Chart 35)

Camelopardalis, the Giraffe. Bartsch first outlined this constellation, claiming that it represented the camel that brought Rebecca to Isaac. The constellation lies in the large space between Perseus, Auriga, and the Bears. (Atlas Charts 2 and 3)

Canes Venatici, the Hunting Dogs. Hevelius formed this constellation out of stars between Ursa Major and Boötes, to represent the two greyhounds held in leash by Boötes (see p. 138; Atlas Chart 15)

Carina, the Keel [of Argo]. See Argo Navis, p. 138. (Atlas Charts 47–49) See the drawing on p. 38.

Chamaeleon, the Chameleon. This small constellation lies below Carina, separated from the south celestial pole by Octans. (Atlas Charts 48 and 49)

Circinus, the Drawing Compass. This constellation, south of Lupus, was added by Lacaille. (Atlas Chart 50)

Columba, the Dove. Petrus Plancius, a 16th-century Dutch theologian and mapmaker, formed this constellation south of Lepus to represent the dove that Noah sent out from the ark. (Atlas Charts 35 and 36)

Coma Berenices, Berenice's Hair. Long recognized as an asterism, Coma Berenices was first listed as a separate constellation in 1602 by Tycho Brahe. Berenice was the wife of Ptolemy Euergetes of Egypt in the middle of the 3rd century B.C. She vowed to sacrifice her hair to Venus if her husband returned safely from war. After his safe return she honored her vow, but her hair disappeared overnight. A Greek astronomer pointed to the constellation, claiming it to be the missing hair, which Venus must have placed in the sky. Coma Berenices contains the north galactic pole (the north pole with respect to the orientation of our Milky Way Galaxy). (Atlas Charts 15, 27, and 28)

Crux, the Cross. The ancient Greeks considered the four chief stars of Crux as part of the Centaur, which surrounds Crux on three sides. There is no central star to the cross, so it looks more like a kite. (Atlas Chart 49)

Dorado, the Swordfish. The Large Magellanic Cloud lies within this constellation. (Atlas Chart 47)

Fornax, the Furnace. Lacaille formed this group from stars within the southern bend of the River Eridanus. (Atlas Chart 34)

Grus, the Crane. A southern constellation. (*Grus americana* is the scientific name for the whooping crane.) (Atlas Charts 43–45 and 52)

Horologium, the Clock. One of Lacaille's constellations. (Atlas Charts 34 and 46)

Hydrus, the Water Snake. Not to be confused with the Ptolemaic constellation Hydra, Hydrus lies between the Large and Small Magellanic Clouds. (Atlas Chart 46)

Indus, the Indian. This constellation is supposed to represent a native American, with arrows in both hands. (Atlas Charts 43 and 52)

Lacerta, the Lizard. Hevelius formed this constellation from stars lying between Cygnus and Andromeda. The shape supposedly was determined by the available space between the older constellations. (Atlas Charts 1, 8, and 20)

Leo Minor, the Lesser Lion. Hevelius formed this constellation from stars lying between the zodiacal constellations Leo and Ursa Major. The name reflects his belief that this star grouping was similar in nature to the two other groups. (Atlas Charts 13 and 14)

Lynx. Hevelius chose this name, explaining that only those with the eyes of a lynx could discern this star group. (Atlas Charts 3, 4, 12, and 13)

Mensa, the Table. Lacaille named this constellation Mons Mensae, after Table Mountain, south of Cape Town, South Africa, where he did much of his work. (Atlas Chart 47)

Microscopium, the Microscope. Lacaille formed this constellation from the stars south of Capricornus and west of Piscis Austrinus. (Atlas Chart 43)

Monoceros, the Unicorn. The Unicorn is generally attributed to Bartsch, but some claim that it is older. (Atlas Charts 24 and 25)

Musca, the Fly. In early catalogues, this group, south of the Southern Cross and northeast of Chamaeleon, was sometimes also called the Bee. (Atlas Chart 49)

Norma, the Square. One of Lacaille's constellations, Norma lies immediately to the north of the Southern Triangle, Triangulum Australe (see below). (Atlas Charts 40 and 50)

Octans, the Octant. Lacaille named this constellation to recognize John Hadley's invention of the octant in 1730. It includes the south celestial pole. (Atlas Charts 45–52)

Pavo, the Peacock. According to myth, Argos, the builder of the ship Argo, was changed into a peacock by Hera after she brought his ship to the heavens. So it was fitting that one of the 12 new constellations in the southern skies should be named after the peacock, thus reuniting Argos and his ship. (Atlas Charts 51 and 52)

Phoenix. Another one of the 12 new constellations in the southern skies, named after the mythical bird. The phoenix was said to live 500 or 600 years in the Arabian wilderness, to burn itself on a funeral

Fig. 4-3 Cygnus, the Swan, from the 1603 star atlas of Bayer. (Jay M. Pasachoff)

pyre, and to rise from its ashes to live again. In ancient China, Egypt, India, and Persia, the phoenix was an astronomical symbol representing natural cycles. (Atlas Charts 33, 45, and 46)

Pictor, the Easel. Lacaille named this grouping Equuleus Pictoris, or Painter's Easel. (Equuleus also means "small horse.") The name has been shortened to Pictor. The constellation lies south of Columba. (Atlas Charts 35 and 47)

Puppis, the Stern [of Argo]. See Argo Navis. (Atlas Charts 25, 36–37) See the drawing on p. 38.

Pyxis, the Compass [of Argo]. See Argo Navis. (Atlas Chart 37) See the drawing on p. 38.

Reticulum, the Reticle. This constellation was named by Lacaille in honor of his reticle, the network of fine lines he placed in the focus of his telescope in order to make his observations in the southern hemisphere. The constellation, however, had been drawn earlier by Isaak Habrecht of Strasbourg. (Atlas Chart 46)

Sagittarius, the Archer. Zodiacal; see above.

Scorpius, the Scorpion. Zodiacal; see above.

Sculptor. Lacaille named this grouping l'Atelier du Sculpteur, the Sculptor's Studio, but the name has been shortened. The constellation lies between Cetus and Phoenix and contains the south galactic pole. (Atlas Charts 33 and 44)

Scutum, the Shield. Hevelius formed this constellation from several stars in the Milky Way, between the tail of Serpens and the head of Sagittarius. The constellation is supposed to represent the coat of arms of John Sobieski, king of Poland, in honor of his successful resistance against the Turkish attack on Vienna in 1683. (Atlas Chart 30)

Sextans, the Sextant. Hevelius formed this constellation, between Leo and Hydra, to recognize the importance of the sextant to his measurements of the stars. (Atlas Chart 26)

Telescopium, the Telescope. Lacaille's original formation of this constellation, between Ara and Sagittarius, encroached upon several older constellations. For example, the telescope's stand was in Sagittarius. Later cataloguers redrew the outlines to avoid this kind of overlapping. (Atlas Charts 42, 51, and 52)

Triangulum Australe, the Southern Triangle. Much more prominent than its northern counterpart, Triangulum (p. 143), this group lies south of Norma. (Atlas Chart 50)

Tucana, the Toucan. Another one of the southern constellations named for exotic birds, this constellation is home to the Small Magellanic Cloud. (Atlas Chart 45)

Vela, the Sails [of Argo]. See Argo Navis (Atlas Charts 37, 38, 48, and 49). See the drawing on p. 38.

Virgo, the Virgin. Zodiacal; see above.

Volans, the Flying [Fish]. Shortened from its original name, Piscis Volans. (Atlas Chart 48)

Vulpecula, the Fox. A constellation added by Hevelius, Vulpecula is home to the Dumbbell Nebula (p. 153). Shortened from Vulpecula cum Ansere, the Fox with the Goose. (Atlas Charts 18 and 19)

5

STARS, NEBULAE, AND GALAXIES

The universe contains many types of objects, and most of them are shown on the Atlas Charts in Chapter 7. In this chapter, we will give a brief description of the different types of objects whose positions in the sky are fixed to the celestial sphere, a fictitious bowl that appears to rotate around the celestial poles. (The sun, moon, and planets, on the other hand, change positions with respect to the stars.) At the end of the chapter, we provide lists and graphic displays of a selection of the most interesting objects in the sky and when they are visible. For your convenience, we have chosen the objects so that some of them will be visible at each time of the year.

Stars

You have already seen the brightest stars on the Monthly Sky Maps in Chapter 3; Appendix 2 provides a fuller list. Astronomers measure the brightness of stars and other celestial objects on the magnitude scale, which is described in Chapter 3 (pp. 56–58).

Both the Monthly Sky Maps and the detailed Atlas Charts in Chapter 7 use circles of different sizes to represent the magnitudes of the stars. Remember that the higher the magnitude, the fainter the star. Stars as faint as 6th magnitude can be seen with the unaided ("naked") eye under perfect conditions, but depending on your eyesight and the brightness of the night sky from streetlights and other sources of "light pollution," the visual limit is usually much lower. It would not be uncommon if your sky were bright enough to prevent you from seeing stars any fainter than 3rd magnitude. Indeed, in cities, the sky itself may be so bright that you cannot see any stars at all!

Star Temperatures

All stars are balls of gas, so hot that they are glowing. Stars have different temperatures, ranging from about 2100°C (about 3800°F) up to about 50,000°C (about 90,000°F). Just as an iron poker glows more and more as it is heated, starting with red hot and then becoming white hot as it grows even hotter, a star's reddish color also indicates its temperature. The coolest stars are reddish balls of glowing gas; the hottest stars glow blue-white. These colors can even be seen with the naked eye. In the constellation Orion, for example, it is not hard to see that the star Betelgeuse, in Orion's shoulder, looks much redder and is therefore much cooler than the star Rigel, in Orion's heel.

Astronomers give star temperatures using the kelvin scale, which uses Celsius degrees but begins at absolute zero, the coldest temperature possible. Absolute zero, 0 kelvin (0 K), is –273°C = –459.4°F.

Spectral Types

Depending on its temperature, each star has its own *spectral type,* which is determined by analyzing its spectrum—the band of colors into which the light from the star can be broken down. The rainbow displays the visible part of the spectrum: red, orange, yellow, green, blue, indigo, and violet; a mnemonic for the order of colors is the name of an imaginary fellow, ROY G. BIV.

When a narrow band of light from the sun or another star is spread out into its spectrum, with blue, say, at the left and red at the right, the spectrum turns out to be crossed by dark lines, each indicating the absence of some particular color. These *spectral lines* are the signatures of different chemical elements at different temperatures. Each element has unique sets of spectral lines for various temperature ranges, so the spectrum of a star reveals the chemical composition of the star's atmosphere. These spectral lines are dark because they are absorbing some of the energy from deeper layers of the sun or the star; they are thus called *absorption lines.* All stars have spectra that are continuous bands of radiation crossed by absorption lines.

When hot gas shines by itself, it may give off *emission lines,* specific colors that are brighter than adjacent colors. A few stars have some emission lines in addition to their absorption lines; the presence of emission lines is noteworthy because it usually shows that there is hot gas surrounding the star. Although emission lines are rare in the spectra of stars, the hot gas in most nebulae is so tenuous that these nebulae have emission-line spectra. They are, therefore, called *emission nebulae,* and appear reddish because the red emission line from heated hydrogen gas is the strongest contributor to the visible part of their spectra.

In this book, we discuss mainly the visible part of the spectrum because our discussions are meant for optical observers. But professional astronomers are increasingly studying other parts of the spectrum. The whole spectrum is a set of waves of different wavelengths. Gamma rays, x-rays, and ultraviolet have wavelengths shorter than those of visible light. Infrared and radio waves have wavelengths longer than those of visible light. Of those other parts of the spectrum, only some radio studies can be carried out by amateur observers; along with a few parts of the infrared, radio waves are the only part of the spectrum besides the visible part that comes through the earth's atmosphere.

Over the past decades, a set of space missions has joined ground-based observing to cover the entire range of the spectrum. Two of NASA's Great Observatories—the Compton Gamma-Ray Observatory and the Hubble Space Telescope—cover gamma rays, the ultraviolet, and the visible. The Advanced X-Ray Facility and the Space

Infrared Telescope Facility are planned Great Observatories. New optical telescopes with mirrors up to 10 meters in diameter (the Keck Telescope in Hawaii), and new, large radio telescopes, have also extended our ability to observe. Advances in electronics are enabling us to use even existing telescopes to get more sensitivity than was previously possible.

In the original determination of spectral types of stars, capital letters were assigned in alphabetical order to indicate the strength of hydrogen's spectral lines relative to the spectral lines from other elements (Fig. 5-1), with A representing the greatest strength. But astronomers later realized that hydrogen radiation is strongest for stars of intermediate temperature rather than for the hottest or coolest stars. So the modern list in order of temperature is out of alphabetical order. From the hottest to the coolest, the order is: O B A F G K M, remembered by generations from the mnemonic "Oh, be a fine girl, kiss me." The actual temperatures and other properties corresponding to the spectral types are given in Appendix 3. Appendix 2 gives spectral types and other data for the 287 brightest stars in the sky.

Double and Variable Stars

Most stars in the sky that appear to be single are actually made up of two or more objects revolving around each other. Sirius, for example, is really a *double* or *binary star*; the bright, bluish-white star we see with the naked eye has a much fainter companion (known as Sirius B) revolving around it. Double stars (which are called "double" even when three or more stars are present) can be interesting to observe, especially when the stars in a pair or multiple system present a beautiful contrast of colors in binoculars or a telescope (see Table 7, p. 185). In some double-star systems, the stars periodically block each other as they orbit, making the total brightness we see vary. These particular binary star systems are examples of *eclipsing binaries.*

Some stars vary in brightness all by themselves. Sometimes a star actually periodically changes in size and therefore brightness. These stars are called *variable stars* (see Table 8, p. 185).

Since double stars and variable stars are particularly interesting for casual star observers and amateur astronomers to observe, we devote a whole chapter (Chapter 6) to them. Two short tables of the double and variable stars that are easiest to observe appear at the end of this chapter; the times when they are visible above the horizon are shown in a Graphic Timetable (p. 187). You will find more charts that will help you observe interesting doubles and variables in Chapter 6.

The Life Histories of Stars

Much of the astronomical research over the last few decades has been devoted to studying the life cycles of stars. Stars begin as collapsing clouds of gas in interstellar space, and become stars when nuclear fusion begins in their interiors, fusing hydrogen into helium. At that point, stars join the *main sequence.* During this period of

Fig. 5-1 A computer simulation of spectral types in order of temperature, omitting the hottest (O and B) and coolest (M). The dark vertical lines are spectral absorption lines. From top to bottom, we see spectral types A0, A5, F0, F5, G0, G5, K0, K5. The series of absorption lines from hydrogen are strongest in spectral type A. (R. A. Bell, University of Maryland)

their lives, energy from the fusion creates a pressure that pushes outward, balancing the inward force of gravity. Depending on how hot and bright a star is, it spends more or less time as a main-sequence star. The hottest stars, though more massive than the sun, use their fuel at such a furious pace that they have relatively short lifetimes—perhaps only 100,000 years. Stars like the sun live on the main sequence for about 10 billion years; the sun is now about halfway through that lifetime. Stars cooler and fainter than the sun can live much longer, 50 billion years or more.

In the type of nuclear fusion that goes on inside the sun and most other stars, four hydrogen nuclei—the central parts of hydrogen atoms—fuse to become one helium nucleus. The resulting helium has slightly less mass than the four hydrogens that went into forming it. The difference is converted into energy in the amount $E = mc^2$, a fact and formula discovered by Albert Einstein in 1905.

When a star begins to die, its fate depends on how much mass it has. Let us first consider stars with about as much mass as the sun, ranging from the least massive stars (with 0.07—7% of—the mass of the sun) to stars with about twice as much mass as the sun. As the stars use up all the hydrogen in their interiors, and so can no longer fuse hydrogen into helium, they can no longer fight off gravity, and their interiors begin to contract. During the contraction, energy is released and their outer layers are pushed out. These outer layers become large and cool, and the stars become *red giants*.

Eventually, the outer layers of some of the red giants become disconnected and float outward, carrying perhaps 20% of the star's mass out into space. The expanding shell of gas is known as a *planetary nebula*. Planetary nebulae are marked with a special symbol on the Atlas Charts in Chapter 7. The escaped nebula bares the inner layers of the star, so the remaining "central stars" appear blue because they are so hot, hotter even than the hottest normal stars. The most commonly observed planetary nebula is the Ring Nebula in Lyrae (Fig. 5-2), which appears as a hazy, white smoke ring through a telescope but which reveals its colors to photography.

Throughout this chapter, we show many objects that can be photographed with small telescopes. They are often identified by their numbers in the Messier catalogue (M) or the later and more extensive (and thus less exclusive) New General Catalogue (NGC) and its Index Catalogue (IC).

After only 50,000 years or so—a twinkling of an eye in the lifetime of a star—the planetary nebula drifts away, and the central star cools. Eventually the central star contracts until it is about the size of the earth. If a mass less than 1.4 times the mass of the sun is left, the star remains at this stage indefinitely. It is then a *white dwarf.*

Fig. 5-2 The Ring Nebula in Lyra, seen through a small telescope. It is not an impressive object to the eye (Atlas Chart 18). (© 1980 Ben Mayer)

Fig. 5-3 A large telescope reveals more of the Ring Nebula's beauty. It is also known as M57. (© 1959, California Institute of Technology)

Fig. 5-4 M76, a planetary nebula in Perseus (Atlas Charts 2, 9, 10). (© 1980 Ben Mayer)

Fig. 5-5 The Dumbbell Nebula, M27, a planetary nebula in Vulpecula (Atlas Charts 18, 19). (© 1979 Ben Mayer)

Fig. 5-6 NGC 6781, a faint planetary nebula in Aquila (Atlas Chart 31). (© 1965 California Institute of Technology)

Fig. 5-7 The Owl Nebula, M97, a faint planetary nebula in Ursa Major (Atlas Chart 5). (© 1980 Ben Mayer)

Fig. 5-8 The Helix Nebula, NGC 7293, in Aquarius. It is 400 light-years away, making it the nearest planetary nebula to us. Its diameter in the sky is about the same as the moon's, but it is too faint to be seen with the unaided eye (Atlas Chart 44). (© 1979 Anglo-Australian Telescope Board)

White dwarfs are faint because they are so small. Thus we see that objects like red giants, planetary nebulae, and white dwarfs, originally discovered as independent classes of objects, are really different stages in the lifetimes of ordinary stars.

Sometimes a white dwarf is part of a double-star system, and its gravity attracts material from the other star in the system. When this material hits the surface of a white dwarf, it may begin nuclear fusion briefly, and the system brightens considerably. We see it as a *nova*. Novae were originally thought of as new stars, but are now known to be stars that suddenly become brighter or visible because of this effect. A few famous novae are marked on the charts.

A star that contains more than about twice as much mass as the sun comes to a more spectacular end. After it becomes a red giant, it grows bigger yet and becomes a supergiant. At that point it may explode completely, becoming a *supernova*. A supernova may rival in brightness the whole galaxy it is in (Fig. 5-9). It was only in the 1920s that it was realized that supernovae and novae are completely different phenomena. A supernova completely devastates the star, forming heavy elements because of the high temperature and then

Fig. 5-9 The spiral galaxy NGC 3110, without (left) and with (right) a supernova. You must get current briefings if you want to photograph a supernova—unless you find one for yourself. (National Optical Astronomy Observatories/N.A. Sharp and G. Jacoby)

spewing these elements out into space. The heavier elements in the human body (all those heavier than iron) were formed in supernovae that exploded before our solar system formed. When our sun and planets formed, they incorporated these heavy elements. Also, it seems increasingly likely that our solar system formed when a nearby supernova caused a cloud of gas and dust to collapse. So supernovae were important to the existence of humanity.

In a few cases, the remnants of a supernova can still be seen in space, as in the Crab Nebula (Fig. 5-10), which exploded in A.D. 1054. The Veil Nebula is part of the Cygnus Loop (Fig. 5-11), the visible remnant of a supernova that exploded even longer ago. Astronomers detect still other supernovae from their radio or x-ray emissions.

In 1987, the first supernova visible to the naked eye since 1604 erupted in the Large Magellanic Cloud. Unfortunately for northern-hemisphere denizens, it is only visible fairly far south on the earth; it was not visible in midnorthern latitudes. Astronomers have been able to make detailed observations as the supernova brightened and faded. They have verified that heavy elements like iron, cobalt, and nickel were formed, and are learning many details about stellar evo-

Fig. 5-10 The Crab Nebula, M1, in Taurus (Atlas Chart 11), the remnant of the A.D. 1054 supernova. (From Palomar Observatory plates, California Institute of Technology, © 1990 Anglo-Australian Telescope Board and Jay M. Pasachoff, from a collaboration between David F. Malin and Jay M. Pasachoff)

Fig. 5-11 The Veil Nebula in Cygnus (Atlas Chart 19). NGC 6992–95 are at left and NGC 6960 is at right in this supernova remnant. (© 1977 Hans Vehrenberg)

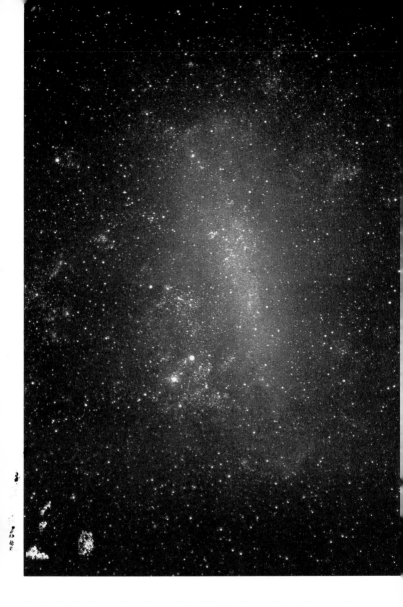

Fig. 5-12 The Large Magellanic Cloud (Atlas Chart 47), with the reddish Tarantula Nebula and, near it in the sky, the supernova that exploded in 1987, known as SN 1987A. It has since faded below naked-eye visibility but continues to be widely studied. North is at the left. (Akira Fujii)

Fig. 5-13 Supernova 1987A in the Large Magellanic Cloud, in the upper right middle of the photo, to the lower right of the Tarantula Nebula. Before the supernova, only a faint star, like hundreds of others on the picture, was detectable. (© 1989 Royal Observatory Edinburgh/Science Photo Library/Photo Researchers)

lution. Their basic idea of how massive stars explode to become supernovae was verified, though there were many surprises. For example, the star that exploded was a blue supergiant, and it had been thought that only red supergiants would make supernovae.

During a supernova explosion, the center of the star can be extremely compressed and can collapse until it is quite small. Stars that have 1.4 to 4 times the mass of the sun collapse until they are only about 12 miles (20 km) across. At that point, the neutrons in the star cannot be pushed closer together. Most of the star is then a gas containing neutrons only, or perhaps the still smaller particles called quarks that make up neutrons. The star is now a *neutron star.*

Neutron stars are too small and faint to be seen directly in visible light. But some neutron stars give off beams of radio radiation. As the star rotates very rapidly—once every second or so—in some cases this beam of radiation sweeps by the earth, the way a lighthouse beacon apparently gives pulses of light as it turns. We detect pulses of radio waves from the neutron star, and so call the object a *pulsar.* Even though we can't see pulsars, we have marked a few prominent pulsars on the Atlas Charts in Chapter 7. Over 500 pulsars are known.

Other neutron stars exist in binary systems (double stars). The gravity of the neutron star sometimes pulls mass off the other star. This mass falls on the neutron star with such force that it heats up enough to give off x-rays. X-ray telescopes in orbit have detected signs of a number of these *binary x-ray sources.*

In a few cases, a mass greater than about four times that of the sun remains after a supernova explosion. Then nothing can stop the collapse of the star. Because of its gravity, it becomes more and more compressed. In cases where the gravity is so high, scientists must use the theory of gravity developed by Einstein in 1917 to explain the situation. Einstein's theory is called the general theory of relativity. The theory predicts that even light will be bent so much by the strong gravity that the light will no longer be able to escape. Neither could any object escape. The star has become a *black hole.*

Black holes are even fainter than neutron stars, so we must look for signs of their presence other than their optical appearance. They are too small to hope to see them block out light from behind. Our best chance of detecting a black hole is if it is located in a binary system. Then the black hole should be attracting material from its companion star. The matter will swirl around the black hole before it enters, and heat up until it gives off x-rays. So x-ray sources are candidates we must study in order to see if other evidence tells us that they are black holes. We conclude that they are black holes if we find that they have too much mass to be neutron stars. We measure the mass of the invisible star in a binary by studying the motions of its visible companion star. The effect is similar to deducing that an invisible dancer is present by watching the movements of the companion. The most likely black-hole candidate in our galaxy is in the constellation Cygnus and is known as Cygnus X-1; its location is marked on Atlas Chart 19 in Chapter 7.

Star Clusters

Sometimes stars form in groups. With binoculars or a small telescope, we might see a dozen or so stars in an irregular grouping in a certain area, though the cluster may actually contain hundreds of stars. The stars are contained within a region about 30 light-years across. Usually, using a larger telescope or making a longer photographic exposure will reveal more stars. The Pleiades and the Hyades in Taurus (Fig. 2-15, p. 37) are among the most famous examples of this type of cluster, which is often called an *open cluster*. Such groupings are also called *galactic clusters*, because they lie in the plane of our galaxy. Open clusters are relatively young on a cosmic scale; the Pleiades formed only 100 million years ago. Long-exposure photos of this cluster (Fig. 2-8, p. 29) show lots of gas and dust present nearby. Though it was once thought that the Pleiades formed out of this cloud of gas and dust, we now realize that the Pleiades is moving through a cloud of gas and dust it happened to encounter. Many other open clusters can be observed in the sky, some with the naked eye, some with binoculars, and others with telescopes (Figs. 5-14 to 5-18).

Fig. 5-14 The open cluster M11 in Scutum (Atlas Chart 30). (© 1980 Ben Mayer)

Fig. 5-15 The open cluster and nebula M16, often known as the Eagle Nebula, in Serpens (Atlas Chart 30). (© 1980 Ben Mayer)

Fig. 5-16 The open cluster M103 in Cassiopeia (Atlas Chart 1). (© 1980 Ben Mayer)

Fig. 5-17 The open cluster NGC 6231 (center) and the nearby nebula IC 4628 in Scorpius (Atlas Chart 41). (© 1977 Hans Vehrenberg)

Fig. 5-18 The open cluster NGC 6520 (Atlas Chart 42, top right) in Sagittarius is near the dark dust cloud Barnard 86. The dust shields molecules from ultraviolet radiation that breaks it apart. Radio telescopes and infrared telescopes allow us to penetrate the dust to detect stars forming inside clouds like this one. (© 1980 Anglo-Australian Telescope Board)

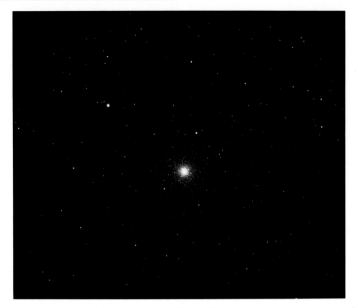

Fig. 5-19 The globular cluster M3 in Canes Venatici (Atlas Chart 15). (Akira Fujii)

In other places in the sky, thousands or hundreds of thousands of stars of a common origin may be located within 300 light-years or so, forming a huge spherical ball. These groupings are called *globular clusters*. In the northern sky, the globular clusters M3 in Canes Venatici (Fig. 5-19), M13 in Hercules (Fig. 2-7), and M15 in Pegasus are among the brightest and thus the easiest to see. A globular cluster looks like a hazy mothball to the naked eye or when viewed through a small telescope; larger telescopes are necessary to see individual stars in this type of cluster. The nearest globular cluster to us is M4 in Scorpius, near the bright star Antares in the sky (Fig. 5-20). Photographs of the region reveal gas and dust around several of the stars in the region, including Antares and rho Ophiuchi. The globular cluster is at a different distance, however, and is free of dust.

Scientists have found that all the globular clusters are very old—perhaps 10 billion years old. Thus they are free of dust. Open clusters, on the other hand, have a wide range of ages. Some may even be forming now. Often, we see around them the dust and gas from which they have formed. A number of interesting open and globular clusters that can be seen at various times of year are listed in Table 9, p. 186; the times when the clusters are visible are plotted on the Graphic Timetable on p. 188.

Fig. 5-20 M4, the nearest globular cluster to us, is at lower right. The rest of the image is taken up with gas and dust around the star rho (ρ) Ophiuchi. It is in the blue "reflection nebula," a cloud of gas reflecting the star's bluish light, at top. The bright star Antares is surrounded by yellow and red nebulosity, with the colors caused by the glowing gas (Atlas Chart 41). (© 1979 Royal Observatory Edinburgh/Anglo-Australian Telescope Board)

Nebulae

Nebulae—clouds of gas and dust that appear hazy to our view—are some of the most beautiful objects to observe in space. The word nebulae (singular, *nebula*) comes from the Greek word for cloud. A few particularly interesting nebulae are listed in Table 10 at the end of this chapter; the times when they can be observed are shown on a Graphic Timetable there.

Some nebulae represent shells of gas thrown off by dying stars. Planetary nebulae (p. 152) and the remnants of supernovae (p. 155) are examples. Planetary nebulae—often called planetaries, for short—got their name because they often appear in small telescopes as small greenish disks; their telescopic images resemble those of the planets Uranus and Neptune, but they have no other similarity to planets. Planetary nebulae often appear greenish because hot oxygen in a certain condition emits a lot of green radiation. Two planetary nebulae are included in Table 10; others are listed in Appendix 5.

Other nebulae represent gas and dust still surrounding young stars. The dust reflects the starlight to us, making a *reflection nebula*. The nebulae surrounding the stars in the Pleiades (Fig. 2-8, page 29) are reflection nebulae, as is dust around other stars (Fig. 5-21).

Some nebulae glow; we call them *emission nebulae*. Other nebu-

Fig. 5-21 Dust and gas in Sagittarius, including the bluish reflection nebulae NGC 6589 and NGC 6590. The reddish glow is from the nebulae IC 1283 and IC 1284 (Atlas Charts 30, 42). (© 1981 Anglo-Australian Telescope Board)

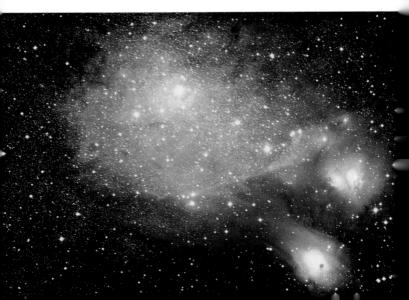

Fig. 5-22 The Lagoon Nebula, M8 (Atlas Charts 41, 42). (© 1978 Ben Mayer)

lae are dark, and absorb radiation from behind. We call them *dark nebulae* or *absorption nebulae*. The Lagoon Nebula, M8, glows with the red light of hydrogen and has a dark, absorbing band across it (Fig. 5-22).

Some nebulae contain small dark nebulae in which stars may be forming. The nebula M16 in Serpens (Fig. 5-15) is a good example. Since radio waves and infrared rays penetrate the nebulae better than visible light does, scientists interested in the birth of stars are now studying nebulae not only in visible light (Figs. 5-23 to 5-30) but also in other parts of the spectrum.

The North America Nebula (Fig. 5-28) in the constellation Cygnus is an example of an emission nebula with an absorption nebula that defines the boundaries we see. The part of the emission nebula we see is roughly the same shape as the continent of North America. Notice how few stars are visible in what would be the Gulf of Mexico because of the dark absorption nebula there.

The Great Nebula in Orion (Figs. 2-9 to 2-12) turns out to be a particularly exciting place. The emission nebula we see is a blister sticking out toward us from a large cloud of dust and gas in which stars are actually forming now. Though we can't see through the emission nebula with visible light, infrared and radio waves penetrate the dark cloud behind it. The absorbing gas and dust in that cloud prevent radiation from the emission nebula from entering and breaking up the gas clouds from which stars will soon form.

Fig. 5-23 The Omega Nebula, M17, in Sagittarius (Atlas Chart 30, bottom left). (© 1980 Ben Mayer)

Fig. 5-24 The Trifid Nebula, M20, and a separate blue reflection nebula (Atlas Charts 41, 42). (© 1979 Ben Mayer)

Fig. 5-25 The California Nebula, NGC 1499 (Atlas Chart 10), named because of its shape. (© 1977 Hans Vehrenberg)

Fig. 5-26 IC 2177 (Atlas Chart 25, lower right), with nearby open clusters. (© 1977 Hans Vehrenberg)

Fig. 5-27 The Cone Nebula, NGC 2264 (Atlas Chart 24). (© 1977 Hans Vehrenberg)

Fig. 5-28 The North America Nebula, NGC 7000, glows red because of the red emission from hydrogen; dark dust absorbs light in the region that corresponds to the Gulf of Mexico. The Pelican Nebula, IC 5067–70, is to the right (Atlas Chart 19). (© 1977 Hans Vehrenberg)

Fig. 5-29 The Rosette Nebula, NGC 2237, in Monoceros, around the cluster NGC 2244 (Atlas Chart 24). (© 1965 California Institute of Technology)

Fig. 5-30 The Eta Carinae Nebula, NGC 3372 (Atlas Chart 49). (© 1977 Hans Vehrenberg)

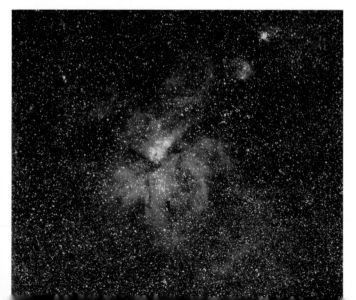

The Milky Way Galaxy

A galaxy is an island of matter in space—a giant collection of gas, dust, and millions or billions of stars. The galaxy we live in, which includes about a trillion (a thousand billion) stars, is called the Milky Way Galaxy. Most of the Milky Way Galaxy is in the shape of a disk; the earth is approximately halfway out from the center. Since the earth is located inside the Milky Way Galaxy, various parts of the galaxy are always visible in our sky. The disk of the Milky Way Galaxy is thin. When we look toward or away from the center or in any other direction in the plane of that disk, we see many stars and much gas and dust; in those directions we see a band of white across the sky, mottled with some dark material. People have long called the band of light that appears to cross the sky by the name the *Milky*

Fig. 5-31 This drawing of the entire sky shows 7000 stars plus the Milky Way. (Lund Observatory, Sweden)

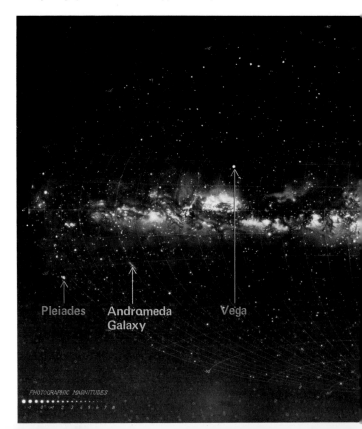

Way because of its appearance (Fig. 5-31); it is the Milky Way from which our galaxy draws its name.

If we look in directions other than that of the plane of our galaxy, our line of sight quickly passes out of the galaxy, and we do not see many stars or much gas or dust; in those directions we see only some of the nearer stars against a dark background. Imagine living deep in a groove of a phonograph record: when you look toward the center or toward the outside edge of the record, you look through a lot of vinyl; when you look upward or downward, though, you quickly see out of the record.

Most of the open clusters lie in the disk of our galaxy, so we see them in or near the Milky Way. Most of the nebulae lie in the disk as well. The globular clusters, though, form a large spherical halo centered at the center of our galaxy. The halo extends far above and below the center of our galaxy; thus these globular clusters do not, for the most part, lie in or near the Milky Way. Indeed, it was the realization around 1920 that the globular clusters seemed to be

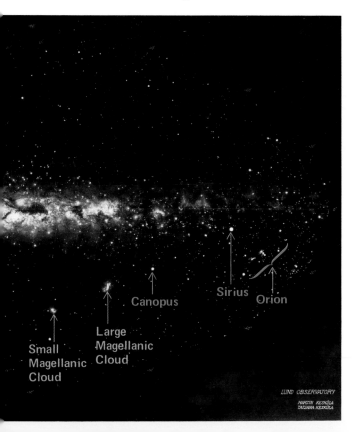

Small
Magellanic
Cloud

Large
Magellanic
Cloud

Canopus

Sirius

Orion

LUND OBSERVATORY

MARTIN KESKÜLA
TATJANA KESKÜLA

forming a spherical halo around something that led Harlow Shapley to deduce that whatever was at the center of that halo was the center of our galaxy. This observation was the proof that the sun does not lie in the center of the galaxy or of the universe.

When we look away from the Milky Way, we are able to look out of our galaxy and see more distant objects, such as other galaxies. (Galaxies and nebulae are known as *deep-sky objects.*) Still, when we look at photographs of these distant objects, the individual points of light we see are usually stars in the foreground, stars that are relatively close to us—in our galaxy, rather than in distant galaxies.

In 1989, the Cosmic Background Explorer spacecraft was launched by NASA to study the universe in the infrared and on the border of the spectrum with the radio. The view it sent back in the infrared of our galaxy (Fig. 5-32) gave us a remarkable view of the plane of the Milky Way and the bulge at our galaxy's center.

Fig. 5-32 Our Milky Way Galaxy, as observed in three infrared wavelengths by the Cosmic Background Explorer and reproduced here in three colors as visible light. The cooler dust, shown as yellow, extends through the plane of our galaxy. (COBE Science Team, NASA)

Galaxies

The Milky Way is only one of millions of galaxies in the universe. Most galaxies outside our own are too faint and distant to be seen with the naked eye or binoculars, but it is fascinating to study their shapes in a telescope. A few interesting examples of galaxies are listed in Table 10 at the end of this chapter; the times of the year when they are visible are shown on the Graphic Timetable on p. 189.

Classes of Galaxies

A basic scheme for classifying galaxies was worked out in the 1920s by Edwin Hubble. More recent and elaborate methods, such as those of Gerard de Vaucouleurs, have also been developed. The Milky Way Galaxy is an example of a *spiral galaxy*—a galaxy in which several "arms" seem to unwind from a central region. Hubble classified the spiral galaxies with an *S* (for *spiral*) followed by an *a, b,* or *c,* depending on the increasing looseness of the arms of the galaxy. Thus a galaxy with tightly wound arms is classified as an Sa; one with less tightly wound arms, like our galaxy or the Andromeda Galaxy (Fig. 5-33), is an Sb; and one with loosely wound arms is an Sc (Figs. 5-34 and 5-35).

We cannot move around to different sides of a galaxy to see it from different perspectives. A telescope reveals so many galaxies, though,

Fig. 5-33 *(left)* The Andromeda Galaxy, M31 (Atlas Chart 9), with the elliptical galaxies NGC 205 (above it) and M32. (© 1959 California Institute of Technology)

Fig. 5-34 *(right)* The inner part of the spiral galaxy M33 in Triangulum, seen face-on (Atlas Chart 9). (© 1979 Ben Mayer)

Fig. 5-35 *(left)* The Whirlpool Galaxy, M51, in Canes Venatici (Atlas Chart 15). (© 1980 Ben Mayer)

Fig. 5-36 *(right)* The spiral galaxy M61 in Virgo (Atlas Chart 27A). (© 1980 James D. Wray, McDonald Observatory)

that we can see examples of each class from different angles—broadside (face-on), somewhat tilted (Fig. 5-43), or edge-on (Figs. 5-42, 5-51, and 5-52). From studying all these galaxies we know, for example, that an Sa galaxy usually has a larger bulge at its center than an Sc galaxy does.

The youngest stars and most of the gas and dust are located in the arms of a spiral galaxy. Since the hottest stars burn out quickly, whenever we see a hot star (which we can recognize by its blue color), it must be relatively young. Color photographs of galaxies (such as Fig. 5-34) show that the central regions are relatively yellow, indicating that older stars are dominant there, while the arms are relatively blue and therefore contain relatively young stars.

Some spiral galaxies have a central bar from which the arms unwind. They are classified with a *B* (for *bar*): SBa, SBb, and SBc (Fig. 5-46).

Most galaxies do not have spiral arms, but have an elliptical shape instead. They are classified with an *E* (for *elliptical*), with a number from 0-7, showing how far out of round they appear. E0 galaxies appear spherical (Fig. 5-40), while E7 galaxies appear quite oblong. Elliptical galaxies are quite old, contain only old stars, and have no gas or dust. They come in a wide range of sizes, from huge to relatively small on a galactic scale.

In between the most elliptical of the elliptical galaxies and the spiral galaxies with the most tightly wound arms is a transitional class of galaxy: S0. An S0 galaxy has a disk but no arms. It is currently thought that the shapes of galaxies result from the different conditions under which they formed, and that galaxies do not evolve from one type to another. It may be, though, that some or all elliptical galaxies are the result of collisions between spirals.

Some galaxies of each type have a noticeable peculiarity in addition to one of the basic shapes described above. A galaxy might have a jet of gas (Fig. 5-40), for example, or be wrapped with extra dust (Fig. 5-50). These galaxies are labelled (*pec*), for *peculiar*, as in "E7 (*pec*)."

Other galaxies have no special shape, and are known as *irregular (Irr)*. Some irregular galaxies seem to have a trace of spiral structure, and might really be the equivalent of Sd spirals (that is, spirals with very loose arms). Others are truly irregular. The nearest type-Irr galaxies to us are the two small satellite galaxies of the Milky Way Galaxy. Since they were first seen by Magellan's crew as they sailed far enough south, these satellite galaxies are known as the Magellanic Clouds. They are best visible from southern latitudes, and cannot be seen from the continental United States. In a telescope, the Large Magellanic Cloud (LMC) seems to show traces of spiral structure (Fig. 5-47), while the Small Magellanic Cloud (SMC) seems completely irregular (Fig. 5-48).

All galaxies except the very closest ones are moving away from us. We can tell this by studying their spectra, which are shifted toward the red end of the spectrum. A *redshift*—a lengthening of the wavelength of any wave—results from motion away from you, just as the length of a sound wave increases as a motorcycle passes you and starts to recede from you. Edwin Hubble discovered that the farther away a galaxy is, the faster it is receding. We measure how fast galaxies are receding by studying the redshifts in their spectra. This method works no matter how far away the galaxy is, as long as we can take a long enough exposure to measure a redshift. Once we measure the redshift, we use *Hubble's Law*, which links redshift with distance, to find out how far away galaxies are. This is the only method we have for finding the distances to the farthest objects in the universe.

The enormous distances to galaxies give us an indication of the immense scale of the universe. The nearest galaxy that northern-hemisphere observers can see is the Great Galaxy in Andromeda, sometimes simply called the Andromeda Galaxy. The center of this galaxy is dimly visible to the naked eye, but it is so far away that this light has been travelling for 2.2 million years—at a speed of more than 186,000 miles per second—to reach us. When we observe the Andromeda Galaxy, we are looking 2.2 million years back in time.

All galaxies apparently come in groups. Our Milky Way Galaxy, the Andromeda Galaxy, and M33 are the three spirals in our Local Group of some two dozen galaxies, which also includes two giant elliptical galaxies and many dwarf elliptical and irregular galaxies.

The Local Group is an outlying member of a large *cluster of galaxies* that covers much of the constellation Virgo and is thus known as the Virgo Cluster (Fig. 5-54). The bulk of the galaxies in the Virgo Cluster are about 60 million light-years away. Other prominent clusters are in Coma Berenices, about 300 million light-years away, and in Hercules, about 500 million light-years away. (These values are

Fig. 5-37 The spiral galaxy M64 in Coma Berenices (Atlas Chart 15). (© 1980 Ben Mayer)

Fig. 5-38 The irregular galaxy M82 in Ursa Major (Atlas Charts 4, 5). (Lick Observatory photo)

Fig. 5-39 The spiral galaxy M83 in Hydra (Atlas Chart 39). (© 1979 Ben Mayer)

Fig. 5-40 The elliptical galaxy M87 in Virgo, with its jet of gas (Atlas Chart 27A). (© James D. Wray, McDonald Observatory)

Fig. 5-41 The face-on spiral galaxy M101 in Ursa Major (Atlas Chart 6). (© 1980 Ben Mayer)

Fig. 5-42 The Sombrero Galaxy, M104, in Virgo, a spiral galaxy seen edge-on (Atlas Chart 27). (© 1979 Ben Mayer)

Fig. 5-43 The spiral galaxy M106 in Canes Venatici (Atlas Chart 15). (© James D. Wray, McDonald Observatory)

Fig. 5-44 The edge-on spiral galaxy M108 in Ursa Major (Atlas Charts 5, 14). (© 1980 Ben Mayer)

Fig. 5-45 The spiral galaxy NGC 253 (Atlas Chart 33) with its light-absorbing dust lanes. (© 1980 Anglo-Australian Telescope Board)

Fig. 5-46 The barred spiral galaxy NGC 1365. (European Southern Observatory)

Fig. 5-47 The Large Magellanic Cloud, with its reddish Tarantula Nebula, NGC 2070 (Atlas Chart 47). The LMC is 169,000 light-years away. (Hans Vehrenberg)

Fig. 5-48 The Small Magellanic Cloud (Atlas Chart 45). To the right is the globular cluster 47 Tucanae (also known as NGC 104) and toward the top is the globular cluster NGC 362. These globular clusters are in our own galaxy, and we are looking past them to see the LMC. (© 1977, Hans Vehrenberg)

Fig. 5-49 NGC 2997, a spiral galaxy in Antlia (Atlas Chart 37). (© 1980 Anglo-Australian Telescope Board)

Fig. 5-50 NGC 5128, a galaxy wrapped with a tremendous dust lane (Atlas Chart 39), corresponds to the strong radio source Centaurus A. North is at upper left. (© 1979 R. J. Dufour)

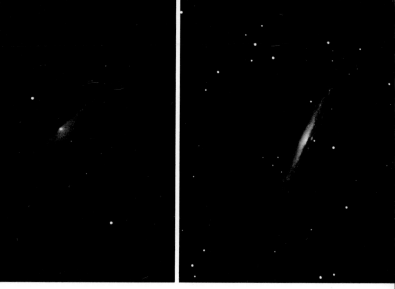

Fig. 5-51 The edge-on spiral galaxy NGC 4565 in Coma Berenices (Atlas Chart 15). (U.S. Naval Observatory)

Fig. 5-52 The spiral galaxy NGC 5907 in Draco (Atlas Chart 6), seen edge-on. (U.S. Naval Observatory)

Fig. 5-53 NGC 6946, a spiral galaxy in Cepheus (Atlas Chart 8). (U.S. Naval Observatory)

Fig. 5-54 Part of the Virgo Cluster of galaxies, including the elliptical galaxies M86 (upper center) and M84 (far right). NGC 4438 is the distorted galaxy at upper left. The positions of these galaxies are shown on Atlas Chart 27A. (© 1987 Royal Observatory Edinburgh/ Anglo-Australian Telescope Board)

computed assuming that Hubble's constant—the rate at which velocity increases with distance—is 75 km/sec/megaparsec = 23 km/sec per million light-years.) Clusters of galaxies have recently been studied particularly well from x-ray telescope observations, which have revealed the presence of gas between the galaxies.

Many clusters of galaxies are linked together in *superclusters.* In between the superclusters are giant voids where no galaxies are found. Modern electronic detectors are revealing huge structures, with one—"the Great Wall"—at least 250 million light-years away.

Quasars

It came as a surprise in 1960 when some of the sources of celestial radio waves appeared to be pointlike—"quasi-stellar"—instead of looking like galaxies. These "quasi-stellar radio sources"—*quasars,* for short—were discovered three years later to be extremely far away, when Maarten Schmidt discovered that the spectrum of one of them showed an extreme redshift. A class of radio-quiet quasars— quasi-stellar objects with huge redshifts—has since been discovered. We now know of over a thousand quasars.

The redshift can be expressed as the fraction or percentage by which the wavelengths of light are shifted. For speeds much slower than the speed of light, this fraction is the same as the fraction that the recession speed of the quasar is of the speed of light. For example, a redshift (called z) of 0.2 means that the wavelengths are shifted toward the red by 0.2 times (20% of) the original wavelength. It is also true that the galaxy or quasar emitting such light is receding from us at 0.2 times the speed of light, or 60,000 km/sec. A quasar with a redshift of 1.0 has its wavelengths shifted by 1.0 times (100% of) the original wavelength; each wavelength is doubled. But Einstein's formulas from the special theory of relativity must be used to calculate how fast the quasars are receding; their velocities are always less than the speed of light.

The most distant quasar known is redshifted by $z = 3.9$. Few quasars with redshifts greater than 3 (300%) have been found, even though instruments exist that would be sensitive enough to do so. The farther out the quasar is, the farther back in time the light reaching us was emitted. That few quasars of the largest redshifts are found indicates that we are seeing back to the instant at which the first quasars were formed—somewhat over 10 billion years ago.

Since quasars are so far away, yet still send us some visible light and relatively strong radio radiation, the quasars must be astonishingly bright. Astronomers now agree that giant black holes are probably present in the centers of quasars. These black holes would contain millions of times the mass of the sun. As gas is sucked into the black holes, it heats up and gives off energy. Quasars may be a stage in the evolution of galaxies, for there is evidence that some quasars have structure around them not unlike that of galaxies. Since we see most quasars quite far away, we are seeing them far back in time, and we can conclude that the epoch at which quasars were brightest took place long ago.

Only one quasar—3C 273, in the constellation Virgo (Fig. 5-55)—is bright enough to be accessible for visual observing with amateur

Fig. 5-55 The quasar 3C 273, in Virgo, is magnitude 13.6. (See also Atlas Chart 27A.) The long jet of gas coming from it is a sign of violent activity there.

telescopes, but we have plotted a handful of quasars on the Atlas Charts in Chapter 7 since they are such astonishing objects that it is exciting even to look in their directions. Electronic detectors allow even amateur astronomers to observe quasars.

Cosmology

Hubble's observations that the most distant galaxies are receding from us faster than closer galaxies can be explained if the universe were expanding in a way similar to the way a giant raisin cake rises (Fig. 5-56). If you picture yourself as sitting on a raisin, all the other raisins will recede from you as the cake rises. Since there is more dough between you and the more distant raisins, the dough will expand more and the distant raisins will recede more rapidly than closer ones. Similarly, the universe is expanding. We have the same view no matter which raisin or galaxy we are on, so the fact that all raisins and galaxies seem to be receding doesn't say that we are at the center of the universe. Indeed, the universe has no center. (We would have to picture a raisin cake extending infinitely in all directions to get a more accurate analogy.)

Since the universe is uniformly expanding now, we can ask what happened in the past. As we go back in time, the universe must have been more compressed, until it was at quite a high density 15 billion or so years ago. Most models of the origin of the universe say that there then was a *big bang* that started the expansion. A new model— the *inflationary universe*—holds that the early universe grew larger rapidly for a short time before it settled down to its current rate of expansion. We cannot see back to the big bang itself; the first matter could have formed as a chance fluctuation in the nothingness of space.

The temperatures were so high in the first microsecond of the universe that not even the chemical elements had formed. But as the universe cooled, first basic atomic particles, such as protons (hydrogen nuclei), and then heavier atoms formed. Still, the universe was opaque until it cooled down to 3,000°C. When it reached that temperature, protons and electrons combined to make hydrogen atoms and the universe became transparent. The hot radiation that permeated the universe at that time has cooled as the universe has continued to expand, and is now detectable as a faint glow in sensitive

Fig. 5-56 A raisin cake rising is analogous to the expansion of the universe. (Jay M. Pasachoff)

radio telescopes. The glow has a temperature of only 3 kelvins (3°C above absolute zero), and is our best evidence that the early universe was hot and dense. Slight ripples in the glow are probably the seeds from which the galaxies formed.

Astronomers ask what will happen to the universe in the future. The evidence is not all in. One possibility is that the universe is *open*—it will continue to expand forever. Another possibility is that the universe will eventually stop its expansion and begin to contract. We know that this cannot happen for at least 50 billion years more—at least three times longer than the current age of the universe—because we can observe the rate at which the universe is now expanding. Still, if the universe does contract in the long run, then we will have a *closed universe* that will wind up in a *big crunch.* The inflationary model indicates that the universe will expand forever, but at a decreasing rate.

Observations from new telescopes on the ground, from the Hubble Space Telescope in orbit, from the Very Long Baseline Array of radio telescopes stretching over the whole United States, and from other instruments will help us forecast the future of the universe.

Table 7: Selected Double Stars

Name	Atlas Chart	Magnitudes	Color	Separation of Components (in arc sec)
gamma Andromedae	9	2.2, 5.1	orange & blue	10"
beta Monocerotis	24	4.6, 5.1, & 5.4	blue	2.8" & 7.2"
iota Cancri	13	4.0 & 6.6	yellow & blue	30"
gamma Virginis	27	3.5 & 3.5	yellow	2"
beta Scorpii	29	2.7 & 4.9		14"
beta Cygni (Albireo)	18	3.2 & 5.4	yellow & green	54"

Note: The times when these doubles are visible are shown in the Graphic Timetable of Double and Variable Stars (p. 187). The positions of these and other double stars are given in Appendix 6, p. 458, and are plotted on the Atlas Charts in Chapter 7.

Table 8: Selected Variable Stars

Name	Atlas Chart	Type (see Ch. 6)	Magnitude (Range)	Period (Days)
Mira (omicron Ceti)	22	long-period	2.6–10.1	332
Algol (beta Persei)	10	eclipsing binary	2.1–3.4	2.9
delta Cephei	8	Cepheid variable	3.5–4.4	5.4
zeta Geminorum	12	Cepheid variable	3.7–4.2	10.2
beta Lyrae	18	eclipsing binary	3.3–4.3	12.9
RR Lyrae	18	RR Lyrae variable	7.0–8.1	0.6

Note: The times when these variables are visible are shown in the Graphic Timetable of Double and Variable Stars (p. 187). The positions of these and other variable stars are given in Appendix 7, p. 460, and Appendix 8, p. 461; they are also plotted on the Atlas Charts in Chapter 7. Special finding charts for Mira, Algol, and beta Lyrae appear at the end of Chapter 6 (pp. 199–200).

Table 9: Selected Open and Globular Clusters

Name	Constellation	Type	Mag.	Diam.	r.a. dec. (2000.0)
M103	Cassiopeia	open	7	6'	01^{h}33^m +60°42'
h and χ Persei	Perseus	open*	4	30', 30'	02^{h}22^m +57°07'
M45 (Pleiades)	Taurus	open	1	110'	03^{h}47^m +24°07'
M79	Lepus	globular	8	9$^+$	05^{h}25^m –24°33'
M35	Gemini	open	5	28'	06^{h}09^m +24°20
M44 (Praesepe)	Cancer	open	3	95'	08^{h}40^m +19°59'
M3	Canes Venatici	globular	6	16'	13^{h}42^m +28°23'
M5	Serpens	globular	6	17'	15^{h}19^m +02°05'
M13	Hercules	globular	6	17'	16^{h}42^m +36°28'
M92	Hercules	globular	7	11'	17^{h}17^m +43°08'
M23	Sagittarius	open	6	27'	17^{h}57^m –19°01'
M24	Sagittarius†	open	6	5'	18^{h}17^m –18°29'
M11	Scutum	open	6	14'	18^{h}51^m –06°16'
M15	Pegasus	globular	6	12'	21^{h}30^m +12°10'
M39	Cygnus	open	5	32'	21^{h}32^m +48°26'
M22	Sagittarius	globular	5	24'	18^{h}36^m –23°54'

The following objects are visible only from southern latitudes:

Name	Constellation	Type	Mag.	Diam.	r.a. dec. (2000.0)
ω Cen	Centaurus	globular	4	36'	13^{h}27^m –47°29'
47 Tuc	Tucana	globular	4	31'	0^{h}24^m –72°05'

*The double cluster; a 1° field is necessary to include both.
†M24 is the star cloud in the direction of the galactic center.

Table 10: Selected Nebulae and Galaxies

Name	Constellation	Type	Diam.	r.a. dec. (2000.0)
M31	Andromeda	spiral	2° × 40'	00^{h}43^m +41°16°
M1 (Crab)	Taurus	supernova	6' × 4'	05^{h}35^m +22°01'
M42 (Orion)	Orion	emission	60'	05^{h}35^m –05°27'
M81	Ursa Major	spiral	16' × 10'	09^{h}56^m +69°04'
M49	Virgo	elliptical	4'	12^{h}30^m +08°00'
M51 (Whirlpool)	Canes Venatici	spiral	12' × 6'	13^{h}30^m +47°12'
M20 (Trifid)	Sagittarius	emission	29'	18^{h}03^m –23°02'
M57 (Ring)	Lyra	planetary	1'	18^{h}54^m +33°02'
M27 (Dumbbell)	Vulpecula	planetary	8' × 4'	20^{h}00^m +22°43'

Notes: Diameters are expressed in degrees (°) and arc minutes ('); the dimensions are a guide to the size of the object when seen through a 6–8" reflector in average conditions. Abbreviations; spiral = spiral galaxy; supernova = supernova remnant; emission = emission nebula; elliptical = elliptical galaxy; planetary = planetary nebula.

THE GRAPHIC TIMETABLE OF THE HEAVENS
DOUBLE STARS AND VARIABLES
Local Standard Time

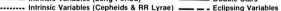

- - - Intrinsic Variables (Long Period)   ——— Double Stars
········· Intrinsic Variables (Cepheids & RR Lyrae)   — - — Eclipsing Variables

(© 1982 Scientia, Inc.)

THE GRAPHIC TIMETABLE OF THE HEAVENS
OPEN AND GLOBULAR CLUSTERS

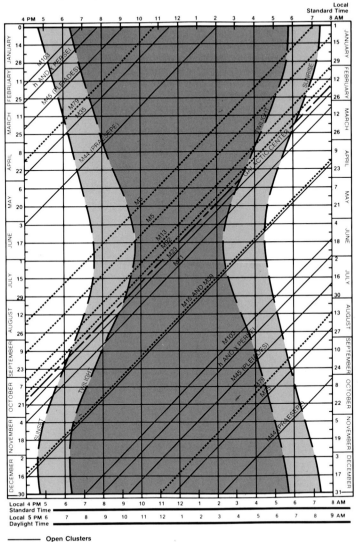

——— Open Clusters

·········· Globular Clusters

(© 1982 Scientia, Inc.)

THE GRAPHIC TIMETABLE OF THE HEAVENS
GALAXIES AND NEBULAE

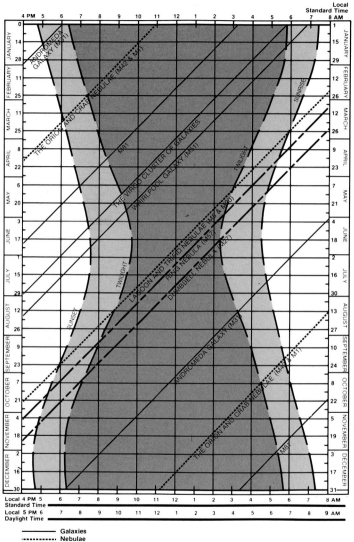

Galaxies
Nebulae
Planetary Nebulae

6

DOUBLE AND VARIABLE STARS

Double Stars

When we look at the sky, most of the stars we see seem to be single points of light. But more detailed investigation has revealed that most of the stars in our galaxy are actually in *double star* systems— systems containing two or more stars. The periods with which the components of double star systems orbit each other range from hours up through centuries.

In some cases, the stars are distant enough from each other and the star system is close enough to us that we can actually see that the star system contains more than one object. A system of this type is called a *visual binary.* In other cases, even though we may not be able to actually see more than one star, we can tell that the system is a double star because the component stars sometimes block each other as they orbit, making the total brightness of the system vary. This type of variable is an *eclipsing binary star* (Fig. 6-2). Sometimes the fact that a star is double can be told only by examination of its spectrum, the breakup of its light into its component colors. The spectrum might show distinct contributions from each of the member stars or might show signs of the stars' motions. A double star that has been identified as such through variations of its spectrum is called a *spectroscopic binary.* Still another possibility is that we can see one star appear to wobble in the sky slightly from side to side over the years, as a result of the gravity of an otherwise invisible companion. This type of double star is called an *astrometric binary,* since it is the delicate measurements of the science of astrometry ("star measuring") that reveals it to us as a double.

Sometimes we see something that looks like a double star, but that is really two stars that happen to be almost in the same line of sight, even though they are at quite different distances from us and therefore are not close to each other. These stars, which are not physically linked, are called *optical doubles,* but are not considered true double stars.

Double stars can be recognized on Atlas Charts in the next chapter by the horizontal lines drawn through the dots that indicate their brightnesses. Many interesting doubles are listed in Appendix 6. A few double stars, including a selection of doubles that are visible at different times around the year, are listed in Table 7, Chapter 5 (p. 185); the times when they are highest in the sky are shown in the

Graphic Timetable on p. 187. Appendix 6 includes information on the *position angle*—the angle measured eastward (counterclockwise), with the brighter star at the center of the "clock," for convenience, from the direction north around to the fainter star. The position angle and the apparent separation (in angular units—minutes or seconds of arc) between components of double systems change over time.

Some double star systems are particularly beautiful to observe with a telescope, even a small one, because the component stars are of different colors. Whenever a contrast of colors is seen in the members of a double, it results from the different temperatures of the individual stars.

One eclipsing binary system, Algol, is particularly easy to observe. It is also known as beta Persei because it is the second brightest star in Perseus. The name Algol, meaning "the demon star," comes from the Arabic words *ras-al-ghul*, meaning "the head of the demon." Figure 6-2 shows Algol's variations in brightness over a 2.9-day period. Algol is such a popular object to observe that we have listed some of the times of its minima in Table 11 (p. 192). A finding chart for Algol (Fig. 6-10) appears at the end of this chapter. On this and other finding charts there, decimal points are omitted from the magnitudes listed, since the decimal points might be confused with stars.

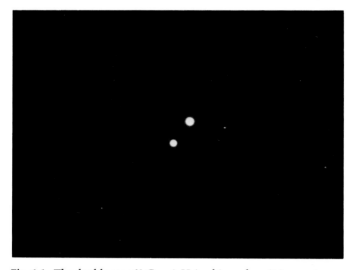

Fig. 6-1 The double star 61 Cygni. Using binoculars, it is easy to see that this is a double. Its components, of magnitudes 5.2 and 6.0, are separated by 30 arc seconds. The components of this system orbit each other every 722 years. The system is only 11 light-years from earth. (Lick Observatory photo)

Table 11: Minima of Algol

1992 January 2, 0:37; February 2, 13:39; March 2, 5:53; April 2, 18:54; May 1, 11:06; June 2, 0:04; July 3, 13:00; August 1, 5:06; September 1, 18:00; October 3, 6:55; November 3, 19:51; December 2, 12:01.

1993 January 3, 1:01; February 3, 14:03; March 1, 9:27; April 1, 22:29; May 3, 11:29; June 1, 3:38; July 2, 16:35; August 3, 5:29; September 3, 18:24; October 2, 10:30; November 2, 23:26, December 1, 15:35.

1994 January 2, 4:36; February 2, 17:38; March 3, 9:51; April 1, 2:03; May 2, 15:04; June 3, 4:02; July 1, 20:09; August 2, 9:04; September 2, 21:58; October 1, 14:04; November 2, 3:01; December 3, 15:59.

1995 January 1, 8:10; February 1, 21:12; March 2, 13:25; April 3, 2:27; May 1, 18:38; June 2, 7:36; July 3, 20:33; August 1, 12:39; September 2, 1:33; October 3, 14:28; November 1, 6:35; December 2, 19:33.

1996 January 3, 8:34; February 1, 0:46; March 3, 13:49; April 1, 6:01; May 2, 19:02; June 3, 8:00; July 2, 0:07; August 2, 13:02; September 3, 1:56; October 1, 18:02; November 2, 6:59; December 3, 19:57.

1997 January 1, 12:08; February 2, 1:10; March 2, 17:23; April 3, 6:25; May 1, 22:36; June 2, 11:35; July 1, 3:42; August 1, 16:37; September 2, 5:31; October 3, 18:26; November 1, 10:33; December 2, 23:31.

Note: The first minimum of each month is given; add 2 days 20 hours 49 minutes successively to find other minima in a given month. (Calculations by Roger W. Sinnott, *Sky & Telescope*)

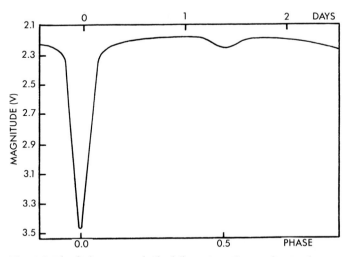

Fig. 6-2 The light curve of Algol (beta Persei), an eclipsing binary. Algol is popular with variable-star observers because of its wide range in brightness over a conveniently short period. (Anthony D. Mallama)

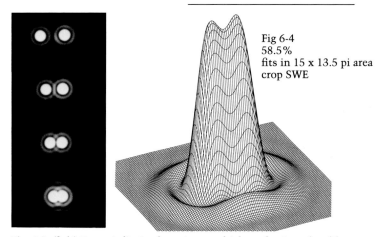

Fig 6-4
58.5%
fits in 15 x 13.5 pi area
crop SWE

Fig. 6-3 *(left)* Dawes's limit, the point at which we begin to be able to distinguish that two objects are present, falls between parts A (top left) and B (bottom left). (Chris Jones, Union College)
Fig. 6-4 *(right)* Dawes's limit corresponds to the brightness distribution at right. (Raymond G. Wilson and Diane Bootz, Illinois Wesleyan University)

An English astronomer in the last century, William Dawes, worked out a rule of thumb to give the telescope aperture (the diameter of the lens or mirror) necessary to separate (resolve) double stars into their components, that is, to tell that two stars are present in a system (Figs. 6-3 and 6-4). His rule is that an aperture of I inches should make barely detectable the presence of a pair of 6th-magnitude stars separated by $4.6/I$ seconds of arc; in the metric system, an aperture of C centimeters should resolve the pair of stars separated by $11.7/C$ seconds of arc. Dawes's rule assumes good sky conditions for viewing, and that the stars are not too different in magnitude.

Variable Stars

In addition to eclipsing binaries—stars that vary because they eclipse each other periodically—there are many stars that vary in brightness all by themselves. All such stars are known as *variable stars.*

The first variable star to be discovered in each constellation has usually been given the letter R, followed by the genitive (possessive) form in Latin of the constellation's name (see Appendix 1). For example, R Andromedae, the first variable star discovered in Andromeda, is a long-period variable. The second variable star in each constellation was given the name S; S Andromedae was apparently a bright star that newly appeared in Andromeda in 1885, though we now know that it was a supernova. The next variable was T, and so on up to Z. Then the lettering scheme started over again with RR and continued to RZ, then SS (not SR) up to SZ, TT up to TZ, and so on up to YY, YZ, and ZZ. Following are AA to AZ, BB to BZ, and so on up to QZ, omitting the letter J (which might be confused with I). This lettering scheme provides names for up to 334 variable stars in each constellation. Additional variables in each constellation are numbered following a V, for variable: V1500 Cygni. Stars that have Bayer designations have retained them, even when they are variables.

Plotting a star's brightness over a period of time is called "finding its light curve." A star's light curve is a graph of its brightness as it varies over time. The light curve of SS Cygni (Fig. 6-5), for example, shows that this variable star changes irregularly in brightness, increasing every 50 days or so from its normal level of 12th magnitude up to 8th magnitude. A finding chart for SS Cygni (Fig. 6-9) appears at the end of this chapter. SS Cygni is an example of a *dwarf nova*. U Geminorum and AY Lyrae are other prominent members of the class; in fact, dwarf novae are often called *U Gem stars.*

Sometimes stars are variable as a result of an actual change in a

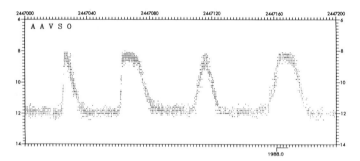

Fig. 6-5 The light curve of SS Cygni, a dwarf nova whose outbursts occur about every 50 days. (AAVSO)

star's size and therefore its brightness. One type of variable, known as a *long-period variable,* takes weeks to complete a cycle of variation. This type of variable is also called a *Mira variable,* after the prototype star Mira (omicron Ceti) in the constellation Cetus, the Whale. Sixteen cycles of variation for Mira are shown at the top of Figure 6-6; a finding chart for this star (Fig. 6-11) also appears at the end of this chapter.

Mira was the very first variable star (except for novae and supernovae) to be discovered. It was noticed as a variable with the naked eye in 1596, even before the invention of the telescope. Since it changed from 9th magnitude, which is invisible to the naked eye, to 3rd magnitude, this star seemed to appear anew in the sky from time to time.

It was named "Mira," the Latin word for "wonderful," because of its wonderful changes in brightness. R Boötis, which ranges from 7th to 13th magnitude (Fig. 6-6), is another example of this class.

RR Lyrae variables, named after the prototype star RR Lyrae in the constellation Lyra (Atlas Chart 18), on the other hand, have very short, regular periods of less than one day (Fig. 6-7). Since RR Lyrae stars are found mostly in globular clusters, they are also known as *cluster variables.* The fact that all variables of this type have essentially the same absolute magnitude—about 0.5—was important for measuring the distance to the globular clusters in which RR Lyrae stars are located. This, in turn, led to Harlow Shapley's discovery in the 1920s that the sun is not at the center of our galaxy.

Cepheid variables, named after the star δ (delta) Cephei, have a distinct pattern to their variations (Fig. 6-8), with periods (cycles) that can range from about one day up to a few days. RR Lyrae stars and Cepheids are two types of variables that have been very important in helping astronomers determine the scale of distances in the universe. All RR Lyrae stars have about the same intrinsic brightness, so any differences in apparent brightness from one RR Lyrae star to the next result only from differences in their distances from

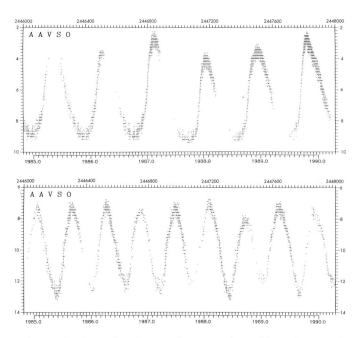

Fig. 6-6 *(top)* 8 cycles of Mira, a long-period variable with a period of about 11 months. *(bottom)* The light curve of R Boötes, a Mira variable with a period of 223 days. (AAVSO)

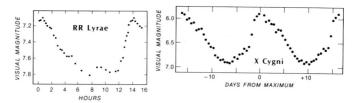

Fig. 6-7 *(left)* RR Lyrae, the prototype of the cluster variables, has a period of 13.6 hours. It rises rapidly to maximum brightness and declines more slowly. This light curve is based on 330 visual observations by Erich Leiner, a German amateur astronomer. *(Sky & Telescope)*

Fig. 6-8 (right) The light curve of X Cygni, a Cepheid variable with a 17-day period. (AAVSO)

us. Each Cepheid variable, on the other hand, can have a different intrinsic brightness, but it is fairly easy for astronomers to calculate the distance to a Cepheid once they know its period of variation. (The period of variation can be measured easily at a telescope; then the intrinsic brightness can be calculated from the star's period. From a comparison of this intrinsic brightness with the star's apparent brightness, astronomers can calculate the distance to the star.) Cepheid variables are giant stars, so large that they can be detected in some of the nearby galaxies; they provide the major method we have of measuring distances to these galaxies. All measurements to more distant galaxies depend, in turn, on the measurements of distances to nearby galaxies.

A star like R Coronae Borealis (abbreviated *R CrB* and informally pronounced "R Cor Bor") varies in brightness because it occasionally gives off a cloud of opaque material—essentially soot—that masks the surface that we ordinarily see. The namesake for *R CrB*-class stars thus fades from 6th magnitude to 11th magnitude or even fainter (see the light curve facing Atlas Chart 16 in Chapter 7, and the finding chart for this star at the end of this chapter). RY Sagittarii, which covers about the same range in magnitude, is another example of the class.

Flare stars, such as UV Ceti or YZ Canis Minoris, occasionally flare up within minutes by one to six magnitudes.

RV Tauri stars, such as R Scuti and V Vulpeculae, vary with a period of one to five months. During each period these stars have one deep minimum and one shallow minimum; at a deep minimum, the brightness of these yellow supergiants may drop by as much as three magnitudes.

For several periods, *semiregular variables* have periods lasting months or years; then they are very irregular for a while.

Variable double stars such as RS Canum Venaticorum (abbreviated *RS CVn* and informally pronounced "R S Can Ven") are unusual eclipsing binaries that are especially interesting to study for those who have photoelectric equipment available. (Photoelectric equipment that can measure magnitudes accurately to 0.01 magnitude is needed.) RS CVn is a binary in which both stars are somewhat more massive than our sun, but generally one member is smaller and hotter and the other is a larger and cooler subgiant. The stars orbit each other very closely every 4.8 days. Every time the hotter star is eclipsed by the subgiant, the light drops by about 1 magnitude. One of the brightest RS CVn-type binaries is λ (lambda) Andromedae, which varies between visual magnitudes 3.70 and 4.05 every 54 days. Other RS CVn stars have periods between 0.6 and 80 days. The light variations arise as one star, with large starspots (comparable to the sunspots on our sun) darkening up to 40% of one hemisphere, rotates on its axis. Enormous bursts of radio waves coincide with the violent flare-ups of the star's extremely active outer atmosphere.

Variable stars are marked on the Atlas Charts in Chapter 7 with both inner and outer circles whenever possible. The inner circles give their faintest magnitude and the outer circles give their brightest magnitude. A number of variables are listed in Appendices 7 and 8; several also appeared in Table 8 and the Graphic Timetable for Double and Variable Stars in Chapter 5. The stars listed in Table 7 and Appendix 8 have shorter periods, and are thus easier to observe as variables, than the stars listed in Appendix 7.

Novae—newly visible stars—can be considered as variables in one sense; they are marked with special symbols on the Atlas Charts, however. A nova brightens when gas from a large companion star falls on the white-dwarf member of a binary system, triggering nuclear fusion on the white dwarf's surface.

Supernovae—stars that explode—are also a sort of variable star. The supernovae that went off in the years 1572 (Atlas Chart 1), 1604 (Atlas Chart 41), and 1987 (Atlas Chart 47) are marked.

Do not confuse *pulsars*—neutron stars that give off regular pulses of radio waves and are not ordinarily detectable optically—with variable stars, stars that vary in brightness in visible light.

Variable-star observers often give dates in terms of *Julian days,* a system of calendar-keeping in which the days are numbered consecutively from January 1, 4713 B.C. The Julian day system eliminates the need to calculate the number of days in a month or the effects of leap years. It also eliminates the need to worry about changes from the Julian to the Gregorian or other calendars. Also, Julian days begin at noon, so the Julian date does not change in the course of a night's observing. Portions of a day are customarily indicated by decimals in this system, instead of by hours, minutes, and seconds. For example, noon on January 1, 1995 is the beginning of Julian Day 2,449,719.0. Every tenth Julian Day is listed in Appendix 11.

The American Association of Variable Star Observers (25 Birch St., Cambridge, MA 02138) is an international organization of amateur astronomers devoted to the study and cataloguing of variable stars. The light curves and special observing projects set up in collaboration with the AAVSO and the International Amateur-Professional Photoelectric Photometry association (IAPPP) often provide important scientific data. The address for the IAPPP is Dyer Observatory, Vanderbilt University, Nashville, TN 37235.

Fig. 6-9. SS Cygni. (Wil Tirion) *Note:* Decimal points are omitted from magnitudes to avoid confusion with points representing stars.

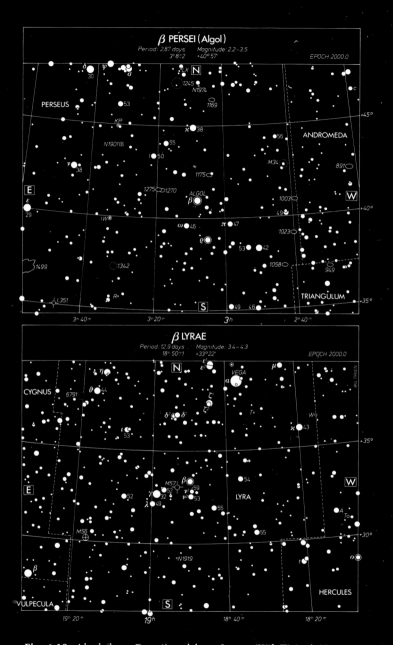

Fig. 6-10. Algol (beta Persei) and beta Lyrae. (Wil Tirion) *Note:* Decimal points are omitted from magnitudes to avoid confusion with points representing stars.

Fig. 6-11. Mira (omicron Ceti). (Wil Tirion) *Note:* Decimal points are omitted from magnitudes to avoid confusion with points representing stars.

Fig. 6-12. R Coronae Borealis. (Wil Tirion) *Note:* Decimal points are omitted from magnitudes to avoid confusion with points representing stars.

7

ATLAS OF THE SKY

On the following pages are 52 Atlas Charts that together cover the entire sky, accompanied by 4 charts showing close-ups of areas of special interest (the Pleiades, the Orion Nebula, the Virgo Cluster, and Proxima Centauri). A visual key to the Atlas Charts appears on the endpapers; Appendix 13 outlines the regions of sky covered by each chart.

The charts have been drawn with high precision by Wil Tirion to show positions of celestial objects as they will appear in epoch 2000.0, that is, at the beginning of the year 2000. The charts contain 25,000 stars down to visual magnitude 7.5, and about 2500 deep-sky objects (star clusters, nebulae, galaxies, and other objects among and beyond the stars). A key to the symbols for these objects and a list of lower-case Greek letters (which are used to label the brightest stars) appear below every chart.

The Greek letters were used to name the brightest stars in constellations by Johann Bayer in his sky atlas of 1603. On the whole, the stars were lettered in order of brightness, with α (alpha) usually being the brightest star in a constellation. This rule was not always followed; for example, the stars in the Big Dipper (which is part of the constellation Ursa Major) are lettered in order around the bowl and handle. Some of the fainter stars are labelled with lower-case Roman (regular) or italic letters or with numbers from the star catalogue John Flamsteed compiled in 1725.

Astronomers mark positions in the sky using coordinates comparable to those we use to plot positions on earth. In astronomy, *right ascension* is celestial longitude, analogous to terrestrial longitude. *Declination* is celestial latitude, analogous to terrestrial latitude. The Atlas Charts in this chapter are marked in right ascension and declination. Right ascension is marked in hours, minutes, and seconds (abbreviated ^{h}, ^{m}, and ^{sec}) of time, with each 24 hours representing a full rotation of 360°. Declination is marked in degrees, minutes, and seconds (°, ', and ") north (+) or south (−) of the celestial equator.

The positions of celestial objects take account of *precession*—the drifting of the direction of the earth's axis of rotation and thus of the celestial coordinate system. Current positions of stars and deep-sky objects and constellation boundaries differ from the positions for the year 2000.0 (as shown on the charts) by less than one-quarter degree. Chapter 15 gives further details on right ascension, declination, precession, and matters of time and calendars.

Constellation figures are outlined, and the official constellation boundaries are marked with dotted lines. The line connecting stars is dotted when a star that has traditionally been part of an asterism or constellation is no longer considered an official part of it; for example, one of the four stars marking the Great Square of Pegasus is really in the constellation Andromeda (see Atlas Charts 20 and 9).

Stellar magnitudes (see Table 3) are represented by dots of different sizes. Each size represents one whole magnitude, including a range of $1/2$ magnitude on each side of the integer (whole number) given, as shown in the key beneath each chart. The relative brightness of stars is shown as they appear to the eye rather than as they appear on a photographic plate, which is usually sensitive to a different range of colors (wavelengths).

Double stars (Chapter 6) are marked with a horizontal line through the dot that represents the total magnitude of the components. Only visual binaries—those systems in which two or more stars can be seen through a telescope (as opposed to stars that have been identified as binaries by studying their spectrum or in some other way)—are marked as doubles. The members of double star systems are plotted as separate stars, though, if they are separated by more than one minute of arc. A few double stars are listed on the charts using the letter A (for Aitken) followed by their numbers in the Aitken Double Star (ADS) catalogue. Sometimes several members of a binary system share the same letter but each component is marked with a different superscript, as in ι^1 (iota-1) and ι^2 (iota-2).

Variable stars (Chapter 6) whose maximum brightness is within the range of magnitude covered on these charts are indicated by a dot surrounded by a concentric circle to show the range of brightness; no inside dot appears if the minimum brightness is fainter than magnitude 7.5. Only variables whose brightness varies by more than 0.1 magnitude are marked.

Deep-sky objects. In 1784, Charles Messier compiled a list (Table 12) of fuzzy objects in the sky, so that he would not be confused by them when searching for comets. A few additional objects were added later. The list turns out to contain many of the most interesting objects in the sky that are accessible to amateur observers. Most deep-sky objects are marked with their numbers in the Messier list, in J.L.E. Dreyer's *New General Catalogue* (NGC) of 1888, or in the supplemental *Index Catalogues* (ICs) of 1895 and 1908. Messier numbers are preceded by an M, NGC numbers are written (on the charts) without prefixes, and IC numbers are preceded by the letter *I* and a period. A few objects are also labeled with their popular names.

The **Milky Way** is outlined by a dotted line on the charts.

Open star clusters (also known as *galactic clusters*) are marked with dotted circles, whose size signifies the size of each cluster. A special chart, facing Chart 10, shows the stars of the Pleiades at a larger scale. Some star clusters are often referred to by their numbers in special catalogues, such as the Trumpler Catalogue (*e.g,* Tr 1) or the Melotte Catalogue (*e.g.,* Mel 71).

Globular star clusters are marked with symbols showing three size ranges.

Planetary nebulae, shells of gas given off when stars like the sun end their lives, are marked with circles bearing four external spikes.

Pulsars, tiny neutron stars that give off regular pulses of radio waves, representing the death of stars somewhat more massive than the sun, and **black holes,** representing the death of extremely massive stars, also have their own symbols. The most likely black-hole candidate is Cygnus X-1 on Atlas Chart 19. The name Cygnus X-1 means that it was the first x-ray source to be discovered in the constellation Cygnus, a discovery that was not possible until observations could be made from x-ray telescopes orbiting above the earth's atmosphere. Even though pulsars and black holes cannot usually be seen in visible light (only two pulsars have been detected optically, even with large telescopes), these objects are so fascinating that it is interesting to know that one is nearby when you are observing.

Novae—sudden brightenings of stars—are listed with the year in which they went off, such as Nova Herculis 1934 (for the nova visible in that location in the year 1934), shown with both variable star and nebula symbols (Atlas Charts 18 and 19). Nova Cygni 1975 and Nova Cygni 1992 are marked on Atlas Chart 19. We now know that novae are events that take place in binary star systems containing a white dwarf. Three **supernovae** are also marked. These supernovae— the one Tycho saw in 1572 (Atlas Chart 1), the one Kepler saw in 1604 (Atlas Chart 41), and the supernova that occurred in 1987 (Atlas Chart 47) in the Large Magellanic Cloud—represented the explosive deaths of massive stars. Their remnants are not easy to see; the Crab Nebula and S147 in Taurus (Atlas Chart 11) and the Veil Nebula in Cygnus (Atlas Chart 19) are much more interesting supernova remnants to see with small telescopes.

The shapes of other **nebulae,** regions of gas and dust in space, are drawn on the charts when they are more than 10 minutes of arc across; a square signifies nebulae smaller than 10 minutes of arc across. A special chart opposite Atlas Chart 24 shows at an enlarged scale the complex of stars and nebulae in Orion's sword (including the Orion Nebula), which are beautiful objects.

Galaxies are drawn as ovals, in four size ranges. They are labelled down to magnitude 13.0 and fainter. The central part of the nearest cluster of galaxies, the Virgo Cluster, is featured on a larger-scale chart, 27A (p. 265).

A few selected **quasars** are marked with triangles. Quasars are farther from us than most galaxies marked on the charts, and all are optically fainter than the normal limit of our charts. These days, many quasars are observable by amateur astronomers using telescopes and electronic detectors. Some of the quasars are listed by their commonly used *3C numbers,* that is, their numbers in the Third Cambridge Catalogue of radio sources. Others are named for their position in other catalogues.

Radio astronomers—astronomers using radio telescopes— originally named objects emitting radio waves with a capital letter and the name of the constellation, such as Taurus A for the first radio source discovered in Taurus. We now know that Taurus A is the Crab Nebula, named for its shape. It is also known as M1, because it was the first object in Messier's list (see Table 11).

The Atlas Charts are in the following order: the north polar charts come first, then the midnorthern charts, equatorial charts, midsouthern charts, and south polar charts. In order to minimize distortion on these charts, Tirion has used a conic projection for the polar regions and intermediate declinations, and a cylindrical projection for the equatorial region.

Numbers set in triangles at the borders of each map direct you to adjacent charts. (The adjacent charts in each group are in order of right ascension.) North is up, west is to the right, south is down, and east is to the left on the charts. (If you hold a paper overhead facing north, you will have north down and west at the left. When you hold the paper with north up, as in the charts, you will find west at the right.)

Keep a life list of the Messier objects you have seen, recording the date on which you observed each one and sketching what it looked like. In March each year, it is possible (though difficult) to see all the Messier objects in a single night, a "Messier marathon."

Table 12: Messier Catalogue

M	NGC	r.a. (2000.0) h m	dec. °	Mag.	Visual Description	Atlas Chart
1	1952	05 34.5	+22 01	8.4	Crab Nebula	11
2	7089	21 33.5	−00 49	6.5	Globular cluster	32
3	5272	13 42.2	+28 23	6.4	Globular cluster	15
4	6121	16 23.6	−26 32	5.9	Globular cluster	41
5	5904	15 18.6	+02 05	5.8	Globular cluster	29
6	6405	17 40.1	−32 13	4.2	Open cluster	41
7	6475	17 53.9	−34 49	3.3	Open cluster	41
8	6523	18 03.8	−24 23	5.8	Lagoon Nebula	42
9	6333	17 19.2	−18 31	7.9	Globular cluster	30
10	6254	16 57.1	−04 06	6.6	Globular cluster	29, 30
11	6705	18 51.1	−06 16	5.8	Open cluster	30
12	6218	16 47.2	−01 57	6.6	Globular cluster	29
13	6205	16 41.7	+36 28	5.9	Globular cluster	17
14	6402	17 37.6	−03 15	7.6	Globular cluster	30
15	7078	21 30.0	+12 10	6.4	Globular cluster	32
16	6611	18 18.8	−13 47	6.0	Open cluster, nebula	30
17	6618	18 20.8	−16 11	7	Omega Nebula	30
18	6613	18 19 9	−17 08	6.9	Open cluster	30
19	6273	17 02.6	−26 16	7.2	Globular cluster	41
20	6514	18 02.6	−23 02	8.5	Trifid Nebula	41, 42
21	6531	18 04.6	−22 30	5.9	Open cluster	41, 42
22	6656	18 36.4	−23 54	5.1	Globular cluster	42
23	6494	17 56.8	−19 01	5.5	Open cluster	30, 41

Note: Magnitudes based on a table in *Sky Catalogue 2000.0* (vol. 2).

Table 12: Messier Catalogue (Continued)

M	NGC	r.a. (2000.0) h	m	dec. °	Mag.	Visual Description	Atlas Chart
24	6603	18	16.9	−18 29	4.5	Open cluster	30
25	IC4725	18	31.6	−19 15	4.6	Open cluster	30
26	6694	18	45.2	−09 24	8	Open cluster	30
27	6853	19	59.6	+22 43	8.1	Dumbbell Nebula	18, 19
28	6626	18	24.5	−24 52	6.9	Globular cluster	42
29	6913	20	23.9	+38 32	6.6	Open cluster	18, 19
30	7099	21	40.4	−23 11	7.5	Globular cluster	43
31	224	00	42.7	+41 16	3.4	Andromeda Galaxy	9
32	221	00	42.7	+40 52	8.2	Elliptical galaxy	9
33	598	01	33.9	+30 39	5.7	Spiral galaxy (Sc)	9
34	1039	02	42.0	+42 47	5.2	Open cluster	10
35	2168	06	08.9	+24 20	5.1	Open cluster	11, 12
36	1960	05	36.1	+34 08	6.0	Open cluster	11
37	2099	05	52.4	+32 33	5.6	Open cluster	11, 12
38	1912	05	28.7	+35 50	6.4	Open cluster	11
39	7092	21	32.2	+48 26	4.6	Open cluster	19
40	WNC4	12	22.4	+58 05	8	Double star	
41	2287	06	47.0	−20 44	4.5	Open cluster	36
42	1976	05	35.4	−05 27	4	Orion Nebula	24
43	1982	05	35.6	−05 16		Orion Nebula; smaller part	24
44	2632	08	40.1	+19 59	3.1	Praesepe; open cluster	13, 25
45	—	03	47.0	+24 07	1.2	The Pleiades; open cluster	10, 11
46	2437	07	41.8	−14 49	6.1	Open cluster	25
47	2422	07	36.6	−14 30	4.4	Open cluster	25
48	2548	08	13.8	−05 48	5.8	Open cluster	25
49	4472	12	29.8	+08 00	8.4	Elliptical galaxy	27A
50	2323	07	03.2	−08 20	5.9	Open cluster	24, 25
51	5194-5	13	29.9	+47 12	8.1	Whirlpool Galaxy	15
52	7654	23	24.2	+61 35	6.9	Open cluster	1
53	5024	13	12.9	+18 10	7.7	Globular cluster	15
54	6715	18	55.1	−30 29	7.7	Globular cluster	42
55	6809	19	40.0	−30 58	7.0	Globular cluster	42
56	6779	19	16.6	+30 11	8.2	Globular cluster	18
57	6720	18	53.6	+33 02	9.0	Ring Nebula	18
58	4579	12	37.7	+11 49	9.8	Spiral galaxy (SBb)	27A
59	4621	12	42.0	+11 39	9.8	Elliptical galaxy	27A
60	4649	12	43.7	+11 33	8.8	Elliptical galaxy	27A
61	4303	12	21.9	+04 28	9.7	Spiral galaxy (Sc)	27A
62	6266	17	01.2	−30 07	6.6	Globular cluster	41
63	5055	13	15.8	+42 02	8.6	Spiral galaxy (Sb)	15
64	4826	12	56.7	+21 41	8.5	Spiral galaxy (Sb)	15
65	3623	11	18.9	+13 05	9.3	Spiral galaxy (Sa)	27
66	3627	11	20.2	+12 59	9.0	Spiral galaxy (Sb)	27

Note: Magnitudes based on a table in *Sky Catalogue 2000.0* (vol. 2).

Table 12: Messier Catalogue (Continued)

M	NGC	r.a. (2000.0) h	m	dec. (2000.0) °	Mag.	Visual Description	Atlas Chart
67	2682	08	50.4	+11 49	6.9	Open cluster	25
68	4590	12	39.5	−26 45	8.2	Globular cluster	39
69	6637	18	31.4	−32 21	7.7	Globular cluster	42
70	6681	18	43.2	−32 18	8.1	Globular cluster	42
71	6838	19	53.8	+18 47	8.3	Globular cluster	19, 31
72	6981	20	53.5	−12 32	9.4	Globular cluster	31, 32
73	6994	20	58.9	−12 38		Open cluster	31, 32
74	628	01	36.7	+15 47	9.2	Spiral galaxy (Sc)	9, 22
75	6864	20	06.1	−21 55	8.6	Globular cluster	42, 43
76	650-1	01	42.4	+51 34	11.5	Planetary nebula	1, 2, 9, 10
77	1068	02	42.7	−00 01	8.8	Spiral galaxy (Sb)	22
78	2068	05	46.7	+00 03	8	Emission nebula	24
79	1904	05	24.5	−24 33	8.0	Globular cluster	35
80	6093	16	17.0	−22 59	7.2	Globular cluster	41
81	3031	09	55.6	+69 04	6.8	Spiral galaxy (Sb)	4, 5
82	3034	09	55.8	+69 41	8.4	Irregular galaxy (Irr)	4, 5
83	5236	13	37.0	−29 52	7.6	Spiral galaxy (Sc)	39
84	4374	12	25.1	+12 53	9.3	Elliptical galaxy	27A
85	4382	12	25.4	+18 11	9.2	Ellip./lenticular galaxy	15, 27
86	4406	12	26.2	+12 57	9.2	Elliptical galaxy	27A
87	4486	12	30.8	+12 24	8.6	Elliptical galaxy	27A
88	4501	12	32.0	+14 25	9.5	Spiral galaxy (Sb)	27A
89	4552	12	35.7	+12 33	9.8	Elliptical galaxy	27A
90	4569	12	36.8	+13 10	9.5	Spiral galaxy (Sb)	27A
91	4548	12	35.4	+14 30	10.2	Spiral galaxy or M58?	27A
92	6341	17	17.1	+43 08	6.5	Globular cluster	17
93	2447	07	44.6	−23 52	6.2	Open cluster	36
94	4736	12	50.9	+41 07	8.1	Spiral galaxy (Sb)	15
95	3351	10	44.0	+11 42	9.7	Barred spiral galaxy (SBb)	26
96	3368	10	46.8	+11 49	9.2	Spiral galaxy (Sa)	26
97	3587	11	14.8	+55 01	11.2	Owl Nebula	5, 14
98	4192	12	13.8	+14 54	10.1	Spiral galaxy (Sb)	27A
99	4254	12	18.8	+14 25	9.8	Spiral galaxy (Sc)	27A
100	4321	12	22.9	+15 49	9.4	Spiral galaxy (Sc)	15, 27A
101	5457	14	03.2	+54 21	7.7	Spiral galaxy (Sc)	6, 15, 16
102	—	—	—	—		M101	
103	581	01	33.2	+60 42	7.4	Open cluster	1, 2
104	4594	12	40.0	−11 37	8.3	Sombrero Galaxy	27
105	3379	10	47.8	+12 35	9.3	Elliptical galaxy	26
106	4258	12	19.0	+47 18	8.3	Spiral galaxy (Sb)	14, 15
107	6171	16	32.5	−13 03	8.1	Globular cluster	29
108	3556	11	11.5	+55 40	10.0	Spiral galaxy (Sb)	5, 14
109	3992	11	57.6	+53 23	9.8	Barred spiral galaxy (SBc)	5, 14, 15

Note: Magnitudes based on a table in *Sky Catalogue 2000.0* (vol. 2).

ATLAS CHART 1. Bubble Nebula, Tycho's Supernova The Milky Way in Cassiopeia, with its rich fields of clouds, gas, and dust, and star clusters, is an interesting area to scan with low-power telescopes or binoculars. Several open clusters are easy to find because they lie close to bright stars. NGC 457 is an especially bright open cluster in the same field of view as φ (phi) Cas, which lies southwest of δ (delta) Cas in the W of Cassiopeia. Even a small telescope gives a good view of the stars in this cluster; more stars are visible with telescopes of higher power. Close by is the open cluster NGC 436. Since binoculars or telescopes with small apertures show only a few stars here, NGC 436 is more suitable for viewing with larger telescopes. M103 (NGC 581) is a fan-shaped, 7th-magnitude cluster (Fig. 5-16) located northeast of δ (delta) Cas.

About 5° northwest of β (beta) Cas, near the border of Cepheus, is M52 (NGC 7654), a rich, 7th-magnitude open cluster. Close to M52 is the Bubble Nebula, NGC 7635, which has a high total brightness even though it is spread over so much sky that its average surface brightness is low. Southwest of β (beta) Cas, about halfway between ρ (rho) and σ (sigma) Cas, is the open cluster NGC 7789. Its diameter is about the same as the moon's. You can detect this cluster with binoculars, and telescopes resolve many of its 1000 stars.

Northeast of β (beta) Cas is κ (kappa) Cas, with the two open clusters NGC 133 and NGC 146 nearby. NGC 146 has about 50 stars within a 6 arc min diameter; this cluster should be viewed with high power because of the richness of the Milky Way in this part of the sky.

Tycho's Supernova of 1572, 0^h25^m +63°, appeared slightly to the northwest of NGC 146, growing so bright that it was visible to the naked eye for about six months. Since the appearance of a new star showed that the sky changed, contrary to Ptolemaic theory, this object was important for the acceptance of Copernicus's heliocentric theory. The remnant of the supernova is now only faintly visible with large telescopes, appearing as thin filaments that form an incomplete ring 8 arc minutes across. Radio telescopes, however, detect strong signals.

Fig. 7-1 The Bubble Nebula (NGC 7635) in Cassiopeia. (Lick Observatory photo)

MAGNITUDES		OPEN CLUSTERS				QUASAR		GREEK ALPHABET	
●	>-04		>10', TO SCALE		<10'	PULSAR		α Alpha	ν Nu
●	-04–05	GLOBULAR CLUSTERS				BLACK HOLE		β Beta	ξ Xi
●	06–15		>10'	5-10'	<5'	MILKY WAY		γ Gamma	ο Omicron
●	16–25	PLANETARY NEBULAE						δ Delta	π Pi
●	26–35		>1'	05'-1'	<05'	GALACTIC EQUATOR		ε Epsilon	ϱ Rho
●	36–45	BRIGHT DIFFUSE NEB.						ζ Zeta	σ Sigma
●	46–55			>10', TO SCALE	<10'	ECLIPTIC		η Eta	τ Tau
●	56–65	GALAXIES						θ ϑ Theta	υ Upsilon
●	66–75		>30'	20'-30' 10'-20'	<10'	CONSTELLATION BOUNDARIES		ι Iota	φ ϕ Phi
DOUBLE or MULTIPLE								κ ϰ Kappa	χ Chi
VARIABLE								λ Lambda	ψ Psi
								μ Mu	ω Omega

ATLAS CHART 2. Polaris, double cluster in Perseus Polaris, α (alpha) Ursa Minoris, the North Star, lies about 1° from the true north celestial pole and circles the pole once every 24 hours. Polaris is a double star, with a 9th-magnitude companion at a distance of 18 arc sec. The pair can be resolved by a good small telescope.

In the Milky Way in Perseus, we find the famous "double cluster," also known as h and χ (chi) Persei, and marked on the chart as NGC 869 and NGC 884. The double cluster is a favorite of amateurs because it is so easy to observe. Binoculars reveal its many stars. A small telescope used with a low-power, wide-angle eyepiece (field of 1°) shows both clusters. Each cluster has a diameter of about 70 light-years. NGC 869 is the younger of the two, only about 10 million years old, which makes it one of the youngest clusters known; it lies over 7000 light-years away from us.

About $1\frac{1}{2}$° east is the smaller open cluster NGC 957. At lower right in Perseus is M76 (NGC 650), a planetary nebula whose integrated magnitude is 11.5. Near the chart's right border, at 58°, we find the binary η (eta) Cas. Its components show a beautiful color contrast, sometimes reported as gold and purple or as yellow and red.

As we move from Cassiopeia to Camelopardalis, we go further from the Milky Way and into less interesting regions of the sky.

Fig. 7-2 The double open cluster in Perseus, h and chi Persei (NGC 869 and 884). (Lick Observatory photo)

MAGNITUDES		OPEN CLUSTERS				QUASAR	△	GREEK ALPHABET			
	>-0.4		>10'	TO SCALE	<10'	PULSAR	⚡	α Alpha		ν Nu	
	-0.4-+0.5					BLACK HOLE		β Beta		ξ Xi	
	0.6-1.5	GLOBULAR CLUSTERS	⊕	⊕	⊕	MILKY WAY		γ Gamma		ο Omicron	
	1.6-2.5		>10'	5'-10'	<5'			δ Delta		π Pi	
	2.6-3.5	PLANETARY NEBULAE	-◇-	-◇-	-◇-	GALACTIC EQUATOR		ε Epsilon		ρ Rho	
	3.6-4.5		>1'	0.5'-1'	<0.5'			ζ Zeta		σ Sigma	
	4.6-5.5							η Eta		τ Tau	
	5.6-6.5	BRIGHT DIFFUSE NEB.			▫	ECLIPTIC		θ ϑ Theta		υ Upsilon	
	6.6-7.5		>10'	TO SCALE	<10'			ι Iota		φ φ Phi	
DOUBLE or MULTIPLE	●							κ ϰ Kappa		χ Chi	
		GALAXIES	◯	○	○	CONSTELLATION BOUNDARIES		λ Lambda		ψ Psi	
VARIABLE	◉ ○		>30'	20'-30'	10'-20' <10'			μ Mu		ω Omega	

ATLAS CHART 3. Camelopardalis Camelopardalis, the Giraffe, has very few bright stars. In Lynx, a trio of multiple stars lies just right of 7^h and just below +60°. The multiple system farthest to the right is an interesting triple. The double star 19 Lyn (ADS6012), near 7^h23^m +55°, is surrounded by several faint companions.

The galaxy NGC 2403 (7^h34^m +65°40') is one of the nearest spiral galaxies outside of our Local Group of galaxies. Binoculars show it as a large hazy spot, while large telescopes hint at spiral structure. NGC 2403 is 8 million light-years away and 37,000 light-years across. The galaxy is easily seen even with small telescopes at low power, and the view with larger telescopes is striking.

Further down in Camelopardalis, at 4^h08^m +62°, is the open cluster NGC 1502, readily visible through small telescopes. Larger telescopes show it to be tightly packed with many stars of differing magnitudes. On nights with good seeing, the cluster is visible even through binoculars.

Six degrees above NGC 1502 is the large beautiful spiral galaxy IC 342. Though it can be seen with small telescopes, larger ones are needed to show any spiral structure. The planetary nebula NGC 1501, located in Camelopardalis slightly below NGC 1502, is about 1 arc min in diameter and slightly oval. Because it is dim, at least a medium aperture is needed for a good view.

Fig. 7-3 Camelopardalis, the Giraffe, from the star atlas of Hevelius (1690). The constellation is drawn backwards from the way it appears in the sky because Hevelius drew the celestial sphere as it would appear from the outside.

MAGNITUDES		OPEN CLUSTERS	⃝ ⃝ ∘ ∘		QUASAR	△	GREEK ALPHABET			
	>-0.4		>10' TO SCALE <10'		PULSAR	⚡	α	Alpha	ν	Nu
	-0.4-+0.5	GLOBULAR CLUSTERS	⊕ ⊕ ⊛		BLACK HOLE	Y	β	Beta	ξ	Xi
	0.6-1.5		>10' 5'-10' <5'		MILKY WAY		γ	Gamma	ο	Omicron
	1.6-2.5						δ	Delta	π	Pi
	2.6-3.5	PLANETARY NEBULAE	⋄ ⋄ ⋄				ε	Epsilon	ρ	Rho
	3.6-4.5		>1' 0.5'-1' <0.5'		GALACTIC EQUATOR		ζ	Zeta	σ	Sigma
	4.6-5.5						η	Eta	τ	Tau
	5.5-6.5	BRIGHT DIFFUSE NEB.	⬚		ECLIPTIC		θ ϑ	Theta	υ	Upsilon
	6.6-7.5		>10' TO SCALE <10'				ι	Iota	φ ϕ	Phi
DOUBLE or TRIPLE	●━●	GALAXIES	⬭ ∘ ∘ ∘		CONSTELLATION BOUNDARIES		κ ϰ	Kappa	χ	Chi
			>30' 20'-30' 10'-20' <10'				λ	Lambda	ψ	Psi
VARIABLE	⦿ ○						μ	Mu	ω	Omega

ATLAS CHART 4. M81 AND M82 The galaxies M81 (NGC 3031) and M82 (NGC 3034) appear at the center of this chart, just short of 10^h and below 70°. They are members of the Ursa Major cluster of galaxies. M81 is one of the prettiest spirals in the sky. M82 (Fig. 5-38) appears as though gas is exploding from it, but there has been continual controversy over whether we are seeing gas exploding or light reflected from relatively stationary gas. These galaxies are two of the most easily observed galaxies in the sky, and are visible through a small telescope or a good pair of binoculars. Nearby galaxies NGC 3077 and NGC 2976 are easily visible with low-power instruments.

QSO 0957+561, at lower left, is the "double quasar," the first known example of a "gravitational lens." The light and radio waves from this quasar are bent by the gravity of an intervening galaxy as they pass it, making us see at least two images separated by only 6 arc sec. The optical objects are 17th magnitude and have a redshift of 1.41 (141%), making them some of the most distant ones known.

Fig. 7-4 M81 (NGC 3031), a type Sb spiral galaxy in Ursa Major, with M82 (NGC 3034) above it, NGC 3077 to its lower left, and NGC 2976 at bottom right. (Palomar Observatory photo)

MAGNITUDES				OPEN CLUSTERS					QUASAR	△	GREEK ALPHABET			
					>10'	TO SCALE	<10'				α Alpha		ν Nu	
	> -0.4								PULSAR	⚡	β Beta		ξ Xi	
	-0.4 - +0.5			GLOBULAR CLUSTERS	⊕	⊕	⊕		BLACK HOLE		γ Gamma		o Omicron	
	0.5 - 1.5				>10'	5'-10'	<5'				δ Delta		π Pi	
	1.6 - 2.5								MILKY WAY		ϵ Epsilon		ϱ Rho	
	2.6 - 3.5			PLANETARY NEBULAE	⋄	⋄	⋄				ζ Zeta		σ Sigma	
	3.6 - 4.5				>1'	0.5'-1'	<0.5'		GALACTIC EQUATOR		η Eta		τ Tau	
	4.6 - 5.5										θ ϑ Theta		υ Upsilon	
	5.6 - 6.5			BRIGHT DIFFUSE NEB.			▫		ECLIPTIC		ι Iota		ϕ φ Phi	
	6.6 - 7.5				>10'	TO SCALE	<10'				κ $\varkappa$ Kappa		χ Chi	
LE or PLE	● ●								CONSTELLATION BOUNDARIES		λ Lambda		ψ Psi	
BLE	⊙ ○			GALAXIES	⬭	○	○				μ Mu		ω Omega	
					>30'	20'-30'	10'-20'	<10'						

ATLAS CHART 5. Big Dipper, Owl Nebula At lower right in Ursa Major—about $2^{1}/_{2}°$ southeast of β (beta) UMa—is M97 (NGC 3587), the Owl Nebula (Fig. 5-7), one of the largest of the planetary nebulae. Small telescopes show a featureless circular disk, but the image in large telescopes suggests the face of an owl. Within 1° of M97 is the galaxy M108 (NGC 3556), shown in Figure 5-44.

Mizar, ζ (zeta) UMa, is the second star from the end of the handle of the Big Dipper and is located near $13^{h}30^{m}$ +55°. Mizar is one of the most interesting doubles in the sky. Its companion, Alcor (labelled *g* on the chart), lies about 12 arc min away (a distance equal to about $^{1}/_{3}$ of the moon's diameter) and is just barely visible with the naked eye. Both components of Mizar, called Mizar A and Mizar B, are in turn double stars, though their components cannot be resolved by telescopes. The motions of the components show up in spectra. The American Indians referred to Mizar and Alcor as the Horse and Rider.

Magnitudes around the Big Dipper, from handle to bowl, are 1.9 for Alkaid, 4.0 for Alcor, 1.8 for Alioth, 3.3 for Megrez, 2.4 for Phecda, 2.4 for Merak, and 1.8 for Dubhe.

M109 (NGC 3992), a bright barred spiral galaxy in Ursa Major, lies near γ (gamma) Ursa Majoris, at 12^{h} and above +50°. Another easily observed galaxy, NGC 3953, lies nearby. These and other galaxies are part of the Ursa Major cluster of galaxies. Another cluster of galaxies can be observed in Draco.

An interesting variable to observe is RY in Draco, at 13^{h} +65°, which varies with a 6-month period.

Fig. 7-5 The Owl Nebula, M97 (NGC 3587) in Ursa Major. (Courtesy of the Observatories of the Carnegie Institution of Washington)

FROM "SKY ATLAS 2000.0" BY WIL TIRION

ATLAS CHART 6. M101, Little Dipper M101 (NGC 5457) is an exceptionally beautiful spiral galaxy in Ursa Major, near 14^h +54°. It is seen face-on, and at almost 8th magnitude, it is one of the brightest galaxies in the sky (Fig. 5-41). M101's spiral arms can barely be seen on a very clear night through a medium-sized telescope, but because the galaxy is so spread out, it is hard to find unless conditions are perfect. M102 was one of Messier's few mistakes; it was really a second reference to M101. Many other members of the Ursa Major cluster of galaxies, such as NGC 5907 (Fig. 5-52), also appear on this chart, near 15^h20^m +56°.

The Little Dipper in Ursa Minor lies in the central region of this chart. The bowl contains β (Kochab), γ (Pherkad), η, and ζ, and the handle is ε, δ, and α (Polaris) UMi. Apparent magnitudes, in the same order, are 2.1, 3.1, 5.0, 4.3, 4.2 , 4.4, and 2.0. These stars can thus make a good test of the quality of your sky, and of your eyes' sensitivity.

Few other objects of special interest are in this region. One double star worth observing is κ (kappa) Boötes, near 14^h13^m +52°.

Thuban, alpha Draconis, was the pole star when the Pyramids were being built, and so was worshipped by the Egyptians.

Fig. 7-6 M101 (NGC 5457), a type Sc spiral galaxy in Ursa Major. (Palomar Observatory photo)

FROM "SKY ATLAS 2000.0" BY WIL TIRION

MAGNITUDES		OPEN CLUSTERS					QUASAR	△		GREEK ALPHABET		
	>-0.4						PULSAR		α	Alpha	ν	Nu
	-0.4-+0.5		>10' TO SCALE	<10'			BLACK HOLE		β	Beta	ξ	Xi
	0.6-1.5	GLOBULAR CLUSTERS	⊕	⊕	⊕		MILKY WAY		γ	Gamma	ο	Omicron
	1.6-2.5		>10'	5-10'	<5'				δ	Delta	π	Pi
	2.6-3.5	PLANETARY NEBULAE					GALACTIC EQUATOR		ε	Epsilon	ϱ	Rho
	3.6-4.5		>1'	0.5-1'	<0.5'				ζ	Zeta	σ	Sigma
	4.6-5.5								η	Eta	τ	Tau
	5.5-6.5	BRIGHT DIFFUSE NEB.					ECLIPTIC		θ ϑ	Theta	υ	Upsilon
	6.6-7.5		>10' TO SCALE	<10'					ι	Iota	φ φ	Phi
DOUBLE or MULTIPLE							CONSTELLATION BOUNDARIES		κ ϰ	Kappa	χ	Chi
VARIABLE		GALAXIES							λ	Lambda	ψ	Psi
			>30'	20'-30'	10'-20'	<10'			μ	Mu	ω	Omega

ATLAS CHART 7. Draco The four stars in the head of Draco—ξ, ν, β, and γ Dra (xi, nu, beta, and gamma Dra)—form a conspicuous asterism, the Lozenge, at the bottom of this chart. They are not far from the bright star Vega (see Atlas Chart 18) and are close to the foot of Hercules. The Lozenge and other areas of Draco contain several interesting doubles. Binoculars resolve the star ν (nu) Dra in the Lozenge, and a good small telescope resolves the nearby star μ (mu) Dra, at $17^h +55°$.

Several other doubles appear toward the center of the chart, including φ (phi) Dra, near $18^h20^m +71°$, and the pair at $18^h +80°$, whose members have Flamsteed numbers 40 and 41 Dra. Due east (left) of φ (phi) Dra is ε (epsilon) Dra, a good double to observe at moderate magnifications since its components are only about 3 arc sec apart.

The planetary nebula NGC 6543, at magnitude 8.8, is one of the brightest in the sky. It is located almost in the center of this chart, about halfway between δ (delta) and ζ (zeta) Dra. NGC 6543 was the first planetary nebula to be observed with a spectroscope; the fact that emission lines were present settled the controversy about whether planetaries were numerous stars or—as they turned out to be—clouds of diffuse gas. A small telescope at moderate magnification shows the disk, but more powerful telescopes are needed to show the internal structure, a bright irregular helix. Since NGC 6543 is a circumpolar object for most northern hemisphere observers, you can view it throughout the year.

The quasar 3C 351 lies at $17^h +60°$. It is magnitude 15.3 and has a redshift of 0.371 (37.1%), making it about 7 billion light-years away.

Fig. 7-7 Draco, the Dragon, (drawn backwards) snakes across the sky in this drawing from the star atlas of Hevelius (1690)

OM "SKY ATLAS 2000.0" BY WIL TIRION

MAGNITUDES		OPEN CLUSTERS			QUASAR	△	GREEK ALPHABET			
	>-0.4		>10' TO SCALE <10'		PULSAR	⚡	α	Alpha	ν	Nu
	-0.4--0.5	GLOBULAR CLUSTERS			BLACK HOLE		β	Beta	ξ	Xi
	0.6-1.5		>10' 5'-10' <5'		MILKY WAY		γ	Gamma	o	Omicron
	1.6-2.5						δ	Delta	π	Pi
	2.6-3.5	PLANETARY NEBULAE			GALACTIC EQUATOR		ε	Epsilon	ϱ	Rho
	3.6-4.5		>1' 0.5'-1' <0.5'			70°	ζ	Zeta	σ	Sigma
	4.6-5.5						η	Eta	τ	Tau
	5.6-6.5	BRIGHT DIFFUSE NEB.			ECLIPTIC		$\theta\ \vartheta$	Theta	υ	Upsilon
	6.6-7.5		>10' TO SCALE <10'			100°	ι	Iota	$\phi\ \varphi$	Phi
BLE or PLE							$\kappa\ \varkappa$	Kappa	χ	Chi
		GALAXIES			CONSTELLATION BOUNDARIES		λ	Lambda	ψ	Psi
ABLE	◎ ○		>30' 20'-30' 10'-20' <10'				μ	Mu	ω	Omega

ATLAS CHART 8. delta Cephei The Milky Way passes through Cepheus and Cygnus in this chart, and presents a very rich star field for observing. The region contains a number of open clusters, planetary nebulae, and gaseous nebulae. Look in Cepheus, near 21^h50^m +58°, for the variable star μ (mu) Cep, one of the reddest stars visible to the naked eye. It is sometimes called the Garnet Star because of its deep red color. Just south of μ Cep is a large faint structure, IC 1396, a region of extended nebulosity. 1^h15^m to the right of μ Cep and slightly north, at about 20^h30^m +60°, are the open cluster NGC 6939 and the spiral galaxy NGC 6946 (Fig. 5-53). Above μ Cep, near 22^h +64°, is one of the best double stars in this constellation, ξ (xi) Cep.

Near the galactic equator, at 22^h30^m +58°, is the famous star δ (delta) Cephei, a variable star whose discovery led to the first measurements of the distances to galaxies and thus to our subsequent understanding of the immense scale of the universe (Chapter 5). This star is the prototype of the *Cepheid variables* (Chapter 6). δ Cephei has a 5.4-day period, during which it varies by about one magnitude in brightness. By observing δ Cephei every night, you can easily detect the variation. Small telescopes also reveal that δ Cephei is a double star.

Toward the top of the chart, near 21^h30^m +78°, is a red variable, S Cep, which is visible through small telescopes. Closer to Polaris is the open cluster NGC 188, one of the oldest open clusters known, at 14 billion years of age. About 70 stars can be seen in this cluster with a medium-sized telescope at low power.

This completes the set of 8 Atlas Charts covering the region from +50° to the north celestial pole. The next 12 Atlas Charts cover the region from +20° to +50°.

Fig. 7-8 Cepheus, from the star atlas of Bode. (Jay M. Pasachoff)

Polaris ·90° 4 URSA MINOR
·75° ·80° ·85° ·85° ·80° ·75° β
3h 15h
2 6
δ ζ ϑ
2h 188 16h
U ε 6217
RX AR V η
CASSIOPEIA YZ 41 AZ
I454 40
2h 6412
70° 6340 70°
1h γ 17h
40 ϱ 6643
π S UX 6503 χ
CAS 7822 CEPHEUS ψ φ ω τ
7762 VW1 τ υ
5° AF DRACO
o DM 6543
CAS EK ε σ 18h
1 β 65° δ
l T 7023 AC ϱ π
AH 7133 6951
7129 ϑ
M52 7142
7635 NY 7139 60° o
67538 ξ VV η 6939
I510 7160 6946 W
I470 7149 α CN 19h
7354 55°
7380 W λ ν μ
7281 δ κ x
67261 ζ ε d
67235 I1395 CYGNUS ψ
RW FZ CH
LACERTA 7235 7127 DO 7008 ζ R
7296 β 7126 RU 6826 RT
β 7128 Nova 1992 6833
I5217 7026
α π¹ 6883
7243 7025
20 22h π² 21h 19 20h 18

MAGNITUDES

●	>-0·4
●	-0·4--0·5
●	0·6-1·5
●	1·6-2·5
●	2·6-3·5
·	3·6-4·5
·	4·6-5·5
·	5·6-6·5
·	6·6-7·5

DOUBLE or MULTIPLE
VARIABLE ◉ ○

OPEN CLUSTERS	⊙ ⊙ ⊙ ○
	>10' TO SCALE <10'
GLOBULAR CLUSTERS	⊕ ⊕ ⊛
	>10' 5'-10' <5'
PLANETARY NEBULAE	◇ ◇ ◇
	>1' 0·5'-1' <0·5'
BRIGHT DIFFUSE NEB.	▭
	>10', TO SCALE <10'
GALAXIES	⬭ ⬬ ○ ○
	>30' 20'-30' 10'-20' <10'

QUASAR	△
PULSAR	⚡
BLACK HOLE	⌖
MILKY WAY	∿
GALACTIC EQUATOR	
	·0°
ECLIPTIC	
	100°
CONSTELLATION BOUNDARIES	

GREEK ALPHABET

α	Alpha	ν	Nu
β	Beta	ξ	Xi
γ	Gamma	o	Omicron
δ	Delta	π	Pi
ε	Epsilon	ϱ	Rho
ζ	Zeta	σ	Sigma
η	Eta	τ	Tau
θ ϑ	Theta	υ	Upsilon
ι	Iota	φ ϕ	Phi
κ ϰ	Kappa	χ	Chi
λ	Lambda	ψ	Psi
μ	Mu	ω	Omega

W

ATLAS CHART 9. M31 (Andromeda Galaxy) M31 (NGC 224), the Great Galaxy in Andromeda (Fig. 5-33), lies in the center of the chart, near 0^h45^m +41°. At a distance of 2.2 million light-years from earth, M31 is the largest neighboring galaxy. It is visible to the naked eye as a hazy glow. It appears in telescopes as a yellowish oval glow, brighter toward the center; the dust lane below its center may be seen or photographed. If you slowly sweep the field with medium power you will see more detail in outer regions of this spiral galaxy. M31 has two faint elliptical companions, M32 (NGC 221) and NGC 205, sometimes known as M110. M32 usually appears as a bright roundish haze, while NGC 205 looks a bit larger, though not as bright.

At left in Triangulum is the face-on spiral galaxy M33 (NGC 598), the brightest spiral in the northern sky (Fig. 5-34) except for M31. M33 covers an area about the same size as the moon but can be difficult to find. (Try testing a telescope on M33 before attempting to find dimmer objects.) With a low-power, wide-field telescope, the galaxy appears as an oval glow covering a large area. On nights of particularly good seeing, you can observe it with binoculars and may even be able to just barely detect it with the naked eye.

3C 48, one of the first quasars discovered, lies at about 1^h40^m +34°, above M33. It has a magnitude of 16.2 and a redshift of 0.367 (36.7%), making it about 7 billion light-years away.

M76 (NGC 650), a prominent planetary nebula (Fig. 5-4), lies near the boundary of Perseus and Andromeda. M76 is difficult to find, though it is easiest to observe in early fall. Many consider it to be the faintest of all the Messier objects. Because it has two distinct components, M76 looks like a smaller version of the Dumbbell Nebula and is sometimes called the Barbell Nebula.

Some noteworthy double stars in this area of the sky are: ι (iota) Tri (yellow and blue) at left center; 1 Ari (ADS1457) (white and green), above and to the right of β (beta) Ari; and γ (gamma) And, at 2^h +43° (orange and yellow). γ (gamma) Ari is one of the most beautiful doubles in the sky, with contrasting orange and green components.

Fig. 7-9 M31 (NGC 224), a type Sb spiral galaxy in Andromeda, photographed with an amateur-grade Schmidt telescope by a student during a freshman observing session. (Hopkins Observatory, Williams College)

D FROM 'SKY ATLAS 2000.0' BY WIL TIRION

MAGNITUDES		OPEN CLUSTERS				QUASAR	△	GREEK ALPHABET			
●	>-0.4		>10'	TO SCALE	<10'	PULSAR	⋇	α	Alpha	ν	Nu
●	-0.4-0.5					BLACK HOLE	⋎	β	Beta	ξ	Xi
●	0.6-1.5	GLOBULAR CLUSTERS	⊕	⊕	⊛	MILKY WAY		γ	Gamma	ο	Omicron
●	1.6-2.5		>10'	5'-10'	<5'			δ	Delta	π	Pi
●	2.6-3.5	PLANETARY NEBULAE	✧	✧	✧	GALACTIC EQUATOR		ε	Epsilon	ϱ	Rho
•	3.6-4.5		>1'	0.5'-1'	<0.5'			ζ	Zeta	σ	Sigma
•	4.6-5.5							η	Eta	τ	Tau
•	5.6-6.5	BRIGHT DIFFUSE NEB.		>10' TO SCALE	<10'	ECLIPTIC		θ ϑ	Theta	υ	Upsilon
·	6.6-7.5							ι	Iota	φ φ	Phi
DOUBLE or MULTIPLE	●-	GALAXIES	◯	◯	◯	CONSTELLATION BOUNDARIES		κ ϰ	Kappa	χ	Chi
VARIABLE	◉ ◯		>30'	20'-30'	10'-20' <10'			λ	Lambda	ψ	Psi
								μ	Mu	ω	Omega

ATLAS CHART 10. The Pleiades, Algol Algol, β (beta) Per, is sometimes called the Demon Star (Chapter 6). It is the most famous of the eclipsing binaries, and the easiest of these variable stars to observe. The eclipses occur approximately every 69 hours, dropping the total brightness of the system from about magnitude 2.1 to a minimum of magnitude 3.4 within a five-hour period; the system returns to its normal brightness after about 20 minutes. The eclipses are fun to observe with the naked eye (see Fig. 6-2 and Appendix 7).

M34 (NGC 1039) is an open cluster in Perseus, about halfway between the two bright stars Algol (β Per) and γ (gamma) Per. It appears to the naked eye as a hazy object. About 80 stars are loosely grouped in M34, and many of these are blue-white doubles. M34 is beautiful in binoculars and small telescopes with wide fields.

M45, the Pleiades, one of the most spectacular and most obvious open clusters in the sky, is in Taurus. Six or seven of its stars, arranged roughly in the shape of a little dipper, are visible to the naked eye. Binoculars clearly show numerous faint stars (see Fig. 7-10 below), and even a small telescope shows more than 100 stars. Wisps of nebulosity, reflection nebulae, cover the group and are especially bright near the more luminous stars (see Fig. 2-8). The nebulous background shows clearly on long-exposure photographs, but you will probably not be able to see it visually.

North of the Pleiades, in Perseus, are NGC 1499—the California Nebula (Fig. 5-25)—a large, faint nebula even more difficult to find than M76; and IC 348, a bright diffuse nebula. NGC 1220, a small open cluster that appears in binoculars as a hazy patch, is at the top center of the chart, near γ (gamma) Per. NGC 1528, a large open cluster visible to the naked eye on clear nights, is at the top left of the chart.

Fig. 7-10 A close-up of the Pleiades. (Wil Tirion)

MAGNITUDES

●	> -0.4
●	-0.4 - -0.5
●	0.6 - 1.5
●	1.6 - 2.5
●	2.6 - 3.5
•	3.6 - 4.5
·	4.6 - 5.5
·	5.6 - 6.5
·	6.6 - 7.5

DOUBLE or MULTIPLE

VARIABLE

OPEN CLUSTERS			
	>10'	TO SCALE	<10'

GLOBULAR CLUSTERS			
⊕	⊕	⊕	
>10'	5'-10'	<5'	

PLANETARY NEBULAE			
	>1'	0.5'-1'	<0.5'

BRIGHT DIFFUSE NEB.
>10'. TO SCALE   <10'

GALAXIES			
	>30'	20'-30'	10'-20' <10'

QUASAR △

PULSAR ⚡

BLACK HOLE

MILKY WAY

GALACTIC EQUATOR
10°

ECLIPTIC
100°

CONSTELLATION BOUNDARIES

GREEK ALPHABET

α	Alpha	ν	Nu
β	Beta	ξ	Xi
γ	Gamma	ο	Omicron
δ	Delta	π	Pi
ε	Epsilon	ϱ	Rho
ζ	Zeta	σ	Sigma
η	Eta	τ	Tau
θ ϑ	Theta	υ	Upsilon
ι	Iota	φ ϕ	Phi
κ ϰ	Kappa	χ	Chi
λ	Lambda	ψ	Psi
μ	Mu	ω	Omega

ATLAS CHART 11. Crab Nebula, Hyades, Aldebaran With binoculars or a rich-field telescope, sweep along the Milky Way through Perseus, Auriga, and Gemini. Many rich star fields, including numerous nebulae and open clusters, will reward your search. M36, M37, and M38 are all open clusters in Auriga. In the same region of Auriga, several gaseous nebulae of interest can be seen. IC 405 is sometimes called the Flaming Star; IC 410 is a cluster with surrounding nebulosity.

The most famous object on the chart is M1 (NGC 1952), the Crab Nebula in Taurus. The Crab is the remnant of a supernova, a star whose explosion the Chinese recorded in 1054 A.D. The Crab is still rapidly expanding, with gas travelling outward at about 1000 km per second. Small telescopes disappointingly show only an oval nebulosity; increasing the magnification reveals more shape. Only with a large aperture might you detect some of the filamentary structure that appears in photographs (Fig. 5-10).

A spectacular open cluster, the Hyades, outlines the bull's face in Taurus. It appears at the bottom edge of the chart, near 4^h30^m +15°. The Hyades is an older and looser cluster than the Pleiades and contains fewer stars. Use low power or good binoculars to see this extended V-shaped group; it is so large that it is not circled on the chart. The stars in this cluster are approximately 140 light-years away and formed about a billion years ago. Their white color contrasts with the red of the star Aldebaran, α (alpha) Tau. Aldebaran is less than half as far from us as the Hyades stars.

Northeast of the Hyades, near 4^h45^m +18°, is the open cluster NGC 1647; it includes about 50 stars spread across an area about the size of the moon's diameter.

In Auriga, at about 5^h10^m +45°, is Capella, α (alpha) Aur, the sixth brightest star in the sky. Near Capella, ε (epsilon) Aur is an eclipsing variable with a period of 27 years, one of the longest periods known. Below ε Aur is ζ (zeta) Aur, another eclipsing variable with a fairly long period of $2\frac{2}{3}$ years.

Fig. 7-11 Taurus, the Bull, from the star atlas of Bode. (Jay M. Pasachoff)

ED FROM "SKY ATLAS 2000.0" BY WIL TIRION

ATLAS CHART 12. Castor and Pollux Gemini is marked by the heavenly twins, Castor and Pollux. The fainter of the two, Castor, α (alpha) Gem, is one of the most beautiful double stars easily resolved in small telescopes. The two stars, of magnitudes 1.9 and 2.9, slowly revolve around each other with a period of 510 years; a third, fainter star called Castor C is also present. Castor is actually a sextuple system, since each of its three components has been found by spectroscopy to be double. Castor C is not only a spectroscopic double but also an eclipsing binary, and is known as YY Gem. Pollux, β (beta) Gem, is brighter than Castor by about $1/2$ magnitude and is yellower.

Southwest of Pollux is δ (delta) Gem, a bright double star. Nearby is NGC 2392, the Eskimo or Clown Face Nebula (Fig. 7-12). The distinctive greenish "face" of this planetary nebula is visible only in large telescopes. ζ (zeta) Gem, to the right of the Eskimo Nebula, near 7^h $+20°$, is one of the brightest Cepheid variables. It changes in brightness by more than $1/2$ magnitude during its 10-day period.

Toward the other side of the chart, near 6^h9^m $+22°$, is η (eta) Gem, a variable red giant. Slightly above η Gem is M35 (NGC 2168), a beautiful open cluster, and its companion NGC 2158. M35 is about 40 arc min in diameter and contains about 200 stars. It is sometimes visible to the naked eye as a hazy, faint patch; any telescope or even binoculars will reveal a fine open cluster. It can be seen best with an eyepiece with at least 1° field. High power tends to reduce the beauty of M35 but is fine for observing its companion about $1/2°$ to the southwest, NGC 2158. NCG 2158 is a very rich open cluster; in its center, about 40 stars are crowded into an area only 4 arc min across, making it look almost like a globular cluster. Although M35 and NGC 2158 appear close to each other, they are completely unrelated physically: M35 is only 2200 light-years away, while NGC 2158 is 16,000 light-years away, near the edge of our galaxy.

NGC 2419 in Lynx, about 7° north of Castor, is so far from the center of our galaxy that it has been called an "intergalactic tramp." On a clear dark night, you can see it in a small telescope.

Fig. 7-12 The Eskimo Nebula (NGC 2392), a planetary nebula. The "face" (upside-down when north is up, as here) is visible only in large telescopes. (Lick Observatory photo)

MAGNITUDES

- \> -0.4
- -0.4·+0.5
- 0.6-1.5
- 1.6-2.5
- 2.6-3.5
- 3.6-4.5
- 4.6-5.5
- 5.6-6.5
- 6.6-7.5

LE or
PLE

BLE ◉ ○

OPEN CLUSTERS	○ >10'	○ TO SCALE	○ <10'
GLOBULAR CLUSTERS	⊕ >10'	⊕ 5'-10'	⊕ <5'
PLANETARY NEBULAE	⬦ >1'	⬦ 0.5'-1'	⬦ <0.5'
BRIGHT DIFFUSE NEB.	▢ >10'	⬭ TO SCALE	□ <10'
GALAXIES	⬭ >30'	⬭ 20'-30'	⬭ 10'-20'	○ <10'

QUASAR △

PULSAR ⭐

BLACK HOLE ⅄

MILKY WAY 〰

GALACTIC EQUATOR
– – – – – – 70°
+

ECLIPTIC
– – – – – – 100°
+

CONSTELLATION
BOUNDARIES ⌐

GREEK ALPHABET

α Alpha	ν Nu
β Beta	ξ Xi
γ Gamma	ο Omicron
δ Delta	π Pi
ε Epsilon	ϱ Rho
ζ Zeta	σ Sigma
η Eta	τ Tau
θ ϑ Theta	υ Upsilon
ι Iota	φ ϕ Phi
κ ϰ Kappa	χ Chi
λ Lambda	ψ Psi
μ Mu	ω Omega

M "SKY ATLAS 2000.0" BY WIL TIRION

ATLAS CHART 13. Praesepe The four stars, γ, η, θ, and δ (gamma, eta, theta, and delta) Cancri (Cnc) at lower right outline the irregular shape that forms the body of Cancer, the Crab. Within the crab's body lies the open cluster M44 (NGC 2632), also called Praesepe or the Beehive Cluster (Fig. 7-13). M44 covers more than 80 arc min—an area almost three times the diameter of the moon—and is one of the most spectacular clusters in the sky. Although M44 is visible to the naked eye only as a hazy patch, a small telescope or binoculars will resolve it into its component stars, many of which are multiples. It is about 520 light-years from us. Praesepe means "the manger"; γ (gamma) and δ (delta) Cnc, which are nearby, are known as "the asses," from a story in Greek mythology.

To the west of M44 is ζ (zeta) Cnc (at about 8^h55^m +18°), an unusual triple star with three yellow components. This system can be viewed in medium-sized or large telescopes. $ι^1$ (iota^1) Cnc (at about 8^h47^m +29°) is an interesting orange-green double with 30" separation, outstanding in even a small telescope because of the beautiful color contrast between its components. Located slightly to the northeast, $ι^2$ (iota^2) Cnc is a triple.

R Leo Minoris is a long-period variable, ranging in brightness from magnitude 6.3 to magnitude 13.2 with a period of 372 days. Its deep red color, especially when near maximum, makes this star an interesting telescopic object.

A noteworthy galaxy in Lynx is NGC 2683 at 8^h55^m +33°, a galaxy seen almost edge-on. Near the boundary between Lynx (Lyn) and Leo Minor, at 9^h20^m + 35°, are several other galaxies, easy for beginners to find by sweeping near α (alpha) Lyn. The brightest of these galaxies is NGC 2859, a barred spiral in Leo Minor. NGC 2903 is an isolated spiral in Leo.

Fig. 7-13 M44 (NGC 2632), also known as Praesepe, the Beehive Cluster. (Hopkins Observatory, Williams College)

MAGNITUDES		OPEN CLUSTERS	● ○ ⊙ ∘ >10' TO SCALE <10'	QUASAR	△	GREEK ALPHABET			
> 0.4				PULSAR	✳	α Alpha		ν	Nu
−0.4 – 0.5		GLOBULAR CLUSTERS	⊕ ⊖ ⊙ >10' 5-10' <5'	BLACK HOLE	⅄	β Beta		ξ	Xi
0.6 – 1.5				MILKY WAY	〰	γ Gamma		ο	Omicron
1.6 – 2.5		PLANETARY NEBULAE	⊹ ⊹ ⊹ >1' 0.5-1' <0.5'			δ Delta		π	Pi
2.6 – 3.5				GALACTIC EQUATOR		ε Epsilon		ϱ	Rho
3.6 – 4.5						ζ Zeta		σ	Sigma
4.6 – 5.5		BRIGHT DIFFUSE NEB.	▱ □ >10' TO SCALE <10'	ECLIPTIC		η Eta		τ	Tau
5.5 – 6.5						θ ϑ Theta		υ	Upsilon
6.5 – 7.5						ι Iota		φ φ	Phi
DBLE or MPLE	●–●			CONSTELLATION BOUNDARIES		κ ϰ Kappa		χ	Chi
		GALAXIES	◯ ◯ ○ ∘ >30' 20'-30' 10'-20' <10'			λ Lambda		ψ	Psi
ABLE	◉ ○					μ Mu		ω	Omega

ATLAS CHART 14. Leo, M64 Leo Minor and Leo contain a number of interesting doubles. One of the most striking is γ (gamma) Leo, one of the stars in the sickle that makes up Leo, actually a double with magnitudes 2.2 and 3.5. This golden-yellow pair is easily resolved and provides a good view even in small telescopes. ζ (zeta) Leo, located in the sickle above γ Leo, is a bright pair of stars far enough apart to be detected with binoculars.

Nearby, at about 11^h $+25°$, is another double star, 54 Leo, that can be resolved with very low power into a pair with magnitudes 4.5 and 6.4. The star Denebola—β (beta) Leo—at the tip of the lion's tail and just below the bottom of the chart at left, is a beautiful blue-orange pair. However, it is merely an optical double—the stars are actually far apart in space. The pulsar CP 1133 nearby was one of the original four pulsars discovered by Jocelyn Bell and Antony Hewish in 1968.

To the lower left of the chart's center is the double star ξ (xi) Ursa Majoris; it is only 26 light-years away and is a good object to observe with small telescopes. The 60-year elliptical orbit of the two visual components, magnitudes 4.3 and 4.8, is tilted 57° to our line of sight. The pair reached their maximum separation of 2.9 arc min as seen from earth in 1980. Each of these two components is in turn a double. The stars in one of the pairs are separated by only 0.5 A.U.—half the distance between the earth and the sun—and orbit each other in 1.8 years. The stars in the other pair are separated by only the distance from the earth to the moon and orbit each other every 4 days.

Since this chart includes an area close to the north galactic pole (which is on the next chart), we are looking as far away as possible from the Milky Way and can thus see many galaxies (Fig. 7-14). Scanning the nearby region of Leo Minor reveals a hard-to-see group of galaxies. NGC 3158, at 10^h20^m $+38°$, is the brightest of this group and should be visible in a medium-sized telescope.

We will discuss the cluster of galaxies at upper left with the next chart. M97 and M108 are discussed with Atlas Chart 5.

Fig. 7-14 Four galaxies in Leo, from Atlas Chart 14 (lower right): NGC 3193 (type E2, upper left), NGC 3187 (type SBc, upper right), NGC 3190 (type Sb, upper center, with dust lane), and NGC 3185 (type SBa, bottom right). (Palomar Observatory photo)

MAGNITUDES		OPEN CLUSTERS				QUASAR	△	GREEK ALPHABET			
●	>-0.4		○ ○ ○ ○			PULSAR	☆	α	Alpha	ν	Nu
●	-0.4-+0.5		>10' TO SCALE <10'			BLACK HOLE	Y	β	Beta	ξ	Xi
●	0.6-1.5	GLOBULAR CLUSTERS	⊕ ⊕ ⊕			MILKY WAY		γ	Gamma	ο	Omicron
●	1.6-2.5		>10' 5-10' <5'					δ	Delta	π	Pi
●	2.6-3.5	PLANETARY NEBULAE	✧ ✧ ✧			GALACTIC EQUATOR		ε	Epsilon	ϱ	Rho
●	3.6-4.5		>1' 0.5'-1' <0.5'					ζ	Zeta	σ	Sigma
●	4.6-5.5							η	Eta	τ	Tau
●	5.6-6.5	BRIGHT DIFFUSE NEB.				ECLIPTIC		θ ϑ	Theta	υ	Upsilon
●	6.6-7.5		>10' TO SCALE <10'					ι	Iota	φ φ	Phi
								κ ϰ	Kappa	χ	Chi
VARIABLE or MULTIPLE	✦	GALAXIES	○ ○ ○ ○			CONSTELLATION BOUNDARIES		λ	Lambda	ψ	Psi
VARIABLE	◉ ○		>30' 20'-30' 10'-20' <10'					μ	Mu	ω	Omega

ATLAS CHART 15. Whirlpool Galaxy Characteristic of this part of the sky is the large number of galaxies, most of them millions of light-years distant. Relatively close to us is one of the brightest galaxies, M51 (NGC 5194)—also known as the Whirlpool Galaxy (Fig. 5-35)—at upper left-center in Canes Venatici. Located a few degrees south of the handle of the Big Dipper, M51 is a face-on spiral about 15 million light-years distant, with a companion galaxy, NGC 5195. Other galaxies nearby to the south and west include M63 (NGC 5055), M94 (NGC 4736), and M106 (NGC 4258), all spirals of type Sb that can be observed with small telescopes. M106 is shown in Figure 5-43. Far beyond are the clusters of galaxies in Ursa Major and Canes Venatici.

At 12^{h}52^m +27° in Coma Berenices, we come to the region around the north galactic pole. Since we are looking away from the Milky Way at this point, there is minimum interference from gas and dust in our galaxy, and many galaxies are visible here. M64 (NGC 4826), at lower center in Coma Berenices, is a spiral known as the Black-eye Galaxy because the dark dust lane across its center is so prominent. The galaxy is relatively bright and can be detected in binoculars. Also located here are the spiral galaxy M100 (NGC 4321)—shown in Figure 5-9—and the elliptical galaxy M85 (NGC 4382). Ten degrees to the north are NGC 4559 and NGC 4565 (Fig. 5-51), an edge-on spiral tilted only 4° from our line of sight. These galaxies are all in the Virgo Cluster of galaxies (see Atlas Charts 27 and 28). Much farther away is the Coma Cluster of galaxies, in which only NGC 4889 and NGC 4874, near 13^h +28°, are bright enough to be seen by most amateur observers.

In this area of the sky we also find several globular clusters. At magnitude 6.4, the globular cluster M3 (NGC 5272)—located at 13^{h}40^m +28° in Canes Venatici—is one of the brightest in the sky (Fig. 5-19). Two other globular clusters, M53 (NGC 5024) and NGC 5053, appear lower in the sky in Coma Berenices. M53, near α (alpha) Com, is twice as far away as M3 and therefore twice as large, since both star clusters have roughly the same apparent size in the sky.

Mel 111 (at 12^{h}20^m +27° in Coma Berenices) is a large, diffuse open cluster of 5th- to 10th-magnitude stars.

This part of the sky is best placed for viewing in the spring.

Fig. 7-15 The Whirlpool Galaxy, M51 (NGC 5194), a type Sb spiral, with the irregular companion galaxy NGC 5195 at the end of one of its spiral arms. (National Optical Astronomy Observatories/ KPNO)

MAGNITUDES			OPEN CLUSTERS					QUASAR	△		GREEK ALPHABET		
	> -0.4				>10' TO SCALE		<10'	PULSAR		α	Alpha	ν	Nu
	-0.4 - +0.5							BLACK HOLE		β	Beta	ξ	Xi
	0.6 - 1.5		GLOBULAR CLUSTERS	⊕	⊕	⊕		MILKY WAY		γ	Gamma	o	Omicron
	1.6 - 2.5			>10'	5-10'	<5'				δ	Delta	π	Pi
	2.6 - 3.5							GALACTIC EQUATOR		ε	Epsilon	ϱ	Rho
	3.6 - 4.5		PLANETARY NEBULAE	◇	◇	◇				ζ	Zeta	σ	Sigma
	4.6 - 5.5			>1'	0.5'-1'	<0.5'				η	Eta	τ	Tau
	5.6 - 6.5							ECLIPTIC		θ ϑ	Theta	υ	Upsilon
	6.6 - 7.5		BRIGHT DIFFUSE NEB.							ι	Iota	ϕ φ	Phi
DOUBLE or MULTIPLE					>10' TO SCALE		<10'			κ $\varkappa$	Kappa	χ	Chi
								CONSTELLATION BOUNDARIES		λ	Lambda	ψ	Psi
VARIABLE			GALAXIES	◯						μ	Mu	ω	Omega

ATLAS CHART 16. Arcturus At lower right is the third brightest star in the sky, Arcturus, α (alpha) Boötes. It is 36 light-years away and about 25 times the diameter of the sun. ξ (xi) Boo (at 14^h45^m +19°) is a double star with widely spaced, contrasting orange and blue components that orbit each other with a period of 152 years. Further to the northeast, μ (mu) Boo (at 15^h25^m +37°) is a widely spaced, white-orange pair with fainter companions.

To the south, in Corona Borealis (the Northern Crown), η (eta) CrB is a close double, with components orbiting each other in about 42 years. ζ (zeta) CrB is a wide pair of blue stars, separated from each other by over 6 arc sec. σ (sigma) CrB is also a wide pair. γ (gamma) CrB is a very close pair, orbiting in about 100 years. o (omicron) CrB has several faint companions and a period of 215 years.

R Coronae Borealis (R CrB) is one of the most unusual stars in the sky. It stays at 6th magnitude for a period ranging from months to years and then precipitously drops to 11th magnitude or even fainter for a period that lasts only weeks (see light curve below). At the same time, its spectrum of absorption lines is obscured and a spectrum of emission lines appears. R CrB is a carbon-rich star, and apparently it sometimes throws off clouds of carbon soot that obscure its photosphere, making spectral lines from its higher and relatively hotter chromosphere appear as emission lines. The clouds of soot have been detected in the infrared. A finding chart for R CrB appears at the end of Chapter 6.

Fig. 7-16 Light curve for R Coronae Borealis. (AAVSO)

ATLAS CHART 17. M13   At the center of the chart in Hercules we find the Keystone, an asterism formed by the stars η, ζ, ε, and π (eta, zeta, epsilon, and pi) Herculis. About $1/3$ of the way from η (eta) to ζ (zeta) Herculis is the spectacular globular cluster, M13 (NGC 6205), shown in Figure 2-7. M13 lies about 25,000 light-years away. It is faintly visible to the naked eye as a fuzzy mothball of about 6th magnitude. You can resolve the outer edges of M13 into its member stars with a medium-sized telescope.

About $1/2°$ northeast of M13 is the faint spiral galaxy NGC 6207, sometimes visible in the same field at low power.

At 17^h15^m +42°, about 7° north of π (pi) Her, is the globular cluster M92 (NGC 6341), about $1/2$ magnitude fainter than M13 but still a good object for small telescopes. A third globular cluster, NGC 6229 (at 16^h45^m +47°), lies about 10° above M13; it is much smaller and fainter (9th magnitude) than the other two clusters.

By sweeping with low power near β (beta) Her at the bottom of the chart, you can find NGC 6210, a bluish-green planetary nebula. NGC 6210 has a fairly bright inner ring with a faint outer ring that measures 20 by 43 arc sec. The nebula can be detected with a small telescope, although a larger telescope is needed to distinguish the rings. The planetary nebula NGC 6058 (at 16^h +41°) is more difficult to locate.

δ (delta) Her is an optical double for which many different colors have been reported. ρ (rho) Her is a pair of blue-white stars that differ in brightness by 1 magnitude. Only 30 light-years away from us is ζ (zeta) Her, a pair with magnitudes 2.9 and 5.5. All lie on the constellation outline drawn.

The quasar 3C 345 is 16th magnitude and has a redshift of 0.6 (60%), placing it about 8 billion light-years away.

Fig. 7-17   Hercules, from the star atlas of Bayer. (Jay M. Pasachoff)

UW
ν
μ
γ
β
DRACO
Al
BP
+50°
BOÖTES
z
y
x
St
6229
τ
υ
χ
+45°
Nova 1934
OP
ι
φ
LYRA
M92
6239
σ
g
χ
6058
ν2 ν1
+40°
GC 345
φ
ν
μ
RR
η
λ
ζ
16
ϑ
ϱ e
π
6207
M13
κ
+35°
UW
c
CORONA
BOREALIS
W
HERCULES
ϱ u
ν1
ν2
σ
ϱ
π
d
w
b
ε
ζ
ξ
υ
ι
+30°
o
ν
μ
ξ
V645
R
γ
λ
ε
δ
+25°
δ
τ
SERPENS
CAPUT
6482
6210
LQ
ϱ
6027
RS
+20°
β
6052
γ
6181
U
Ton 256
κ
γ
+15°

FROM "SKY ATLAS 2000.0" BY WIL TIRION

MAGNITUDES	OPEN CLUSTERS				QUASAR △	GREEK ALPHABET	
>-0.4		>10' TO SCALE	<10'		PULSAR	α Alpha	ν Nu
-0.4-+0.5					BLACK HOLE	β Beta	ξ Xi
0.6-1.5	GLOBULAR CLUSTERS	⊕ ⊕ ⊕				γ Gamma	o Omicron
1.6-2.5		>10' 5-10' <5'			MILKY WAY	δ Delta	π Pi
2.6-3.5						ε Epsilon	ϱ Rho
3.6-4.5	PLANETARY NEBULAE	✧ ✧ ✧			GALACTIC EQUATOR	ζ Zeta	σ Sigma
4.6-5.5		>1' 0.5-1' <0.5'				η Eta	τ Tau
5.6-6.5					ECLIPTIC	θ ϑ Theta	υ Upsilon
6.6-7.5	BRIGHT DIFFUSE NEB.		□			ι Iota	φ φ Phi
DOUBLE or MULTIPLE		>10' TO SCALE	<10'			κ κ Kappa	χ Chi
VARIABLE	GALAXIES	○ ○	○ ○		CONSTELLATION BOUNDARIES	λ Lambda	ψ Psi
		>30' 20'-30'	10'-20' <10'			μ Mu	ω Omega

ATLAS CHART 18. Ring Nebula, Dumbbell Nebula The brightest star on this chart is Vega, α (alpha) Lyrae. Vega is a pure white star of magnitude 0 and is dazzlingly beautiful in a telescope. With ε (epsilon) and ζ (zeta) Lyr, Vega forms a small equilateral triangle. A person with acute eyesight can barely detect the two components of ε (epsilon) Lyr, each of which is about 5th magnitude. Even a small telescope separates the pair and splits each component into a second pair, making four white stars in all.

β (beta) Lyr, a spectroscopic double and an eclipsing binary, varies between magnitudes 3.3 and 4.3 every 12.9 days. The variations are easy to follow by comparing the magnitude of this double with that of γ (gamma) Lyr, magnitude 3.2 (see finding chart for β Lyr, end of Chapter 6). Other nearby stars in Lyra to compare are η (eta) at magnitude 4.4, θ (theta) at 4.4, $ζ^1$ (zeta^1) at 4.4, κ (kappa) at 4.3, λ (lambda) at 4.9, and ι (iota) at 5.3.

Albireo—β (beta) Cygni—at the nose of the Swan, is one of the prettiest doubles. Binoculars split it into orange and blue components. The components of δ (delta) Cygni, whose orbital period is 830 years, differ by 3 magnitudes.

RR Lyrae (at 19^h25^m +43°) is the prototype of a class of variable stars with regular periods of less than one day (see p. 195).

β, γ, δ, and ζ Lyr form a parallelogram. About halfway between β and γ Lyr, on a short side of this parallogram, is M57 (NGC 6720), the Ring Nebula. This most famous of the planetary nebulae has a shell of gas expanding from a central star. The shell represents the outer quarter of the star's mass and bares the core of the star, which appears bluish because it is so hot. This is the end that our sun will reach one day, in about 5 billion years. A small telescope shows the nebula clearly (Fig. 5-2), although a larger one is necessary to reveal structural details (Fig. 5-3). The colors show up only in long-exposure photographs.

To the south and east of M57, near 19^h20^m +30°, is the globular cluster M56 (NGC 6779). This small, highly concentrated cluster is easily visible with small telescopes. Further south and east in Vulpecula, near 20^h +23°, is M27 (NGC 6853), the second largest planetary nebula, about 3 light-years in diameter. Because of its shape, M27 is commonly called the Dumbbell Nebula (Fig. 5-5). Though its total brightness is great, M27 is spread over such a large area that the average brightness of its surface remains fairly low. A dark sky is needed to view it well. Low power shows its shape and greenish color; higher power begins to show some structure. To the west are the pulsars PSR 1937+215 and CP 1919, which can be detected only in the radio spectrum. PSR 1937+215 gives off over 600 pulses of radio waves per second.

Below M27, in Sagitta, is the globular cluster M71 (NGC 6838), which is rich in stars despite its relatively small diameter.

On the boundary between Lyra and Hercules, at 18^h20^m +46°, is the remnant of Nova Herculis 1934.

NITUDES		OPEN					QUASAR	△		GREEK ALPHABET	
	> -0·4	CLUSTERS		>10'	TO SCALE	<10'	PULSAR		α	Alpha	ν	Nu
	-0·4 - +0·5						BLACK HOLE		β	Beta	ξ	Xi
	0·6 - 1·5	GLOBULAR	⊕	⊕	⊕				γ	Gamma	o	Omicron
	1·6 - 2·5	CLUSTERS		>10'	5'-10'	<5'	MILKY WAY		δ	Delta	π	Pi
	2·6 - 3·5								ε	Epsilon	ϱ	Rho
	3·6 - 4·5	PLANETARY	✧	✧	✧		GALACTIC EQUATOR		ζ	Zeta	σ	Sigma
	4·6 - 5·5	NEBULAE		>1'	0·5'-1'	<0·5'			η	Eta	τ	Tau
	5·6 - 6·5								θ ϑ	Theta	υ	Upsilon
	6·6 - 7·5	BRIGHT					ECLIPTIC		ι	Iota	φ φ	Phi
LE or		DIFFUSE NEB.		>10'	TO SCALE	<10'			κ ϰ	Kappa	χ	Chi
PLE									λ	Lambda	ψ	Psi
BLE		GALAXIES	⬭	◯	○	○	CONSTELLATION		μ	Mu	ω	Omega
				> 30'	20'-30'	10'-20'	<10'	BOUNDARIES				

ATLAS CHART 19.   Deneb, North America Nebula, Veil Nebula, Cygnus Loop In the center of the chart near the bright star Deneb, α (alpha) Cyg, is the North America Nebula (NGC 7000), named because of its shape. Although this nebula and its neighbor, the Pelican Nebula (IC 5067–5070), are extremely hard to observe telescopically, long-exposure photography or electronic imaging makes them visible. The Pelican's beak is facing the North America Nebula (Fig. 5-28). Another region of nebulosity lies around γ (gamma) Cyg, southwest of Deneb, near 20^h20^m +40°.

Cygnus contained the two brightest novae of the past decades. Nova Cygni 1975, on the diagonal galactic equator near 21^h15^m +48°, rivalled Deneb by surpassing 2nd magnitude. Nova Cygni 1992, near 20^h30^m +52°, reached magnitude 4.4

On the 20^h meridian is Cygnus X-1, invisible in ordinary light but the brightest x-ray source in Cygnus. The x-rays probably come from gas swirling around a black hole; the presence of the black hole is inferred from its gravitational effect on the 9th-magnitude star HDE 226868 that is observed at that location.

Southeast of this region, near 21^h +30°, is another area of diffuse nebulae. NGC 6960 appears close to the double star 52 Cygni, whose orange and blue components are separated by $6^1/_2$ arc sec. NGC 6960, 6992, 6995, and 6979 are jointly known as the Veil Nebula, which makes up most of the Cygnus Loop, a faint circular nebula about $2^1/_2$° across. The Cygnus Loop is the remnant of a supernova that exploded over 100,000 years ago. The Veil Nebula is visible through a wide range of optical instruments, from binoculars to large telescopes, but its structure and beautiful colors show only in long-exposure photographs (Fig. 5-11).

Within the triangle formed by α, γ, and ε (alpha, gamma, and epsilon) Cyg is the Northern Coalsack, an opaque patch of nebulosity that obscures the Milky Way behind it.

Near the upper right of the chart, at 19^h40^m +50°, is the planetary nebula NGC 6826. This nebula is often called the Blinking Nebula because its central star, which is relatively bright, appears to blink on and off if you look rapidly toward and away from it.

M39 (NGC 7092) is an open cluster in northern Cygnus (near 21^h30^m +48°), with about 30 stars scattered across its 7 light-year diameter. This cluster is a fine object to view with binoculars or low-power, wide-field telescopes.

Near 21^h40^m +43° is the variable star SS Cygni, which rises sharply to its maximum about once every 50 days, on a somewhat irregular schedule (Fig. 6-5). It is very interesting to follow as it rapidly increases in brightness from 12th to 8th magnitude. You can see its brightness change markedly in two or three hours during certain parts of its cycle. SS Cyg is too faint to be shown on this chart, but its position is marked on a finding chart in Chapter 6.

To the southwest, near 21^h20^m +39°, is 61 Cyg, the first star whose distance from the sun was measured (from its parallax). 61 Cyg is an orange pair of stars only 11 light-years away from us.

MAGNITUDES		OPEN CLUSTERS				QUASAR	△	GREEK ALPHABET			
●	>-04		●>10'	●TO SCALE	○<10'	PULSAR	✦	α Alpha		ν Nu	
●	-04–-05	GLOBULAR CLUSTERS	⊕>10'	⊕5-10'	⊛<5'	BLACK HOLE	⅄	β Beta		ξ Xi	
●	06–15					MILKY WAY		γ Gamma		ο Omicron	
●	16–25	PLANETARY NEBULAE	◇>1'	◇0.5-1'	◇<0.5'			δ Delta		π Pi	
●	26–35					GALACTIC EQUATOR		ε Epsilon		ϱ Rho	
●	36–45	BRIGHT DIFFUSE NEB.						ζ Zeta		σ Sigma	
•	46–55		▱>10' TO SCALE		□<10'			η Eta		τ Tau	
•	55–65					ECLIPTIC		θ ϑ Theta		υ Upsilon	
•	66–75	GALAXIES	◯>30'	◯20'-30'	○10'-20' ○<10'	CONSTELLATION BOUNDARIES		ι Iota		φ ϕ Phi	
BLE or PLE ●—								κ ϰ Kappa		χ Chi	
ABLE ◉ ○								λ Lambda		ψ Psi	
								μ Mu		ω Omega	

ATLAS CHART 20. Pegasus As we move away from the Milky Way into Lacerta, Andromeda, and Pegasus, the star fields thin out. The bright star β (beta) Peg—below the center of the chart, near 23^h $+27°$—marks the northwest corner of the Great Square of Pegasus. β Peg, also called Scheat, is a red-giant star that varies with an irregular period from magnitude 2.3 to 2.7. One corner of the square is not in Pegasus; α (alpha) Andromedae (And) marks the northeast corner of the Square. About halfway between these two stars is the double star 78 Peg, a close pair with magnitudes 5 and 8. The third star in the Square, α (alpha) Peg, is drawn just outside the chart boundary at the bottom center; the fourth star does not show on this chart.

About 5° to the northwest of β Peg is η (eta) Peg. Follow the line from β to η Peg about 7° further to a pair of double stars, $π^1$ (pi^1) and $π^2$. $π^2$ is an optical double—two yellow stars at different distances from earth that are apparently separated in the sky by only 15 minutes of arc. The pair can be seen well in binoculars.

Just to the right of the center of the chart, about 5° north and slightly west of η Peg, is the spiral galaxy NGC 7331 (Fig. 7-18). This galaxy can be found by sweeping the area with low power.

The planetary nebula NGC 7662 lies near 23^h26^m $+42.5°$ in Andromeda, about 3° southwest of ι (iota) And. One of the best planetaries for observing, NGC 7662 appears round, slightly ring-like, and bluish-green. About 3 arc min south of NGC 7662 is NGC 7640, a barred spiral galaxy that is fairly easy to locate.

Sweeping the northern area of Lacerta with a low-power telescope reveals several deep-sky objects. Binoculars give a good view of the open cluster NGC 7243, west of α (alpha) Lac, near 22^h15^m $+50°$. Large telescopes show about 50 of the cluster's stars. About 4° southwest is another open cluster, NGC 7209, smaller and fainter than NGC 7243. Many of its stars are 9th to 10th magnitude; they provide a beautiful view in a medium-sized telescope. East of β (beta) Lac is a third open cluster, NGC 7296.

Fig. 7-18 NGC 7331, a type Sb spiral galaxy in Pegasus. The dust lane surrounding its disk shows clearly. Three other spirals are visible beyond it. (National Optical Astronomy Observatories/KPNO)

FROM "SKY ATLAS 2000.0" BY WIL TIRION

MAGNITUDES

●	>-04
●	-04--05
●	06-15
●	16-25
●	26-35
•	36-45
•	46-55
•	56-65
•	66-75

DOUBLE or MULTIPLE

VARIABLE

OPEN CLUSTERS
>10' TO SCALE <10'

GLOBULAR CLUSTERS
>10' 5-10' <5'

PLANETARY NEBULAE
>1' 05'-1' <05'

BRIGHT DIFFUSE NEB.
>10' TO SCALE <10'

GALAXIES
> 30' 20'-30' 10'-20' <10'

QUASAR △

PULSAR ⋇

BLACK HOLE

MILKY WAY

GALACTIC EQUATOR
70°

ECLIPTIC
100°

CONSTELLATION BOUNDARIES

GREEK ALPHABET

α	Alpha	ν	Nu
β	Beta	ξ	Xi
γ	Gamma	ο	Omicron
δ	Delta	π	Pi
ε	Epsilon	ϱ	Rho
ζ	Zeta	σ	Sigma
η	Eta	τ	Tau
θ ϑ	Theta	υ	Upsilon
ι	Iota	φ φ	Phi
κ ϰ	Kappa	χ	Chi
λ	Lambda	ψ	Psi
μ	Mu	ω	Omega

ATLAS CHART 21. Pisces The next group of star charts shows the region of the sky surrounding the celestial equator. Near the top of this chart are γ (gamma) and α (alpha) Peg, the southernmost stars of the Great Square of Pegasus (Atlas Chart 20).

In Pisces, in the middle of the right-hand side of the chart, the stars ι, θ, γ, κ, and λ (iota, theta, gamma, kappa, and lambda) Psc form a distinctive asterism shaped like a small, irregular pentagon. This asterism, called the Circlet, marks the western fish in Pisces, and lies directly south of the Great Square of Pegasus. The Circlet covers an area about 7° by 5° and also includes fainter stars.

Due west of δ (delta) Psc is UU Psc, a wide pair with components of 6th and 8th magnitudes.

Below the Circlet, at −10°, is the triple system ψ^1, ψ^2, and ψ^3 (psi[1], psi[2], and psi[3]) in Aquarius. About $4\frac{1}{2}$° south of ψ^3 Aqr is the double star 94 Aqr, a pair of white and yellow-white stars with magnitudes 5.3 and 7.3. Even a small telescope at low power resolves this wide pair.

To the southeast, R Aqr lies south of ω^1 (omega[1]) and ω^2 (omega[2]) Aqr. R Aqr is a long-period (Mira-type) variable that changes in brightness from about 6th to 12th magnitude and back to 6th magnitude again during its 387-day period. The double star 107 Aqr can be found 4° south and slightly east of R Aqr. The white and yellow-white components of 6th and 7th magnitude are separated by about 6 arc sec.

In Cetus we find ϕ^1, ϕ^2, and ϕ^3 (phi[1], phi[2], and phi[3]) about 7° north of β (beta) Cet. ϕ^1 and ϕ^2 form an equilateral triangle with the planetary nebula NGC 246. The planetary looks like a dim oval through small telescopes but looks like a ring with a 12th-magnitude central star through large telescopes.

Fig. 7-19 Pisces the Fish, from the star atlas of Bayer. (Jay M. Pasachoff)

NITUDES		OPEN CLUSTERS				QUASAR	△	GREEK ALPHABET			
>-0.4			○	○	⋄						
			>10' TO SCALE		<10'	PULSAR	☼	α Alpha		ν	Nu
-0.4 - +0.5						BLACK HOLE	Y	β Beta		ξ	Xi
0.6-1.5		GLOBULAR CLUSTERS	⊕	⊕	⊕			γ Gamma		o	Omicron
1.6-2.5			>10'	5'-10'	<5'	MILKY WAY		δ Delta		π	Pi
2.6-3.5								ε Epsilon		ϱ	Rho
3.6-4.5		PLANETARY NEBULAE	✧	✧	✧	GALACTIC EQUATOR		ζ Zeta		σ	Sigma
4.6-5.5			>1'	0.5'-1'	<0.5'			η Eta		τ	Tau
5.6-6.5								$\theta \; \vartheta$ Theta		υ	Upsilon
6.6-7.5		BRIGHT DIFFUSE NEB.			▫	ECLIPTIC		ι Iota		$\phi \; \varphi$	Phi
			>10' TO SCALE		<10'		100°	$\kappa \; \varkappa$ Kappa		χ	Chi
BLE or PLE	●					CONSTELLATION BOUNDARIES		λ Lambda		ψ	Psi
ABLE	◉ ○	GALAXIES	○	○	⋄			μ Mu		ω	Omega
			>30'	20'-30'	10'-20'	<10'					

ATLAS CHART 22. Cetus, M77 Just above the center of the chart, the "cords" of Pisces—the "cords" holding the two fish together—converge to form an acute angle at α (alpha) Psc, also called El Rischa, the Knot. With components of magnitudes 4.2 and 5.1 separated by about 2 arc sec, α Psc can be observed with a medium-sized telescope.

The cords point to the lower left toward Mira, o (omicron) Ceti, the variable star about halfway down the neck of Cetus, the Whale. The first variable discovered, in 1596, Mira ("the Wonderful") is the prototype of long-period variables (Chapter 6). At its maximum magnitude of about 2.0, it is the brightest star in this constellation, shining with a deep red color. During its 332-day cycle, Mira slowly fades to 10th magnitude, far below naked-eye visibility, then gradually returns to maximum. (See Figs. 6-6 and 6-11.)

About 6°—three fingers' width at arm's length—northeast of Mira is δ (delta) Cet, and about ½° southeast of this star is M77 (NGC 1068), one of the brighter spiral galaxies. M77's bright nucleus can be seen with a small telescope, but observations of its face-on spiral structure require a large telescope.

α (alpha) Cet, at left center, is an optical double. The two components, separated by 16 arc min, can be resolved with binoculars.

ζ (zeta) Cet lies near 1^h15^m −10°, toward the bottom of the neck of Cetus. About 5° northwest of ζ Cet is NGC 615, a spiral galaxy.

This field contains two of the stars closest to us. The flare star UV Ceti near the bottom of the chart is the fifth nearest star system. It is too faint to see easily when at its normal 13th magnitude, but sometimes it brightens within about five minutes to almost 6th magnitude, a change of nearly 250 times in brightness. To its upper left is τ (tau) Ceti, the 20th closest star to earth. τ Cet, magnitude 3.5, is the nearest solar-type star (that is, a star with the same type of spectrum, temperature, and other properties as our sun). It is thus one of the prime objects in the search for life elsewhere in the universe.

Fig. 7-20 M77 (NGC 1068), a type Sb spiral galaxy in Cetus. At magnitude 8.8, it is a difficult object to detect in small telescopes. (Lick Observatory)

ATLAS CHART 23.   Aldebaran, Hyades As we move toward the western edge of the Milky Way in Taurus and Eridanus, the star fields become richer. On winter evenings, sweep southward with binoculars from the Hyades (at top; see also Atlas Chart 11) through the shield of Orion.

Just north of the Hyades is T Tauri (at 4^h22^m +19°32', but unmarked because it is too faint to be included on our chart), one of the most interesting stars in the sky. T Tauri varies in brightness because it is extremely young and has not settled down to a steady existence. It fluctuates between 8th and 13th magnitudes. T Tauri stars, the youngest stars, are being studied by optical, infrared, and radio techniques. T Tauri is near a diffuse nebula, NGC 1554–55, known as Hind's Variable Nebula. Over the last century, the nebula faded from view, then brightened considerably.

Slightly northwest of μ (mu) Eri, at 4^h46^m –3°, is NGC 1637, a galaxy visible with medium-sized telescopes. The planetary nebula NGC 1535 lies 12° southwest, near γ (gamma) Eri, at lower center; it consists of a bright inner ring and a faint outer ring with a 12.2-magnitude central star.

At 4^h15^m –8° is the triple system o^2 (omicron^2) Eri, also known as 40 Eridani. It is less than 16 light-years from us. It contains a 9th-magnitude white dwarf, 40 Eri B, the easiest white dwarf to study with a small telescope. Astronomers have measured the mass of the white dwarf and verified the theoretical prediction that its mass is about that of the sun. The system has also provided a test of Einstein's theory of relativity, since the white dwarf's spectral lines are redshifted by gravity, as Einstein predicted. 11th-magnitude 40 Eri C, which forms a visual binary with the white dwarf, is a small red star, one of the least massive stars known. The pair is separated from the bright (4th-magnitude) 40 Eri A by 84 arc sec.

About 6° northwest of o^1 (omicron^1), just to the right of the chart's center, lies w Eri. This star is also known as 32 Eri (double star number ADS2850). Its greenish and yellowish components are 5th and 6th magnitude.

The cluster of galaxies at the bottom edge of the chart includes NGC 1300, a fine example of a barred spiral galaxy.

Fig. 7-21 T Tauri, with Hind's Variable Nebula (NGC 1555) clearly visible as nebulosity 45 arc sec to its west (right). Another nebulous patch surrounds the star itself and is known as Burnham's Nebula. (Lick Observatory photo)

FROM 'SKY ATLAS 2000 0' BY WIL TIRION

MAGNITUDES

OPEN
CLUSTERS   >10 TO SCALE <10

GLOBULAR
CLUSTERS   >10   5-10' <5'

PLANETARY
NEBULAE   >1' 0.5-1' <0.5'

BRIGHT
DIFFUSE NEB.   >10 TO SCALE <10'

DOUBLE or
TRIPLE

VARIABLE   ◎ ○

QUASAR   △

PULSAR   ☆

BLACK HOLE

MILKY WAY

GALACTIC EQUATOR

ECLIPTIC

CONSTELLATION
BOUNDARIES

GALAXIES   > 30' 20'-30' 10'-20' <10'

GREEK ALPHABET			
α	Alpha	ν	Nu
β	Beta	ξ	Xi
γ	Gamma	ο	Omicron
δ	Delta	π	Pi
ε	Epsilon	ρ	Rho
ζ	Zeta	σ	Sigma
η	Eta	τ	Tau
θ ϑ	Theta	υ	Upsilon
ι	Iota	φ φ	Phi
κ ϰ	Kappa	χ	Chi
λ	Lambda	ψ	Psi
μ	Mu	ω	Omega

ATLAS CHART 24. Orion Nebula The entire region of Orion and Monoceros is interesting to sweep with a low-power telescope or binoculars. The region of Orion is one of the most fascinating areas in the sky because it contains both the youngest known stars and many beautiful nebulae.

Orion's belt, three stars in a line, is one of the easiest asterisms to locate (Fig. 2-9). In Orion's shoulder is Betelgeuse, α (alpha) Ori, a supergiant star whose reddish color is apparent to the naked eye. The 10th brightest star in the sky, Betelgeuse varies in brightness about 1 magnitude during its 5.8-year period. Rigel, the bright bluish star β (beta) Ori, marks Orion's heel. Rigel, a blue-white double, is the 7th brightest star in the sky. Because it is so bright, the secondary is hard to find.

From Orion's belt extends his sword (Fig. 2-10). M42 (NGC 1976), the Great Nebula in Orion, is a magnificent luminous cloud surrounding θ¹ (theta¹) Ori in the sword. It is often simply called the Orion Nebula (Fig. 2-11). Even the smallest optical aid reveals the wispy structure of this nebula. Small telescopes readily resolve θ¹ into four components, which are called the Trapezium. The four stars (magnitudes 5.1, 6.7, 6.7, and 7.9) are very hot and provide the energy to illuminate the nebula. Larger telescopes also show two additional components of 11th magnitude and reveal more of the nebula's structure. The colors, though, show only with time expo-

Fig. 7-22. *(left)* Orion Nebula region. (Karl-Schwarzschild-Observatory, FRG).

Fig. 7-23. *(right)* A chart of the Orion Nebula region. (Wil Tirion)

GREAT ORION NEBULA

MAGNITUDES		OPEN CLUSTERS				QUASAR	△	GREEK ALPHABET			
	> - 0.4		>10'	TO SCALE	<10'	PULSAR		α	Alpha	ν	Nu
	-0.4 - +0.5					BLACK HOLE		β	Beta	ξ	Xi
	0.6 - 1.5	GLOBULAR CLUSTERS						γ	Gamma	ο	Omicron
	1.6 - 2.5		>10'	5'-10'	<5'	MILKY WAY		δ	Delta	π	Pi
	2.6 - 3.5	PLANETARY NEBULAE				GALACTIC EQUATOR		ε	Epsilon	ϱ	Rho
	3.6 - 4.5		>1'	0.5'-1'	<0.5'		70°	ζ	Zeta	σ	Sigma
	4.6 - 5.5							η	Eta	τ	Tau
	5.6 - 6.5	BRIGHT DIFFUSE NEB.				ECLIPTIC	100°	θ ϑ	Theta	υ	Upsilon
	6.6 - 7.5		>10'	TO SCALE	<10'			ι	Iota	φ φ	Phi
BLE or PLE						CONSTELLATION BOUNDARIES		κ ϰ	Kappa	χ	Chi
ABLE		GALAXIES	>30'	20'-30'	10'-20' <10'			λ	Lambda	ψ	Psi
								μ	Mu	ω	Omega

sures. Even a short time exposure with a tripod-mounted 35-mm camera, using an ordinary 50-mm or 35-mm lens, shows the nebula as red, and allows the principal stars in Orion to be picked out. Photographs taken through equatorially driven telescopes look very different depending on the exposure time; short exposures show only the bright inner core of the nebula, while longer ones overexpose the inner parts but show outer contours.

The Orion Nebula lies about 1500 light-years from the sun. The nebula is a blister on the side of the Orion Molecular Cloud that is closer to us. In the Orion Molecular Cloud, dust shields molecules from being broken apart by the ultraviolet light from the hot stars. Astronomers study the molecules with radio telescopes; objects that are probably stars in formation are studied in the infrared.

NGC 1973–75–77 refers to the nebulosity and open cluster around the northern end of Orion's sword. NGC 1981 is an open cluster slightly farther north, with about 12 widely scattered members. NGC 1980 is a faint nebula around ι (iota) Ori, south of the Orion Nebula.

Extending downward from the star at the far left of Orion's belt— ζ (zeta) Ori—is IC 434, which contains the famous Horsehead Nebula (Fig. 2-13). The horsehead shape is formed by dark, absorbing gas and dust that blocks our view of a bright reddish emission nebula beyond. Northeast of the Horsehead, the nebula NGC 2023 is partially covered by the same dust cloud. Many beautiful photographs of the Orion Nebula and the Horsehead Nebula have been taken by amateur astronomers.

M78 (NGC 2068) is a wispy cloud north of Orion's belt, found by sweeping the area with low power. Long exposures show Barnard's Loop, which rings the northeast side of the Orion complex.

With low power, sweep the triangle formed by β (beta) Ori, η (eta) Ori (about 5° up toward Orion's belt), and β (beta) Eridani (Eri). The triangle contains many faint irregular patches of nebulosity. IC 2118, the Witch Head Nebula, lies about $1^1/_2°$ west of Rigel. γ (gamma) Ori has faint nebulosity around it.

Continue sweeping northeast from the Orion and Horsehead Nebulae into Monoceros. About 2° east of ε (epsilon) Mon is NGC 2244, a loose open cluster visible to the naked eye and resolvable into its member stars with good binoculars. NGC 2244 has about 24 member stars in an area 40 arc min across. Around NGC 2244 is NGC 2237, the Rosette Nebula. It is relatively large—1° across—and hard to locate. With low power it often shows just as a halo or glow around the open cluster; photographed in color, it looks spectacular (Fig. 5-29).

Nearby, further northeast, NGC 2264 is a nebulous cluster around S Mon, a variable double star. The cluster contains about 20 stars in an area close to the size of the full moon. The Cone Nebula (Fig. 5-27), like the Rosette, is difficult to find, but can be located with a medium-sized telescope.

To the south is NGC 2261, Hubble's Variable Nebula (Fig. 7-24). This nebula is so interesting that it was the first object photographed

Fig. 7-24 Hubble's Variable Nebula (NGC 2261). (Palomar Observatory photo)

with the huge 5-m telescope when it opened at Palomar Observatory. The nebula reflects light from the irregular variable R Mon, which varies from 10th to 13th magnitude. The nebula has the shape of a comet's tail. The shape sometimes changes in a matter of weeks. It is hard to observe with small telescopes.

Moving farther south in the sky, near 6^h50^m $0°$, is the open cluster NGC 2301, which consists of several overlapping groups of stars. This cluster has about 50 stars, including many bright ones.

Toward the bottom of the chart in Canis Major is Sirius, α (alpha) CMa, the Dog Star. Millennia ago, its dates of first visibility in the evening sky gave its name to the "dog days" of summer. At magnitude −1.46, Sirius is the brightest star in the sky.

In Orion's sword, ι (iota) and $θ^2$ (theta^2) are interesting doubles, as is η (eta) to the northwest. ζ (zeta) Ori, the easternmost star in Orion's belt, is a triple system with blue-white components of magnitudes 2, 4, and 10. σ (sigma) Ori, south of ζ, is a multiple with at least 5 components. The two brightest components, of magnitudes 4.0 and 6.0, are separated by only $1/4$ arc sec and so are difficult to resolve, but a small telescope can separate the other components. Two other components are 8th- and 10th-magnitude stars; they are about 12 arc sec away, on opposite sides of the brighter pair. Another companion (7th magnitude) is 40 arc sec away.

The components of the double star ε (epsilon) Mon, 7° southeast of Betelgeuse, show as blue and gold. The two components are separated by about 13 arc sec and are accompanied by a third companion. Low power should be used to find ε Mon because the surrounding star field is so rich.

About 12° south is β (beta) Mon, an easily resolved triple that is visible to the naked eye. Its three blue components are of magnitudes 4.6, 5.1, and 5.4.

ATLAS CHART 25. Procyon   A number of open clusters appear in this region, which is worth sweeping with low power. The most spectacular is the Beehive Cluster (M44), called Praesepe, which is described opposite Atlas Chart 13. Southeast of ζ (zeta) Mon, near 8^h13^m –6° in Hydra, the rich open cluster M48 (NGC 2548) is bright enough to be visible to the naked eye but difficult to locate. On the right of the chart, near 7^h03^m –8° in Monoceros, M50 (NGC 2682) is a rich open cluster west of α (alpha) Cancri.

A beautiful open cluster in Puppis is M46 (NGC 2437), somewhat fainter than M67 but containing more stars. On the northern edge of M46 is the planetary nebula NGC 2438, an irregular patchy ring. Nearby is M47 (NGC 2422), an open cluster that is faintly visible to the naked eye because of its many 6th-magnitude stars. Both M46 and M47 are only about 20 million years old. NGC 2539 is another rich open cluster in Puppis. Low power should be used to view the open cluster NGC 2506 in Monoceros, slightly northwest of NGC 2539.

Near 7^h40^m –18° in Puppis is the planetary nebula NGC 2440, best viewed with high power.

At the lower right of the chart (at –12°), extending from Canis Major into Monoceros, is IC 2177 (Fig. 5-26), a nebulous patch more than 3° across. This nebula was called the Eagle Nebula in older references, though that name is now usually applied to M16 (NGC 6611) instead (Atlas Chart 30). Toward the upper tip of IC 2177 are two open clusters, NGC 2335 and NGC 2343.

Procyon, α (alpha) Canis Minoris, is the 8th brightest star in the sky (magnitude 0.38) and one of the closest stars to us (about 11 light-years away). Procyon has a faint (13th-magnitude) white-dwarf companion, the second closest white dwarf to us.

Fig. 7-25 Monoceros plus the head of Canis Major, from the atlas of Bode (1801). Note the star Procyon. (Jay M. Pasachoff)

MAGNITUDES

- $\bullet$ >-0.4
- $\bullet$ -0.4 - +0.5
- $\bullet$ 0.6 - 1.5
- $\bullet$ 1.6 - 2.5
- $\bullet$ 2.6 - 3.5
- $\bullet$ 3.6 - 4.5
- • 4.6 - 5.5
- $\cdot$ 5.6 - 6.5
- $\cdot$ 6.6 - 7.5

DOUBLE or MULTIPLE ●–●

VARIABLE ◎ ○

OPEN CLUSTERS	○	○	○	◌
	>10'	TO SCALE	<10'	

GLOBULAR CLUSTERS	⊕	⊕	⊕
	>10'	5-10'	<5'

PLANETARY NEBULAE	◇	◇	◇
	>1'	0.5'-1'	<0.5'

BRIGHT DIFFUSE NEB. □
>10', TO SCALE   <10'

GALAXIES	⬭	○	○	○
	>30'	20'-30'	10'-20'	<10'

QUASAR △

PULSAR ✳

BLACK HOLE Υ

MILKY WAY 〰

GALACTIC EQUATOR
70°

ECLIPTIC
100°
+

CONSTELLATION BOUNDARIES

GREEK ALPHABET

α	Alpha	ν	Nu
β	Beta	ξ	Xi
γ	Gamma	o	Omicron
δ	Delta	π	Pi
ε	Epsilon	ϱ	Rho
ζ	Zeta	σ	Sigma
η	Eta	τ	Tau
θ ϑ	Theta	υ	Upsilon
ι	Iota	φ φ	Phi
κ ϰ	Kappa	χ	Chi
λ	Lambda	ψ	Psi
μ	Mu	ω	Omega

ATLAS CHART 26. Regulus As we move away from the obscuring dust clouds of the Milky Way, the more distant galaxies become visible. In Leo we see an outer edge of the huge cluster of galaxies—the Virgo Cluster—that extends through Virgo, Coma Berenices, and Corvus. Three of the brighter galaxies in Leo are M95 (NGC 3351), M96 (NGC 3368), and M105 (NGC 3379), located about 30 million light-years from the Milky Way Galaxy. M95 (magnitude 9.7) is a barred spiral and M96 (magnitude 9.2) is a regular spiral; both are relatively large. M105 is a small elliptical galaxy of magnitude 9.3. If you use a wide-angle, medium-power telescope to sweep about 9° east of Regulus, you can see these galaxies in the same field of view.

Regulus, α (alpha) Leo, lies directly on the ecliptic. Regulus is at the base of the "sickle" that many people see as part of the constellation's shape; it marks the lion's heart. The 21st brightest star in the sky at magnitude 1.35, Regulus is visible for most of the year, and can be seen in the eastern sky in spring. It has a faint companion that can sometimes be detected with binoculars.

γ (gamma) Leo, the brightest star in the sickle, is a binary located about 8° northeast of Regulus. One of the best doubles in the sky, γ Leo consists of two yellow components of magnitudes 2.2 and 3.5 that orbit with a period of 620 years. The components are fairly close, so they are difficult to resolve with a small telescope. The gap between the pair is currently widening, though; these stars will be about 5 arc sec apart by the year 2100.

This chart includes Wolf 359, the third closest star to the sun, after the α (alpha) Centauri system and Barnard's Star. At magnitude 13.5, Wolf 359 is too faint to be marked on this chart, but it is located near VY Leo, at 10^h56^m +7°. It is one of the least luminous stars known, but has been discovered because its rapid proper motion (motion across the sky—see p. 19) makes its closeness (only 7.8 light-years from earth) apparent.

The radiant of the Leonid meteor shower (Table 19), which reaches its maximum frequency on November 17 each year, lies about 2° northwest of γ Leo. This shower peaks every 33 years, as the earth passes through the part of a defunct comet's orbit where the remaining particles from the comet are bunched. The last spectacular display of Leonids occurred in 1966; the next might occur in 1998 or 1999.

In the Lion's foreleg, R Leo is one of the brightest of the long-period variables; it ranges from magnitude 11.3 to 4.4 over a period of 312 days. Located about 5° west of Regulus, R Leo forms a triangle with two westward stars of magnitudes 9.0 and 9.6.

Although the constellation Hydra is not particularly rich in stars, sweeping the region with low-power binoculars does show some objects of interest. NGC 3242 is a planetary nebula located about 1.8° south of μ (mu) Hydra at the lower left of the chart. In a small telescope the planetary appears as a pale blue disk; a large telescope reveals a bright inner ring and a faint outer shell.

FROM "SKY ATLAS 2000.0" BY WIL TIRION

ATLAS CHART 27.   Sombrero Galaxy, Virgo Cluster of Galaxies
Here·we find the greatest concentration of galaxies in the Virgo Cluster of galaxies that extends north into Canes Venatici and south into Corvus. The Virgo Cluster is an average of about 65 million light-years away. Our Milky Way Galaxy is part of the Local Group which, in turn, is an outlying part of the Virgo Cluster. Many of the galaxies in the main part of the Virgo Cluster are shown on an expanded chart (27A) of the area outlined in the upper-left region of this chart.

Just above the outlined area is M85 (NGC 4382), an elliptical galaxy in Coma Berenices, at 12^h25^m +18°. One of the brightest galaxies in the Virgo Cluster, M85 shows in a small telescope as a bright oval patch.

In the Leo Cluster of galaxies at upper right, M65 (NGC 3623) and M66 (NGC 3627) are two bright spiral galaxies about 20 arc min apart, located about halfway between θ (theta) and ι (iota) Leo. Both galaxies appear similar to the Andromeda Galaxy. At magnitude 9.0, M66 is about 0.3 magnitude brighter than M65. M65 and M66 can be seen in the same field of view with low-power telescopes. On a clear night, you may be able to glimpse both galaxies with a good pair of binoculars. Two nearby spirals, NGC 3628 and NGC 3593, may be visible in the same telescopic field.

On the border of Virgo and Corvus, near 12^h40^m −12°, is M104 (NGC 4594), another of the brighter members of the cluster. M104 is called the Sombrero Galaxy (Fig. 5-42) because of its distinctive large center and the dark lane of dust that runs along the equatorial plane of this spiral galaxy, seen only 6° from edge-on. These features are hard to see in small telescopes, though the galaxy can be readily detected as a hazy oval patch. In larger telescopes, the dust lane can be detected under good observing conditions.

In Corvus, about 4° southwest of γ (gamma) Corvi, near 12^h −18°, are a pair of peculiar galaxies, NGC 4038 and NGC 4039, known as the Antennae. Each of these elliptical galaxies appears to have a long curving tail; computer models show that the tails may have formed by gravity as a result of a collision of the two galaxies. The Antennae are a source of radio waves and lie about 90 million light-years away.

One of the finest double stars in the sky and a favorite of amateurs is γ (gamma) Vir (at 12^h42^m −1°). Its two almost equal components (magnitudes 3.5) are separated by less than 3 arc seconds and are closing rapidly.

Located about 4° south of σ (sigma) Leo, near the ecliptic (at about 11^h27^m +3°), is τ (tau) Leo, a pair of yellow and blue stars of 5th and 8th magnitudes, separated by 90 arc sec. δ (delta) Crv, whose components are magnitudes 3.0 and 9.2, is also easily resolved.

MAGNITUDES					OPEN CLUSTERS					QUASAR		GREEK ALPHABET			

MAGNITUDES

- >-0.4
- -0.4 - +0.5
- 0.6 - 1.5
- 1.6 - 2.5
- 2.6 - 3.5
- 3.6 - 4.5
- 4.6 - 5.5
- 5.6 - 6.5
- 6.6 - 7.5

DOUBLE or MULTIPLE

VARIABLE

OPEN CLUSTERS   >10' TO SCALE <10'

GLOBULAR CLUSTERS   >10' 5-10' <5'

PLANETARY NEBULAE   >1' 0.5'-1' <0.5'

BRIGHT DIFFUSE NEB.   >10' TO SCALE <10'

GALAXIES   >30' 20'-30' 10'-20' <10'

QUASAR

PULSAR

BLACK HOLE

MILKY WAY

GALACTIC EQUATOR   70°

ECLIPTIC   100°

CONSTELLATION BOUNDARIES

GREEK ALPHABET

α	Alpha	ν	Nu
β	Beta	ξ	Xi
γ	Gamma	ο	Omicron
δ	Delta	π	Pi
ε	Epsilon	ρ	Rho
ζ	Zeta	σ	Sigma
η	Eta	τ	Tau
θ ϑ	Theta	υ	Upsilon
ι	Iota	φ φ	Phi
κ ϰ	Kappa	χ	Chi
λ	Lambda	ψ	Psi
μ	Mu	ω	Omega

ATLAS CHART 27A. Virgo Cluster of Galaxies This chart shows the heart of the Virgo Cluster. About 75% of the brightest galaxies in this cluster are spirals.

Since the Virgo Cluster is the closest rich cluster of galaxies to us, it is the easiest to observe. In small telescopes most of the galaxies appear as faint patches of light. But on a clear dark night in the summer, over 100 galaxies can be viewed with a medium-sized telescope. It is best to locate a galaxy with low power first and then switch to higher magnifications.

Some outstanding galaxies in Coma Berenices include: M98 (NGC 4192) at 12^h19^m +15°, a bright, elongated spiral seen nearly edge-on; M99 (NGC 4254)—about 1.5° southeast of M98, near 12^h19^m +14°— a bright, round spiral seen face-on; and M88 (NGC 4501)—about 4° east of M99, near 12^h32^m +14°—a spiral that can be located by searching for the two faint stars near its edge. M100 (NGC 4321), near 12^h23^m +16°, is the largest spiral in the Virgo Cluster (Fig. 5-9).

In Virgo, noteworthy galaxies include: M49 (NGC 4472), M58 (NGC 4579), M59 (NGC 4621), M60 (NGC 4649), M61 (NGC 4303), M84 (NGC 4374), M86 (NGC 4406), M89 (NGC 4552), and M90 (NGC 4569). M49, one of the brightest ellipticals, is fairly easy to find near 12^h30^m +8°. M61, about 6° southwest of M49, near 12^h22^m +4°30', is a beautiful face-on spiral (Fig. 5-36). M84 and M86 are nearly identical ellipticals separated by less than 20 arc min. M90 is an edge-on spiral with a bright nucleus.

One of the brighter and most interesting galaxies in the Virgo Cluster is M87 (NGC 4486), a huge peculiar elliptical galaxy at 12^h31^m +13°. The best photographs taken with large telescopes show the more than 1000 globular clusters that surround this galaxy. Short-exposure photographs taken with large telescopes have also revealed an unusual jet of gas (Fig. 5-40). M87 has been identified as the radio source Virgo A, and many astronomers think that a giant black hole containing millions of times more mass than the sun lies at its center.

Near 12^h30^m +2°, about $3\frac{1}{2}$° northeast of η (eta) Vir, is 3C 273 (Fig. 5-55), the brightest and one of the first known quasars. The easiest quasar to observe, 3C 273 ranges in magnitude from about 12.2 and 13.0. Depending on its magnitude and on observing conditions, 3C 273 can sometimes be glimpsed in medium to large telescopes with the aid of an accurate finding chart. It appears almost starlike, not nebulous, and is thus "quasi-stellar." From the enormous redshift in its spectrum, astronomers have calculated that this bluish object is receding at the tremendous speed of 50,000 km per second, 16% of the speed of light. Hubble's Law tells us that 3C 273 is out among the distant galaxies.

MAGNITUDES

3   4   5   6   7   >8¹

DOUBLE or
MULTIPLE

VARIABLE   ⊙ ○

QUASAR   △

GALAXIES   ⬭   ○   ○   ○
              >30' 20'-30' 10'-20' <10'

ATLAS CHART 28. Arcturus, Spica   Arcturus, α (alpha) Boötes, at magnitude 0.0 the third brightest single star in the sky, and 1st-magnitude Spica, α (alpha) Virginis, are the most prominent objects in this region. Arcturus is a cool red giant. Spica, the 16th brightest star, is extremely hot and therefore bluish. It is an eclipsing spectroscopic binary that drops about one magnitude from its usual magnitude of 1.0 during a four-day period. These objects are easily found in the sky from the curve in the handle of the Big Dipper. Following the curve backward from the bowl, you "arc to Arcturus."   Then, from Arcturus, you can continue straight on: "spike to Spica." These two stars are so bright that they stand out.

In the Virgo Cluster of galaxies, NGC 5364 is a spiral galaxy of 10th magnitude (Fig. 7-26). NGC 5746 (at 14^h45^m +2°) is an edge-on spiral of 11th magnitude, best seen with small telescopes; its companion, NGC 5740, a little over $1/4$° south, is a spiral of magnitude 11.9. To the left of the chart, the galaxies NGC 5806 (spiral), NGC 5813 (elliptical), and NGC 5831 (elliptical) are visible in medium-sized telescopes. The dim galaxies NGC 5838, NGC 5854, and NGC 5864 are slightly further east. The nearby spiral NGC 5846 is brighter. Another spiral galaxy located slightly to the southeast, NGC 5850, is dimmer but about twice as large as NGC 5846.

Of the double stars shown on this chart, ζ (zeta) Boo, at upper left, is a beautiful pair of white stars with magnitudes 4.5 and 4.6, which orbit each other with a period of 123 years. They can be resolved with a medium-sized telescope. π (pi) Boo, above ζ Boo, is another double, more easily resolved.

S Vir, about halfway between Spica and ζ (zeta) Vir, is a long-period variable ranging from 6th to 13th magnitude, with an average period of 377 days. As it nears maximum brightness, its red color makes it an especially interesting telescopic object.

This chart contains 3C 279, one of the brightest quasars. It has reached an absolute magnitude as high as –31, which is 10,000 times brighter than the Andromeda Galaxy. 3C 279 is on the ecliptic at extreme right.

Fig. 7-26 NGC 5364 in Virgo, a spiral galaxy, type Sc. (National Optical Astronomy Observatories/KPNO)

MAGNITUDES

- >-0.4
- -0.4-+0.5
- 0.6-1.5
- 1.6-2.5
- 2.6-3.5
- 3.6-4.5
- 4.6-5.5
- 5.6-6.5
- 6.6-7.5

VARIABLE or MULTIPLE ●←

VARIABLE ◎○

OPEN CLUSTERS

>10', TO SCALE   <10'

GLOBULAR CLUSTERS

>10'   5-10'   <5'

PLANETARY NEBULAE

>1'   0.5'-1'   <0.5'

BRIGHT DIFFUSE NEB.

>10', TO SCALE   <10'

GALAXIES

>30'   20'-30'   10'-20'   <10'

QUASAR   △

PULSAR   ⚡

BLACK HOLE   ⌇

MILKY WAY

GALACTIC EQUATOR
——— 70° —+—

ECLIPTIC
——— 100° —+—

CONSTELLATION BOUNDARIES

GREEK ALPHABET

α	Alpha	ν	Nu
β	Beta	ξ	Xi
γ	Gamma	ο	Omicron
δ	Delta	π	Pi
ε	Epsilon	ϱ	Rho
ζ	Zeta	σ	Sigma
η	Eta	τ	Tau
θ ϑ	Theta	υ	Upsilon
ι	Iota	φ φ	Phi
κ ϰ	Kappa	χ	Chi
λ	Lambda	ψ	Psi
μ	Mu	ω	Omega

FROM "SKY ATLAS 2000.0" BY WIL TIRION

ATLAS CHART 29. Globular Clusters M5, M10, M12 In Serpens, the globular cluster M5 (NGC 5904) is one of the finest in the sky, surpassed only by 47 Tuc, w (omega) Cen, and possibly M13. During the summer months it is easily located in the sparse area near 15^h18^m +2°, slightly northwest of the naked-eye star 5 Ser. Under very good conditions, M5 (Fig. 7-27) is also visible to the naked eye. With binoculars, it appears as a hazy star, while small telescopes show it as a bright, circular glow. Larger telescopes begin to resolve its stars. Nearby, 5 Ser is a double with 5th- and 10th-magnitude components that are separated by 11 arc sec.

M10 and M12, two very similar globular clusters in Ophiuchus, are also outstanding. Both brighter than 7th magnitude, they are visible to the naked eye. Located about 5° northeast of z (zeta) Oph, near 16^h57^m -4°, M10 (NGC 6254) is a rich cluster with a diameter of about 12 arc min, and medium-sized telescopes begin to resolve its stars. M12 (NGC 6218) lies about 3° northwest of M10 and is a bit larger. Since M12 has a relatively loose structure, its stars are more readily resolved.

M107 (NGC 6171), a third globular cluster in Ophiuchus, lies about 3° south of z (zeta) Oph. At magnitude 9 and about 8 arc min across, M107 is much fainter and smaller than M10 or M12.

See Atlas Chart 28 for the galaxies in Virgo shown here west of M5.

During the summer months scan the region of Serpens Caput (the Serpent's Head); the tail, Serpens Cauda, is on Atlas Chart 30. Use binoculars or a low-power telescope near b (beta) Ser. d (delta) Ser is a fine double with components of magnitudes 4.1 and 5.2, easily resolved by a small telescope. About 1° east of b (beta) Ser near 15^h46^m +15°, R Ser is a long-period variable, ranging from magnitude 5.6 to 14.0 over an average period of 356 days. Its color near maximum, when it can sometimes be seen with the naked eye, is crimson.

S Her, a long-period variable located near 16^h50^m +15° in Hercules, ranges from magnitude 5.9 to 13.6 in 307 days.

Fig. 7-27 M5 (NGC 5904), a globular cluster in Serpens. (National Optical Astronomy Observatories/KPNO)

9

17h · 17 · 40m · 20m · 16h · 40m · 20m · 16 · 15h

+20°
6182 ⚬s
·U γ
HERCULES
q κ
✕ ⚬Ton256
+5° V451 ⚬oS ·ω
h I4593
✕ ι
k
γ o
n· •m
λ
σ ⚬6070
+M12 ⚬6118
+M10 δ
ε
OPHIUCHUS υ
ζ· ψ
·χ ξ
·V107 ⚬v ·ι
⚬R ·φ SCORPIUS χ
⚬V1010 φ ψ ·I4593
I4601
20m

ι
κ τ7
τ8 τ3
⚬5962
γ⚬R β τ6 τ5 τ2
φ ρτ4 τ1
υ ⚬5984
χ 5936⚬
⚬5970
δ
λ SERPENS CAPUT
α
ε ⚬5921
ω ψ
+M5
A1
A2
b μ
FZ2 β
ε ⚬5885 LIBRA
5915 ·ES
γ ⚬5878
η ·RU
ζ o ⚬F703
230° κ ν
ϑ
λ
16h 40m 20m

+20°
ξ
BOOTES +15°
+10°
VIRGO
+5°
28
5775
5864
⚬5854
5838⚬ ⚬5806
5845⚬ 5813
5850 5831 0°
M
⚬5792 W
5768⚬
-5°
⚬5812
δ
ξ2
ξ1
·FY -15°
τ4 α1
⚬5796
5791⚬
40 15h
-20°

FROM "SKY ATLAS 2000.0" BY WIL TIRION

MAGNITUDES		OPEN CLUSTERS				QUASAR △		GREEK ALPHABET		
●	>-0.4		⬭ ○ ○ ○					α Alpha		ν Nu
●	-0.4-·0.5		>10' TO SCALE <10'			PULSAR ☆		β Beta		ξ Xi
●	0.6-1.5	GLOBULAR CLUSTERS	⊕ ⊕ ⊕			BLACK HOLE ⋉		γ Gamma		o Omicron
●	1.6-2.5		>10' 5-10' <5'			MILKY WAY 〰		δ Delta		π Pi
●	2.6-3.5	PLANETARY NEBULAE	◇ ◇ ◇					ε Epsilon		ϱ Rho
●	3.6-4.5		>1' 0.5'-1' <0.5'			GALACTIC EQUATOR		ζ Zeta		σ Sigma
•	4.6-5.5							η Eta		τ Tau
•	5.6-6.5	BRIGHT DIFFUSE NEB.	⬭ □			ECLIPTIC		θ ϑ Theta		⌄ υ Upsilon
•	6.5-7.5		>10' TO SCALE <10'					ι Iota		φ φ Phi
DOUBLE or TRIPLE ●–●–								κ ✕ Kappa		χ Chi
VARIABLE ◎ ○		GALAXIES	⬭ ○ ○ ○			CONSTELLATION BOUNDARIES		λ Lambda		ψ Psi
			>30' 20'-30' 10'-20' <10'					μ Mu		ω Omega

ATLAS CHART 30. Omega Nebula The star fields begin to increase in brilliance toward the Milky Way in Aquila, Scutum, and Sagittarius. The area provides good views in binoculars or low-power telescopes.

The open clusters NGC 6633 in Ophiuchus (at 18^h28^m +7°) and IC 4756 in Serpens (at 18^h40^m +6°) are easily resolved at relatively low power. About 5° southwest of ζ (zeta) Aquilae at upper left, you can see the open cluster NGC 6709 with medium power. Another rich field lies about 1° northeast of β (beta) Oph, in the open cluster IC 4665 (at 17^h47^m +6°).

The rich open cluster M11 (NGC 6705), the Wild Duck, is located near 18^h50^m −6° on the northern edge of the Scutum star cloud, a bright region of the Milky Way. M11 is magnificent in both small and large telescopes (Fig. 5-14); it can sometimes be seen with the naked eye. A medium-sized telescope resolves its edges, while larger telescopes resolve hundreds of its stars. About $3^1/2$° south of M11 is the open cluster M26 (NGC 6694), which can also be observed easily in small telescopes.

In Sagittarius, M23 (NGC 6494) is a large open cluster that appears prominent against a dark nebula. Its bright stars are outstanding even when viewed through binoculars. The open clusters M18 (NGC 6613), M24 (NGC 6603), and M25 (IC 4725) also lie among the dark nebulae in Sagittarius. M24 is actually a part of the Milky Way and includes the open cluster NGC 6603. Nearby are the reflection nebulae NGC 6589 and NGC 6590 (Fig. 5-21).

An interesting planetary, NGC 6572, is in Ophiuchus. Use high power to observe the globular clusters M9 (NGC 6333), NGC 6356, and NGC 6342.

In Serpens, near 18^h20^m −14°, is M16 (NGC 6611), the Eagle Nebula, an easily located nebulous cluster (Fig. 5-15). To the southeast in Sagittarius near 18^h20^m −16° is the Omega Nebula, M17 (NGC 6618), also called the Horseshoe or Swan Nebula (Fig. 5-23). The star background in this region is particularly rich. In Scutum, the nebula IC 1287, 2° south of α (alpha) Sct, requires slightly higher power.

Barnard's Star (just above the Chart's center, at 18^h +5°), magnitude 9.5, is the second closest star to our solar system, counting the whole α Centauri system as the first. It has the greatest apparent angular motion across the sky (proper motion) of any star (Fig. 2-2).

Fig. 7-28 M16.
(Lick Observatory photo)

FROM "SKY ATLAS 2000.0" BY WIL TIRION

GNITUDES		OPEN CLUSTERS	○ ○ ○ ○		QUASAR	△		GREEK ALPHABET			
●	>-0.4		>10' TO SCALE <10'		PULSAR	⚡		α Alpha	ν Nu		
●	-0.4--0.5	GLOBULAR CLUSTERS	⊕ ⊕ ⊖		BLACK HOLE	Y		β Beta	ξ Xi		
●	0.6-1.5		>10' 5'-10' <5'		MILKY WAY			γ Gamma	o Omicron		
●	1.6-2.5							δ Delta	π Pi		
●	2.6-3.5	PLANETARY NEBULAE	◇ ◇ ◇		GALACTIC EQUATOR			ε Epsilon	ϱ Rho		
●	3.6-4.5		>1' 0.5'-1' <0.5'			70°		ζ Zeta	σ Sigma		
●	4.6-5.5					+		η Eta	τ Tau		
●	5.6-6.5	BRIGHT DIFFUSE NEB.	◻		ECLIPTIC	100°		θ ϑ Theta	υ Upsilon		
●	6.6-7.5		>10' TO SCALE <10'			+		ι Iota	ϕ φ Phi		
UBLE or TIPLE	●-●	GALAXIES	⬭ ○ ○ ○		CONSTELLATION BOUNDARIES			κ $\varkappa$ Kappa	χ Chi		
IABLE	◉○		>30' 20'-30' 10'-20' <10'					λ Lambda	ψ Psi		
								μ Mu	ω Omega		

ATLAS CHART 31. Altair From Cygnus into Aquila, the Milky Way appears to be divided lengthwise by enormous dust clouds. These clouds form a band called the Great Rift, which lies along the central plane of our galaxy in a lane like the equatorial lanes visible in photographs of edge-on galaxies. The dark nebulae and rich star fields provide beautiful views during the summer months.

Near the top of the chart in Sagitta (the Arrow), about halfway between γ (gamma) and δ (delta) Sge, is the rich globular cluster M71 (NGC 6838), which is magnitude 8.3.

Above the center of the chart is α (alpha) Aquilae, Altair, the 12th brightest star in the sky. About 2° north of Altair is γ (gamma) Aql. Slightly northwest of γ Aql is B143, a dark nebula about 30 arc min in diameter that is visible in medium-sized telescopes. About 5° to the west, the planetary nebula NGC 6803 shows a small disk, as does the fainter planetary, NGC 6804, nearby. The planetary nebula NGC 6891, 7° northeast of Altair, appears as a bright disk surrounded by a fainter ring. Eight degrees west-southwest of Altair is the planetary nebula NGC 6781; it can be photographed only with large apertures.

At lower center, close to the Milky Way in Sagittarius, is NGC 6822, an irregular dwarf galaxy and one of the few members of the Local Group that is readily visible. Use a rich-field telescope to view it. Although it is one of the nearer and apparently larger galaxies, an intervening dust cloud reduces its brightness.

Slightly northwest of NGC 6822 and visible in the same field is NGC 6818, the Little Gem, one of the closest planetary nebulae. Use a large telescope to observe its 13th-magnitude central star; smaller telescopes show its pale blue-green disk.

Double stars in this region include: π (pi) Aql, a 6th-magnitude double about 3° north of Altair; γ (gamma) Del (at 20^h47^m +16°), a wide double located at the northeast corner of the lozenge-shaped asterism formed by α, β, δ, and γ (alpha, beta, delta, and gamma) Del; and 15 Aql, a wide double lying northeast of the Scutum star cloud, about 1 arc min north and slightly west of λ (lambda) Aql (at 19^h05^m −5°).

Among the variable stars on the chart are: η (eta) Aql, a Cepheid variable that ranges from magnitude 3.5 to 4.4 during a period of slightly more than 7 days; σ (sigma) Aql, an eclipsing variable that drops about 0.2 magnitudes within a period of 47 hours; R Aql, a reddish, long-period variable often visible to the naked eye at maximum brightness; and U Sagittae, an Algol-type eclipsing binary. The brightness of U Sge ranges from 6.6 to 9.2 with a period of 3 days, 9 hours.

One of the most unusual objects in our galaxy, SS 433 (at 19^h15^m +5°), is too faint (14th magnitude) for small telescopes. Its spectrum shows that it is emitting jets of gas in opposite directions at 25% of the speed of light, a speed otherwise unknown in our galaxy. Astronomers have concluded that it is a binary system containing a neutron star.

MAGNITUDES		OPEN CLUSTERS				QUASAR	△		GREEK ALPHABET		
	>-0.4		○	○	○	⋄	PULSAR	✦	α	Alpha	ν	Nu
	-0.4 - +0.5		>10'	TO SCALE	<10'	BLACK HOLE	⅄	β	Beta	ξ	Xi
	0.6-1.5	GLOBULAR CLUSTERS	⊕	⊕	⊕			γ	Gamma	ο	Omicron
	1.6-2.5		>10'	5'-10'	<5'	MILKY WAY		δ	Delta	π	Pi
	2.6-3.5	PLANETARY NEBULAE	⋄	⋄	⋄			ε	Epsilon	ρ	Rho
	3.6-4.5		>1'	0.5'-1'	<0.5'	GALACTIC EQUATOR		ζ	Zeta	σ	Sigma
	4.6-5.5							η	Eta	τ	Tau
	5.6-6.5	BRIGHT DIFFUSE NEB.			□	ECLIPTIC		θ ϑ	Theta	υ	Upsilon
	6.6-7.5		>10'	TO SCALE	<10'			ι	Iota	φ φ	Phi
DOUBLE or MULTIPLE	●-					CONSTELLATION BOUNDARIES		κ ϰ	Kappa	χ	Chi
		GALAXIES	○	○	○			λ	Lambda	ψ	Psi
VARIABLE	◉○		>30'	20'-30'	10'-20' <10'			μ	Mu	ω	Omega

ATLAS CHART 32. Saturn Nebula NGC 7009, one of the brightest planetary nebulae, is located near 21^h $-11°$, about 1° west of ν (nu) Aquarii (Aqr). It consists of a bright inner ring surrounded by an outer disk with faint extensions. It is sometimes called the Saturn Nebula (Fig. 7-29). Small telescopes show it only as starlike.

Slightly southwest of NGC 7009 is M72 (NGC 6981), a small globular cluster difficult to resolve even with large telescopes and high power. The open cluster M73 (NGC 6994) is nearby.

Two globular clusters on this chart, M15 (NGC 7078) and M2 (NGC 7089), are among the brightest in the sky. Both are clearly visible to the naked eye, and even the smallest optical aid shows them as hazy patches that are condensed toward the centers. M15 (at 21^h30^m $+12°$) is located about 4° northwest of ε (epsilon) Pegasi. An unusually rich and compact cluster, M15 has been identified as an x-ray source. M2 is located just below the celestial equator, about 5° north of β (beta) Aqr. Since M2 has such a highly condensed center, even large telescopes resolve only its outer edges.

The globular cluster NGC 7006 in Delphinus is very remote; it lies about 185,000 light-years from the solar system, about the same distance as the Magellanic Clouds. The cluster is very difficult to resolve; in a medium-sized telescope, it appears as a hazy spot about 1 arc min in diameter.

East of α (alpha) Aqr, the four stars γ, ζ, η, and π (gamma, zeta, eta, and pi Aqr) form a small Y-shaped asterism called the Water Jar, a characteristic feature of this constellation. The star ζ Aqr at the center of the Y is one of the finest doubles in the sky, with components of magnitudes 4.3 and 4.5.

This ends the set of equatorial charts; we now turn to charts of intermediate southern declinations.

Fig. 7-29 NGC 7009, the Saturn Nebula, a planetary nebula in Aquarius. (National Optical Astronomy Observatories/KPNO)

FROM "SKY ATLAS 2000.0" BY WIL TIRION

MAGNITUDES		OPEN CLUSTERS					QUASAR	△		GREEK ALPHABET			
●	> -0.4		>10'	TO SCALE	<10'		PULSAR	☆		α	Alpha	ν	Nu
●	-0.4 – +0.5						BLACK HOLE	⅄		β	Beta	ξ	Xi
●	0.6 – 1.5	GLOBULAR CLUSTERS	⊕	⊕	⊛					γ	Gamma	ο	Omicron
●	1.6 – 2.5		>10'	5'–10'	<5'		MILKY WAY			δ	Delta	π	Pi
●	2.6 – 3.5	PLANETARY NEBULAE	✧	✧	✧					ε	Epsilon	ϱ	Rho
●	3.6 – 4.5		>1'	0.5'–1'	<0.5'		GALACTIC EQUATOR			ζ	Zeta	σ	Sigma
•	4.6 – 5.5						─ ─ ─ ─ ─	70°		η	Eta	τ	Tau
•	5.6 – 6.5	BRIGHT DIFFUSE NEB.		>10'. TO SCALE	<10'	□	ECLIPTIC	100°		θ ϑ	Theta	υ	Upsilon
•	6.6 – 7.5						─ ─ ─ ─ ─			ι	Iota	φ φ	Phi
DOUBLE or MULTIPLE										κ ϰ	Kappa	χ	Chi
VARIABLE	◉ ○	GALAXIES	⬭	○	○	○	CONSTELLATION BOUNDARIES	⌐ ¬		λ	Lambda	ψ	Psi
			>30'	20'–30'	10'–20'	<10'				μ	Mu	ω	Omega

ATLAS CHART 33. South Galactic Pole The stellar background in this region is thin, and even galaxies are rare. The galaxy NGC 253, near the south galactic pole in Sculptor, is a large and bright spiral (Fig. 5-45), often considered the finest in the sky except for the Andromeda Galaxy. Because NGC 253 is at such a southern declination, observers in midnorthern latitudes need a medium-sized telescope and good viewing conditions to see it well.

The spiral galaxy NGC 247, about 4° north of NGC 253, is nearly as large as NGC 253 but about two magnitudes fainter. NGC 247 may be found most easily by looking with low power about 3° south of β (beta) Ceti and then waiting for the galaxy to drift into view. NGC 247 and NGC 253 are very close to us (for galaxies)—only about 12 million light-years away.

About 4° northwest of α (alpha) Phe, near the border between Sculptor and Phoenix, NGC 55 is another prominent galaxy in the southern sky, though difficult for northern observers. It is a large, nearly edge-on spiral that shows in small telescopes as an oval patch of light. All three galaxies belong to the Sculptor group, most of which are loose, large spirals.

The globular cluster NGC 288 near the south galactic pole is relatively uninteresting.

SX Phe, about 7° west of α Phe, is one of the best-known dwarf Cepheid variables. During its 79-minute period, it varies from magnitude 6.8 to about 7.5.

Fig. 7-30 Sculptor, from the atlas of Bode (1801). In modern atlases, we find Fornax, the Furnace, to the left of Sculptor, but Bode showed the then-modern apparatus of the time. (Jay M. Pasachoff)

FROM "SKY ATLAS 2000.0" BY WIL TIRION

Star Chart Legend

MAGNITUDES

- > -0.4
- $-0.4 - +0.5$
- $0.6 - 1.5$
- $1.6 - 2.5$
- $2.6 - 3.5$
- $3.6 - 4.5$
- $4.6 - 5.5$
- $5.6 - 6.5$
- $6.6 - 7.5$

DOUBLE or MULTIPLE

VARIABLE

OPEN CLUSTERS — $>10'$ TO SCALE $<10'$

GLOBULAR CLUSTERS — $>10'$ $5'-10'$ $<5'$

PLANETARY NEBULAE — $>1'$ $0.5'-1'$ $<0.5'$

BRIGHT DIFFUSE NEB. — $>10'$ TO SCALE $<10'$

GALAXIES — $>30'$ $20'-30'$ $10'-20'$ $<10'$

QUASAR

PULSAR

BLACK HOLE

MILKY WAY

GALACTIC EQUATOR — 70°

ECLIPTIC — 100°

CONSTELLATION BOUNDARIES

GREEK ALPHABET

α	Alpha	ν	Nu
β	Beta	ξ	Xi
γ	Gamma	o	Omicron
δ	Delta	π	Pi
ε	Epsilon	ϱ	Rho
ζ	Zeta	σ	Sigma
η	Eta	τ	Tau
$\theta\ \vartheta$	Theta	υ	Upsilon
ι	Iota	$\phi\ \varphi$	Phi
$\kappa\ \varkappa$	Kappa	χ	Chi
λ	Lambda	ψ	Psi
μ	Mu	ω	Omega

Constellations shown: CETUS, AQUARIUS, FORNAX, SCULPTOR, PHOENIX, HOROLOGIUM, ERIDANUS, GRUS

ATLAS CHART 34. NGC 1300 Left of the center of the chart, near the border between Fornax and Eridanus, is the Fornax Cluster of galaxies. The cluster consists of a number of faint galaxies as well as 18 bright ones. Nine of these bright galaxies can be seen in the same 1° field of view.

NGC 1316, an elliptical or S0 galaxy at a distance of about 55 million light-years, is the brightest member of the group. It has been identified as the radio source Fornax A and may be undergoing some type of nuclear outburst. Its companion galaxy, NGC 1317, is a spiral with a bright nucleus.

NGC 1365, the second brightest galaxy of the Fornax Cluster, is an excellent example of a barred spiral galaxy. Its central bar extends about 45,000 light-years and appears to be about 3° long.

Near 3^h20^m −20° is NGC 1300, the prototype of a barred spiral galaxy with moderately wide arms (called SBb).

Just to the right of the chart's center, southwest of β (beta) Fornacis, is the globular cluster NGC 1049. It is part of the Fornax System, a faint dwarf galaxy that is a member of our Local Group of galaxies. The system contains five groups of stars that somewhat resemble the globular clusters in our galaxy. The clusters in Fornax, though, differ in density, brightness, and size. For example, NGC 1049 (at 2^h40^m −34°) is 50 times larger than the largest globular cluster in our galaxy. It is 630,000 light-years away.

θ (theta) Eri (at 2^h58^m −40°) is a wide double that can be resolved with binoculars. Its components are bright, of magnitudes 3.4 and 4.5. The double star f Eri (at 3^h48^m −38°) has widely spaced components of magnitudes 4.8 and 5.3.

Fig. 7-31 NGC 1300, a typical barred spiral galaxy with moderately wide arms (type SBb) in Eridanus. (Palomar Observatory photo)

ERIDANUS

CETUS

FORNAX

SCULPTOR

CAELUM

ERIDANUS

PHOENIX

DORADO

RETICULUM

HOROLOGIUM

PICTOR

MAP FROM 'SKY ATLAS 2000.0' BY WIL TIRION

MAGNITUDES				
◯	> -0.4			
◯	-0.4 - +0.5			
◯	0.6 - 1.5			
●	1.6 - 2.5			
●	2.6 - 3.5			
•	3.6 - 4.5			
·	4.6 - 5.5			
·	5.6 - 6.5			
·	6.6 - 7.5			

| DOUBLE or MULTIPLE | ●— |
| VARIABLE | ◉ ◯ |

OPEN CLUSTERS	◌ ◌ ◌ ◌
	>10' TO SCALE <10'
GLOBULAR CLUSTERS	⊕ ⊕ ⊕
	>10' 5-10' <5'
PLANETARY NEBULAE	-◇- -◇- -◇-
	>1' 0.5'-1' <0.5'
BRIGHT DIFFUSE NEB.	▭ □
	>10' TO SCALE <10'
GALAXIES	◯ ◯ ◯ ◦
	>30' 20'-30' 10'-20' <10'

QUASAR	△
PULSAR	☆
BLACK HOLE	⌐
MILKY WAY	〰
GALACTIC EQUATOR	—·—·—
	70° +
ECLIPTIC	———————
	100°
CONSTELLATION BOUNDARIES	⌐ ⌐

GREEK ALPHABET			
α	Alpha	ν	Nu
β	Beta	ξ	Xi
γ	Gamma	o	Omicron
δ	Delta	π	Pi
ε	Epsilon	ρ	Rho
ζ	Zeta	σ	Sigma
η	Eta	τ	Tau
θ ϑ	Theta	υ	Upsilon
ι	Iota	φ φ	Phi
κ ϰ	Kappa	χ	Chi
λ	Lambda	ψ	Psi
μ	Mu	ω	Omega

ATLAS CHART 35. M79, Lepus, Columba, Caelum, Eridanus In the constellation Lepus, the Hare, we find M79 (NGC 1904), one of the few globular clusters visible during the winter. Under good conditions it can be detected even with binoculars. M79 is not very impressive with small or medium-sized telescopes; only larger instruments begin to resolve its edges into their component stars. Located near 5^h24^m –25°, M79 forms an isosceles triangle with β (beta) Lep and ε (epsilon) Lep. M79 is an 8th-magnitude cluster about 3 arc min in diameter and lies about 50,000 light-years away.

In the constellation Columba, the Dove, about 1° east of α (alpha) Col, is the 12th-magnitude spiral galaxy NGC 2090. Because of its extreme southern declination, NGC 2090 is difficult for northern-hemisphere observers to find; it can be glimpsed only when the sky about the southern horizon is exceptionally clear. If you can find NGC 2090, try to find the brighter spiral NGC 1792, which lies even farther south. NGC 1792 lies on the border of Columba and Caelum, about 3° south and slightly east of the 4.6-magnitude star γ (gamma) Caeli.

Further south of NGC 1792, near 5^h14^m –40° in Columba, the globular cluster NGC 1851 is barely visible to the eye but is an interesting object through a telescope.

Among the double stars visible in this region, γ (gamma) Lep is an easily resolved double that offers a nice color contrast even in small telescopes. Its components are magnitudes 3.7 and 6.3, separated by 95 arc sec.

About $1/2$° to the southwest of M79 is ADS 3954, a double star with components of magnitudes 5.4 and 6.6, separated by 3.2 arc sec. This double can be resolved with small telescopes.

μ (mu) Columbae is a well-known "runaway star" that seems to be moving at high speed—for a star in our galaxy—away from the Orion Molecular Cloud, the star nursery that lies behind the Orion Nebula. Two similar hot stars are known. All three lie at the same distance from the Orion Molecular Cloud, where infrared and radio studies have found stars in formation (see p. 30). The hot stars may have been ejected from that region during the last few million years.

Fig. 7-32. Lepus, the Hare, from the atlas of Bayer (1603). (Jay M. Pasachoff)

Star chart showing constellations: LEPUS, ERIDANUS, CAELUM, FORNAX, COLUMBA, CMA, PUPPIS, HOROLOGIUM, PICTOR, CARINA, DORADO, RETICULUM

Coordinate markers: 6h, 40m, 24, 20m, 5h, RX, 40m, 20m, 23, 4h
-15°, -20°, -25°, -30°, W, -35°, 34, -40°, -45°, -50°, 46
40m, 47, 6h, γ, 40m, 20m, 5h, 40m, 20m, 4h, 40m, 46

Selected labels: θ, η, ζ, µ, R, SS, 2017, α, δ, β, ε, 1964, γ, LEPUS, T, M79, ADS.3954, 2179, 2196, 2139, S, 1744, DM 1540, 1521, 1518, τ6, T, τ7, τ8, τ9, ν1, ν2, ζ, ERIDANUS, ν1, ν2, σ, ϱ, 1425, 1406, 1537, 1531, 1532, ν3, ν4, FORNAX, µ, λ2090, α, 1800, o, γ, CAELUM, β, R, 1380, 1379, 1381, 1387, 1389, 1386, ε, o, 1808, 1792, 2005, 1427, 1400, 1406, 1437, CMA, δ, κ, 2185, γ, β, ξ, COLUMBA, ϑ, 1851, ν, λ, α, QQ.020-388, QQ.347-383, α, δ, 1487, 1512, HOROLOGIUM, 1411, 2035, 1448, ϑ, 1493, π2, π1, η, β, PUPPIS, G, S, η1, η2, PICTOR, ζ, 1527, 1433, 1494, R, ϑ, λ, β, γ, 1705, ι, DORADO, 1954, 1933, α, Canopus, CARINA, δ, 1617, 1596, 1566, 1549, 1515, RETICULUM, 1249, γ, W

OM "SKY ATLAS 2000.0" BY WIL TIRION

ATLAS CHART 36. Sirius, M93, M41, Canis Major, Puppis In the winter Milky Way, many beautiful star fields are visible low in the southern sky. In particular, Canis Major and Puppis are worth sweeping with a telescope or binoculars.

The open cluster M41 (NGC 2287) is one of the finest in the sky, located near 6^h47^m $-21°$, about 4° south of Sirius in Canis Major. At magnitude 4.5 it is sometimes visible with the naked eye. M41 is a good object for viewing with binoculars and is easy to resolve with medium power. It is a fairly rich cluster, with about 25 bright stars and many fainter ones in a field about the size of the full moon.

A second open cluster suitable for viewing with a low-power telescope is M93 (NGC 2447), about 2° northwest of 3rd-magnitude ξ (xi) Pup, near the galactic equator at 7^h45^m $-24°$. M93 lies in a dense star field at a distance of about 3300 light-years. It is a very rich cluster, with about 300 component stars. About 2° on the other side of ξ Pup is the diffuse nebula NGC 2467.

A third outstanding open cluster in this region is NGC 2477, located 15° south of M93 in Puppis, near 7^h52^m $-39°$. It is rich and compact, with about 300 stars in a field 20 arc min across.

ε (epsilon) Canis Majoris lies above the center of the chart, near 7^h $-29°$. Its 7th-magnitude companion is about 7 arc sec away.

Northeast, near τ (tau) CMa, is the variable star UW CMa, near 7^h19^m $-25°$. About 5° to the east, the double star n Pup has two widely-separated components of almost equal magnitude.

k Pup, near 7^h39^m $-27°$, is a bright double easily resolved with small telescopes. Its bluish components are about magnitudes 4.5 and 4.6, separated by 9.8 arc sec. Near 7^h29^m $-43°$, σ (sigma) Pup is a double with orange and white components of magnitudes 3.3 and 9.4, separated by 22.4 arc sec.

About 3° southwest of σ Pup, near 7^h14^m $-45°$, L^2 Pup is one of the brightest red variables. Since its minimum brightness is about 6th magnitude, L^2 Pup is visible to the naked eye during most of its cycle. Another variable star visible to the naked eye is V Pup, about 3° southwest of γ (gamma) Velorum. V Pup is an eclipsing variable, ranging in magnitude from 4.7 to 5.2.

Fig. 7-33 Canis Major, the Big Dog, from the star atlas of Bayer (1603). (Jay M. Pasachoff)

MAGNITUDES		OPEN CLUSTERS				QUASAR		GREEK ALPHABET			
	>-0.4		>10'	TO SCALE	<10'			α	Alpha	ν	Nu
	-0.4 - +0.5					PULSAR		β	Beta	ξ	Xi
	0.6 - 1.5	GLOBULAR CLUSTERS				BLACK HOLE		γ	Gamma	ο	Omicron
	1.6 - 2.5		>10'	5-10'	<5'	MILKY WAY		δ	Delta	π	Pi
	2.6 - 3.5							ε	Epsilon	ϱ	Rho
	3.6 - 4.5	PLANETARY NEBULAE				GALACTIC EQUATOR		ζ	Zeta	σ	Sigma
	4.6 - 5.5		>1'	0.5-1'	<0.5'			η	Eta	τ	Tau
	5.6 - 6.5						70°	θ ϑ	Theta	υ	Upsilon
	6.6 - 7.5	BRIGHT DIFFUSE NEB.				ECLIPTIC		ι	Iota	φ φ	Phi
DOUBLE or			>10' TO SCALE		<10'		100°	κ ϰ	Kappa	χ	Chi
MULTIPLE						CONSTELLATION BOUNDARIES		λ	Lambda	ψ	Psi
VARIABLE		GALAXIES	>30'	20'-30' 10'-20'	<10'			μ	Mu	ω	Omega

ATLAS CHART 37. Gum Nebula In this region of the southern sky, we are looking toward the Milky Way along the galactic equator. Unlike other regions of the Milky Way, though, this region includes few interesting objects.

The Gum Nebula is too large to mark on the chart; it is a huge emission nebula that extends through the constellations Puppis and Vela over an area at least 35° in diameter. It is named after its discoverer, Colin Gum. The object that provides the energy for the central part of the nebula is probably PSR 0833–45 (the pulsar that also provides the energy for the x-ray source Vela X), near 8^h30^m –45°. The pulsar emits both radio and optical pulses with a period of 0.09 seconds, and lies about 1500 light-years distant.

ζ (zeta) Pup, left of 8^h at –40°, is a star of spectral type O, one of the hottest stars in the sky. About 5° north-northeast of ζ Pup, near 8^h12^m –35°, is the site where Nova Puppis 1942 erupted. One of the brightest novae in modern times, it rapidly reached a maximum of about 0.3 magnitude.

About 4° east-northeast of α (alpha) Pyxidis is T Pyx, near 9^h05^m –32°. T Pyx is one of the few recurrent novae. It is normally about 14th magnitude but may rise to magnitude 6.3 or 7 at maximum. More eruptions have been observed in this source than in any other. Its five maxima were recorded in 1890, 1902, 1920, 1944, and 1966. Given this average interval of 19 years, we might have expected another eruption in about 1985, but as of 1991, none had occurred. Check T Pyx regularly.

NGC 2997, a spiral galaxy in Antlia, is shown in Figure 5-49.

Fig. 7-34 A part of the Gum Nebula in Vela. (Bart Bok)

MAGNITUDES		OPEN CLUSTERS			QUASAR	△	GREEK ALPHABET			
●	>-0.4		>10' TO SCALE <10'		PULSAR	☆	α	Alpha	ν	Nu
●	-0.4 - +0.5				BLACK HOLE		β	Beta	ξ	Xi
●	0.6-1.5	GLOBULAR CLUSTERS	⊕ ⊕ ⊛		MILKY WAY		γ	Gamma	o	Omicron
●	1.6-2.5		>10' 5'-10' <5'				δ	Delta	π	Pi
●	2.6-3.5	PLANETARY NEBULAE	✧ ✧ ✧		GALACTIC EQUATOR		ε	Epsilon	ρ	Rho
•	3.6-4.5		>1' 0.5'-1' <0.5'				ζ	Zeta	σ	Sigma
•	4.6-5.5						η	Eta	τ	Tau
.	5.6-6.5	BRIGHT DIFFUSE NEB.			ECLIPTIC		θ ϑ	Theta	υ	Upsilon
.	6.6-7.5		>10' TO SCALE <10'				ι	Iota	φ φ	Phi
DOUBLE or MULTIPLE	●	GALAXIES	⬭ ○ ○ ⚬		CONSTELLATION BOUNDARIES		κ ϰ	Kappa	χ	Chi
			>30' 20'-30' 10'-20' <10'				λ	Lambda	ψ	Psi
VARIABLE	◎ ○						μ	Mu	ω	Omega

ATLAS CHART 38. NGC 3132 The number of stars in this area diminishes with increasing distance from the Milky Way. Antlia, the Water Pump, is one of the least interesting regions of the sky, both to the telescope and the naked eye. Hydra and the northern part of Centaurus also contain few noteworthy objects.

One notable object is NGC 3132, one of the few planetary nebulae visible in the spring, located right on the Vela/Antlia border, near 10^h07^m –40°. This planetary is about 8th magnitude in total brightness and has a bright central star of about 10th magnitude. It is nearly the same size as the Ring Nebula in Lyra. Though brighter than the Ring Nebula, NGC 3132 is harder to find and not as well known because of its southern declination and the lack of nearby stars to aid in finding it. One method for locating NGC 3132 is to wait for Regulus in Leo to reach your meridian and then point your telescope about 52° south.

NGC 3132 shows more detail than the Ring Nebula. On photographs, its elliptical disk looks as though several oval rings have been superimposed and tilted at different angles. Because of this appearance, it is sometimes called the Eight-Burst Nebula.

N Hydrae (ADS 8202), at 11^h32^m –29°, is a wide pair of closely matched yellow stars of magnitudes 5.8 and 5.9. Another interesting double is β (beta) Hya (at 11^h53^m –34°). Its components of magnitudes 4.7 and 5.5 can be resolved in a medium-sized telescope.

Fig. 7-35 Centaurus, the Centaur (drawn backwards), from the star atlas of Bayer (1603). (Jay M. Pasachoff)

8

12 h · 27 · 40m · 20m · 11 h · 40m · 20m · 10 h

CRATER

CORVUS

HYDRA

ANTLIA

CENTAURUS

VELA

FROM "SKY ATLAS 2000.0" BY WIL TIRION

40m · 20m · 49 · 12h · 40m · 20m · 11h · 40m · 20m · 10h · 48

W

26

37

ATLAS CHART 39. Omega Centauri, M83, NGC 5128 Here we find one of the most spectacular objects within range of amateur telescopes: NGC 5139, ω (omega) Centauri, one of the brightest and largest globular clusters. Its apparent diameter is about the size of the full moon. Because it is so far south of the celestial equator, ω Cen is visible in the U.S. only from the southernmost states. Observers there can sometimes detect it low on the horizon on clear spring and summer evenings, about 36° almost due south of Spica, near 13^h27^m –47°. Binoculars may help you find it. To the naked eye, ω Cen looks like a fuzzy 4th-magnitude star. Through small telescopes or binoculars, it looks like a hazy patch (Fig. 7-36, p. 290). The cluster contains over one million stars. To locate it from a southern site, find ε Cen 7° northwest of β Cen, and then note that ε, ζ, and ω form an isosceles triangle.

An outstanding galaxy in the summer sky is the spiral M83 (NGC 5236), near 13^h37^m –30° on the Hydra/Centaurus border, about 18° south of Spica and nearly halfway between γ (gamma) Hya and θ (theta) Cen. A spiral seen face-on (Fig. 5-39), it is one of the 10 largest galaxies and one of the 25 brightest. M83 is hard for northern observers to see because it lies very low in the southern sky, in a field rich with star clouds and dust.

About 3° south of M83 is NGC 5253, another bright galaxy. A medium-sized telescope shows it as an oval with a bright center. Two of the brightest extragalactic supernovae ever recorded erupted in this galaxy. The first, in 1895, reached magnitude 7.2; another, in 1972, reached magnitude 7.9.

Perhaps the most famous galaxy in this field is NGC 5128, located at 13^h25^m –43°, about $4^1/_2$° north of ω Cen. NGC 5128 is a giant peculiar galaxy, one of the largest and most luminous galaxies known. It looks like a glowing sphere of 7th magnitude crossed by a thick dust lane (Fig. 5-50) and shows well in medium-sized telescopes and sometimes in good binoculars. A jet of gas extends from the galaxy's center. NGC 5128 has been identified as the powerful radio source Centaurus A. Both the jet of gas and the radio waves and x-rays may result from matter falling into a giant black hole at the galaxy's center.

The globular cluster M68 (NGC 4590) is relatively bright even though it is small and highly concentrated. It is located at 12^h40^m –27° near ADS 8612, a 5th-magnitude double star slightly to the southwest—the only nearby star visible to the naked eye. M68 appears as a fuzzy glowing ball of 8th magnitude, about 3 arc min across. To locate it, sweep with binoculars from δ (delta) Crv through β (beta) Crv and continue about 4° farther south. NGC 5367 is a nebula with an embedded open cluster.

R Hya is a notable long-period variable about 3° east of γ Hya, at 13^h30^m –23°. The third long-period variable discovered, R Hya is one of the easiest to observe. It ranges from magnitude 3 to 11 with a period of 390 days and is noted for its deep red color.

MAGNITUDES

- >-0.4
- -0.4 - +0.5
- 0.6 - 1.5
- 1.6 - 2.5
- 2.6 - 3.5
- 3.6 - 4.5
- 4.6 - 5.5
- 5.6 - 6.5
- 6.6 - 7.5

DOUBLE or MULTIPLE

VARIABLE

OPEN CLUSTERS			
	>10'	TO SCALE	<10'

GLOBULAR CLUSTERS			
	⊕ >10'	⊕ 5-10'	• <5'

PLANETARY NEBULAE			
	>1'	0.5'-1'	<0.5'

BRIGHT DIFFUSE NEB.
>10' TO SCALE <10'

GALAXIES
> 30' 20'-30' 10'-20' <10'

QUASAR △

PULSAR ✷

BLACK HOLE ⅄

MILKY WAY

GALACTIC EQUATOR
70°

ECLIPTIC
100°

CONSTELLATION BOUNDARIES

GREEK ALPHABET

α	Alpha	ν	Nu
β	Beta	ξ	Xi
γ	Gamma	ο	Omicron
δ	Delta	π	Pi
ε	Epsilon	ϱ	Rho
ζ	Zeta	σ	Sigma
η	Eta	τ	Tau
θ ϑ	Theta	υ	Upsilon
ι	Iota	φ ϕ	Phi
κ ϰ	Kappa	χ	Chi
λ	Lambda	ψ	Psi
μ	Mu	ω	Omega

Constellations labeled: VIRGO, CORVUS, CRATER, HYDRA, CENTAURUS, LUPUS, CRUX

ATLAS CHART 40. Centaurus, Lupus, Libra Few interesting objects lie in this area of the southern sky, which is dominated by sparse regions in Centaurus, Lupus, and Libra. We discussed the globular cluster ω Centauri with Atlas Chart 39.

The globular cluster NGC 5694 is located in the upper right-hand part of the chart, at the eastern tip of the tail of Hydra, almost halfway between σ (sigma) Lup and π (pi) Hya, near 14^h40^m $-27°$. NGC 5694 is difficult to resolve because of its small apparent diameter. Its total magnitude is 10.2, though none of its 10 brightest stars is brighter than about 16th magnitude. Lying about 100,000 light-years away, on the far side of our galaxy, NGC 5694 is one of the most distant globular clusters.

Toward the bottom of the chart, near 14^h08^m $-48°$, is the open cluster NGC 5460. Its total magnitude is 5.6, and none of its members is brighter than 8th magnitude. Though sparse, this cluster covers an area about the size of the full moon. NGC 5460 is best observed with a rich-field telescope or binoculars.

Though it is very hard to observe visually, an extended region of nebulosity can be detected in Scorpius, between δ (delta) and π (pi) Sco. δ Sco is an extremely hot star, spectral type B0. It lies about 540 light-years away and is one of the brighter members of the Scorpio-Centaurus Association. The Scorpio-Centaurus Association is a scattered group of stars that extends over 90° of the southern sky and includes many of the brighter stars in the constellations Scorpius, Lupus, Centaurus, and Crux. This group of stars is part of a larger group of about 100 stars often called the Local Star Cloud, located in one of the spiral arms in our galaxy. Typically, the stars in the group are spectral type B, about 20 million years old. The reddish Antares, α (alpha) Sco, about 7° southeast of δ Sco (Atlas Chart 41), is the brightest member of this group.

Many double stars lie in the constellation Lupus. One of these is π (pi) Lupi (near 15^h05^m $-47°$), with components of magnitudes 4.1 and 6.0. ε (epsilon) Lup, east of λ (lambda) Lup, near 15^h23^m $-45°$, can be resolved with a medium-sized telescope. κ (kappa) Lup, southeast of π Lup, near 15^h12^m $-49°$, is a very wide pair, of magnitudes 4.6 and 4.7. ξ (xi) Lup, northeast in Lupus, near 15^h57^m $-34°$, is a wide double, with stars of magnitudes 5.3 and 5.8.

Fig. 7-36 ω (omega) Centauri, one of the largest, brightest globular clusters (Atlas Chart 39). (© 1974 Anglo-Australian Telescope Board)

ED FROM "SKY ATLAS 2000.0" BY WIL TIRION

MAGNITUDES		OPEN CLUSTERS				QUASAR	△	GREEK ALPHABET			
⬤	>-0.4		>10'	TO SCALE	<10'	PULSAR	✳	α Alpha		ν Nu	
⬤	-0.4 - -0.5					BLACK HOLE	⌇	β Beta		ξ Xi	
⬤	0.6-1.5	GLOBULAR CLUSTERS	⊕	⊕	⊕	MILKY WAY		γ Gamma		ο Omicron	
⬤	1.6-2.5		>10'	5'-10'	<5'			δ Delta		π Pi	
⬤	2.6-3.5	PLANETARY NEBULAE	✧	✧	✦	GALACTIC EQUATOR		ε Epsilon		ϱ Rho	
•	3.6-4.5		>1'	0.5'-1'	<0.5'			ζ Zeta		σ Sigma	
•	4.6-5.5					------ 70°		η Eta		τ Tau	
•	5.6-6.5	BRIGHT DIFFUSE NEB.			▢	ECLIPTIC		θ ϑ Theta		υ Upsilon	
·	6.6-7.5		>10' TO SCALE		<10'	------ 100°		ι Iota		φ φ Phi	
								κ ϰ Kappa		χ Chi	
DOUBLE or MULTIPLE	•-•	GALAXIES	⬭	○	○	CONSTELLATION BOUNDARIES		λ Lambda		ψ Psi	
VARIABLE	◎ ○		>30'	20'-30'	10'-20' <10'			μ Mu		ω Omega	

ATLAS CHART 41. Antares, Southern Milky Way One of the most exciting regions of the entire sky, this area offers outstanding sights for summer observers. Brilliant star fields lie among the dark clouds and winding dust lanes of the Milky Way, and many open and globular clusters are present. First sweep the area with binoculars or a telescope at low power and then switch to higher magnifications for individual objects.

A good starting point is the most prominent object in this region—Antares, α (alpha) Scorpii, near $16^h29^m -26°$. At magnitude 0.96, the reddish Antares (its name means "compared to Mars," the reddish planet) is the 15th-brightest star. It becomes visible in midspring or early summer in the southeastern sky. IC 4606, a reddish nebula about 5 light-years in diameter, surrounds Antares (Fig. 5-20). IC 4604, a reflection nebula around ρ (rho) Ophiuchi, about 3° north-northwest of Antares, is too faint for visual observations but shows up as a rich bluish-purple cloud in long-exposure photographs through large telescopes. In between, IC 4603 is a reflection nebula around a fainter star.

Less than 2° due west of Antares is M4 (NGC 6121), one of the largest and nearest globular clusters. At 6th magnitude, M4 is visible with binoculars and can sometimes be detected with the naked eye. M4 is one of the easiest globular clusters to locate. Because of its very loose structure, small telescopes can resolve its edges and medium-sized telescopes under high power can completely resolve its stars.

Less than 1° northeast of M4 in the same field is NGC 6144, a smaller and fainter globular cluster. To observe this cluster, use high power.

A little over 4° northwest of Antares, sweep about halfway between Antares and β (beta) Sco to find M80 (NGC 6093), a globular cluster that looks smaller and brighter than M4. It lies on the western border of a dark cloud. Because M80 is very compact, it is much harder to resolve than M4.

About 8° east of Antares is M19 (NGC 6273), a compact globular cluster. To find M19, point at Antares, then sweep east and slightly north. Alternatively, point your telescope at Antares and wait about 33 minutes for M19 to drift into view. It is one of the most oval globular clusters, with an apparent diameter of 5 arc min and a magnitude of 7.2. Its outer edges can be easily resolved.

About 7° southeast of Antares and about 5° south of M19 is another pretty globular, M62 (NGC 6266). M62 is about the same size and slightly brighter than M19, though it looks round in a small telescope. However, M62 is one of the most asymmetrical clusters, as large telescopes show. Its nucleus lies southeast of the center of the cluster, making it look somewhat like a comet.

Slightly east and about $1^1/2°$ north of M19 is NGC 6284, a small, bright globular cluster that looks like a 9th-magnitude star in a medium telescope. The 8th-magnitude globular cluster NGC 6293 can be found about $1^3/4°$ east-southeast of M19.

FROM "SKY ATLAS 2000.0" BY WIL TIRION

MAGNITUDES		OPEN CLUSTERS				QUASAR	△	GREEK ALPHABET			
●	>-0.4		○ ○ ○	⋄				α Alpha		ν Nu	
			>10' TO SCALE <10'			PULSAR	☆	β Beta		ξ Xi	
●	-0.4-+0.5							γ Gamma		ο Omicron	
●	0.6-1.5	GLOBULAR CLUSTERS	⊕	⊕	⊛	BLACK HOLE	Y	δ Delta		π Pi	
●	1.6-2.5		>10'	5'-10'	<5'	MILKY WAY		ε Epsilon		ϱ Rho	
●	2.6-3.5							ζ Zeta		σ Sigma	
•	3.6-4.5	PLANETARY NEBULAE	⋄	⋄	⋄	GALACTIC EQUATOR		η Eta		τ Tau	
•	4.6-5.5		>1'	0.5'-1'	<0.5'		70°	θ ϑ Theta		υ Upsilon	
•	5.6-6.5						┼	ι Iota		φ φ Phi	
•	6.6-7.5	BRIGHT DIFFUSE NEB.			▢	ECLIPTIC		κ ϰ Kappa		χ Chi	
			>10' TO SCALE		<10'		100°	λ Lambda		ψ Psi	
DOUBLE or MULTIPLE	●–●							μ Mu		ω Omega	
VARIABLE	◎ ○	GALAXIES	◯	○	○	○	CONSTELLATION BOUNDARIES				
			>30'	20'-30'	10'-20'	<10'					

East of Antares and north of M19, the southern part of Ophiuchus is one of the most striking regions of the Milky Way, with a vast expanse of dark nebulae lit by bright stars. Here we are looking through the spiral arms of our galaxy toward the galactic center. A good star to help you orient yourself in this area is θ (theta) Ophiuchi, a 3rd-magnitude star near 17^h22^m $-25°$. About 2° east and below θ Oph, the huge Pipe Nebula extends about 7°. It is readily visible to the naked eye and is one of the largest dark clouds in the Milky Way. Absorption from the Pipe Nebula obscures the stars in an area several degrees across.

For northern-hemisphere observers, the finest portions of the Milky Way lie in Sagittarius. Moonless nights in the summer are ideal for sweeping the region with binoculars or viewing with medium-sized telescopes. The brightest part is the Great Sagittarius Star Cloud, just north of γ (gamma) Sgr. Farther west, star clouds are obscured by the Great Rift, which marks the equatorial plane of our galaxy. In this region, we are looking directly toward the center of our galaxy (the *galactic center*), about 30,000 light-years from earth. The galactic center is hidden from our optical view by interstellar dust and dark nebulae. It lies about $1\frac{1}{2}°$ southwest of the 4th-magnitude Cepheid variable X Sgr, a foreground object. The galactic center can be detected as part of the radio source Sgr A. Infrared, x-rays, and gamma rays from the galactic center also penetrate the absorbing dust, providing ways to study this part of our galaxy, which may contain a giant black hole.

About $2\frac{1}{2}°$ north and slightly west of γ (gamma) Sgr is one of the few dark nebulae that can be seen in amateur telescopes.

Farther southwest along the galactic equator in Scorpius, M6 (NGC 6405) and M7 (NGC 6475) are two large bright open clusters, both beautiful in small telescopes. Looking somewhat like the Pleiades, M6 (at 17^h40^m $-32°$) has a total magnitude brighter than 4, and contains many stars between 8th and 12th magnitude. Even a small telescope resolves M6 into its member stars.

Easily located about 3° southeast of M6, near 17^h50^m $-35°$, M7 is a brilliant cluster of 3rd magnitude, sometimes visible to the naked eye on a dark night. To the naked eye, M7 looks like a hazy glow with a rich star cloud in the background. It is one of the few open clusters that look impressive in binoculars. Medium-sized tele-

Fig. 7-37 Two globular clusters, NGC 6522 and NGC 6528, close to each other in Sagittarius at 18^h02^m and 18^h03^m, respectively, and $-30°$. (National Optical Astronomy Observatories/KPNO)

Fig. 7-38 The Milky Way in Sagittarius and Scorpius. (Harvard College Observatory)

scopes with higher power completely resolve the cluster. M7 is much larger than M6, with many stars from 6th to 8th magnitude. On the northwest edge of M7 is the globular cluster NGC 6453, visible in the same field of view under low power.

Still farther southwest—near the galactic equator at $16^h55^m -41°$, about $1/2°$ north of ζ (zeta) Sco—is NGC 6231 (Fig. 5-17), another fine open cluster (though it is unfavorably located for northern-hemisphere observers). Under good conditions, it can be seen with the naked eye by observers who are far enough south; it looks like a miniature version of the Pleiades because of its central group of seven or so brilliant white stars. NGC 6231 lies about 6000 light-years away; if it were as close to us as the Pleiades, it would look almost the same size but would be about 50 times brighter.

NGC 6231 appears to be the center of a large group of bright stars of spectral types O and B. About 1° north and slightly east of NGC 6231 lies H12, the richest part of this group, with about 200 stars. A small telescope shows the stars of H12 as a trail extending northeast from NGC 6231, ending in a bright nebulous region. This extended group of stars marks one of the spiral arms of our galaxy, which lies over 5000 light-years from us—closer to the galactic center than the arm that contains our sun. IC 4628 is a faint nebula about $1 1/2°$ north of NGC 6231. A much larger loop of nebulosity about 300 light-years in diameter circles this entire association of stars in a giant irregular ring about 4° wide. The nebula is one of the giant regions of glowing hydrogen that outline the spiral arms in our own galaxy and other spirals.

Other open clusters in this region include: NGC 6242, a compact cluster about 1° north of H12; NGC 6281, about $2 1/2°$ further to the northeast, a compact and elongated cluster; NGC 6124, a rich cluster about 6° west of H12 near $16^h25^m -41°$; and NGC 6193, a large cluster located about 7° south-southwest of ζ (zeta) Sco.

The remnant of the supernova that Kepler saw as a nova in 1604 is at upper left, $17^h40^m -18°$. It is faint even in photographs.

ATLAS CHART 42. Lagoon Nebula, Trifid Nebula In this region we are still looking toward the center of our galaxy from our vantage point more than halfway out on an outer spiral arm. Moonless nights in July are best for viewing the bright star clouds, open and globular clusters, and curious nebulae (Fig. 5-21) in this area of the Milky Way, visible low above the southern horizon. Sagittarius is located by its "Teapot" of stars: σ, τ, ζ, and φ make its handle; to the southwest δ, γ, and ε make the spout; and λ marks the top.

γ (gamma) Sgr marks the top of the Archer's arrow in the figure of Sagittarius, on the right-hand side of the chart near 18^{h}06^m –30°. North and west of γ Sgr, just off the mainstream of the Milky Way near 18^{h}02^m –23°, are two outstanding emission nebulae—the Lagoon Nebula and the Trifid Nebula. Both are about 2500 light-years away and, like M42 (the Orion Nebula), get their energy from ultraviolet radiation from young, hot stars in their midst.

M8 (NGC 6523), the Lagoon Nebula, is the more spectacular of the two, visible to the naked eye as a cometlike glow. It is an irregular nebula about the size of the full moon, crossed by a broad absorbing band of dust that gives the nebula its name (Fig. 5-22). Smaller dust clouds can also be seen. Because of the nebula's great extent, it is best viewed with a wide-field eyepiece. The Lagoon Nebula contains dust and gas clouds where new stars form and a region of glowing hydrogen resulting from the presence of the hot stars that can be seen in its midst. The eastern half of the nebula contains the prominent star cluster NGC 6530, a scattered open cluster about 10 arc min in diameter. It is one of the youngest clusters known, not more than a few million years old, and includes several T Tauri stars (variable stars with irregular fluctuations, indicating that they have not yet settled down to a regular existence).

About 1½° north-northwest of the Lagoon Nebula is M20 (NGC 6514), the Trifid Nebula. The lower part of the Trifid is a diffuse emission nebula. In photographs we see the reddish radiation from the cloud of glowing hydrogen, which is divided into three parts by dust lanes (Fig. 5-24). Where the three dark lanes overlap, we find a central triple star. These lanes are fairly easy to detect with a medium-sized telescope at medium power. The bluish upper part of M20, unconnected to the lower part, is a reflection nebula.

M21 is a small, rich open cluster of magnitude 5.9, located in the same low-power field as M20 (the Trifid). About 1° southeast of M8 (the Lagoon) is NGC 6544—a small, very remote globular cluster that is difficult to find. One degree farther southeast is NGC 6553, another globular cluster; it is very difficult to resolve in part because thick obscuring dust dims it by about 6 magnitudes. About 1½° east-northeast of M8 are several irregular nebulae, possibly connected to the Lagoon Nebula by a faint gaseous haze.

λ (lambda) Sgr, a few degrees to the east of M8 near 18^{h}28^m –25°, also lies in a rich field. M22 (NGC 6656) is an impressive globular cluster, 2° northeast of λ Sgr, near 18^{h}36^m –24°. At 5th magnitude, M22 is the third brightest and most easily resolved globular cluster in the sky. Its only equal in the northern sky is M13, the Hercules

FROM "SKY ATLAS 2000.0" BY WIL TIRION

MAGNITUDES

●	>-0·4
●	-0·4—0·5
●	0·6—1·5
●	1·6—2·5
●	2·6—3·5
•	3·6—4·5
·	4·6—5·5
·	5·6—6·5
·	6·6—7·5

●● DOUBLE or MULTIPLE

◉○ VARIABLE

OPEN CLUSTERS ○ ○ ○ ⊙
>10′ TO SCALE <10′

GLOBULAR CLUSTERS ⊕ ⊕ ⊙
>10′ 5–10′ <5′

PLANETARY NEBULAE ◇ ◇ ◇
>1′ 0·5–1′ <0·5′

BRIGHT DIFFUSE NEB. ▭ □
>10′ TO SCALE <10′

GALAXIES ⬭ ○ ○ ○
>30′ 20′–30′ 10′–20′ <10′

QUASAR △

PULSAR ⵦ

BLACK HOLE ⵦ

MILKY WAY 〰

GALACTIC EQUATOR ⌐ 70°

ECLIPTIC ⵦ 100°

CONSTELLATION BOUNDARIES ⌐⌐

GREEK ALPHABET

α	Alpha	ν	Nu
β	Beta	ξ	Xi
γ	Gamma	ο	Omicron
δ	Delta	π	Pi
ε	Epsilon	ϱ	Rho
ζ	Zeta	σ	Sigma
η	Eta	τ	Tau
θ ϑ	Theta	υ	Upsilon
ι	Iota	φ φ	Phi
κ ϰ	Kappa	χ	Chi
λ	Lambda	ψ	Psi
μ	Mu	ω	Omega

Fig. 7-39 *(left)* The Lagoon Nebula, M8 (NGC 6523), in Sagittarius. The shorter exposure, **Fig. 7-40** *(right)*, shows the "hourglass" structure near its center. (Lick Observatory photos)

Cluster (see Atlas Chart 17). M22's brightest stars are 11th magnitude, and it has a total population of at least half a million stars. It is one of the nearest globular clusters, only about 9600 light-years away. Since it is less than 1° from the ecliptic, we can sometimes see a planet in the same field.

About 1° west-northwest of M22 is NGC 6642, a small, faint globular cluster that looks like a hazy spot.

Slightly northwest of λ (lambda) Sgr, at 18^h24^m –25° in the same low-power field, is M28 (NGC 6626), a bright globular cluster that looks like a star in a rich star background. It is one of the more compact globulars, not very striking in a medium-sized telescope because it is hard to resolve. Slightly closer on the east side of λ Sgr is NGC 6638, a small, remote globular cluster that is difficult to resolve.

About 5° southwest of λ Sgr is δ (delta) Sgr, with the faint globular cluster NGC 6624 located slightly to the southeast. About 3° southeast of δ and about $2^1/2$° northeast of ε (epsilon) Sgr, near 18^h30^m –32°, is M69 (NGC 6637), a small, 8th-magnitude globular cluster resolved only with large telescopes. About 2° east of M69 and almost halfway between ζ (zeta) and ε Sgr is the globular cluster M70 (NGC 6681), similar in size and brightness to M69. A third, smaller globular cluster is NGC 6652, about 1° southeast of M69. All three globular clusters look like bright stars in a uniformly rich star field and lie on the far side of our galaxy.

Northeast of M70 and about 2° southwest of ζ Sgr, near 18^h55^m –31°, is M54 (NGC 6715), a small, bright globular cluster of 8th magnitude. Because M54 is highly concentrated, though, only large telescopes begin to resolve it.

About $7\tfrac{1}{2}°$ south of ζ Sgr is a field of bright and dark nebulae and obscuring dust in Corona Australis. NGC 6726–27 is the brightest part of the field. Slightly southeast is the reflection nebula NGC 6729, whose variations in brightness follow the variations of its illuminating star, R CrA.

Farther east in Sagittarius the richness of the star fields diminishes rapidly. Sweeping through this region does reveal one noteworthy globular cluster, M55 (NGC 6809), near 19^h40^m –31°, about 7° east from ζ Sgr and slightly to the south. Readily visible to the naked eye, M55 looks like a hazy star; in a small telescope it looks like a circular glow about 10 arc min in diameter. Since M55 appears so low in the sky to northern observers, it is difficult to resolve when viewed from northern latitudes.

Fig. 7-41 Sagittarius, the Archer, from the star atlas of Hevelius (1690). It is drawn backwards from its appearance in the sky because Hevelius drew the celestial sphere as it would appear on a star globe seen from the outside.

ATLAS CHART 43. Capricornus In the rather barren area near the borders of Capricornus and Sagittarius, it is easy to locate M75 (NGC 6864), near 20^h06^m $-22°$ and less than 7° southwest of β (beta) Cap (drawn above the top border of the chart). M75 is a small, rich globular cluster of 8th magnitude, bright enough to be readily visible in good binoculars when it is low in the southern sky on clear August nights. Since it is one of the most compact globular clusters, it can be resolved only in telescopes of fairly large aperture. M75 lies on the far side of our galaxy, about 95,000 light-years away.

The most prominent globular cluster in Capricorn is M30 (NGC 7099), found on the top left side of this chart. It is easily found with binoculars or small telescopes, about 4° southeast of ζ (zeta) Cap and slightly northwest of the 5th-magnitude star 41 Cap, near 21^h40^m $-23°$. Like M75, though, M30 is difficult to resolve even with larger telescopes because of its extremely compact center. It lies about 40,000 light-years away.

One of the farthest objects known in the universe, the quasar PKS 2000–330, is at the right middle of the chart. Because of the expansion of the universe, it is receding from us so rapidly that its spectral lines are redshifted by 3.7 times (370% of) their original wavelengths. That puts this quasar over 12 billion light-years away, which means that we are seeing it as it was 12 billion years ago.

Fig. 7-42 Capricornus, the Goat (drawn backwards), from the star atlas of Hevelius (1690).

MAGNITUDES		OPEN CLUSTERS				QUASAR	△	GREEK ALPHABET			
●	>-0.4	○	○	○	◌			α Alpha		ν Nu	
●	-0.4--0.5		>10' TO SCALE		<10'	PULSAR	☆	β Beta		ξ Xi	
●	0.6-1.5	GLOBULAR CLUSTERS	⊕	⊕	⊛	BLACK HOLE	Y	γ Gamma		o Omicron	
●	1.6-2.5		>10'	5'-10'	<5'	MILKY WAY	〰	δ Delta		π Pi	
●	2.6-3.5							ε Epsilon		ϱ Rho	
●	3.6-4.5	PLANETARY NEBULAE	◇	◇	◇			ζ Zeta		σ Sigma	
●	4.6-5.5		>1'	0.5'-1'	<0.5'	GALACTIC EQUATOR		η Eta		τ Tau	
●	5.6-6.5							θ ϑ Theta		υ Upsilon	
●	6.6-7.5	BRIGHT DIFFUSE NEB.	⬭		▫	ECLIPTIC		ι Iota		φ φ Phi	
			>10' TO SCALE		<10'			κ ϰ Kappa		χ Chi	
DOUBLE or TRIPLE	●—					CONSTELLATION BOUNDARIES		λ Lambda		ψ Psi	
VARIABLE	◎ ○	GALAXIES	⬭	○	○			μ Mu		ω Omega	

ATLAS CHART 44. Fomalhaut, Helix Nebula This region is uninteresting except for α (alpha) Piscis Austrini, a bright white star whose brilliance is intensified by the comparative darkness of the starless background. α PsA is also called Fomalhaut, a name derived from the Arabic for "mouth of the fish." At magnitude 1.16, Fomalhaut is the 18th brightest star in the sky. To northern-hemisphere observers it is visible in autumn, low above the horizon in an empty region of the southern sky.

Though not readily visible to observers at northern latitudes, an interesting object in this region is the planetary nebula NGC 7293, near 22^h30^m −21° in Aquarius; find it by looking 21° south from ζ (zeta) Aqr. NGC 7293 is the Helix Nebula, a huge bubble of gas about $1\frac{1}{2}$ light-years in diameter surrounding a 13th-magnitude central star (Fig. 5-8 and below). A planetary results from the death of a star containing about as much mass as the sun. The Helix is the largest planetary, about $\frac{1}{2}$ the apparent diameter of the full moon. Although its total brightness is magnitude 6.5, its surface brightness is low because of its large size, making it difficult to detect except with low power on very dark nights. Even on the best nights, the nebula shows only as a faint, circular haze; little structure is visible except in larger telescopes and on long-exposure photographs (Figs. 5-8 and 7-43). To observe it, try the technique of averted vision: look not directly at the nebula but toward one side, which brings its image onto a more sensitive area of your retina.

The double star 41 Aqr lies several degrees west and slightly south of the Helix Nebula. Its contrasting components are magnitudes 5.6 and 7.1. Separated by 5.0 arc sec, the components can be resolved in small telescopes.

Southern constellations like Grus, the Crane, are relatively unfamiliar to most northern-hemisphere observers. θ (theta) Gru (at 23^h07^m −44°) is another double star that can be separated in a small telescope, with components of magnitudes 4.5 and 7.0.

In the constellation Phoenix, SX Phe, a dwarf Cepheid variable, lies about $7\frac{1}{2}$° west of α (alpha) Phe. SX was originally discovered as a star with large proper motion in 1938; it is about 400 light-years away. Its period is about 79 minutes, ranging in magnitude from about 6.8 to 7.5.

Fig. 7-43 The Helix Nebula (NGC 7293), a planetary nebula in Aquarius. See also Figure 5-8. (National Optical Astronomy Observatories/CTIO)

AQUARIUS

MR2251-178

7218○

7392○

g1
g2
v 7293
(Helix neb.)

CAP

41

7184

○7377

○7252

7314○

ε

7507○

Fomalhaut
α

7361○

λ

η

PISCIS AUSTRINUS

δ *γ* *β*

τ
μ
υ

7172○
7173-74-76

θ

7154
7135
I.5156

ι

I.5135

SCULPTOR

○7755

μ

γ

○7793

S

x1

δ

ζ

θ

I.5271○

π

I.5332

7713○ *β*

I.5269

I.1459
I.5273○

7418
7421○

○I.5186

υ

7456○

○7410

ν *φ*

λ

γ

○7462

7599○7582
7590○
I.5325○

φ

7424
7412○

σ2 *π*
○7307

μ1

μ2

GRUS

ξ

MIC

7097○

○P7763

○SX

7744

7552○
7531○ *η*

I.5328

7496○

δ1
δ2
I.5267

7166○ 7162○

7070○
7079○
7107○

7070

θ

α

x

ε

θ

I.5240

π2 *π1*
I.5201○ 7232
7233

7213○ *β*

α

7119
R

○7099

MIC

New6

PHOENIX

κ2
λ1

τ

σ

I.5152
I.5152○ ○7196

τ3
τ2 *τ1*

ε

○S

7145○
7141○

7155○

○7124

70490

π

7690○

○*o*

ζ

η

○7168

INDUS

7689○

x

δ

○7JS4 *θ*

7090○

SKY ATLAS 2000.0 BY WIL TIRION

0h · 21 · R 40m · 20m · 23h · 40m · 20m · 32 · 22h
-15°
-20°
-25°
-30° W
-35° 43
-40°
-45°
-50°
40m · 20m · 45 · 0h · 40m · 20m · 23h · 40m · 20m · 22h · 40m · 52

MAGNITUDES

●	> -0.4
●	-0.4 - +0.5
●	0.6 - 1.5
●	1.6 - 2.5
●	2.6 - 3.5
•	3.6 - 4.5
•	4.6 - 5.5
·	5.6 - 6.5
·	6.6 - 7.5

DOUBLE or MULTIPLE ●-● ●

VARIABLE ⊙ ○

OPEN CLUSTERS   ○ ○ ○ ○
>10' TO SCALE <10'

GLOBULAR CLUSTERS   ⊕ ⊕ ⊙
>10' 5-10' <5'

PLANETARY NEBULAE   ✧ ✧ ✧
>1' 0.5'-1' <0.5'

BRIGHT DIFFUSE NEB.   ▱ □
>10' TO SCALE <10'

GALAXIES   ◯ ◯ ○ ·
> 30' 20'-30' 10'-20' <10'

QUASAR   △

PULSAR   ☿

BLACK HOLE   ⅄

MILKY WAY   〰

GALACTIC EQUATOR   ---70°--+--

ECLIPTIC   ---100°--+--

CONSTELLATION BOUNDARIES

GREEK ALPHABET

α	Alpha	*ν*	Nu
β	Beta	*ξ*	Xi
γ	Gamma	*o*	Omicron
δ	Delta	*π*	Pi
ε	Epsilon	*ϱ*	Rho
ζ	Zeta	*σ*	Sigma
η	Eta	*τ*	Tau
θ *ϑ*	Theta	*υ*	Upsilon
ι	Iota	*φ* *φ*	Phi
κ *ϰ*	Kappa	*χ*	Chi
λ	Lambda	*ψ*	Psi
μ	Mu	*ω*	Omega

ATLAS CHART 45. Small Magellanic Cloud, 47 Tucanae We begin here a series of eight polar charts showing the region surrounding the south celestial pole. The most interesting objects in this chart are the Small Magellanic Cloud and the bright globular cluster 47 Tucanae (NGC 104). Both can be found slightly below the center of the chart, near 0^h30^m –72°.

The Small Magellanic Cloud and its companion galaxy, the Large Magellanic Cloud (see Atlas Chart 47), are two of the closest galaxies to the Milky Way Galaxy. The SMC and the LMC are separated by about 80,000 light-years and are linked by a scattered group of stars and star clusters.

The Small Magellanic Cloud can be observed with all ranges of telescopic power by observers in the southern hemisphere. To the naked eye it looks like a cloud about $3^1/_2$° across, with its hazy outline contrasting with the dark background (Fig. 7-52, p. 320).

Many open and globular clusters have been found in the Small Magellanic Cloud. Both the Small and the Large Magellanic Clouds also contain many Cepheid variables. In 1917 Harlow Shapley, using the relationship between the periods and luminosities of the Cepheid variables, calculated that the Magellanic Clouds were about 150,000 light-years distant. This calculation sparked a tremendous debate about whether the Magellanic Clouds were within our galaxy or were far outside its bounds and therefore were separate galaxies themselves. We now know that they are two of the approximately 24 members of the "Local Group" of galaxies to which our Milky Way Galaxy belongs.

Slightly to the west of the Small Magellanic Cloud, though not connected to it, is 47 Tucanae, a large, highly concentrated globular cluster that is bright enough (total magnitude 4) to be easily visible to the naked eye. 47 Tuc is one of the nearest globular clusters, only 20,000 light-years away.

In a similar direction is a second globular cluster, NGC 362, about twice the distance of 47 Tuc from the Milky Way. It consists of stars of magnitudes 13 to 14 and also is highly compact. NGC 362 is barely visible to the naked eye at magnitude 6.6.

The noteworthy double stars in this region include β (beta) Tuc (at 0^h32^m –63°), a wide double that can be resolved with low power into a pair of 4.4- and 4.8-magnitude stars. This system is actually a sextuple, though the other components are relatively faint. κ (kappa) Tuc, (near 1^h16^m –69°) is a blue-white pair, of magnitudes 5.1 and 7.3, that can be resolved in a small telescope. At least two fainter components are also present.

Fig. 7-44 The globular cluster 47 Tucanae, NGC 104. (National Optical Astronomy Observatories/CTIO)

δ●
● ρ
7690○
π
○ 7796   7689○
PHOENIX   7702○   ○S
●585   ●S
2●●●qт
● ζ
ERIDANUS   ● ω●   η
● ρ
Achernar ● α   ○434
782○
BS● ι   ○BQ β³● β1.2
● α   η
ρ   ● ζ   ● ε
θ
HOR   TUCANA
η² η¹   λ
π²   ● π
π¹●   406○
● δ   362⊕   ϑ
ζ ● ε   6.02 □   ⊕47 Tuc
● ● ●   Small Magellanic
Cloud
HYDRUS   ● κ   λ
ϑ   ○643
● ν   β ζ   ϑ
γ   σ
● ι ● μ τ¹   ψ
τ²   γ³ γη
γ² γ2
MENSA η ● ι   18.41⊕   ξ ε   β
● γ   ξ   OCTANS
● κ π   TZ●   ν
● R   θ
α●   ●B σ ●χ ● S
-75°   -80°   -85°   -90°   49   -85°

GRUS
σ   τ²● τ¹
τ³
● ζ   ● ε
● χ   η
γ   22h
● δ   -55°
7205○ ε
● κ   ● π
● ν
● α
7126○
7125○
ξ ● δ   W
○7329   ○7192   -60°
7096○
7083○
INDUS   7020○
● γ   52
○ρ   21h
-65°
● v
● β
● o   ●SX   ● v
● σ
1.5052○ ○6943
KZ○
PAVO 6876○
● μ¹   20h
α● μ²● θ●   ● ε   -70°
○6808
λ ●   ● τ

APUS   19h
● φ   51
18h
-70°   -75°

FROM "SKY ATLAS 2000.0" BY WIL TIRION

MAGNITUDES		OPEN CLUSTERS	○ ○ ○ ✧		QUASAR	△	GREEK ALPHABET		
●	> -0.4		>10' TO SCALE <10'		PULSAR	⚡	α Alpha	ν Nu	
●	-0.4 - +0.5	GLOBULAR CLUSTERS	⊕ ⊕ ⊛		BLACK HOLE	Y	β Beta	ξ Xi	
●	0.6 - 1.5		>10' 5-10' <5'		MILKY WAY		γ Gamma	ο Omicron	
●	1.6 - 2.5						δ Delta	π Pi	
●	2.6 - 3.5	PLANETARY NEBULAE	✦ ✦ ✦		GALACTIC EQUATOR		ε Epsilon	ρ Rho	
•	3.6 - 4.5		>1' 0.5'-1' <0.5'			-70°	ζ Zeta	σ Sigma	
•	4.6 - 5.5						η Eta	τ Tau	
•	5.6 - 6.5	BRIGHT DIFFUSE NEB.	⌂ □		ECLIPTIC	100°	θ ϑ Theta	υ Upsilon	
•	6.6 - 7.5		>10' TO SCALE <10'				ι Iota	φ ϕ Phi	
DOUBLE or TRIPLE	●—						κ ϰ Kappa	χ Chi	
		GALAXIES	○ ○ ○ ○		CONSTELLATION BOUNDARIES		λ Lambda	ψ Psi	
VARIABLE	◉ ○		>30' 20'-30' 10'-20' <10'				μ Mu	ω Omega	

ATLAS CHART 46. Achernar This chart shows an area with few bright stars, except for Achernar, α (alpha) Eridani, near 1^h38^m $-57°$. Achernar, whose name means "the star at the end of the river," lies at the southernmost point of Eridanus. At magnitude 0.46, it is the ninth brightest star in the sky. Though it is never visible from most of the continental U.S., on autumn evenings it can sometimes be seen just above the southern horizon from southern Texas and Florida, and appears higher in the sky from Hawaii. Achernar is a hot blue giant, about 650 times as bright as the sun and about 120 light-years away. Just north of Achernar is p Eri, a wide orange pair of 6th-magnitude stars.

Below α (alpha) Reticuli (the Net), which is located at 4^h14^m $-62°$, θ (theta) Ret is a double star with components of magnitudes 6.2 and 8.3, separated by 3.9 arc sec. A couple of degrees northeast of θ Ret, R Ret is a long-period variable that ranges in magnitude from 6.5 to 14.0. Its period is 278 days.

Fig. 7-45 Eridanus, the river into which Cygnus dived in search of a friend. Cygnus was then changed by Apollo into a swan and placed in the sky. The sea-serpent Hydrus is nearby. The drawing of the constellation is backwards, as are all drawings from the star atlas of Hevelius.

MAGNITUDES		OPEN CLUSTERS				QUASAR	△	GREEK ALPHABET			
●	>-0.4	○ ○ ○ ∘						α	Alpha	ν	Nu
		>10' TO SCALE <10'				PULSAR	⛢	β	Beta	ξ	Xi
●	-0.4-+0.5					BLACK HOLE	Y	γ	Gamma	o	Omicron
●	0.6-1.5	GLOBULAR CLUSTERS	⊕ ⊕ ✳			MILKY WAY		δ	Delta	π	Pi
●	1.6-2.5		>10' 5'-10' <5'					ε	Epsilon	ϱ	Rho
●	2.6-3.5					GALACTIC EQUATOR		ζ	Zeta	σ	Sigma
●	3.6-4.5	PLANETARY NEBULAE	-◇- -◇- -◇-					η	Eta	τ	Tau
•	4.6-5.5		>1' 0.5'-1' <0.5'					θ ϑ	Theta	υ	Upsilon
•	5.6-6.5					ECLIPTIC		ι	Iota	φ φ	Phi
•	6.6-7.5	BRIGHT DIFFUSE NEB.			□			κ ϰ	Kappa	χ	Chi
			>10' TO SCALE <10'					λ	Lambda	ψ	Psi
DOUBLE or MULTIPLE	●-●					CONSTELLATION BOUNDARIES		μ	Mu	ω	Omega
VARIABLE	◎ ○	GALAXIES	⬭ ○ ∘ ∘								
			>30' 20'-30' 10'-20' <10'								

ATLAS CHART 47. Large Magellanic Cloud, Tarantula Nebula, Canopus In the center of this region is the Large Magellanic Cloud, the huge, irregular companion galaxy to the Small Magellanic Cloud (Atlas Chart 45). Covering a vast area of the sky, the Large Magellanic Cloud (Fig. 5-47) can be resolved even with relatively small telescopes. It looks like a hazy cloud to the naked eye and is bright enough to be visible even under a full moon. (See Fig. 7-52 opposite Atlas Chart 52.)

The central part of the LMC extends over 20,000 light-years in length, while the whole galaxy extends at least 50,000 light-years. It contains at least 30 billion stars, including some supergiants larger than any in our galaxy. At least 400 planetary nebulae and more than 700 open clusters lie within the Large Magellanic Cloud, along with about 60 globular clusters, most of which are similar to those found in our galaxy.

The most striking areas of the LMC are the huge bright regions of glowing hydrogen where supergiant stars provide the energy for emission nebulae. Over 50 diffuse nebulae are visible with medium-sized telescopes. The most outstanding of these is the Tarantula Nebula (NGC 2070), a looped nebula surrounding the star 30 Doradus (in Dorado, the Swordfish). Visible to the naked eye, the Tarantula Nebula is the largest diffuse nebula known in the universe. Its complex structure shows much detail (Fig. 7-46). More than 100 supergiant stars cluster at its center, a region of nebulosity where stars are forming. Nearby, a supernova exploded on February 24, 1987; for a few weeks it was bright enough to be seen with the naked eye. As it fades, astronomers are studying it carefully (Chapter 5). Studies of the supernova have shown that it is 169,000 light-years away.

The brightest star in the Large Magellanic Cloud is S Doradus in the open cluster NGC 1910. S Dor is an irregular variable star that ranges from magnitude 8.6 to 11.7. Its average luminosity is over 500,000 times that of the sun.

Near 6^h24^m $-53°$ is α (alpha) Carinae, also known as Canopus. At magnitude -0.72, Canopus is the second brightest star in the sky, surpassed in brightness only by Sirius. From the southern half of the U.S. it can be seen during the winter months low on the southern horizon, passing south of us about 20 minutes before Sirius does. Because it is so bright and so isolated from other bright stars in the sky, Canopus is often used for navigation by spacecraft going to the outer planets.

Fig. 7-46 The Tarantula Nebula (NGC 2070) and Supernova 1987A. (National Optical Astronomy Observatories/CTIO)

PUPPIS

CAE

CARINA

Canopus

PICTOR

DORADO

VOLANS

Tarantula neb.
SN1987A
Large Magellanic
Cloud

MENSA

RETICULUM

HOR

HYDRUS

CHAMAELEON

Small Magellanic Cloud

TUC

SCA

OCTANS

51

"SKY ATLAS 2000.0" BY WIL TIRION

MAGNITUDES		OPEN CLUSTERS				QUASAR	△	GREEK ALPHABET			
	> -0.4		>10'	TO SCALE	<10'	PULSAR	☆	α	Alpha	ν	Nu
	-0.4 - -0.5					BLACK HOLE	⅄	β	Beta	ξ	Xi
	0.6-1.5	GLOBULAR CLUSTERS	⊕	⊕	⊛			γ	Gamma	ο	Omicron
	1.6-2.5		>10'	5-10'	<5'	MILKY WAY		δ	Delta	π	Pi
	2.6-3.5	PLANETARY NEBULAE	✧	✧	✧			ε	Epsilon	ϱ	Rho
	3.6-4.5		>1'	0.5'-1'	<0.5'	GALACTIC EQUATOR		ζ	Zeta	σ	Sigma
	4.6-5.5							η	Eta	τ	Tau
	5.6-6.5	BRIGHT DIFFUSE NEB.			▫	ECLIPTIC		θ ϑ	Theta	υ	Upsilon
	6.6-7.5		>10' TO SCALE		<10'			ι	Iota	φ φ	Phi
DBLE or MPLE	●─●					CONSTELLATION BOUNDARIES		κ ϰ	Kappa	χ	Chi
		GALAXIES	◯	○	○			λ	Lambda	ψ	Psi
VBLE	◉ ○		>30'	20'-30'	10'-20'			μ	Mu	ω	Omega

ATLAS CHART 48. Southern Milky Way In Carina, Vela, and Centaurus, the southern Milky Way again comes into view. Here, along the galactic equator, the Milky Way's brilliant star fields are extremely rich, rewarding amateurs for hours of random scanning with binoculars or small telescopes.

The numerous open clusters all merit observation. Among these are NGC 3114 (at 10^h03^m –60°), NGC 3293 (at 10^h35^m –58°), and NGC 2516 (at 8^h –61°). One of the finest open clusters visible to observers in the lower latitudes of the northern hemisphere, NGC 2516 should be viewed with a wide-field telescope because of its great size (about 1° or 15 light-years). It lies about 1300 light-years away and is older than the double cluster in Perseus (an extremely young cluster, only 10 million years old), and younger than the Pleiades (still fairly young at 100 million years old, less than 1% of the age of the universe).

One noteworthy globular cluster in this region is NGC 2808, above the center of the chart, near 9^h47^m –65°. It is a large, rich cluster of 13th- to 15th-magnitude stars, covering an area about 5 arc min across. At its center is a brilliant group of loosely packed stars.

Of the double stars, H Vel can be resolved in a small telescope. It is a blue-orange pair with magnitudes 4.9 and 7.7. υ (upsilon) Car (at 9^h47^m –65°), at magnitude 3.1, is another double that can be resolved in small telescopes; its 6th-magnitude secondary component is 5 arc sec away from the third-magnitude primary. t^2 Car, near 10^h40^m –59°, is a wide orange-green pair.

l ("ell") Car (at 9^h45^m –63°) is one of the brightest Cepheid variables. It reaches magnitude 3.3 at maximum and is visible to the naked eye throughout its cycle. It is too far south for most U.S. observers, though. This star is one of the largest Cepheids known, with a diameter about 200 times that of the sun. l Car has a period of $35\frac{1}{2}$ days and is over 3000 light-years away.

Fig. 7-47 Star trails around the south celestial pole, photographed from Australia. At lower left, the bright star Acrux (alpha Crucis) in the foot of the Southern Cross has risen. The Large and Small Magellanic Clouds are also visible, as hazy blurs. This is an unguided 24-minute exposure with a wide-angle (24- mm) lens on ASA 250 film. (Dennis di Cicco/*Sky & Telescope*)

NITUDES	OPEN CLUSTERS				QUASAR	△		GREEK ALPHABET		
>-0.4		○	○	⋅				α Alpha		ν Nu
		>10' TO SCALE <10'			PULSAR	✦		β Beta		ξ Xi
-0.4-+0.5								γ Gamma		o Omicron
0.6-1.5	GLOBULAR CLUSTERS	⊕	⊕	⊕	BLACK HOLE	Y		δ Delta		π Pi
1.6-2.5		>10'	5-10'	<5'	MILKY WAY			ε Epsilon		ϱ Rho
2.6-3.5	PLANETARY NEBULAE	✧	✧	✧				ζ Zeta		σ Sigma
3.6-4.5		>1'	0.5'-1'	<0.5'	GALACTIC EQUATOR			η Eta		τ Tau
4.6-5.5						70°		θ ϑ Theta		υ Upsilon
5.6-6.5	BRIGHT DIFFUSE NEB.			▫	ECLIPTIC			ι Iota		ϕ φ Phi
6.6-7.5		>10' TO SCALE <10'				100°		κ $\varkappa$ Kappa		χ Chi
LE or PLE ●-●					CONSTELLATION BOUNDARIES			λ Lambda		ψ Psi
BLE ⊙○	GALAXIES ◯	○	⊙	○				μ Mu		ω Omega
	>30'	20'-30'	10'-20' <10'							

ATLAS CHART 49. Eta Carinae Nebula, Coalsack Nebula, Southern Cross The Milky Way continues here through Carina, Crux, and Centaurus, offering outstanding sights for observers in southern latitudes. In the upper right-hand corner of the chart, near 10^h45^m $-59°$, the Eta Carinae Nebula (NGC 3372) warrants special attention (Fig. 5-30). Appearing as the brightest part of the Milky Way, this extended nebula shows a highly complex structure with intermingling dark and light lanes and patches. The dark cloud superimposed on the brightest area at the center of the nebula is the Keyhole Nebula (NGC 3324). The brightest star to the left of the Keyhole is the variable star η (eta) Carinae, lying about 4000 light-years from us.

η (eta) Carinae itself is a 6th-magnitude star. On the chart, it is located at the end of a short line that extends to the right and downward from the Greek letter η. η Car is surrounded by a small nebulous shell that is expanding at the rate of about 4 arc sec per century. Although this variable star shows some similarities to most novae, it also shows some peculiar differences: it remained bright for more than a century and was unusually luminous at maximum. First noted by Halley in 1677, it varied in brightness during the 19th century, finally reaching its maximum of magnitude −1 in 1843. The star faded to 8th magnitude and has since brightened to magnitude 6.2. With a mass approximately 100 times that of the sun, it may explode as a supernova; the presence of some of the heavy elements in unusual amounts, discovered by analysis of its spectrum, shows that this star is in an advanced stage of life.

Slightly north of the Eta Carinae Nebula is the open cluster NGC 3293, surrounded by reflection nebulae. The cluster is only 1500 light-years away from us and is not physically connected to the Eta Carinae Nebula. About 3° northeast of Eta Carinae is another open cluster, NGC 3532. Since it is very large and elongated, it is best viewed with a wide-field telescope. This superb cluster contains at least 400 members, of which over 150 stars are 12th magnitude or brighter. About 5° south of the nebula is the scattered open cluster IC 2602. θ (theta) Car is the bright central star of this cluster, which contains 30 stars that are brighter than 9th magnitude and many fainter ones. The cluster is over 1° across and is best viewed with a rich-field telescope or at low power. With its central star θ Car at a distance of only 750 light-years from earth, IC 2602 may be one of the nearest open clusters to us.

Further east (left) along the Milky Way is IC 2944 (at 11^h35^m $-63°$), a faint shell around the star λ (lambda) Cen. IC 2944, along with many other regions of nebulosity visible here, lies in a region of ionized hydrogen that marks one of the spiral arms of our galaxy. Slightly east (left) of IC 2944 is the loose open cluster IC 2948, lying behind the densest part of IC 2944. To the north, on the galactic equator (near 11^h35^m $-62°$), NGC 3766 is a very rich, concentrated open cluster that contains at least 200 stars from 8th to 15th magnitude; it covers an area about 10 arc min across. Beautiful even through binoculars, it is similar in appearance to M37 in Auriga (see Atlas Chart 11). About 5° to the north is the 11th-magnitude plane-

MAGNITUDES			OPEN CLUSTERS				QUASAR	△		GREEK ALPHABET		
	>-0.4			◯	◯	◌	PULSAR	✳		α Alpha		ν Nu
	-0.4 -0.5			>10' TO SCALE		<10'	BLACK HOLE	Y		β Beta		ξ Xi
	0.6-1.5		GLOBULAR CLUSTERS	⊕	⊕	⊕	MILKY WAY			γ Gamma		ο Omicron
	1.6-2.5			>10'	5'-10'	<5'				δ Delta		π Pi
	2.6-3.5		PLANETARY NEBULAE	◇	◇	◇	GALACTIC EQUATOR			ε Epsilon		ϱ Rho
	3.6-4.5			>1'	0.5'-1'	<0.5'				ζ Zeta		σ Sigma
	4.6-5.5									η Eta		τ Tau
	5.6-6.5		BRIGHT DIFFUSE NEB.	◠		▢	ECLIPTIC			θ ϑ Theta		υ Upsilon
	6.6-7.5			>10' TO SCALE		<10'				ι Iota	φ ϕ	Phi
VARIABLE or MULTIPLE	◉		GALAXIES	◯	◯	◯	CONSTELLATION BOUNDARIES			κ ϰ Kappa		χ Chi
VARIABLE	◉ ◯			>30'	20'-30'	10'-20' <10'				λ Lambda		ψ Psi
										μ Mu		ω Omega

tary nebula NGC 3918. It appears as a rich blue, featureless disk and so has been compared to the planet Uranus.

Continuing eastward (to the left) along the Milky Way, we come to Crux, a small constellation nearly surrounded by Centaurus. Crux contains the famous Southern Cross, a diamond-shaped constellation. α (alpha) Cru—Acrux—marks the foot of the cross. β (beta) Cru—Mimosa—to the northeast marks the eastern end of the crosspiece. γ (gamma) Cru—Gacrux—to the northwest (upper right on the chart), marks the head of the cross and is nearly the same brightness as β. δ (delta) Cru, to the southwest of γ, marks the western end of the crosspiece. Three of these stars are among the 30 brightest stars in the sky. Because the cross has no central star, it actually looks more like a kite than a cross.

At 1st magnitude, α Cru (Acrux) lies nearly 400 light-years away. It is an easily resolved double, with two blue stars of magnitudes 1.4 and 1.9, separated by 4½ arc sec. Each of these components is also a spectroscopic double.

β Cru (Mimosa), 20% farther away than α Cru, is the 20th brightest star at magnitude 1.25. Nearly as bright is γ Cru, only about 90 light-years away. Like Antares, it is a red giant, though not so large and bright. An optical double, its components show a striking contrast in both color and magnitude.

Fig. 7-48 The Jewel Box (NGC 4755), an open cluster surrounding the star κ (kappa) Crucis. The 8 brightest stars range from about 6th to 10th magnitude; the cluster is about 10 arc min across. (Gabriel Martin, AURA, Inc.; National Optical Astronomy Observatories/CTIO)

Fig. 7-49 The Milky Way. Acrux (alpha Crucis) is at center, just at the right edge of the dark Coalsack. It is the southernmost point of the kite-like Southern Cross. Mimosa is the bright star to the upper left of Acrux. The other two stars of the southern cross are fainter, and continue around clockwise. The complex of nebulosity around η (eta) Carinae is at right center. (Royal Astronomical Society)

Just to the south of β Cru is a magnificent open cluster called the Jewel Box (NGC 4755). It is one of the finest objects in the southern Milky Way. This cluster contains more than 100 stars scattered over an area 50 light-years across. About 50 of its brightest stars, most notably the 6th-magnitude star κ (kappa) Cru, are concentrated at its center. Many of the cluster's stars are supergiants, including some of the brightest ones known in our galaxy. Most of its members are bluish-white or white, contrasting with a single red supergiant—like diamonds and a ruby. Not more than a few million years old, the Jewel Box is one of the youngest open clusters known. Visible with the naked eye, it should be viewed with low power because of the richness of the surrounding star field.

South of κ Cru and east of α Cru is an almost starless area, caused by a vast dust cloud about 7° by 5° across (60–70 light-years in diameter) that obscures the Milky Way in the background. This is the Coalsack, the most famous of the naked-eye dark nebulae. The few stars visible through telescopes are foreground objects lying between us and the obscuring dust. The Coalsack is one of the nearest dark nebulae, only 500–600 light-years away. It is easily apparent to the naked eye.

ATLAS CHART 50. **Alpha Centauri** Through Centaurus and Norma, the brightness of the Milky Way is divided by clouds of obscuring dust. The most distinctive features in this region are the two bright stars α (alpha) Centauri and β (beta) Centauri (magnitudes 0.0 and 0.6, respectively), located above the center of the chart. The former is known in navigational circles as Rigil Kent (short for Kentaurus), while the latter is sometimes called Hadar or Wazn. A bright pair of stars in the southern sky separated by 4½° (two fingers' width) often turns out to be α and β Centauri (Cen).

The fourth brightest star in the night sky at magnitude 0.0, α Cen A is in the nearest star system to the earth. Alpha is 4.34 light-years away from us. It is a multiple system; its primary star is almost three times as bright as its secondary. A third, fainter companion lies further away from the primary and secondary stars, in a direction closer to the sun. This third component is Proxima Centauri (see Fig. 7-50, below). Proxima ("the nearest") is a red dwarf with a diameter about 1/20 that of the sun. One of the smallest stars known, it is 1/3 the size of Jupiter, though its mass is much greater.

β Centauri is the 11th brightest star at magnitude 0.61. It also has a companion star only 1.3 arc sec away; the pair is difficult to resolve because of the primary's brightness. β Cen is a blue-giant star, about 10,000 times as bright as the sun.

Circinus X-1, an x-ray source, is an interesting object on this chart, though it is not visible to the eye. It probably contains a neutron star, a compact remnant left over by the death of a massive star.

Fig. 7-50 A chart showing the region near Proxima Centauri, the closest star to the sun. Because it is so close, over a period of years we can see it move with respect to more distant stars, as marked. (Wil Tirion)

FROM "SKY ATLAS 2000.0" BY WIL TIRION

MAGNITUDES		OPEN CLUSTERS	⬭ ○ ○ ⬭ >10' TO SCALE <10'	QUASAR	△	GREEK ALPHABET			
●	>-0.4			PULSAR	ⵌ	α	Alpha	ν	Nu
●	-0.4–0.5			BLACK HOLE	Y	β	Beta	ξ	Xi
●	0.6–1.5	GLOBULAR CLUSTERS	⊕ ⊕ ⊛ >10' 5'-10' <5'	MILKY WAY		γ	Gamma	ο	Omicron
●	1.6–2.5					δ	Delta	π	Pi
●	2.6–3.5	PLANETARY NEBULAE	-◇- -◇- -◇- >1' 0.5'-1' <0.5'	GALACTIC EQUATOR		ε	Epsilon	ϱ	Rho
●	3.6–4.5					ζ	Zeta	σ	Sigma
●	4.6–5.5					η	Eta	τ	Tau
●	5.6–6.5	BRIGHT DIFFUSE NEB.	⬭ □ >10' TO SCALE <10'	ECLIPTIC		θ ϑ	Theta	υ	Upsilon
●	6.6–7.5					ι	Iota	φ φ	Phi
DOUBLE or TRIPLE	●-●-●					κ ϰ	Kappa	χ	Chi
VARIABLE	◉ ○	GALAXIES	⬭ ○ ○ ○ >30' 20'-30' 10'-20' <10'	CONSTELLATION BOUNDARIES		λ	Lambda	ψ	Psi
						μ	Mu	ω	Omega

ATLAS CHART 51. Octans, Pavo, Apus, Ara As we move southeast of the Milky Way in this chart, the star fields diminish in richness, though globular clusters become more apparent. NGC 6397 (at 17^h40^m $-54°$) in Ara, the Altar, is a naked-eye globular cluster of exceptional brilliance. It can be found by looking toward the eastern (left) edge of the Milky Way, about $10^1/_2°$ south of θ (theta) Sco, though it can't be seen from most of the U.S. It is a loose scattered group with a total magnitude of 5.7, easily resolved in small telescopes. About 8200 light-years distant, NGC 6397 may be the nearest globular cluster to our solar system.

Another exceptionally bright cluster, NGC 6752 (at 19^h10^m $-60°$), has a total magnitude of 5.4, placing it among the half dozen brightest globular clusters. The third largest in apparent size, exceeded only by ω (omega) Cen and 47 Tuc, NGC 6752 is also one of the nearer globular clusters, about 14,000 light-years away.

A noteworthy double star in this region is ξ (xi) Pav (at 18^h23^m $-62°$), an orange-green pair with a primary component of magnitude 4.4 and a 9th-magnitude secondary.

Fig. 7-51 The constellations near the south celestial pole, from the star atlas of Hevelius (1690). They are reversed from the way they appear in the sky (and on the chart) because this is a view looking on a star globe. Note the beautiful peacock (Pavo).

FROM "SKY ATLAS 2000.0" BY WIL TIRION

MAGNITUDES		OPEN CLUSTERS				QUASAR	△	GREEK ALPHABET			
○	>-0.4	>10'	TO SCALE	<10'		PULSAR	⋇	α	Alpha	ν	Nu
○	-0.4−0.5					BLACK HOLE		β	Beta	ξ	Xi
○	0.6−1.5	GLOBULAR CLUSTERS	⊕	⊕	●			γ	Gamma	ο	Omicron
●	1.6−2.5	>10'	5'−10'	<5'		MILKY WAY		δ	Delta	π	Pi
●	2.6−3.5							ε	Epsilon	ϱ	Rho
●	3.6−4.5	PLANETARY NEBULAE	◇	◇	◇	GALACTIC EQUATOR		ζ	Zeta	σ	Sigma
●	4.6−5.5	>1'	0.5'−1'	<0.5'				η	Eta	τ	Tau
•	5.6−6.5							θ ϑ	Theta	υ	Upsilon
•	6.6−7.5	BRIGHT DIFFUSE NEB.		>10' TO SCALE	<10'	ECLIPTIC		ι	Iota	φ ϕ	Phi
DOUBLE or MULTIPLE								κ ϰ	Kappa	χ	Chi
VARIABLE ⊙ ○		GALAXIES	⬭	○	○	CONSTELLATION BOUNDARIES		λ	Lambda	ψ	Psi
		>30'	20'−30'	10'−20' <10'				μ	Mu	ω	Omega

ATLAS CHART 52. The constellations in this area contain relatively few stars. Here we find only two bright stars, α (alpha) Pavonis, the Peacock Star, and α (alpha) Gruis, Al Na'ir, in Grus, the Crane. Indus, the Indian, is the other constellation that takes up most of this chart.

The region near the south celestial pole is almost barren. Although the number of background stars here does not differ greatly from the number near the north celestial pole, that pole has enough fairly bright stars to at least make the surrounding constellations look interesting. The 5th-magnitude star σ (sigma) Octantis, lying within 1° of the south celestial pole, is the southern pole star. Though it is very inconspicuous compared with Polaris and lacks the Pointers and Little Dipper that make Polaris easy to find, σ Oct is easily visible to the naked eye in a dark sky.

λ (lambda) Oct (at $21^h 51^m -83°$) is a double star easily resolved in a small telescope. It shows constrasting orange and green components of magnitudes 5.4 and 7.7.

Fig. 7-52 The Large and Small Magellanic Clouds are 20° and 40°, respectively, above the horizon in this photograph from Australia, a 45-second exposure on 400 ASA film with a 35-mm lens at $f/1.5$. The south celestial pole is near the right edge of the picture. Canopus is at lower left and Achernar is at top left. (Shigetsugu Fujinami)

8

THE MOON

The moon is often the most prominent object in the nighttime sky. The moon is somewhat more than $1/4$ the diameter of the earth. This makes it the largest satellite (moon) in the solar system in comparison to its parent planet. (Three moons of Jupiter and one each of Neptune and Saturn are physically larger than our moon.)

The moon orbits the earth every $27^1/_3$ days with respect to the stars. But during that time, the earth and moon have moved as a system about $1/_{12}$ of the way in their yearly orbit around the sun. So if the moon at a certain point in its orbit is directly between the earth and the sun, $27^1/_3$ days later it has not quite returned to that point directly between the earth and the sun. The moon must orbit the earth a bit further to get back to the same place with respect to the line between the earth and the sun. The moon reaches this point in a couple of days, making the *synodic period* of the moon equal to $29^1/_2$ days. (The synodic period is the interval between two successive conjunctions—coming to the same celestial longitude—of two celestial bodies, in this case conjunctions of the moon and sun as observed from the earth.) It is the synodic months that are taken into account in lunar calendars.

The Phases of the Moon

The phases of the moon repeat with this $29^1/_2$-day period, since the phases simply depend on the angle between the earth, sun, and moon. One-half of the moon is always illuminated by the sun. To us on earth, the moon appears to go through phases because in the course of the month we see different fractions of its lighted half. When the sun and moon are on opposite sides of the earth, the moon is *full* (Fig. 8-1). Everyone on earth who can see the moon above the horizon sees the same phase of the moon at the same time.

When the sun and moon are on the same side of the earth, we are looking past the moon at the sun. At this time, the far side of the moon is illuminated by the sun, but the side that faces us receives no sunlight. We say that the moon is *new*. Actually, we can often dimly see the dark face of the moon by *earthshine*—sunlight that bounces off the earth and back up to the moon.

In between the new moon and the full moon, the moon is a *crescent* (less than half-illuminated, Fig. 8-2), a *half-moon* (half the face

Fig. 8-1 A full moon. North on the moon is up, as it would be for a northern-hemisphere observer viewing the moon with the naked eye or with binoculars. West is at left. Mare Crisium is the small mare on the northeast limb (just above center at the right). Tycho is the crater at lower center with prominent rays emanating from it. (Lunar and Planetary Laboratory, University of Arizona)

we see illuminated), or is *gibbous* (more than half-illuminated, Fig. 8-3). (Gibbous comes from the Latin word that means "a hump," or "bulging.") The first half-moon after the new moon is called the first quarter, since we are ¼ of the way through the monthly cycle of phases. The half-moon after the moon is full is called the third quarter. While the phases are changing from new to full, with more of the illuminated side of the moon becoming visible, we say the moon is *waxing.* Between full and new phases the moon is *waning.*

Table 13 lists dates for the phases of the moon. Since the moon's orbit is elliptical, the moon's speed around the earth varies, making the period between its phases vary slightly.

The angle between the earth, the moon, and the sun determines which phase will appear, so the time of night the moon rises depends on its phase. A full moon rises when the sun sets. A new moon rises when the sun rises and sets when the sun sets. The moon rises about 50 minutes later each night. A first-quarter moon thus rises at about noon and sets around midnight, and so is at its highest point each day at sunset. An interesting project is to observe the moon on as many days and nights of the months as possible, and to sketch each phase and its orientation with respect to the sun. You can often see the moon in the daytime, especially if you first figure out approximately where to look for it.

Table 13: Phases of the Moon

New Moon d h m (U.T.)			First Quarter d h m (U.T.)			Full Moon d h m (U.T.)			Last Quarter d h m (U.T.)		
1992											
Jan. 4	23	11	Jan. 13	02	33	Jan. 19	21	30	Jan. 26	15	28
Feb. 3	19	00	Feb. 11	16	16	Feb. 18	08	04	Feb. 25	07	57
Mar. 4	13	24	Mar. 12	02	37	Mar. 18	18	19	Mar. 26	02	31
Apr. 3	05	02	Apr. 10	10	07	Apr. 17	04	44	Apr. 24	21	40
May 2	17	46	May 9	15	45	May 16	16	04	May 24	15	54
June 1	03	57	June 7	20	48	June 15	04	51	June 23	08	12
June 30	12	19	July 7	02	45	July 14	19	07	July 22	22	13
July 29	19	36	Aug. 5	10	59	Aug. 13	10	28	Aug. 21	10	02
Aug. 28	02	43	Sept. 3	22	40	Sept. 12	02	17	Sept.19	19	54
Sept. 26	10	41	Oct. 3	14	13	Oct. 11	18	04	Oct. 19	04	13
Oct. 25	20	35	Nov. 2	09	12	Nov.10	09	21	Nov.17	11	40
Nov. 24	09	12	Dec. 2	06	18	Dec. 9	23	41	Dec. 16	19	15
Dec. 24	00	43									
1993											
			Jan. 1	03	39	Jan. 8	12	38	Jan. 15	04	02
Jan. 22	18	28	Jan. 30	23	20	Feb. 6	23	56	Feb. 13	14	58
Feb. 21	13	06	Mar. 1	15	47	Mar. 8	09	47	Mar. 15	04	17
Mar. 23	07	16	Mar. 31	04	11	Apr. 6	18	45	Apr. 13	19	39
Apr. 21	23	49	Apr. 29	12	42	May 6	03	35	May 13	12	20
May 21	14	08	May 28	18	22	June 4	13	03	June 12	05	37
June 20	01	54	June 26	22	45	July 3	23	46	July 11	22	50
July 19	11	25	July 26	03	26	Aug. 2	12	11	Aug. 10	15	20
Aug. 17	19	29	Aug. 24	09	59	Sept. 1	02	34	Sept. 9	06	27
Sept.16	03	12	Sept. 22	19	33	Sept.30	18	54	Oct. 8	19	37
Oct. 15	11	37	Oct. 22	08	53	Oct. 30	12	38	Nov. 7	06	37
Nov.13	21	35	Nov. 21	02	04	Nov. 29	06	32	Dec. 6	15	50
Dec. 13	09	28	Dec. 20	22	26	Dec. 28	23	07			
1994											
									Jan. 5	00	01
Jan. 11	23	11	Jan. 19	20	27	Jan. 27	13	24	Feb. 3	08	07
Feb. 10	14	31	Feb. 18	17	49	Feb. 26	01	16	Mar. 4	16	55
Mar. 12	07	06	Mar. 20	12	15	Mar. 27	11	11	Apr. 3	02	55
Apr. 11	00	18	Apr. 19	02	35	Apr. 25	19	46	May 2	14	33
May 10	17	08	May 18	12	51	May 25	03	40	June 1	04	03
June 9	08	28	June 16	19	57	June 23	11	34	June 30	19	31
July 8	21	39	July 16	01	13	July 22	20	17	July 30	12	41
Aug. 7	08	46	Aug. 14	05	58	Aug. 21	06	48	Aug. 29	06	41

Table 13: Phases of the Moon (Continued)

New Moon			First Quarter			Full Moon			Last Quarter		
d	h	m	d	h	m	d	h	m	d	h	m
(U.T.)			(U.T.)			(U.T.)			(U.T.)		
Sept. 5	18	34	Sept. 12	11	35	Sept.19	20	02	Sept. 28	00	24
Oct. 5	03	56	Oct. 11	19	18	Oct. 19	12	19	Oct. 27	16	45
Nov. 3	13	37	Nov. 10	06	15	Nov. 18	06	58	Nov. 26	07	05
Dec. 2	23	55	Dec. 9	21	08	Dec. 18	02	18	Dec. 25	19	08
					1995						
Jan. 1	10	57	Jan. 8	15	47	Jan. 16	20	27	Jan. 24	04	59
Jan. 30	22	48	Feb. 7	12	55	Feb. 15	12	16	Feb. 22	13	05
Mar. 1	11	49	Mar. 9	10	15	Mar. 17	01	26	Mar. 23	20	11
Mar. 31	02	09	Apr. 8	05	36	Apr. 15	12	09	Apr. 22	03	19
Apr. 29	17	37	May 7	21	45	May 14	20	49	May 21	11	36
May 29	09	28	June 6	10	27	June 13	04	04	June 19	22	02
June 28	00	51	July 5	20	04	July 12	10	50	July 19	11	11
July 27	15	15	Aug. 4	03	17	Aug. 10	18	17	Aug. 18	03	04
Aug. 26	04	33	Sept. 2	09	04	Sept. 9	03	38	Sept. 16	21	10
Sept.24	16	56	Oct. 1	14	36	Oct. 8	15	53	Oct. 16	16	27
Oct. 24	04	37	Oct. 30	21	18	Nov. 7	07	21	Nov.15	11	41
Nov. 22	15	44	Nov. 29	06	29	Dec. 7	01	28	Dec. 15	05	33
Dec. 22	02	24	Dec. 28	19	07						
					1996						
						Jan. 5	20	52	Jan. 13	20	47
Jan. 20	12	51	Jan. 27	11	15	Feb. 4	15	59	Feb. 12	08	37
Feb. 18	23	31	Feb. 26	05	52	Mar. 5	09	24	Mar. 12	17	16
Mar. 19	10	46	Mar. 27	01	32	Apr. 4	00	08	Apr. 10	23	37
Apr. 17	22	50	Apr. 25	20	42	May 3	11	49	May 10	05	05
May 17	11	47	May 25	14	15	June 1	20	48	June 8	11	06
June 16	01	37	June 24	05	25	July 1	03	59	July 7	18	56
July 15	16	16	July 23	17	50	July 30	10	37	Aug. 6	05	26
Aug. 14	07	35	Aug. 22	03	38	Aug. 28	17	53	Sept. 4	19	07
Sept. 12	23	09	Sept. 20	11	24	Sept. 27	02	52	Oct. 4	12	06
Oct. 12	14	16	Oct. 19	18	10	Oct. 26	14	12	Nov. 3	07	52
Nov.11	04	17	Nov. 18	01	10	Nov. 25	04	11	Dec. 3	05	07
Dec. 10	16	58	Dec. 17	09	31	Dec. 24	20	41			
					1997						
									Jan. 2	01	46
Jan. 9	04	26	Jan. 15	20	03	Jan. 23	15	12	Jan. 31	19	41
Feb. 7	15	08	Feb. 14	08	58	Feb. 22	10	28	Mar. 2	09	39
Mar. 9	01	15	Mar. 16	00	07	Mar. 24	04	46	Mar. 31	19	39
Apr. 7	11	03	Apr. 14	17	01	Apr. 22	20	35	Apr. 30	02	37
May 6	20	48	May 14	10	56	May 22	09	14	May 29	07	52
June 5	07	05	June 13	04	53	June 20	19	10	June 27	12	43
July 4	18	41	July 12	21	45	July 20	03	21	July 26	18	30
Aug. 3	08	15	Aug. 11	12	43	Aug. 18	10	57	Aug. 25	02	24
Sept. 1	23	53	Sept. 10	01	22	Sept.16	18	52	Sept. 23	13	37
Oct. 1	16	53	Oct. 9	12	23	Oct. 16	03	47	Oct. 23	04	50

Fig. 8-2 *(left)* A crescent moon, 5 days old (that is, 5 days past new). Mare Crisium is still visible. (Lunar and Planetary Laboratory, University of Arizona)

Fig. 8-3 *(right)* A gibbous moon, 10 days old (that is, 10 days past new). (Lick Observatory photo)

Table 13: Phases of the Moon (Continued)

New Moon d h m (U.T.)		First Quarter d h m (U.T.)		Full Moon d h m (U.T.)		Last Quarter d h m (U.T.)	
Oct. 31	10 02	Nov. 7	21 44	Nov. 14	14 13	Nov. 21	23 59
Nov. 30	02 15	Dec. 7	06 11	Dec. 14	02 38	Dec. 21	21 44
Dec. 29	16 58						

Notes: d = day, *h* = hour, *m* = minute. To convert Universal Time (UT) to time in U.S. time zones, subtract:

  5 hours to get E.S.T, 4 hours to get E.D.T.
  6 hours to get C.S.T., 5 hours to get C.D.T.
  7 hours to get M.S.T., 6 hours to get M.D.T.
  8 hours to get P.S.T., 7 hours to get P.D.T.
  9 hours to get Alaska S.T.
 10 hours to get Hawaii S.T.

The Moon's Surface

Even with the naked eye, we can see that the surface of the moon is varied in structure. The fact that the moon has large flat areas called *mare* (pronounced "MA ray"; plural *maria,* pronounced "MAR ee uh") and craters was discovered by Galileo when he first turned his small telescope to look at the moon in 1609. Maria means "seas," though there is no water in these lunar seas.

The view of the moon through even a small telescope can be breathtaking. You can see that the maria are very flat, and that there are other regions, the *highlands,* that are covered with craters. There are relatively few craters on the maria. These "seas" have, instead, been made flat by volcanic material—lava—that flowed from beneath the lunar surface over 3 billion years ago. This lava covered whatever craters existed at that time, so the craters now visible in the maria were formed by the impact of interplanetary rocks—meteorites—that have hit the moon since then.

When observing the moon with binoculars or with a telescope, you will find it most interesting to observe the *terminator,* the line separating light from dark (day from night, on the moon). At the terminator, we are seeing the region where the sun's rays are hitting the moon at the most oblique angle, and therefore shadows are longest there. This increases the contrast of the surface features. One can even calculate the height of lunar mountains by measuring the lengths of their shadows.

In this chapter, we provide detailed maps of the lunar surface. They are artist's drawings based on National Aeronautics and Space Administration (NASA) photographs, which are able to bring out the structure of features of all parts of the moon. The maps are drawn in a projection that enlarges the areas near the edges (called *limbs*) of the moon, which are otherwise too foreshortened to see clearly. In this projection, a dime held over any portion of the map covers the same area on the moon.

The moon keeps essentially the same face toward the earth as it orbits the earth, presumably because a slight bulge of matter exists in the side of the moon that faces the earth, allowing earth's gravity to capture the moon's rotation. (As a result, the moon turns once on its axis with respect to the stars during each of its orbits around the earth.)

We are not, however, completely limited to seeing only 50% of the moon. The moon is sometimes turned slightly one way and sometimes slightly the other. These variations, called *librations,* enable us to see about $5/9$ of the surface. Because of this fact, the special projection of the lunar maps in this guide may be more useful to an observer than a photograph taken at a certain instant when the moon may have been turned at a different libration angle. The librations result from several causes, the chief of which is the fact that the moon is turning at a constant rate, while it is moving in its elliptical orbit at slightly different speeds, depending on how far away it is from the earth.

When we observe the moon with the naked eye or through a telescope, we see various maria (Fig. 8-4). The largest mare is actually called an ocean, Oceanus Procellarum. Other maria have names such as Palus, signifying a marsh, and Lacus, meaning a lake, though we now know that there is certainly no water on the moon. At the edges of some of the maria we find indentations, each known as a bay—a *sinus.*

Craters of all sizes can be found, ranging up to hundreds of kilometers across. Many of the craters have *central peaks*—raised regions

Fig. 8-4 Huge lava flows in southern Mare Imbrium, photographed from Apollo 15 in orbit around the moon. (NASA)

at their centers. Scientists have been able to duplicate these central peaks in laboratories on earth by shooting bullets at sand; the central peaks arise from a rebound of material. The craters, for the most part, have been formed where meteorites have hit the moon. When the meteorites crash, they release their energy explosively, as though an atomic bomb or tons of TNT have gone off. It is this energy that forms each crater, which explains why the craters on the moon are relatively round, even though the meteorites may have hit at an angle.

The moon has *mountain peaks,* and *mountain ranges,* along with smaller raised *ridges.* A few *valleys* can be seen on the lunar surface. Some small valleys are known as *rilles;* rilles often seem sinuous in form, winding their ways for hundreds of kilometers across the lunar surface.

The photographs show that at certain places, one can see *rays* that appear to radiate outward from a few craters, most prominently from Tycho. These rays consist of material ejected when the craters were formed. Over millions of years, the material in the rays darkens until it matches the surrounding surface. The fact that the rays extending from Tycho are still clearly visible tells us that this is one of the youngest of the large craters on the moon.

For thousands of years, humans had to guess what the moon was like. But in 1969, with the first Apollo landings of U.S. astronauts, we began to acquire first-hand knowledge of the lunar surface. Even such basic knowledge as the fact that the moon has a hard surface with a thin coating of dust had to await the first landings of unmanned spacecraft on the moon and then observations that the Apollo astronauts didn't sink into the surface. Twelve astronauts on six Apollo missions landed on the moon (Table 14) and carried out many types of experiments there. The astronauts measured the flow of heat from beneath the lunar surface, collected particles from the sun that hit the moon, and measured the hardness of rocks on the surface. Of course, the collecting of moon rocks and moon dust for detailed analysis back on earth was the most widely known of the experiments. Three unmanned Soviet landers also brought back to earth a few samples of moon rock and dust, though in far smaller quantities than the 382 kilograms (843 pounds) of material brought back by the American astronauts. Many of the lunar rocks are basalts, a common type of rock on earth formed by vulcanism.

As a result of the analysis of moon rocks on earth, scientists were able to work out an accurate chronology of the moon's history. The oldest rocks were 4.42 billion years old, which presumably represents the time when the moon's surface began to solidify, shortly after the overall formation of the moon 4.6 billion years ago. Then, from about 4.2 to 3.9 billion years ago, the surface was bombarded heavily by meteorites. A hundred thousand years later, radioactive elements inside the moon had generated so much heat that lava flowed onto the moon's surface, filling the largest basins and making the maria that we see today. This era of lunar vulcanism ended about 3.1 billion years ago, and the surface of the moon has changed little since then.

Though pictures of the moon taken from earth are often spectacular, whether taken with small telescopes or with some of the largest ones, any view of the moon from earth is always somewhat blurred by the effect of looking through the earth's atmosphere (Fig. 8-5). The photographs from the Apollo spacecraft therefore can show much finer detail. And from the earth, we see only the moon's near side. The far side was completely unknown to us until spacecraft circled the moon. In this chapter, in addition to providing eight detailed maps of the moon's near side, we present a map of the far side, on a less expanded scale. These maps show some of the names that have

Table 14: Manned Missions to the Moon

Mission	Year	Landing Site—see Moon Map
Apollo 11	1969	6
Apollo 12	1969	3
Apollo 14	1971	3
Apollo 15	1971	6
Apollo 16	1972	2
Apollo 17	1972	6

Fig. 8-5 A photograph taken from earth with a small (3.5-in.) telescope, showing Clavius (near top) and Tycho to the north (lower center). South is up, as in Moon Map 3. (Questar Corporation)

been assigned to craters and other features by the International Astronomical Union, which has the responsibility for naming astronomical features in the universe.

Lunar Eclipses

The plane of the moon's orbit is tilted 5° with respect to the earth's. Thus as the moon orbits the earth each month, it usually passes above or below the earth's shadow. (The earth's shadow is a cone that—at the moon's distance from the earth—is about twice as broad as the moon's diameter.) But every few months, the moon passes either partially or entirely into the earth's shadow, and we have a partial or total *lunar eclipse* (Fig. 8-6).

The earth's shadow has a darker inner cone, the *umbra*, from which the sun cannot be seen at all, and an outer cone, the *penumbra*, from which part of the sun can be seen. Most of the penumbra is not dark enough to have a noticeable effect on the moon's brightness, so penumbral eclipses are largely ignored.

During a partial lunar eclipse, the umbra of the earth's shadow advances onto part of the moon's surface and then moves off the other side. No other effect is seen.

Fig. 8-6 A drawing of a lunar eclipse, showing the umbra of the earth's shadow (the area defined by solid lines) and the penumbra (defined by dotted lines). (Susan Eder)

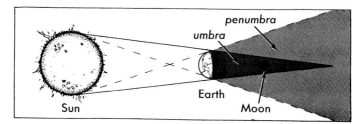

During a total lunar eclipse (Table 15), the umbra hits the moon (first contact) and then gradually covers the moon until the moon is entirely covered (second contact). Then, for an hour or two, the moon is immersed in the earth's shadow. Though no sunlight falls directly on the totally eclipsed moon, some sunlight is bent around the earth's atmosphere. From this refracted sunlight, the blue light is removed when the light is scattered in the earth's atmosphere. This creates blue skies overhead for people on earth; only the red light gets through to the moon. Thus the totally eclipsed moon appears reddish. Just how reddish it looks depends on whether volcanic dust is present in the earth's atmosphere; the dust makes the moon look darker and less reddish. Even giant storms or cloudy regions on earth can affect the earth's shadow, perhaps making the darkness of the shadow appear uneven on the moon. The moon will also appear less evenly illuminated if it passes closer to the sides of the umbra instead of through the umbra's center.

Table 15: Lunar Eclipses

Date	Moon enters shadow	Totality begins	Totality ends	Moon leaves shadow	Maximum magnitude	Overhead at maximum (long.)	(lat.)
6/15/92	3:28	—	—	6:28	0.69	74°	24°S
12/9– 10/92	**22:01**	**23:08**	**0:22**	**1:29**	**1.28**	**357°**	**23°N**
6/4/93	**11:13**	**12:14**	**13:50**	**14:51**	**1.57**	**195°**	**22°S**
11/29/93	**4:41**	**6:03**	**6:49**	**8:11**	**1.09**	**99°**	**21°N**
5/25/94	2:40	—	—	4:24	0.24	53°	20°S
4/15/95	11:43	—	—	12:55	0.12	185°	11°S
4/4/96	**21:37**	**22:32**	**0:54**	**1:59**	**1.38**	**2°**	**6°S**
9/27/96	**1:14**	**2:20**	**3:30**	**4:36**	**1.25**	**46°**	**2°N**
3/24/97	3:00	—	—	6:22	0.92	68°	1°S
9/16/97	**17:09**	**18:16**	**19:18**	**20:25**	**1.20**	**283°**	**3°S**
7/28/99	10:23	—	—	12:45	0.40	172°	18°S

Notes: Entries in **boldface** = totality visible in the U.S. and Canada. All times are given in Universal Time (U.T.). To convert Universal time to time in U.S. time zones, subtract:

   5 hours to get E.S.T, 4 hours to get E.D.T.
   6 hours to get C.S.T., 5 hours to get C.D.T.
   7 hours to get M.S.T., 6 hours to get M.D.T.
   8 hours to get P.S.T., 7 hours to get P.D.T.
   9 hours to get Alaska S.T.
   10 hours to get Hawaii S.T.

The maximum magnitude is the fraction of the moon's diameter that is in the umbra at the deepest part of the eclipse. The whole moon is barely in the umbra for maximum magnitude of 1, and is further in the umbra for maximum magnitude greater than 1.

(Based on *Canon of Lunar Eclipses* by Jean Meeus and Hermann Mucke and *Fifty Year Canon of Lunar Eclipses* by Fred Espenak)

Observers in the eastern U.S. and Canada will be able to see the total lunar eclipse of December 9, 1992, and those in the west can observe the total eclipse of June 4, 1993. That of November 29, 1993 will be visible throughout North America. Observers in the easternmost U.S and Canada will see the total eclipse of April 4, 1996. The continental U.S. and Canada, except for Alaska, will see the total eclipse of September 27, 1996. The total eclipse of September 16, 1997, will be visible in most of the world except the Americas.

To photograph a lunar eclipse, use a telephoto lens with a focal length of at least 200 mm for close-ups, though wide-angle views can also be interesting. During the partial phases, the bright part of the moon is illuminated by the sun; since it is about the same distance from the sun as the earth is, use the same exposure you would use to photograph people outdoors on a sunny day on earth. (For example, a lens setting of $f/11$ at $1/125$ second for ISO/ASA 64 film would be typical.) During the total part of the eclipse, however, the moon is much darker, and time exposures of a minute or more with your lens wide open may be necessary. These will blur because of the moon's motion, unless your camera or telescope is on a tracking mount. For best results, take a wide range of exposures.

The Moon Maps
Descriptions accompanying maps are by Ewen A. Whitaker

Map Projection

As seen from earth, the limb (outer) regions of the moon appear very crowded together (foreshortened) because of the viewing angle; formations situated within 10° of the map edges can be observed only with difficulty, and then only when illumination and libration conditions are favorable. The lunar maps used here (which were prepared in a cooperative effort of the National Geographic Society and the U.S. Geological Survey) are drawn in a projection that spreads out the limb regions and makes them easier to see (Fig. 8-7). The projection preserves the relative areas that features cover on the lunar surface but slightly alters their true dimensions.

Directions on the Moon

Since the moon has north and south poles, these directions are unambiguous. Prior to 1961, east and west on the moon were reckoned in the same directions as the sky, *i.e.*, for an observer in the earth's northern hemisphere facing south (toward the moon, from U.S. and Canadian latitudes), east was to the left and west to the right. However, these directions are opposite to those used universally in terrestrial mapping, and the advent of the Space Age required that a common convention be adopted. Thus east and west in the accompanying moon charts and descriptions, as with all professional documents published since 1961, conform to these true lunar directions. Readers who wish to consult some of the more detailed descriptive works and maps of the moon published before 1961 should be aware that "east" and "west" in these publications refer to directions in the sky. All common astronomical telescopes invert the moon's image, so the enlarged maps of the moon's near side in this guide are oriented with south at the top and lunar east to the left, to make the maps easy to use at the telescope. The orientation chart of the near side, however, is not inverted; it directly corresponds with the view seen with the naked eye or through binoculars.

Fig. 8-7 The moon's near side (North is up). This orientation map shows the location of each of the moon maps that follow.

MOON MAP 1. This area consists largely of the lunar highlands, which are the highly cratered and lighter-toned areas of the moon, although most of Mare Fecunditatis lies within the boundaries of this map, as do portions of Mare Smythii and Mare Australe. The major craters are Humboldt (toward the left edge), Furnerius, Petavius, Vendelinus, and Langrenus.

Humboldt, a relatively fresh crater with a diameter of 125 miles (200 km), would be a very impressive feature if it were situated closer to the center of the moon's face (disk). It is best viewed one night after full moon, but favorable librations are essential. Vendelinus and Furnerius are better placed for good viewing but are older, as evidenced by the number of more recent craters that have overlapped them and by their generally smoother appearance. Petavius, 110 miles (177 km) in diameter, is somewhat younger, and is interesting because of a major rille that runs from its west wall to the imposing group of central peaks. Langrenus, named for (and by!) Van Langren, who produced the first lunar map, is also fresh and clear-cut in appearance, with a small central peak and finely terraced walls. To the southwest (upper right) of Petavius are situated the sources of two extensive systems of bright surface streaks called rays. These are best seen when the terminator lies some distance away, *i.e.*, during the period towards full moon. The rays are remarkable in that their source craters, Furnerius A and Stevinus A, are so small.

Mare Fecunditatis consists of two contiguous, nearly round areas of dark basaltic lavas; the northern part has about three times the diameter of the southern. The larger part of this "sea" displays a typical system of fairly prominent ridges, the result of compressional forces. The small craters Messier and Messier A, situated near the lunar equator, are interesting both because of their somewhat anomalous shapes and their unusual pair of rays, resembling searchlight beams, that stretch westward from Messier A (see Fig. 8-8, lower right). These craters were studied extensively in the past because of suspected changes in their appearance, which are now known to be the result of changes in illumination and viewing angles.

Fig. 8-8 The craters Messier and Messier A, in Mare Fecunditatis, photographed from lunar orbit during the Apollo 8 mission. Messier is 9 miles (14 km) long, 6 miles (9 km) wide, and 7000 feet (2 km) deep. (NASA)

1

S

Jeans

Lyot

Brisbane

Peirescius

Hamilton

Gum

Oken

Vega

VALLIS RHEITA

Marinus

Fraunhofer

MARE AUSTRALE

Abel

Furnerius

Barnard

Adams

Fornerius A

Rheita

Legendre

Hase

Stevinus

Palitzsch

Stevinus A

Phillips

Snellius

Reichenbach

Humboldt

Petavius

Hecataeus

Schorr

Wrottesley

Borda

Gibbs

Balmer

Holden

Biot

Santbech

Behaim

Monge

Ansgarius

Vendelinus

Cook

Colomba

Lamé

Montes Pyrenaeus

La Pérouse

McClure

Kapteyn

Lohse

Crozier

Bellot

Magelhaens

Langrenus

MARE FECUNDITATIS

Goclenius

Kästner

Gilbert

Lubbock

Van Vleck

Maclaurin

Messier A

Weierstrass

Webb

Messier

Luna 16

ess

RE

THI

2

3

MOON MAP 2. This area also consists largely of highlands, but is interesting because of the presence of Mare Nectaris (lower left) and its associated basin, and of the Rheita Valley (Vallis Rheita, upper left). This lunar valley, which is best viewed when the moon is either about 4–5 days old (during the crescent phase), or 2–3 days after the full phase, is about 300 miles (480 km) long. However, there is some evidence that the valley is not a single structure but consists of two segments of different origin. The 200-mile (320-km) northern segment appears to have been caused by a subsidence of the moon's crust; the southern segment, which lies at an angle to the northern one, resembles many of the valleys that appear to radiate from the Imbrium basin (Map 7), such as those southeast of the crater Hipparchus (lower right of this map; Fig. 8-9).

Janssen is one of the largest craters (120 miles—190 km—in diameter) shown on this map (upper left center); most of its floor is very rough. This floor also contains a prominent rille, with many lesser rilles and a clifflike fault branching from it. Maurolycus (70 miles—112 km—in diameter), at center, is one of the deepest (15,000 ft.—4570 m) of the larger craters; it looks very impressive when situated near the terminator. Theophilus (bottom center), with a diameter of 62 miles (100 km), looks somewhat fresher (sharper-edged). It is well situated for observations of part of its *ejecta blanket*—the blanket of material ejected from the crater—that extends in a northerly direction.

A medium-sized telescope will reveal the roughness of this area compared with the fairly smooth surface of Mare Nectaris. Mare Nectaris is a prominent, somewhat circular area of dark, basaltic lavas some 220 miles (354 km) in diameter that displays some concentric ridges on the eastern part. This mare represents a filling by lavas of a pre-existing central depression caused by the impact that formed the Nectaris basin. The outer boundary of this basin is marked, on the southwest, by the fault line named the Altai Scarp (Rupes Altai) and on the east, by the Pyrenees Mountains. These and other segments of scarps and mountain blocks form a circle that is concentric with and has twice the diameter of the mare's surface—a characteristic shared by all the larger impact structures on the moon.

Fig. 8-9 Lunar valleys radial to the Imbrium basin, near the crater Hipparchus (bottom center). (Lunar and Planetary Laboratory, University of Arizona)

Amundsen
Demonax→ Scott Malapert→
←Wexler
Neumayer→
Helmholtz→ →Boguslawsky
Petrov Gill Simpelius→
Boussingault→
Pontécoulant→ Curtius→
Manzinus→
Mutus→ Pentland→
←Hanno Hagecius→
Biela→ ←Nearch Zach→
Rosenberger Kinau→
Reimarus→ Asclepi→ Tannerus→ ←Jacobi
←Watt Hommel→ Lilius→
Steinheil→ Vlacq→ Cuvier→
Mallet→ Pitiscus→ Ideler→ ←Baco
←Young Lockyer→ Dove→ Clairaut→ Heraclitus→
Spallanzani→ Breislak→ Licetus→
Janssen→ Nicolai→ Barocius→ Faraday→
Fabricius→ Maurolycus→
Metius→ Stofler→ Nasireddin→
Rheita Wöhler→ Büsching→ Buch→ ←Fernelius
Stiborius→ Gemma Frisius→ Kaiser→
Neander→ Rabbi Levi→ Celsius→ Nonius→ Walter→
Lindenau→ Gooddcre→
Piccolomini→ Zagut→ Aliacensis→
Weinek→ Rothmann→ Wilkins→ Paisson→ Werner→
Santbech→ Pantanus→ Krusenstern→
Fracastorius→ Pons Sacrobosco→ Blanchinus→
Beaumont→ Azophi→ Playfair→ Delaunay→
MARE Geber→ Abenezra→ Faye→
NECTARIS Almanon→ Airy→
Tacitus→ Argelander→ Vogel→
Cyrillus→ Abulfeda→ Parrot→
Descartes→ Burnham→ Klein→
Gaudibert→ Kant→ Andel→ Albategnius→
Mädler→
Gutenberg→ Theophilus→ Halley→
Capella→ Isidorus→ Zöllner→ Apollo 16 Hind→ Hipparchus→
Torricelli→ Alfraganus→ Taylor→
Hypatia→ Horrocks→ Pickering→ Gylden→
Censorinus→ Delambre→ Seeliger→ Réaumur→
Moltke→ SINUS
MEDII

E
←1
→3
6
Rupes Altai
Catharina
Rheita
Vallis
Rheita
Montes
Pyrenaeus

MOON MAP 3. For an earth-based observer, the area covered by this map is dominated by the dark expanses of maria—Mare Nubium, Mare Cognitum, Mare Humorum, and a portion of Oceanus Procellarum (see also Map 8). The highlands area to the south also displays some interesting formations, including the 55-mile (90-km) diameter crater Tycho (left center). When situated near the terminator, this crater appears both rougher and deeper than its neighbors, with strongly terraced inner walls and a well-formed central peak. At phases near full moon, you can see that Tycho is the center of a very extensive system of bright rays, some of which extend almost a quarter of the way around the moon.

There are several large craters to the south of Tycho, but Clavius (140 miles—225 km—in diameter) is undoubtedly the most eye-catching, with an arc of smaller craters spanning its level floor. A smaller crater to its west, Schiller (upper right of center), is unique because it is noticeably elongated, a condition that is further enhanced by the foreshortening that occurs near the moon's limbs. Nearby (farther west) are the large crater Schickard and the unique formation Wargentin. Wargentin looks like a typical crater, but its interior has been filled to the rim with material. The elevated floor is smooth and flat, with a few low, curving ridges.

Nearer to the center of the moon's disk, at the lower left of this map, we find the large craters Ptolemaeus, Alphonsus, and Arzachel, which gradually decrease in diameter and increase in depth and freshness of appearance. Southwest of Arzachel, near the eastern edge of Mare Nubium, lies the Straight Wall (Rupes Recta), a 70-mile-long (113-km-long) fault in the mare surface that averages almost 1000 ft. (300 m) in height, with a slope of about 40°. When the moon is 8–9 days old, the Wall is impressive at sunrise, for it casts a wide, wedge-shaped shadow.

To the west, Mare Humorum (at right) is a reasonably circular dark area similar in size to Mare Nectaris (Map 2), but the surroundings look more degraded; as a result the edge of the basin is scarcely discernible in a telescopic view. The terrain between the two rings that surround Mare Humorum has been largely flooded with lavas (in Palus Epidemiarum, for example); the area between the rings surrounding Mare Nectaris is largely highlands material. The area lying between Mare Humorum and Palus Epidemiarum includes three parallel, curving rilles that are concentric with the Mare. These rilles are true *graben*—areas of subsidence between parallel faults in the lunar crust. The crater Gassendi, at the northern end of the Mare, is a much-observed and interesting formation. It is about 70 miles (100 km) in diameter, with a cluster of central peaks and a rough floor that displays a complicated network of rilles. Transient Lunar Phenomena (TLPs)—temporary appearances such as apparent obscurations, colorations, glows, etc.—have been reported in this crater on many occasions.

S

3

Drygalski

Malapert Cabeus

Le Gentil

Hausen ←

Newton

Casatus

Short Klaproth

Bailly

Moretus

Wilson

Gruemberger Kircher

Bettinus

Pingré

Cysatus ←

Blancanus

Zucchius

Rutherfurd

Scheiner

Segner

Weigel

Clavius

Rost →

Phocylides

Nasmyth

Porter

Schiller

Wargentin

Deluc

Bayer →

Noeggerath

Maginus

Longomontanus

Schickard

Proctor →

Mee

Drebbel

Pictet

Tycho

Wilhelm

Saussure →

Hainzel

LACUS

Huggins

Surveyor 7

Epimenides

Elger

Clausius

Sasserides

Heinsius

Capuanus

EXCELLENTIAE

Orontius

Ball

Wurzelbauer

Palmieri

Lexell

Cichus

PALUS

Walter

Hell Weiss

EPIDEMIARUM

W

Deslandres

Pitatus

Hesiodus

Campanus

Promontorium Kelvin

4

Kies →

MARE

HUMORUM

Purbach

MARE

König →

Hippalus →

Thebit

NUBIUM

Bulialdus

Gassendi

Alpetragius

Promontorium Taenarium

Lubiniezky

Ranger 9

Alphonsus Davy

MARE

OCEANUS

Ptolemaeus

Ranger 7

COGNITUM

Parry →

Euclides

PROCELLARUM

Herschel

Fra Mauro

Spörer

Apollo 14 Apollo 12 & Surveyor 3

Flammarion

Luna 5

Lansberg

SINUS

MARE

INSULARUM

MEDII

7

MOON MAP 4. Besides Oceanus Procellarum (lower left; see also Moon Map 8), this area contains the eastern half of Mare Orientale, the Orientale basin, and its extensive ejecta blanket (Fig. 8-10). However, these latter formations are too close to the limb to permit good observations from earth; lunar features that are located further from the limb command more interest in the telescope. In the highlands areas these include the crater Grimaldi (lower right), the Sirsalis-Darwin rille system, and the crater Mersenius and its environs (left center). Grimaldi is really a small basin, since it has the characteristic inner and outer concentric scarps. Its floor has also been flooded with mare lavas except toward the north, where they have not reached the crater wall.

The Sirsalis Rille (Rima Sirsalis) is one of the longest graben on the moon, and is contiguous with the Darwin system. Where the rille crosses crater walls, the walls have been cut by the parallel faults, as has the lower terrain.

The crater Mersenius, 51 miles (83 km) in diameter, is unusual in that its floor is noticeably convex—it is more convex than the moon's surface. This bulge is noticeable at sunrise, when the eastern part of the floor is well illuminated while the western part is still largely in shadow.

The western "shores" of Mare Humorum display some interesting features, such as the rough surface northeast of Mersenius, the cliff-like faults southeast of that crater, and a small crater (Liebig F) that sits squarely on one of these faults. The flooded crater Doppelmayer is interesting for its concentric structure.

The dark-floored crater Billy and its companion crater Hansteen, which is of similar size but quite different appearance, are situated near the shoreline of Oceanus Procellarum. Between these craters lies the exceptionally bright mountain Mons Hansteen; special photography has shown it to be notably redder than the highlands surface nearby.

Fig. 8-10 The dark central area is Mare Orientale (Eastern Sea), on the Moon's edge as seen from earth. The basin was caused by the impact of a body that was probably about 30 miles (50 km) across. At right, we see part of the moon's front side. Grimaldi is the small dark region to the right (east) of the Orientale basin, with Oceanus Procellarum above (northeast of) it. The regions on the left are from the moon's far side, which is never visible from earth. North is up in this photo taken in 1990 by NASA's Galileo spacecraft. (NASA)

S

4

Catalan

Vallis Baade

Inghirami

Baade

Graff

Vallis Bouvard

Schickard

Vallis Inghirami

Piazzi

Lagrange

Shaler

Lehmann

Wright

Lacroix

Pettit

Krasnov

Nicholson

Fourier

Vieta

Palmieri

Byrgius

Doppelmayer

Cavendish

Eichstadt

MARE

Liebig F

Lamarck

Liebig

Henry Freres

MONTES

MARE

ORIENTALE

LACUS

VERIS

UMORUM

Henry

Mersenius

Rima Sirsalis

MONTES

CORDILLERA

De Vico

Darwin

Gassendi

Crüger

Kopff

Zupus

Fontana

LACUS

Rocca

AUTUMNI

Billy

Sirsalis

Hansteen

Mons Hansteen

Hartwig

O

Grimaldi

Schlüter

C

Flamsteed

Damoiseau

Orbiter 5

E

Surveyor 1

A

Hermann

Lohrmann

N

Riccioli

U

Hevelius

S

PROCELLARUM

8

W

MOON MAP 5. The most notable feature on this map is Mare Crisium, an oval dark spot that is readily visible to the naked eye. This lunar sea was once named "The Caspian." It is comparable in size with both Mare Nectaris and Mare Humorum, but unlike those two seas, it is totally isolated from the other major maria. The outer ring of the Crisium basin, twice again the diameter of the mare, is visible mostly on the northern (lower) side when the sun is setting on this region, about two days after the full moon. The area between the rings contains several patches of dark lavas, which have been named Mare Anguis (Serpent Sea), Mare Undarum (Sea of Waves), and more recently, Lacus Bonitatis (Lake of Goodness). Although it is only $17^{1}/_{2}$ miles (28 km) in diameter, the crater Proclus, to the west (right) of Mare Crisium, catches the eye during most phases because of its extreme brilliance. As the moon approaches the full phase, a striking ray system, which extends from all but the southwest sector of the crater, also becomes apparent. Similar asymmetrical ray patterns can be reproduced in the laboratory by using low-angle impacts.

At the north end of Mare Fecunditatis lies the crater Taruntius, which displays a weak ray system but has a flooded floor with concentric rilles and a small central peak.

Of the larger craters on the map, Neper (named for Napier, the inventor of logarithms), with its great terraced walls and prominent central peak, would be very impressive if it were situated nearer the central regions. However, it is on the lunar limb and can only be seen either soon after new moon or full moon, and then only if the moon's libration is favorable. Nearby are the dark areas of Mare Marginis and Mare Smythii (Smyth's Sea, Fig. 8-11), equally difficult to observe. The crater Gauss (110 miles—177 km—in diameter), at lower left, is somewhat easier to observe; its floor exhibits some smaller craters and other detail. Burckhardt, north of Mare Crisium, is interesting in that it has partially obliterated two older, slightly smaller craters, which now protrude like ears on opposite sides of it.

Fig. 8-11 The earth is rising over the lunar limb as the Apollo 11 Lunar Module rises to rendezvous with the orbiter. In this westward-looking view, the large, dark area in the background is Smyth's Sea, which is on the moon's east limb as seen from earth. (NASA)

MOON MAP 6. As seen from earth, this area consists mostly of mare surfaces, including Mare Serenitatis and its adjacent Lacus Mortis and Lacus Somniorum, Mare Tranquillitatis and Mare Vaporum, Sinus Medii, and Mare Frigoris. The only reasonably pristine highlands areas on this map are those lying well north of Mare Frigoris. The area towards the center of the moon's face, which lies in Sinus Medii at upper right, abounds with interesting formations. Triesnecker marks the approximate center of a branching system of rilles that can be observed with medium-sized telescopes.

North of this system lies the more prominent Hyginus Rille, which cuts right through the small crater Hyginus. The western arm of this rille is punctuated with a string of craterlets, visible only in large instruments, attesting to some type of lunar volcanic or internal activity here in the past. Hyginus itself is a flat-floored rimless crater, which again indicates a volcanic-tectonic origin.

East of Hyginus lies the Ariadaeus Rille, a great linear graben that cuts through lowlands and mountain ridges alike. The area immediately north of the Hyginus Rille is one of the darkest spots on the moon; from lunar satellites and data acquired from other ground-based studies, we know that this darkness is largely due to a higher than average content of the mineral ilmenite (ferrous titanate) in the soil; in this area the soil consists mostly of the lunar equivalent of volcanic ash (mainly small glass beads).

The full moon appears almost silvery white in a dark sky, but its true color is mostly brownish gray. You can see color variations, however, especially if you view Mare Serenitatis and Mare Tranquillitatis in a telescope at low power when the terminator is not too close by. The rather warm, brownish tone of Serenitatis contrasts noticeably with the more steely gray tones of Tranquillitatis; the grayish color results from the unusually high ilmenite content of the basaltic lavas of Mare Tranquillitatis. This mare has a very strong system of ridges that traverse its western half.

Mare Serenitatis displays the typical concentric ridges of a flooded basin. The landing site of Apollo 17 is situated just off the eastern-most corner of the mare, in a patch of noticeably darker material. Lunokhod 2, carried by the Soviet Luna 21 spacecraft, landed and operated near Le Monnier crater 100 miles (160 km) farther north. Slightly farther north is Posidonius, a prominent crater on the shore of Mare Serenitatis. Both sinuous and graben-type rilles cross the floor of Posidonius. The sinuous rilles follow tortuous paths over the lunar surface and are true lava-flow channels or collapsed lava tubes.

South of Mare Frigoris, craters Aristoteles, Eudoxus, Atlas, and Hercules are the remaining large, easily observable craters in this map area. Atlas (55 miles—88 km—in diameter) is unusual because of the rilles and dark spots on its floor.

E

△2

6

SINUS
MEDII

Menzel

Apollo 11
Surveyor 5
• Ranger 8
← Lamont

MARE

TRANQUILLITATIS

Ranger 6 •
Ross →

Sabine
Ritter
Ariadaeus
Rima Ariadaeus

Hyginus
Rima → Triesnecker
Hyginus

Julius
Caesar

MARE
VAPORUM

Marco
Polo

Lyell ⌐

Franz →⌐
Vitruvius →
Carmichael →
Hill →

Jansen →
Promontorium Archerusia

Apollo 17 →

Franck →
Littrow

Plinius
MONTES HAEMUS

Manilius

Yangel →

MARE

Mons Hadley →
Santos-Dumont

MONTES
APENNINUS

Apollo 15
PALUS
PUTREDINIS

Römer
Luna 21

Le Monnier

SERENITATIS

Luna 2
Autolycus

MONTES

TAURUS

Posidonius →
Chacornac

Luther

MONTES
CAUCASUS

Aristillus
Theaetetus
Galippus

Cassini

G. Bond →
Hall

Dawes
Grove

Maury →
Franklin

Cepheus
Oersted
Shuckburgh →

Chevalier →

Atlas

Hercules

Baily
Aristoteles

LACUS
SOMNIORUM

Williams
Masan
Plana
LACUS
Bürg
MORTIS

Mitchell →

Eudoxus

Alexander
Lamech

MONTES ALPES

Egede

Vallis Alpes →

Galle

Democritus
Thales

Endymion
De La Rue →

Strabo →
Schwabe →

Mbigno →

Arnold

MARE

Gärtner

Kane

Protagoras
Archytas

FRIGORIS

Sheepshanks
C. Mayer

Timaeus

W.
Bond

Nelson
Peters

Barrow

Bel'kovich

Hayn

Cusanus

Petermann →

Baillaud →

Meton

Eudemon
Scoresby

De Sitter →

Challis
Main

Byrd

Nansen

Peary

△5

⊳4

N

MOON MAP 7. This area is dominated by Mare Imbrium, with the mare areas of Mare Insularum, Sinus Aestuum, Mare Frigoris, and Sinus Roris occupying much of the remainder. The Imbrium basin (Fig. 8-12) is second only to the Orientale basin in freshness, with an age (it is believed) of about 3.9 billion years. On the moon's earthside face, only the much older Procellarum basin is larger than this huge Imbrium basin. Its formation therefore had a profound effect on the pre-existing lunar surface, and all craters situated south of Mare Frigoris (on this map) necessarily post-date that event. The mare lavas must also be more recent than the basin. There is strong evidence that all lunar vulcanism that produced dark mare lavas occurred no earlier than about 3.7 billion years ago. The surface of Mare Imbrium displays the usual concentric ridge systems, but under good conditions, lava-flow fronts—sharp demarcations—can be detected. Isolated mountain ranges and peaks, such as the Straight Range (Montes Recti), Montes Teneriffe, Mons Pico, Montes Spitzbergen, and Mons La Hire, lie on a circle that is half the diameter of the circle marked by the Carpathians (Montes Carpatus), Apennines (Montes Apenninus), and Caucasus (Montes Caucasus, Map 6). These inner ranges thus mark the ring that is equivalent to the general shoreline for Mare Crisium, Mare Nectaris, and Mare Humorum.

The craters Archimedes (on the east—to the left—of Mare Imbrium), Aristillus, and Autolycus form a very well-known landmark group. The first crater is flooded with mare lavas and thus is older than the lava flows that filled it, but the other two are clearly more recent than the lavas, displaying typical unflooded impact-crater floors and rough, radial ejecta deposits on top of the mare surface.

The Apennine Scarp (or Mountains, Montes Apenninus) is extremely impressive when viewed just after first quarter or near the last quarter phase. The highest peaks rise some 16,000 ft. (5 km) above the mare surface, but the pinnacle-like drawings of them in older books stem from a misinterpretation of the shapes of their shadows; photographs taken by the Apollo 15 astronauts revealed the generally smooth, rolling nature of the mountains that comprise this range. The Hadley Rille, which was visited by those astronauts, can be glimpsed with small telescopes under steady atmospheric conditions when the moon is about nine days old (past new moon).

The north shore of Mare Imbrium is marked by a strip of highlands that contains the lunar Alps (Montes Alpes), the crater Plato, and the spectacular Sinus Iridum (Bay of Rainbows). The location of this strip is quite anomalous with respect to the rest of the Imbrium basin; there is mounting evidence that the strip is actually a coalesced pair of crustal islands that were torn from their original locations some 100 miles (160 km) to the northeast, during the refilling of the Imbrium crater by magma flowing underneath the moon's crust. The generally parallel-sided shape of Mare Frigoris, the "wrong" placement of the Alps, and other bits of evidence support this conclusion. The Alps, a group of isolated mountains and hills, contain the famous Alpine Valley (Vallis Alpes), a roughly parallel-sided "gash" over 100 miles (160 km) long and averaging 6 miles (10

km) in width (Fig. 8-12). It was once surmised that this valley was formed either by a tangentially travelling meteorite or else by a flying fragment from the Imbrium basin-forming impact, but this idea has long been discounted. It appears to be a graben-like feature, possibly caused by the crustal movements noted above.

Plato, 63 miles (101 km) in diameter, is prominent because of its smooth, level, dark floor, which contrasts strongly with the surrounding lighter highlands materials. The crater's floor contains craters 1½ miles (2½ km) in diameter and smaller; the largest one is located near the center. A medium-sized telescope is needed to show these objects as recognizable craters. Sinus Iridum looks beautiful when the sun is rising on it and its illuminated western edge protrudes far into the unlit surrounding area. This occurs when the moon is about 10 days old.

The crater Copernicus (57 miles—92 km—in diameter), situated at the top of the map in Mare Insularum, is at least as famous and frequently observed as Plato. It is an excellent example of a large, comparatively fresh impact crater. It has a level but somewhat rough floor, with a group of small central peaks. The strongly terraced walls, a result of post-impact slumping, rise some 15,000 ft. (5 km) above the floor. Copernicus is the center of one of the most extensive ray systems anywhere on the moon. The smaller crater Kepler (20 miles—32 km—in diameter), at the top right of the map, also has a notable ray system, the rays of which mingle with those of Copernicus.

Fig. 8-12 The northeast portion of Mare Imbrium, showing Montes Caucasus, Montes Alpes (the Alps), and Vallis Alpes (the Alpine Valley). South is up in this and other photos taken with the 61-in. telescope. (Lunar and Planetary Laboratory, University of Arizona)

MOON MAP 8. This chart is taken up almost entirely by the gray expanse of Oceanus Procellarum, whose western shore is never far removed from the lunar limb. In addition to the usual ridge systems and sprinkling of small craters, this area displays some unique features and interesting formations. The showpiece is undoubtedly the crater Aristarchus, plus the whole Aristarchus Plateau region to the northwest of the crater itself.

Aristarchus is one of the brightest craters of its size anywhere on the moon. It is a relatively fresh impact crater, 28 miles (45 km) in diameter, with a rim rising about 9000 ft. (2700 m) above the floor. It is the center of a major ray system, as are all relatively fresh impact craters. More Transient Lunar Phenomena (TLPs) have been reported in and near Aristarchus than at any other lunar location. In the past, many of these reports undoubtedly stemmed directly or indirectly from effects of the crater's brightness. Thus when the moon is less than a week old, the crater can be seen glowing in the earthlit part of the disk; observed rather low in the sky, the sunlit crater is bright enough against the dark mare background to produce a spectrum as the earth's atmosphere spreads out the lunar light, causing some of the reported color phenomena. However, dedicated observers are now aware of these "red herrings," and not all reports can be dismissed so easily. The whole area is unusual from several standpoints, and rare phenomena, such as emissions of gas, may occur here. Indeed, the orbiting Apollo spacecraft detected more radon gas here than anywhere else on the moon.

Close to the northwest lies the moon's largest volcano and associated lava-flow channel, visible in the smallest telescopes. Although it was discovered by Huygens, this channel is known as Schröter's Valley (Vallis Schröteri), after the German amateur astronomer who first observed it. The volcano itself is the rather unassuming hill immediately northwest of Aristarchus, and the valley's northern flank starts with a depression nicknamed the "Cobra Head," because of the valley's resemblance to the head and body of a snake. The valley cuts through a rough area that is mostly darker than the surrounding mare, despite the presence of a concentration of rays from Aristarchus. Evidence from other investigations indicates that the whole area is covered with a blanket of lunar-type volcanic ash with a high ilmenite content. Although dark, the area is distinctly browner than the surrounding mare, or even other dark, ash-blanketed areas, which are all grayer than their surroundings. It is interesting that this volcanic soil with high ilmenite content can exist in two forms of identical composition but different color. Thus the black and orange soils collected near Shorty crater (which is not shown because of its small size) by the Apollo 17 astronauts are identical apart from color. The difference in color may be due to differing cooling rates, which determine whether the black ilmenite crystallizes out or stays dispersed as an orange coloration in the glass beads in the soil.

The bright marking known as Reiner Gamma (upper right; Fig. 8-13) is an example of a rare type of surface marking; other examples are confined almost entirely to the moon's far side. It is not connected with any visible topography, nor does it have any relief of its own. It does, however, exhibit a magnetic field; this field may shield the surface from the darkening effects of the solar wind and thus preserve the area's brightness. To the northeast lies a large field of rather small volcanic structures known familiarly as the Marius Hills, but the details of their topography only begin to become visible in large telescopes (Fig. 8-13).

In the highlands region at upper right, the crater Hevelius—74 miles (119 km) in diameter—commands the most attention. Its floor is crisscrossed by a lattice of linear rilles, two of which cut through the crater wall and continue into the adjacent terrain.

The crater Lichtenberg, situated in the mare much further to the north, has a ray system that extends only to the north, thus superficially resembling the Proclus system. However, the cause in this case is quite different—the southern portion of the Lichtenberg ray system was covered up by a later lava flow.

Fig. 8-13 The craters Reiner (top), Marius (left), and the unique bright marking called Reiner Gamma, to the west (right) of Reiner. Some details of the Marius Hills are visible to the west-northwest of the crater Marius. South is up. (Lunar and Planetary Laboratory, University of Arizona)

O C E A N U S

Lohrmann→

Hevelius←

←Suess

Hedin

Reiner→

Reiner Gamma

←Cavalerius

Kepler

Luna 7

Luna 9 ·

Olbers←

Marius

Luna 8 ·

Marius Hills

←Galilaei

Vasco da Gama

Cardanus←

P R O C E L L A R U M

* *Luna 13*

Krafft←

Dalton←

Balboa→

Einstein

Bahr

Herodotus

Aristarchus←

Schiaparelli→

Seleucus

Vallis Schröteri

Eddington

Struve

Briggs←

Russell

←Wollaston

Bartels←

Nielsen→

←Lichtenberg

Voskresenskiy→

Naumann→

Ulugh Beigh→

Aston→

Röntgen

Mons Rümker→

Lavoisier→

SINUS RORIS

Harding

Bunsen→

Dechen→

Gerard→

Repsold→

Galvani

Babbage→

Longley

Stokes→

enophanes→

Volta

Regnault→

N

Fig. 8-14 The moon's far side. (North is up.)

The Moon's Far Side

The far side of the moon has been seen only by Apollo astronauts, but it has been photographed both by them (Fig. 8-14) and by unmanned spacecraft, so that its topography is quite well documented. In 1990, the Galileo spacecraft en route to Jupiter also photographed the moon's far side (Fig. 8-10).

The most obvious difference from the near side is the scarcity of dark maria. The far side also displays some remnants of larger basins. The cratered areas of the far side resemble the heavily cratered areas toward the south on the moon's near side, with a range of diameters and degrees of apparent freshness.

The paucity of maria (lava-flooded areas) on the far side means an almost complete absence of the volcanic-related features such as rilles, domes, vents, etc., that diversify the near-side topography.

9

FINDING THE PLANETS

The brightest planets are quite easy to recognize. They often stand out because they are so bright and shine so steadily instead of twinkling. The reddish color of Mars also makes the planet distinctive. When we are observing the sky, these characteristics can help us recognize that we are observing planets instead of stars. The fact that the planets all lie close to the *ecliptic*—an imaginary line drawn across the sky to mark the yearly path of the sun among the stars—also helps us pick out the planets. The ecliptic is marked with a dotted line on the Monthly Sky Maps in Chapter 3 and on the Atlas Charts in Chapter 7.

Most of the planets can be seen with the naked eye; Venus, for example, is often conspicuous as a bright object in the sky near sunrise or sunset—the "morning star" or the "evening star," respectively. The planets are most enjoyable to observe, however, when you turn a telescope on them. In the next chapter, we will describe what each planet looks like in a telescope, and what some of the latest observations from space have revealed about the planets. In this chapter, we will show you how to locate the naked-eye planets in the sky, and how to know in advance which planets will be "up"—visible above the horizon—when you plan to observe. Also, if you see a bright object in the sky, you can use the information in this chapter to determine whether it is a planet.

As they orbit the sun, the planets change their positions with respect to the stars. We display the positions of the planets in the sky from night to night in a series of Graphic Timetables of the Heavens at the end of this chapter. The Graphic Timetables are a compact way of displaying the rising, setting, and transit times of the planets during the night; they show the times for sunrise, sunset, and twilight as well. (An object *transits* when it crosses your *meridian,* the line drawn from the north celestial pole through your zenith and then through the point due south on your horizon to the south celestial pole; thus a planet "transits" when it is passing due north or south of you, and is then at its highest in the sky.) Once you have become familiar with the Graphic Timetables, which takes a little practice, you will then be able to determine quickly which objects are well suited for observing at any given time of the year and at any time of the night; you will also be able to identify the planets you are seeing in the sky. You can also locate the planets by using the information in Appendix 11 to plot their positions along the ecliptic, which is marked (as a dotted line) on the Monthly Sky Maps in Chapter 3 and on the Atlas Charts in Chapter 7.

We have provided one Graphic Timetable for each year. To use any of the Timetables, scan down the left-hand axis to find the date of the year. Then scan across the top or bottom axis to find the time of night in local time for your time zone. An extra line across the bottom shows the time in daylight saving time.

Look along the horizontal line that corresponds to your date to see which planets can be seen. The time of a planet's transit tells you the time when it will appear due south of you. Before that time, the planet will be to the east along the ecliptic; after that time, it will be to the west along the ecliptic. If a planet sets during the night, it will generally be visible from dusk until it sets. If a planet rises during the night, it will generally remain visible until morning twilight.

The Graphic Timetables in this guide are drawn for observers at latitude 40°N; the correction for observers at midnorthern latitudes amounts to only a few minutes, so we do not give it here. The Timetables give rising and setting times for objects assuming a flat horizon; if you have mountains on your horizon, of course, planets will become visible later or will disappear from your view earlier.

Each year's planetary curves are different from those of other years, yet distinct patterns appear. The Timetables show the curves even before sunset and after sunrise, when the planets aren't usually visible (though the brighter ones can sometimes be seen), in order to display the patterns better.

The regular cycling of Mercury's rising and setting times as it rapidly orbits the sun is displayed as distorted sine waves oscillating on either side of the sunrise and sunset lines. Venus displays a similar pattern but over a much longer period. Notice that the rising and setting curves for Venus recur every 19.2 months, the period with which Venus returns to successive *superior conjunctions*—when Venus lines up on the far side of the sun for us on earth. (This is Venus's *synodic period*, as opposed to its *sidereal period*—the time it takes to return to the same position in the sky with respect to the stars.) Whenever Venus sets more than $3/4$ of an hour after sunset, you should be able to spot it easily with the naked eye. Mercury and Venus have orbits smaller than earth's, and are known as *inferior planets*.

The *superior planets* have orbits outside the earth's. They can be seen rising and setting far from the sun in the sky, and the curves showing their positions on the Graphic Timetables are more linear. Mars's pattern repeats every 25–27 months, which means that *oppositions* of Mars—when Mars is opposite the sun in our sky, transiting in the middle of the night, 12 hours after the sun has transited—occur at intervals of about 2 years, 2 months. During an opposition, Mars is on your meridian at midnight, when the sun is as far on the other side of the earth (and thus invisible) as it gets. Mars will come within 58 million miles (94 million km) on January 3, 1993; 63 million miles (101 million km) on February 11, 1995; and 61 million miles (99 million km) on March 20, 1997.

Jupiter returns to opposition every 13 months and Saturn every 12.4 months; in other words, in the 12 months the earth takes to complete an orbit of the sun, Jupiter and Saturn have moved ahead a little and it takes us a few more weeks to catch up.

For practice in using the Graphic Timetable, let us pick an example. Look at the night of May 20, 1994. Draw a horizontal line from left to right, or follow across the Timetable with your finger. First you find the lines for Mars setting and for Jupiter rising. At the bottom, you can see that they come at 5:30 p.m. and 6 p.m., respectively, daylight saving time. (Since daylight saving time is in common use at this time of year, we give times in DST for this example.) At 8 p.m., the light shading shows the onset of twilight. Mercury sets at 10 p.m., shortly before the heavier shading shows that twilight turns into night, and Venus sets about half an hour later. Thus Mercury and Venus have been evening stars. Since the first mentions of these planets you come to are their settings, you know that they must have been up when sunset came (or else you would have seen the lines for their risings). At about 11:30 p.m., Jupiter transits, that is, passes your north-south meridian. Thus Jupiter is well placed for observing almost all night. Saturn rises about 2 a.m. When it rises high enough, often an hour or so later, it becomes visible in the eastern sky. Morning twilight begins about 4 a.m. and Mars rises soon thereafter. Jupiter sets at 5 a.m., about an hour before sunrise. Mercury and Venus rise about 7 a.m., but it is already daylight and they are ordinarily not seen.

You can use a Graphic Timetable in reverse to identify an object in the sky. You must check both the Graphic Timetables of the planets to see if the object is a planet and the Graphic Timetable of the Brightest Stars (Fig. 1-2, p. 9) to see if it is a star. If the object is in the east, check the appropriate Timetable in this chapter for a curve representing a recent rising time of a planet. If it is to the south, then search for a transit curve and compare it with those for the brightest stars, in Figure 1-2. If the object is to the west, look to see what bright planets are about to set at the time when you are observing.

Visibility of the Planets

Descriptions by Robert C. Victor
Graphic Timetables by Scientia, Inc.

1992

VENUS is a "morning star" early in the year, but gradually approaches the sun and becomes harder to see. Venus passes widely north of Antares on January 8 and closely north of Mars on February 19. On February 28 and 29, Venus is closely paired with Saturn, while Mars lingers about 5° to their upper right. By the end of March, Venus is too difficult to observe.

On June 13 Venus passes superior conjunction, behind the sun, and emerges as an "evening star" in the western twilight in August. On the 22nd of that month, Venus is very close to Jupiter. Gradually pulling away from the sun, Venus improves until the year's end.

MERCURY has three good morning appearances in 1992: in early January, when it is to the lower left of Venus, and close to Mars on the 10th; in August; and in December. Good evening apparitions are in February–March and June–July.

MARS opens this year as a faint, difficult 1.6 magnitude "star" very low in the southeast morning twilight, to the lower left of Mercury and Venus. Mars is overtaken by Mercury on January 10 and by Venus on February 19. The reddish planet overtakes slow-moving Saturn on March 6. Then in Capricornus, Mars moves eastward against the stars, brightens slowly, and rises progressively earlier in the night. On July 26 Mars is south of the Pleiades and has brightened to first magnitude. Mars goes north of Aldebaran on August 10 and south of Pollux on November 1. By then Mars has brightened to zero magnitude and rises in the late evening. In late November, Mars begins to retrograde and swing back toward Pollux, which it passes again on Christmas Eve. Mars ends this year gleaming at magnitude −1.2 while rising in the northeast shortly after sunset.

JUPITER opens the year as a brilliant "star" rising in the east a few hours after sunset. Rising earlier as weeks pass, Jupiter reaches opposition (180° from the sun) on February 28, and then gleams at magnitude −2.0 in the sky all night long. Continuing as an evening object, Jupiter sets about 2 hours earlier each month until it fades into the western twilight in August. Passing solar conjunction in September, Jupiter emerges in morning twilight in October.

SATURN is in Capricornus all year. In early January it can be seen low in the southwest in evening twilight. In conjunction with the sun on the 29th, Saturn emerges into the east-southeast morning twilight in late February, when it is passed closely by Venus.

Saturn rises about 2 hours earlier with each passing month. On August 7 it reaches opposition in the east-southeast at dusk and is visible all night as a "star" of magnitude +0.4. Telescopically, the rings are tilted 16°. An evening star for the rest of the year, Saturn is overtaken by Venus on December 21. At year's end, Saturn is low in the southwest at dusk, to the lower right of Venus.

THE GRAPHIC TIMETABLE OF THE HEAVENS
1992

Fig. 9-1 A Graphic Timetable showing the positions of the planets in 1992. The hours shaded in dark gray are most favorable for viewing.

1993

VENUS opens the year as a fine "evening star." On January 19 it reaches its greatest elongation, 47° from the sun, and sets nearly 4 hours after sundown. Venus rapidly gets lower in the western sky during March. Swinging between earth and sun on April 1, Venus leaves the evening sky and becomes visible in the east before sunup as the "morning star." For ten weeks before and after April 1, Venus is especially interesting through telescopes and binoculars as its phase changes from half full to a large thin crescent and back.

In the morning sky, Venus reaches its greatest elongation, 46° from the sun, on June 10. Gradually approaching the sun, Venus passes near Spica on November 4, and Jupiter on November 10. By mid-December Venus is in twilight.

MERCURY has two fine evening apparitions, in February and in May–June. The best morning apparitions come in July–August and in November–December.

MARS reaches opposition (180° from the sun) on January 7. Then shining at magnitude –1.2 in Gemini, Mars rises in the northeast around sunset and is visible all night. Near the end of January, Mars passes directly overhead for late evening viewers at latitude 27° north (southern Texas and central Florida). In only two other years in the 20th century, 1914 and 1961, has Mars appeared so far north of the celestial equator.

Mars remains an "evening star" until early autumn. It fades in twilight in September.

JUPITER is in Virgo for nearly all of 1993. As the year begins, Jupiter rises in the middle of the night and stands high in the south in morning twilight. Rising earlier each month, Jupiter reaches opposition on March 30. Shining at magnitude –2.0, Jupiter is then visible all night long, rising in the east at sunset and setting in the west at dawn.

In the months following opposition, Jupiter remains an "evening star" until it disappears into the western twilight in September. Jupiter passes conjunction with the sun on October 18. Then, at the beginning of November, Jupiter emerges as a "morning star" in the east-southeast, to the lower left of Venus and Spica.

SATURN spends 1993 in Capricornus and Aquarius. As the year opens, Saturn is in the southwest at dusk, to the lower right of Venus. By late January Saturn disappears into the twilight glow.

In March, Saturn emerges as a "morning star" low in the east-southeast at dawn. Saturn rises 2 hours earlier with each passing month and reaches opposition on August 19. Then 180° from the sun, Saturn rises at dusk and is above the horizon all night; the rings are tilted 12° from edge-on. Saturn is an "evening star" for the rest of the year.

THE GRAPHIC TIMETABLE OF THE HEAVENS
1993

Fig. 9-2 A Graphic Timetable showing the positions of the planets in 1993. The hours shaded in dark gray are most favorable for viewing.

1994

VENUS is at superior conjunction (beyond the sun) in mid-January and is not visible for several weeks. It emerges as an "evening star" low in the western twilight by the end of February. In June, Venus reaches its highest position above the western horizon at dusk, and sets $2^1/_2$ hours after sunset. Venus comes within 7° of Jupiter in late September, then swings rapidly toward the sun and disappears in early October.

Venus passes inferior conjunction (nearly between earth and sun) on November 2, then emerges as a "morning star" in the east-southeast by mid-November. On the 14th, Venus is within 5° south of Mercury. By late December, Venus rises more than $3^1/_2$ hours ahead of the sun.

Telescopically, Venus is of greatest interest from September through December, when it passes through crescent phases and appears large because it is close to earth.

MERCURY has two excellent evening apparitions: In January–February (close to Saturn on February 1); and in May–June (about 9° to the lower right of Venus in late May).

In the morning sky, Mercury's March apparition isn't very favorable from midnorthern latitudes. Mercury's July appearance is better, and the one in November is very favorable.

MARS was in conjunction with the sun on December 27, 1993. Mars's emergence as a "morning star" is very gradual; it should be visible to the unaided eye in twilight by the end of April, when the red planet is low in the east, to the lower left of Saturn.

As months pass, Mars brightens and rises progressively earlier in the night. At year's end it rises in late evening.

JUPITER opens the year as a "morning star" in Libra, in the southern sky at dawn. As months pass, Jupiter rises earlier, and by April 30 it reaches opposition. Then visible all night long, Jupiter rises in the east-southeast at sunset and sets at sunrise.

In the following months Jupiter is an evening "star." If you look for it at dusk, you'll see it drift over to the south by June, and to the west-southwest by October, when it fades into the twilight.

Jupiter passes conjunction with the sun on November 17 and emerges as a "morning star" in the east-southeast twilight in early December.

SATURN spends the year in Aquarius. On January 1 it is in the southwest at dusk and sets within a few hours after sunset.

After passing solar conjunction on February 21, Saturn emerges as a "morning star" in the east-southeast twilight in late March. Saturn rises earlier in the night until it reaches opposition on September 1. Then rising at sunset, Saturn is visible all night long.

Saturn remains in the evening sky in the closing months of 1994. In December it is well up in the south at dusk.

THE GRAPHIC TIMETABLE OF THE HEAVENS
1994

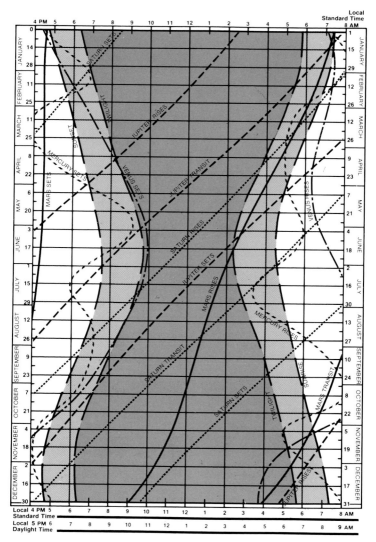

Fig. 9-3 A Graphic Timetable showing the positions of the planets in 1994. The hours shaded in dark gray are most favorable for viewing.

1995

VENUS starts the year as a "morning star," rising more than 3 hours before the sun. Within two weeks it reaches greatest elongation, 47° from the sun. Venus passes 3° N of Jupiter on January 14 and widely north of Antares two days later. On April 13 Venus passes 0.5° N of Saturn, the pair rising just over an hour before sunup. Venus continues to rise ever closer to dawn and is hard to see by July. It passes superior conjunction on August 20, emerging as an "evening star" by late October.

In November Venus passes 1.3° N of Jupiter on the 18th and 0.2° south of Mars on the 22nd; the compact trio sets over an hour after sunset. At year's end Venus sets 2$\frac{1}{2}$ hours after the sun.

MERCURY has a good evening apparition in January (about 20° lower right of Saturn), and an excellent one in April–May. In December, Mercury goes 1.1° S of Mars on the 23rd and closes the year 13° lower right of Venus. In the morning, Mercury lingers 15° lower left of Venus in early March and climbs 8° to Venus's upper right in early July. Mercury's best morning apparition is in October.

MARS opens the year in Leo, 4° NE of Regulus, and rises 4 hours after sunset. Turning retrograde (westward) as earth overtakes it, the red planet reaches opposition and all-night visibility on February 11. Mars backs into Cancer, where in late March it is 17° west of Regulus, high in the eastern evening sky, and then resumes direct motion against the stars. On May 24, Mars, faded to first magnitude, slides only 1° N of Regulus. By late June, Mars is in the west-southwest at dusk, where it sinks slowly for the rest of the year.

Mars goes 2° N of Spica on August 28. On November 15, Mars goes 1.2° S of Jupiter; Venus soon overtakes both. Mars ends the year 18° lower right of Venus and 13° lower right of Mercury.

JUPITER is within 8° of Antares for most of 1995 and performs a triple conjunction with that star, passing 5° N of it in late January, early June, and late September. Near Venus in mid-January, Jupiter rises earlier and higher each morning. By mid-March, it is in the south at dawn. By mid-May it rises in evening twilight. On June 1 it stands at opposition at magnitude –2.1 and is up all night. In July, Jupiter is in the south at dusk, and by October is in the southwest. Sinking into twilight, it is overtaken by Mars and Venus in November (see above). Jupiter departs by early December.

SATURN is in Aquarius all year, though its rings are less visible than usual because they are almost edge-on to us. In the southwest at dusk in January, Saturn sinks into the western twilight in mid-February. After solar conjunction on March 6, Saturn emerges into the morning glow in early April, to the lower left of Venus. After a close conjunction with Venus on April 13, Saturn climbs halfway up the southern sky at dawn in July. By early August, Saturn rises in evening twilight. By September 14 Saturn is at opposition at magnitude +0.9 and is up all night. For the rest of the year Saturn can be seen at dusk, high in the sky in the south by December.

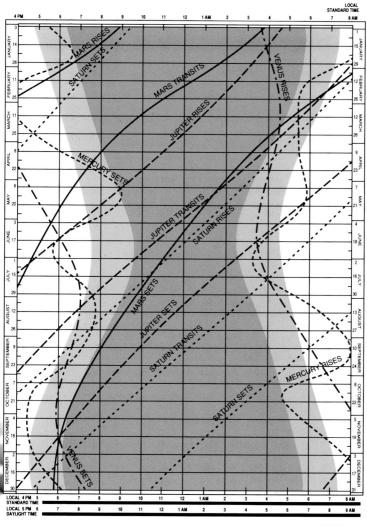

Fig. 9-4 A Graphic Timetable showing the positions of the planets in 1995. The hours shaded in dark gray are most favorable for viewing.

1996

VENUS this year is an "evening star" in the western sky until early June. After passing Saturn on February 2, Venus reaches greatest elongation, 46° from the sun, on April 1, and sets four hours after sundown. On the next two evenings, Venus appears within 1° of the Pleiades. Continuing eastward, Venus passes widely north of Aldebaran on April 12, and stops above the horns of Taurus on May 19. Venus appears in the eastern morning sky from late June on. During June 23–July 4, Venus passes near Mercury, Mars, and Aldebaran. On August 20, Venus reaches greatest elongation again and rises more than 3½ hours before the sun. Venus goes past Pollux on September 1, Mars on September 4, Regulus on October 3, Spica on November 17, and Antares on December 25.

MERCURY has two fine evening apparitions: in early January, low in the southwest at dusk, and in April, low in the west-northwest. In both, Mercury appears to lower right of Venus. At dusk in December, Mercury is very low in the southwest, to lower right of Jupiter. In morning twilight, Mercury can be seen low in the east-southeast, to Jupiter's lower left, in January–February, and low in the east, to the lower left of Venus and Regulus, in September–October.

MARS can be glimpsed (in binoculars) at dusk on January 1, 5° to the lower right of Mercury. Mars reappears in the east-northeast in morning twilight in mid-June, again near Mercury, then passes Venus and Aldebaran near the end of June. Although it remains near magnitude +1.5 all summer, Mars gets easier to see as it rises earlier each month. After passing Pollux on August 30, Mars is overtaken by Venus on September 4. Later that month, on the 21st, Mars passes through the Beehive Cluster. The red planet goes by Regulus on October 29, and at magnitude +1.3 should be a close match in brightness, but not color, to the star. Mars ends the year at magnitude +0.5 in Virgo, high in the south as twilight behind.

JUPITER spends 1996 in Sagittarius, making three passes above the handle of the Teapot. Visible virtually the entire year, Jupiter emerges as a morning star low in southeast twilight near the start of January. Each month, Jupiter rises earlier, reaching opposition on July 4. Then at magnitude –2.7, Jupiter is visible all night, in southeast at dusk and in southwest at dawn. Jupiter can be followed until year's end, when it's very low in the southwest at dusk.

SATURN opens the year high in the south-southwest at dusk and is overtaken by Venus on February 2. In Aquarius south of the Circlet of Pisces, Saturn is unusually faint, at magnitude +1.2, because it appears wingless until earth crosses to the south (illuminated) side of the ring plane on February 11. After sinking into the western twilight in early March, Saturn reappears by late April in Pisces in the eastern morning sky. Saturn makes a foray into Cetus from early June to late August before backing into Pisces. Its rising time shifts 2 hours earlier each month until Saturn comes up at sunset on September 26; it is then at opposition, and up all night. Now closer to earth and with rings tipped about 4°, Saturn shines brighter at +0.5. At year end, Saturn is high in the south at dusk.

THE GRAPHIC TIMETABLE OF THE HEAVENS
1996

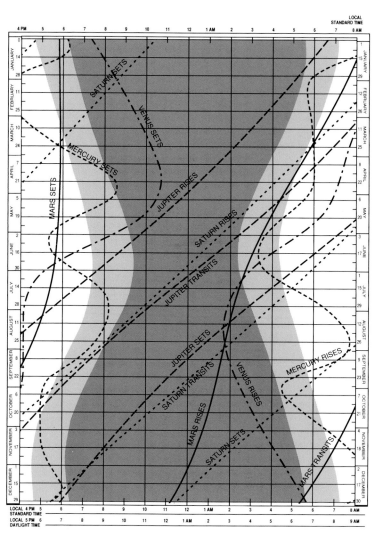

Fig. 9-5 A Graphic Timetable showing the positions of the planets in 1996. The hours shaded in dark gray are most favorable for viewing.

1997

VENUS is an easy "morning star" low in southeast at dawn in January. Approaching the sun, Venus passes emerging Mercury on Jan. 12 and at month's end is far to its lower left. A challenging twilight duo on Feb. 6 is described under Jupiter. Venus goes beyond the sun on April 2 and by mid-May emerges into the west-northwest at dusk. An "evening star" for the rest of the year, it remains low in twilight until autumn. Watch Venus pass Pollux on June 22, Regulus on July 22 (with Mercury trailing within 5° behind Venus for the rest of July), Spica on Sept. 6, Antares on Oct. 16, and Mars on Oct. 24. On Nov. 6, Venus reaches greatest elongation, 47° from the sun, and sets farther south than it will again until 2005. In December, Venus sets as much as 3 hours after the sun early in the month, but slows its eastward progress and is overtaken by Mars on the 21st. For a few days around then, Venus pauses 17° to the lower left of Jupiter.

MERCURY has its best evening apparition of the year in late March and early April, low and north of west at dusk. Also at dusk, in the latter half of July, Mercury forms beautiful groupings with Venus and Regulus that can be enjoyed with binoculars, and at the end of November Mercury can be found very low in the southwest, 23° lower right of Venus. In the morning, you can find Mercury near Venus in January, just below Regulus around September 11, and to the left of Antares in the last week of December.

MARS on January 1 rises an hour before midnight and reaches the southern sky before dawn. Mars comes up earlier each week until opposition on March 16–17, when it gleams at mag. −1.3 and is up all night. Languishing in western Virgo except for a reverse into Leo in April–May, Mars finally passes Spica on August 3. Moving east against the evening zodiacal backdrop with increasing speed, Mars passes its counter-namesake Antares on October 12. For the rest of the year, Mars lingers near Venus, coming closest to it on October 24 and December 21. By year's end, Mars fades to mag. +1.2.

JUPITER, as the year begins, follows the sun over the southwest horizon by only an hour. After weeks of invisibility, Jupiter emerges in the east-southeast morning sky around the middle of February, and remains in Capricornus for the rest of the year. Jupiter's close conjunction with Venus on February 6 will be difficult to observe from midnorthern latitudes, rising barely half an hour before sunup. Jupiter comes up earlier each month until its opposition on August 9, when it will gleam at mag. −2.8 low in the east-southeast at dusk and be up all night. By year's end, Jupiter is in the southwest at dusk, with Mars and Venus to its lower right.

SATURN opens the year high in the south at dusk and spends most of 1997 in Pisces. Saturn sinks into western twilight in mid-March, then emerges around the end of April in the east at dawn. Rising earlier, Saturn reaches opposition (all-night visibility, at mag. +0.2) on October 9–10. Its rings are then tilted 10°. Saturn continues in the evening sky until year's end, when it reaches the meridian before darkness falls.

THE GRAPHIC TIMETABLE OF THE HEAVENS
1997

Fig. 9-6 A Graphic Timetable showing the positions of the planets in 1997. The hours shaded in dark gray are most favorable for viewing.

10

OBSERVING THE PLANETS

In the previous chapter, we explained how to find the planets in the sky. This chapter deals with observing the planets themselves. With even a small telescope, you can see that the planets have shapes and that the apparent shapes of some of the planets change over time. Since the easiest and most impressive planets to observe (in order) are Jupiter, Saturn, Venus, and Mars, we describe the planets in that order here, then discuss the planets that are harder to see—Mercury, Uranus, Neptune, and Pluto.

JUPITER

Jupiter, the largest planet in the solar system, is 11 times the diameter and over a thousand times the volume of the earth. It is about 5.2 times as far away from the sun as the earth is; since the average distance from the earth to the sun is called 1 Astronomical Unit (1 A.U.), Jupiter averages 5.2 A.U. from the sun. When Jupiter is on the same side of the sun as the earth, it is high in the nighttime sky, and is only about 4 A.U. from us (5.2 A.U. minus the earth's orbital radius of 1 A.U. from us (5.2 A.U. minus the earth's orbital radius of 1 A.U. equals 4.2 A.U.). At this distance, the planet covers almost 50 seconds of arc in the sky—$1/40$ the diameter of the full moon—and can be about magnitude –2.5, three times brighter than the brightest star, Sirius.

When a planet is on a line with the earth and sun, the planet and sun appear close together in the sky and we say that the planet is in *conjunction*. The actual time of conjunction is when the planet and the sun appear at the same longitude along the ecliptic (see Appendix 11). Planets can also be in conjunction with each other or with the moon. Jupiter is in conjunction with the sun only when it is on the far side of the sun and consequently appears smaller than it does when it is at opposition.

A planet is at *opposition* when it is on the extension of the line of sight from the sun through the earth. Jupiter and the other outer planets are best observed at opposition, when they are above the horizon all night. They then rise at sunset, are brightest, and show the largest disks.

Fig. 10-1 A montage of planetary images from NASA spacecraft, from Mercury at the top, through Venus, Earth and moon, Mars, Jupiter, Saturn, Uranus, and Neptune. (NASA/JPL)

Fig. 10-2 Jupiter, photographed from the earth, showing its bright horizontal zones and its dark horizontal belts. South is at top, since this is a view through a telescope. The four Galilean satellites are also visible. (Lunar and Planetary Laboratory, University of Arizona)

Jupiter's Disk

With a small telescope, you can see light and dark bands across Jupiter's disk. The number of bands you see depends not only on how close Jupiter is to earth at the time but also on how steady the atmosphere is for your observing location. The bands represent clouds drawn out into long streaks as Jupiter rotates; the planet, which is made entirely of gas, rotates at different speeds at different latitudes. (Solid bodies like the earth don't do this.) Gas near the pole rotates about 5 minutes faster than gas near the equator does during each 10-hour rotation period. (Planets rotate—spin—on their axes but revolve—orbit—around the sun.)

Figure 10-2 is a ground-based photograph of Jupiter and its moons. Even a large telescope does not show much more detail, because of the obscuring effects of the earth's atmosphere. The form of the bands changes slowly over long periods of time. The major bands have been given names, as shown in Figure 10-3. The bright bands are called *zones* and the dark bands are called *belts.* The belts and zones show subtle colors.

Jupiter's rotation causes it to bulge at the equator—to be *oblate*—by 7%. It is obvious in even a small telescope that Jupiter is out-of-round.

Fig. 10-3 A schematic diagram showing the major features of Jupiter.

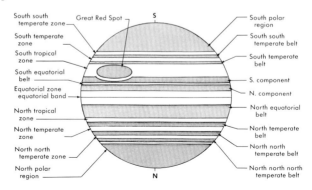

A large reddish region known as the Great Red Spot has been observed on Jupiter from time to time for hundreds of years. The Great Red Spot is about 8400 by 18,000 miles (14,000 by 30,000 km), much larger than the earth. The Great Red Spot is a giant storm in Jupiter's clouds, which is more visible at some times than others. Sometimes its shape changes. Close-up views taken from the Voyager spacecraft revealed the rotation of the Great Red Spot (Fig. 10-4).

Though the Voyagers discovered a thin ring around Jupiter (Fig. 10-5), it is too faint to be detected by ordinary means from earth. The ring was not expected, but scientists looked for it briefly with Voyager 1, and it turned up. Voyager 2 then paid more attention to observing it properly. It showed up best when backlighted, with the sun behind it as seen from the spacecraft.

Jupiter's Moons

The four brightest moons (satellites) of Jupiter can be seen with even a small telescope. Named Io, Europa, Ganymede, and Callisto, after mythological lovers of Jupiter (as are all of Jupiter's more than 16 moons), they range from 1950 to 3270 miles (3138 to 5262 km) in diameter. All but one of the four brightest moons are larger than our own moon. The largest of Jupiter's moons, Ganymede, is even larger than the planet Mercury.

Nonetheless, these four "Galilean satellites," so called because they were discovered by Galileo, were merely points of light in the sky until NASA's two Voyager spacecraft flew nearby in 1979 and 1980, radioing back close-up pictures of the moons' surfaces. Io is covered with volcanoes, of which about 10 are now erupting (Fig. 10-6); it is the most active body in the solar system. Europa is apparently covered with ice. Ganymede—which has the largest surface diameter of any moon in the solar system—may contain water and ice surrounding a core of rock; its surface shows craters and strange grooves (Fig. 10-6, *right*). Callisto is covered with craters, including a huge bull's-eye called Valhalla.

Fig. 10-4 A close-up of Jupiter's Great Red Spot and the turbulence surrounding it. North is up on this and other photos taken from space. (JPL/NASA)

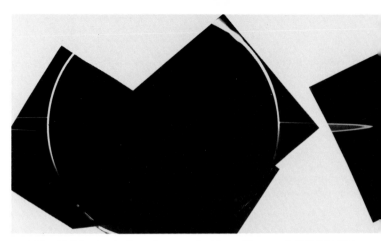

Fig. 10-5 Jupiter's ring, photographed from Voyager 2. (JPL/NASA)

These four bright moons orbit in the plane of Jupiter's equator, so they always seem stretched out close to a line drawn through Jupiter. The period of Io's orbit is 1 day, 18 hours; Europa's period is 3 days, 13 hours; Ganymede's is 7 days, 3 hours; and Callisto's is 16 days, 16 hours. If you observe these moons in a telescope over a night or from night to night, you can see their relative positions change. We sometimes see the moons move in front of or behind Jupiter; when the moons move in front of Jupiter, their shadows fall on the planet. When the moons are at their brightest, Ganymede can reach magnitude 4.6, and the others can be no more than a magnitude fainter.

Each year, the positions of the Galilean moons in relation to the sides of Jupiter are graphed in *The Astronomical Almanac,* and the

Fig. 10-6 *(left)* Volcanoes erupting hundreds of kilometers high above the surface of Io, a satellite of Jupiter. (JPL/NASA)
(Right) A computer-enhanced photo of Ganymede's surface, showing some of its craters (the dark areas) and grooves. (JPL/NASA)

Fig. 10-7 Jupiter, imaged from the Hubble Space Telescope in orbit around the Earth. Images of this quality can now be obtained from the Hubble Space Telescope whenever the priority for observing Jupiter is sufficiently high. The cloud pattern is entirely different from what it was when the Voyagers passed by Jupiter a dozen years earlier. Images like this one are being taken on a regular basis to follow how Jupiter's weather evolves. The computer programs used to predict weather on Earth will be tested with these changing weather patterns on Jupiter, and we hope that forecasts of weather on Earth will improve as a result. At extreme right, we see the Great Red Spot below center and Jupiter's moon Europa disappearing behind the planet above center. (NASA/JPL, California Institute of Technology)

graphs are reprinted in the magazines *Sky & Telescope* and *Astronomy*. Since separate graphs are needed for each month, we will not take space in this field guide to print the maps here. Computer programs that display the configuration of Jupiter's moons are readily available.

Missions to Jupiter

NASA's Ulysses mission to the sun was launched in 1990 via Jupiter. Jupiter's gravity sent the spacecraft out of the ecliptic, the plane in which the planets orbit, so that Ulysses will be able to observe the poles of the sun. It passed Jupiter in 1992; it will be over the sun's south pole in 1994 and, its path bent by the sun's gravity, over the sun's north pole in 1995.

A NASA mission called Galileo was launched in 1989 and will arrive at Jupiter on December 7, 1995. Its goal is to launch a probe that will parachute through Jupiter's clouds and send back data for about an hour. It will also put a spacecraft in orbit around Jupiter for a couple of years. Though its main antenna is stuck in the closed position, Galileo carries a smaller antenna that should enable the mission to carry out a large fraction of its goals.

Observing Jupiter

Count, sketch, and note the colors of belts and zones on the disk. Observe and sketch the Great Red Spot and perhaps other disturbances in Jupiter's atmosphere; notice the oblateness of Jupiter's disk. Observe and identify the Galilean satellites and how they move; observe their occultations by Jupiter (when they pass behind Jupiter's disk), their eclipses, and the transits of the moons and their shadows across Jupiter's disk.

Table 16: Oppositions of Jupiter

Date of Opposition	Diameter of Disk (arc sec)	Distance to Earth A.U.	Distance to Earth km (millions)
February 29, 1992	45	4.41	660
March 30, 1993	44	4.45	666
April 30, 1994	45	4.42	662
June 1, 1995	46	4.32	647
July 4, 1996	47	4.19	626
August 9, 1997	49	4.05	606
September 16, 1998	50	3.96	593

Fig. 10-8 One of the best ground-based photos of Jupiter. The Great Red Spot shows clearly. North is at top. (Lunar and Planetary Laboratory, University of Arizona)

Fig. 10-9 Jupiter, as seen from the Voyager 1 spacecraft. Io appears as a tiny reddish-brown ball suspended in front of the planet, and Europa is at far right. (JPL/NASA)

Fig. 10-10 Jupiter's Great Red Spot, photographed by one of the Voyagers. We also see a white oval, which is another storm like the Great Red Spot. We now know of similar storms on Saturn and Neptune. (JPL/NASA)

Fig. 10-11 Voyager photos of Jupiter's Galilean moons, to scale: Io (top left), made reddish by sulfur from its volcanoes; smooth, icy Europa; Ganymede, the largest solar-system moon (lower left); and Callisto (bottom right), with bright craters. (JPL/NASA)

SATURN

Galileo, with his tiny telescope, could see that Saturn wasn't quite round. Some decades later, astronomers realized that Saturn was surrounded by a ring (Fig. 10-12). As the decades and centuries passed, we realized that Saturn had more and more rings. In the 1970s, we knew of half a dozen rings; now, with the results from the Voyager flybys, we know of hundreds of thousands of rings.

Saturn is 9.4 times the diameter of earth, almost the size of Jupiter. Its ring extends out much farther, up to 81,000 miles (135,000 km) from Saturn's center.

Saturn is 9.5 A.U. from the sun, which means that at best it is twice as far from earth as Jupiter is. Its maximum size is thus about 20 seconds of arc, and it never goes brighter than about zero magnitude.

When the Voyager spacecraft visited Saturn in 1981, they not only observed Saturn's rings and disk in detail but also got closeup views of many of Saturn's moons (Fig. 10-13). They even discovered several new moons; a total of 18 moons are now known.

Fig. 10-12 One of the best ground-based photos of Saturn, taken with a 61-in. telescope. North is at top. (Catalina Observatory, University of Arizona)

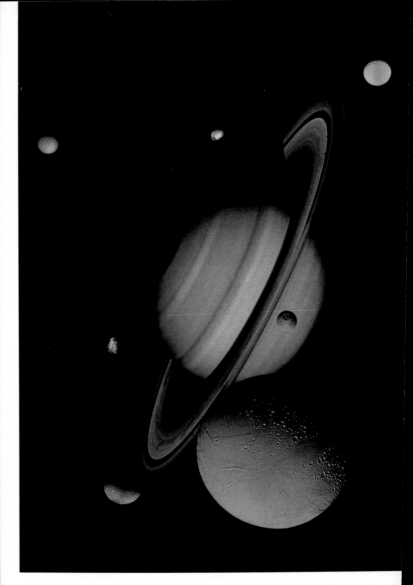

Fig. 10-13 A montage of Saturn and some of its moons, photographed from the Voyager 1 and 2 spacecraft. Clockwise from upper left, the moons are Titan (reddish), Iapetus (with one dark side), Tethys, Mimas (a small moon with a giant crater), Enceladus (lower center), Dione, and Rhea. (JPL/NASA)

Saturn's Rings

Even small telescopes reveal Saturn's rings. They are often the first objects an amateur looks at, and they are certainly among the first things shown to novices. The rings are so glorious that professionals like to look at them too. When you are observing Saturn (or any of the other planets), you will find that waiting for steady air (good "seeing") will give you better images.

The main division between Saturn's bright middle ring (the *B-ring*) and fainter outer ring (the *A-ring*) is called *Cassini's division*, after its 17th-century discoverer. A faint inner *crepe ring* (the *C-ring*) is hard to see. Though Cassini's division looks dark when seen from earth, and therefore resembles a gap in the rings, the Voyagers revealed that it really contains bits of opaque material. A gap called *Encke's division* runs through the A-ring, though it is extremely hard to detect even with large telescopes.

On close examination from Voyager, Saturn's rings break up into thousands of tiny "ringlets" (Fig. 10-14). The rings and ringlets consist of chunks of rock, ranging in size from pebbles to huge boulders, each independently orbiting Saturn.

Saturn's rings and equator are inclined by 27° to Saturn's orbit, so we see them from different aspects at different times. The angle at which we see the rings varies over a 30-year period. The earth last passed through the plane of the rings, when the rings become invisible, in 1979–80, and widened to our view until 1987–88. They will again be edge-on in 1995–96. They are faintest at this edge-on time, so additional moons are sometimes discovered then.

Fig. 10-14 A contrast-enhanced photo showing about 60 of Saturn's rings, taken from Voyager 1. Voyager 2 revealed hundreds of thousands of such "ringlets." (JPL/NASA)

Fig. 10-15 As Voyager 1 left Saturn and looked back, the planet appeared as a crescent inside its rings. The Cassini division is readily visible, and some material can be seen faintly inside it. (JPL/NASA)

Saturn's Disk

Saturn's disk, out-of-round by 10%, shows less contrast in its bands than Jupiter's disk does. The effect may be because Saturn is farther from the sun and thus colder; the cooler temperatures may slow down the chemical reactions that create the colors in the clouds.

Saturn's Moons

Saturn boasts of the second largest moon in the solar system, Titan. With its clouds included, Titan is 3625 km (5150 miles) in diameter, nearly half the size of earth, and is surrounded by an atmosphere that is even thicker than earth's. Titan never becomes brighter than about 8th magnitude; it can, however, be seen as a small, starlike point of light with even a small telescope.

Saturn has another dozen moons over 60 miles (100 km) across, and many smaller ones (Appendix 10). A mnemonic for the major moons and their order of distance from Saturn—Mimas, Enceladus, Tethys, Dione, Rhea, Titan, Hyperion, Iapetus, and Phoebe—is "Met Dr. Thip," remembering that Titan is the second T.

Observing Saturn

Observe the rings and their orientation; observe and sketch Cassini's division; try to observe the bands on Saturn's disk.

Observe Titan, Saturn's largest moon, and plot its changes in position during its 16-day orbital period; see how many other satellites you can observe (such as Rhea, Tethys, and Dione) with, say, a 6-inch telescope.

Oppositions of Saturn occur on August 7, 1992; August 19, 1993; September 1, 1994; September 14, 1995; September 26, 1996; October 10, 1997; September 16, 1998; October 23, 1999.

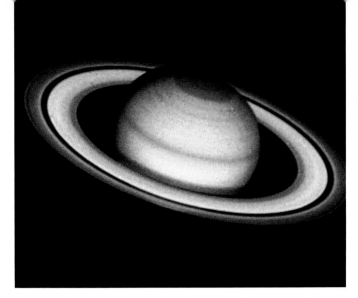

Fig. 10-16 Saturn, photographed from the Hubble Space Telescope. (NASA)

Fig. 10-17 In 1990, an amateur astronomer noticed a white spot on Saturn. This spot grew and grew and eventually covered a wide band on Saturn's surface. Such events occur about every 30 years, though this was the largest in 60 years. The Hubble Space Telescope made this image. (NASA)

VENUS

Venus can be the brightest object in the sky besides the sun and moon. Since its orbit is inside that of the earth, we see Venus only when we are looking in the general direction of the sun. This bright planet is visible only during the first few hours after sunset, when it is known as "the evening star," or before sunrise, when it is known as "the morning star." Venus can be brighter than magnitude –4, and can even cast noticeable shadows.

Venus is covered with thick layers of clouds through which we cannot see. From earth, we see no structure, though we do see Venus go through phases as it orbits the sun (Fig. 10-18). (Only planets that have orbits smaller than earth's—Venus and Mercury—can go through a crescent phase. The fact that Venus goes through a complete cycle of phases, including the crescent phase, was discovered by Galileo and was major proof of the validity of Copernicus's idea that the sun rather than the earth is at the center of the solar system.)

When Venus is just about to pass between the sun and us, it appears as a crescent and is at its largest. We may even see sunlight bent around toward us through its thick atmosphere. When Venus appears at the same longitude along the ecliptic as the sun, it is at *conjunction*. When Venus lies nearly on a line of sight between us and the sun, it is at *inferior conjunction*. When we can see all of Venus's lighted side (its "full" phase), the planet is on the far side of the sun, at its farthest point from us and therefore at its smallest. It is then at *superior conjunction*.

From spacecraft looking through ultraviolet filters from the vicinity of Venus, we have been able to study the circulation of the planet's clouds (Fig. 10-19).

Though the clouds block our view from the earth, the Pioneer Venus Orbiter in 1979 compiled an overall map of Venus's surface, using radar (Fig. 10-20).

Fig. 10-18 The phases of Venus. Note the different size of Venus at its various phases. Whenever we see a crescent, Venus must be on the near side of the sun; as a result, it appears relatively large. (Akira Fujii)

Fig. 10-19 The clouds of Venus show when observed from a spacecraft with ultraviolet light of wavelengths slightly too short to come through the earth's atmosphere. (NASA/Ames)

Fig. 10-20 The overall radar map of Venus compiled by the Pioneer Venus spacecraft; the radar could penetrate the clouds that enshroud Venus. (NASA/Ames, U.S. Geological Survey, and M.I.T.)

Fig. 10-21 Views of Venus from the radar on the Magellan spacecraft. The resolution is as small as 100 meters on Venus's surface. The false color matches the color on Venus. The vertical scale in the computer recreation at right is x10. (NASA)

NASA's Magellan spacecraft went into orbit around Venus in 1990. Its radar—which measures reflected radio waves—has sent back images of Venus's surface much more detailed than those made by earlier spacecraft (Fig. 10-21). The Magellan observations have shown details of the geology of Venus's crust, and have changed our understanding of the processes that shaped Venus's surface.

384 A series of Soviet spacecraft have landed on Venus and sent back photographs of its surface (Fig. 10-22). From studies of the composition of the surface, we know that the same kind of geological processes that formed the earth's surface also were at work on Venus.

Fig. 10-22 The surface of Venus, photographed in 1982 by a Soviet lander, showed flat rocks and soil. The swath photographed is a curved region with horizons appearing diagonally just beyond the upper left and upper right corners. In the center, we look down at the base of the spacecraft. (Image courtesy of Valeriy Barsukov and Arnold Selivanov and the USSR Academy of Sciences)

The earth, though, has several continents and is mostly covered with deep ocean basins. Venus, on the other hand, has only a few small continents and few deep basins; it is mostly covered with a broad rolling plain.

Venus's clouds consist primarily of sulfuric acid droplets. Its atmosphere is mostly carbon dioxide, and the surface pressure is 90 times that on earth. The earth contains about the same amount of carbon dioxide, though on earth it is locked up in carbonate rocks formed under the ocean. So the presence of water on earth apparently saved us from undergoing Venus's fate.

The carbon dioxide in Venus's atmosphere traps sunlight, which enters mostly as visible light but is changed to infrared radiation when it heats Venus's surface. The infrared can't escape, mostly because of the carbon dioxide but also somewhat because of other gases and particles, so the atmosphere heats up to a temperature of 500°C (900°F) on Venus's surface. This effect is known as the "greenhouse effect." If we unbalance our earth's atmosphere in some way, perhaps by burning too much fossil fuel and thus putting too much carbon dioxide into the atmosphere, our atmosphere could become as unlivable as Venus's.

Venus's atmosphere also teaches another lesson about air pollution. If we introduce too many fluorocarbons into the earth's atmosphere by using aerosol cans that contain them or by leakage of air-conditioner or refrigerator coolant, we could destroy a lot of the earth's ozone layer, which protects us from the sun's ultraviolet light. The effects of ozone and other gases are now better understood through comparative studies of the atmospheres of the earth, Venus, and other planets.

Transits of Venus

Only rarely does Venus *transit*—go directly in front of—the sun. It is then visible as a black dot projected on the solar disk; light bent forward to us by Venus's atmosphere makes a bright ring around the planet. Historically, transits of Venus have been important for setting the distance scale in the solar system; we can now find the distance scale more accurately with radar and by tracking spacecraft, so transits of Venus are now merely an observational curiosity.

Transits of Venus come in pairs separated by 8 years; the interval between successive pairs is more than 100 years. The last transits were in 1874 and 1882. The next will be on June 8, 2004, and June 5–6, 2012.

Observing Venus

Observe the phases, especially during the 10 weeks before and after inferior conjunction, when Venus switches from an "evening star" to a "morning star." An ultraviolet filter sometimes adds contrast to photographs of the disk.

MARS

Mars, "the red planet," has long been an object of interest to humanity because of its relatively rapid motion among the stars and because of its reddish color. Over a period of months, Mars's path among the stars apparently reverses itself in a giant loop (Fig. 10-23). In 1543, Copernicus explained this loop in Mars's orbit, called *retrograde* (backwards) *motion*, by showing how it is an effect of perspective. It occurs when the earth passes Mars, as both planets orbit the sun. The orbits of other planets have similar retrograde loops.

Mars's surface, when viewed from earth, shows semipermanent features, which can be followed over the 25-hour period of rotation of Mars, a Martian "day." These features change with the seasons of the year on Mars; the cycle of Martian seasons takes 23 earth months, the period with which Mars orbits the sun. Mars's reddish tinge is obvious even to the naked eye, but a telescope is necessary to see detail on Mars's surface from earth (Fig. 10-24).

Because of Mars's elliptical orbit, at different oppositions Mars is at different distances from us. The angular diameter of its disk at opposition ranges from about 14 arc sec to 25 arc sec, which is $1/130$ to $1/75$ the diameter of the full moon and about the same size as Saturn's disk. The closer the planet is to us, the larger it appears. Mars

Fig 10-23. A planetarium simulation of Mars's motion across the background of stars, showing a retrograde loop. (Geoff Chester, Albert Einstein Planetarium, Smithsonian Institution)

Fig. 10-24 Polar caps and other features on Mars that can be observed from earth. Sinus Meridiani is the horizontal feature on the left photo. Syrtis Major is the triangular feature on the right photo, with the Hellas plain below it. North is at top. (Donald Pearson)

appears still smaller when not at opposition, sometimes as small as 4 arc seconds across.

Because of the seasonal changes on Mars, and because some observers thought they saw thin lines crossing Mars's surface, Percival Lowell and others at the turn of the last century suggested that there was life on Mars. The seasonal changes, they thought, were caused by vegetation, and the lines were "canals" dug by Martians to carry water.

But observations from the ground and later from spacecraft have shown that the seasonal changes are the result of blowing dust during huge seasonal storms generated by the effect of solar heating. When dust is blown off certain surfaces, the dark underlying material is revealed. Close-ups have proved that the "canals" don't really exist; they were presumably the effect of the eye and brain, which tend to imagine connections even when they don't exist. In fact, the features that show up in telescopes as bright and dark to earthbound observers don't necessarily correspond to any physical features on Mars.

The polar caps on Mars, which wax and wane with the seasons of each Martian year, turn out to be largely made of frozen carbon dioxide that condenses over a core of frozen water. The existence of large quantities of water is thought to be essential for life as we know it, so the discovery of signs of water on Mars is encouraging for those who hope to find that life has started there independently of life on earth.

Fig. 10-25 The surface of Mars from one of the Viking orbiters. (NASA/JPL/USGS processing)

Fig. 10-26 Sand dunes and rocks on Mars, photographed by the Viking 1 Lander. (JPL/NASA)

The American Viking missions in 1976 carried out the closest reconnaissance of Mars to date. Each of the two Viking spacecraft had an orbiter that took photographs of Mars's surface over a period of years. The Viking orbiters' photographs revealed giant volcanoes, a huge canyon larger in diameter than the continental United States, many craters in certain regions, and many other geological features. Branching channels appear like streambeds on earth, indicating that water may have flowed on Mars in the past.

Each Viking carried a Lander, which took photographs of the surface (Fig. 10-26), and a small biology laboratory that searched for signs of life. The signs, after much investigation, seem to be negative, though the possibility that life exists cannot be completely ruled out on the basis of these studies.

Mars has two moons, Phobos ("Fear," in Greek) and Deimos ("Terror," in Greek), named after the mythological companions of the Roman war god, Mars. Photographs from the Vikings and from the earlier Mariner 9 spacecraft revealed that both moons are elliptical, with Phobos having a longest diameter of only 16 miles (27 km) and Deimos a longest diameter of only 9 miles (15 km). Phobos was observed most recently close up by the Soviet Phobos mission in 1989. These moons are not large and are not made round by gravity like our moon, which is really a small planet. The moons of Mars are really only small, orbiting chunks of rock, comparable to some of the smaller asteroids. They do not become brighter than 11th and 12th magnitudes, and so are not easily observed from earth.

Observing Mars

Observe the reddish color and features on the disk (such as Syrtis Major, Hellas, and the polar caps) as the planet rotates; notice how the features change with Mars's seasons. Observe seasonal dust storms. An orange filter is useful to accentuate contrast on Mars's surface; a blue filter may reveal the status of dust storms. Morning clouds show best with a green or yellow filter.

Table 17: Oppositions of Mars

Date of Opposition	Nearest to Earth	Diameter of Disk (arc sec)	Distance to Earth A.U.	km (millions)
November 27, 1990	November 20	18	0.52	77
January 7, 1993	January 3	15	0.63	94
February 12, 1995	February 11	14	0.68	101
March 17, 1997	March 20	14	0.66	99
April 24, 1999	May 1	16	0.59	87

MERCURY

Mercury, the closest planet to the sun, is less than half the size of the earth. It has no moons, no atmosphere, and is an exceedingly inhospitable place. The temperature at midday is over 400°C (750°F).

Mercury never appears too far from the sun in the sky, and so is visible only briefly after sunset or before sunrise, as shown in the Graphic Timetables in Chapter 9, or when it passes in front of the sun (Fig. 10-27).

From earth, we can see Mercury's phases, but even the largest telescopes do not reveal any detail on its surface. The surface features are known only from NASA's Mariner 10 spacecraft, which flew close to Mercury three times in 1974 and 1975. The pictures (Fig. 10-28) revealed that Mercury has many craters and resembles our moon. The craters are flatter and have thinner rims on Mercury, because of the higher gravity, but those are subtle effects. We deduce that Mercury's interior was once molten from the lava that once flooded the surface. Also, Mariner 10 found a weak magnetic field. We think magnetic fields can remain only if part of the interior is still molten.

Transits of Mercury

Transits of Mercury are not as rare as those of Venus: by the year 2000, there will have been eleven in this century. The most recent ones were on November 10, 1973; November 13, 1986; and November 6, 1993. The most recent was visible from Europe but not from North America. Mercury takes a few hours to cross the sun's disk. Observers should note the exact times when Mercury first touches the sun, when it moves entirely within the solar disk, when it first touches the other side of the sun, and when it leaves the solar disk entirely.

Following those transits, the next will be a grazing transit—when

Fig. 10-27 The transit of Mercury across the face of the sun in 1973. (Fred Espenak)

Mercury will appear to just graze one edge of the solar disk—on November 15, 1999. This grazing transit will be visible from Antarctica and possibly from southern Australia. The following transit of Mercury will be on May 7, 2003 (just over a year before the next transit of Venus). It will be visible from the U.S. and Canada.

Observing Mercury

Observe the phases. For best viewing, locate Mercury on a favorable morning when it rises well ahead of the sun, and keep your telescope on it until after sunrise.

Fig. 10-28 A mosaic of Mariner 10 images of Mercury, with an artist's conception of Mercury's interior added. Mercury's core is shown in yellow, and may be partly molten. (Courtesy of Robert G. Strom, from his *Mercury: The Elusive Planet*, Smithsonian Institution Press, artwork by Karen Denomy)

URANUS

Uranus reaches magnitude 6 at its brightest, the limit of naked-eye visibility. It is a giant planet, about four times the earth's diameter, and about 15 times its mass. It appears as a tiny greenish or bluish disk in earth-based telescopes because methane in its atmosphere absorbs the other colors, chiefly red. Uranus shows in binoculars or small telescopes as only a dot. Astronomers learned most of what we know about Uranus when the Voyager 2 spacecraft flew by it in 1986.

Uranus's orbit is 19 A.U. in radius, almost twice that of Saturn. Uranus is so distant that it never gets bigger than 4 seconds of arc. Since the best resolution available from earth's surface is about $\frac{1}{2}$ second of arc, even the largest telescopes don't show much detail on its surface.

A mnemonic for the names of Uranus's moons, in order of their distance from the planet—Miranda, Ariel, Umbriel, Titania, and Oberon—is "M-Auto." Uranus's moons are shown in Figs. 10-29 and 10-30.

Fig. 10-29 Uranus and its five largest moons through a large telescope, in one of the best photographs ever taken from earth. Still, the moons appear only as points of light. (William Liller/The Cerro Tololo Inter-American Observatory)

Fig. 10-30 *(opposite)* Uranus and its five major moons, a montage pasted together from photographs taken with the spacecraft Voyager 2. Uranus is the bluish object at center. Ariel is at lower right foreground, Umbriel is reproduced small to its left, Oberon appears small above it and to the left of Uranus, Titania appears at top left, and Miranda overlaps the top of Uranus. (NASA/JPL)

Fig. 10-31 *(left)* The rings of Uranus seen frontlighted, as we see them from earth. *(right)* The rings of Uranus seen backlighted, after Voyager 2 passed Uranus. Fine dust in the rings shows up especially well. (NASA/JPL)

When Uranus occulted (that is, passed in front of and therefore hid) a star in 1977, the light from the star winked off and on a few times before and after the star was occulted by the planet itself. This marked the discovery of a set of nine thin rings around Uranus, which have been studied further at subsequent occultations.

Voyager 2 photographed the rings as it passed by. As it approached, it had the same view we have from earth, with the sun over its shoulder. After it passed, it could look through the rings, which stood out when backlighted (Fig. 10-31).

Each of Uranus's moons turned out to have a different personality. They are all made out of frozen mixtures of rock and ice, and all are fairly dark, reflecting only a small percentage of the sunlight that hits them. The most interesting is Miranda (Fig. 10-32), whose surface is so varied though it is only 300 miles (500 km) across, it is like the old joke about the animal that was put together by a committee. Apparently, Miranda was completely broken up in the past in a collision and came together with its parts jumbled.

Fig. 10-32 Voyager 2's view of a canyon on the edge of Miranda, seen before its photograph of Uranus and with an artist's conception of a ring. (NASA/JPL)

Fig. 10-33 *(top left)* Ariel. *(top right)* Umbriel. *(bottom left)* Titania. *(bottom right)* Oberon. *(center)* Miranda. All were photographed by Voyager 2 and are shown at their relative sizes and darknesses (a property known as albedo). (NASA and USGS — Flagstaff, courtesy of S.K. Croft and L. Soderblom)

The surface of Ariel, 720 miles (1200 km) across, shows few craters or other old features, and so must have been reshaped by geological activity. Umbriel, also 720 miles (1200 km) across though darker, is covered with craters, and its surface may otherwise be unchanged since it was formed 4.5 billion years ago. Titania and Oberon are each somewhat bigger, 960 miles (1600 km) across. Titania shows no large craters, which must have been covered over at some time, perhaps by material that flowed out from the interior. Oberon has many large craters. Voyager 2 also discovered 10 additional moons.

Observing Uranus

Observe its greenish disk. Uranus starts the 1990s in Sagittarius above the "Teapot" and ends the decade in Capricornus as it moves along the ecliptic. (A chart that will help you find Uranus appears in the January issue of *Sky & Telescope* each year.)

NEPTUNE

Neptune, another of the giant planets, is about the same size as Uranus. It is 30 A.U. from the sun and gets no larger in the sky than 2.5 arc sec. Thus from earth we have been able to see very little detail on its surface.

Until 1999, Neptune is actually the farthest of the nine planets from the sun, since Pluto's elliptical orbit brings it closer to the sun than Neptune. However, we rank planets by the overall sizes of their orbits, so it is still legitimate to say that Neptune is the eighth planet.

Most of what we have learned about Neptune came from the 1989 flyby by the Voyager 2 spacecraft (Fig. 10-34).

Fig. 10-34 Neptune, as seen from the Voyager 2 spacecraft. The atmospheric storm known as the Great Dark Spot is clearly visible, as is a bright methane ice cloud. (NASA/JPL)

Neptune shows a lot of activity on its surface, unlike bland Uranus. Neptune's surface activity results from an internal source of energy. We do not know why Jupiter, Saturn, and Neptune have such additional energy while Uranus does not.

Neptune, like Uranus, gets its color from the traces of methane in its atmosphere, which is mainly made of hydrogen and helium. The methane absorbs the red part of the spectrum, leaving the blue for us to see. The most obvious feature on Neptune's surface is the Great Dark Spot. The Great Dark Spot is a circulating storm, similar in many ways to the Great Red Spot on Jupiter. The Great Dark Spot is about the size of the earth. It is a high-pressure region, and rotates every 17 days. Methane ice clouds at greater heights appear bright.

Once Uranus's rings were discovered from earth when they occulted stars, astronomers started searching for rings about Neptune. Over several years, astronomers sometimes detected drops in the brightness of stars when they passed near Neptune, and sometimes did not detect such drops. They deduced that Neptune might have partial rings, perhaps ring arcs.

Voyager 2 found, however, that Neptune does have complete rings around it (Fig. 10-35). The material is not evenly distributed in the rings, though, and in some places the ring material is so thin that it does not noticeably hide a star. Voyager found two clumpy rings at 31,800 and 37,800 miles (53,000 and 63,000 km) from Neptune's center, far above its equator, which is 14,860 miles (24,760 km) from the center. Voyager also photographed a faint, inner ring 25,200 miles (42,000 km) from the center and a broad ring extending from the inner clumpy ring halfway to the outer one.

Fig. 10-35 The rings of Neptune, photographed by Voyager 2. The left half and the right half were photographed separately. The two major rings plus additional material forming broad rings are visible in these backlighted images. The dark bar in the center provides the appropriate space for the part missing from the photographs. The clumps were on the side of Neptune for each photograph that did not show. (NASA/JPL)

Fig. 10-36 Triton, Neptune's largest moon. We see its southern region. The lowest part of the image is its polar ice cap, probably of nitrogen ice. Ultraviolet sunlight and radiation from Neptune's magnetosphere may have interacted with the ice to turn it pinkish. The image also shows many dark, elongated streaks that are the results of eruptions from under Triton's surface. (NASA/USGS)

From earth, we had known that Neptune had two moons. The largest, Triton, is one of the largest moons of the solar system, somewhat larger than our own moon though not as large as the Galilean satellites of Jupiter. It was named after a sea god, a son of Poseidon. Triton orbits Neptune in the opposite direction from all the other major moons in the solar system around their planets, which indicates that it was formed elsewhere and then was captured by Neptune's gravity.

Voyager 2 was able to pass extremely close to Triton, and the views it sent back were astounding (Fig. 10-36). The broad southern polar cap is pinkish, and plumes of dust were seen erupting. The result of these plumes is the black streaks that are visible on the surface, presumably in the downwind direction. The rest of the surface of Triton that was seen is known as the "cantaloupe" terrain from its puckered appearance.

Nereid, the second moon of Neptune that was known from earth, is much smaller. Its name means "sea nymph" in Greek. Voyager 2 discovered six additional moons of Neptune. One of them is even larger than Nereid's 360-mile (600-km) diameter.

The magnetic fields of both Neptune and Uranus were big surprises. They are both very tilted from the planets' axes of rotation and are offset from the planets' centers. The earth's magnetic field, on the other hand, is tilted only slightly. We have a lot to learn about how magnetic fields are generated. Probably, those of Uranus and Neptune are formed in shells far from center.

Observing Neptune

With a telescope of at least moderate size, notice Neptune's blue-greenish color and the fact that it has a slight disk. Neptune, like Uranus, starts the 1990s in Sagittarius above the "Teapot" and ends the decade in Capricornus as it moves along the ecliptic. (A chart that will help you find Neptune appears in the January issue of *Sky & Telescope* each year.)

Fig. 10-37 Neptune and Triton, seen as crescents as Voyager 2 receded into more distant space. (NASA/JPL)

PLUTO

Tiny, distant Pluto is so far away and so small that we know little about it. Its orbit is very elliptical and has an average radius of 39 A.U. Pluto is now on the part of its orbit that is within the orbit of Neptune. Pluto will be within Neptune's orbit, closer than Neptune both to the sun and to the earth, until the year 1999.

Pluto—like Neptune's moon, Triton—has methane ice or snow on its surface and an atmosphere consisting of methane gas plus traces of other substances. Pluto is about magnitude 13.7 and was only slightly brighter in 1989, when it reached *perihelion*, the closest point ("peri-") of its orbit to the sun ("helios"). Though Pluto is as bright as it has been for centuries, it is still much too faint to be seen in small telescopes. For keen observers, though, it may be seen as a point of light in 20-cm (8-inch) telescopes. No detail at all is detectable on its surface, even in the largest telescopes (Fig. 10-38).

Photographing Pluto on different nights, though, reveals its slow motion among the stars. Pluto was found from such motion in 1930 by Clyde Tombaugh, the only planet to be discovered in modern times. Tombaugh studied hundreds of thousand of pairs of star images, comparing one night's observations with another's, before he noticed Pluto. Tombaugh studied the part of the sky where he found Pluto because of predictions that gravity from a planet there could explain why Uranus did not follow exactly in the orbit it otherwise should. (Neptune had not been studied for long enough to use for such a study.) Though the predictions led Tombaugh to find Pluto, if Pluto were entirely responsible for the deviations in Uranus's orbit, it would have to have nearly as much mass as the earth. Whether there is still another planet out there, or our measurements are too inaccurate to tell, is not known.

Fig. 10-38 Even with the 5-m Hale telescope on Palomar Mountain, Pluto shows as only a dot. (California Institute of Technology)

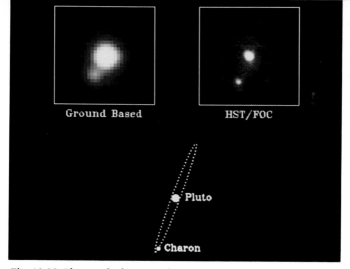

Fig. 10-39 Pluto and Charon, in both a ground-based view and in an image taken with the Hubble Space Telescope. Only the Space Telescope has been able to show them as completely distinct objects. (NASA and Canada-France-Hawaii Telescope Corp.)

A ground-based photograph taken in 1978 revealed that the image of Pluto was not quite round. A bulge at the edge of Pluto's image turned out to be a previously unsuspected moon, which was named Charon (Fig. 10-39). The third law of Johannes Kepler as emended by Isaac Newton, both in the 17th century, links the period of revolution of a moon with the mass of its central object. Studies of the orbit of Pluto's moon have shown us that Pluto is only $1/500$ the mass of earth, nowhere near enough mass to cause the measured deviations in Uranus's orbit.

It remains quite difficult to observe Charon, and no ground-based image has shown it as an object completely separate from Pluto. Finally, in 1990 the Hubble Space Telescope provided an image that showed Pluto and Charon as separate objects. This and later images are enabling astronomers to measure the size of Charon's orbit and Pluto's mass more accurately.

Other observations indicate that Pluto is less than $1/5$ the size of earth, even smaller than our moon. The most interesting of these observations are from mutual occultations of Pluto and Charon, observed as Pluto and Charon passed in front of each other twice every 6-hour orbital period from 1985 to 1990. Studying the way the total brightness from the pair changes enables not only the sizes of each to be accurately determined but also gives an idea of the darkness of different regions on their surfaces (Fig. 10-40). Pluto is only 2300 kilometers in diameter and Charon is only 1186 kilometers across. Thus Pluto and Charon are closer in size to each other than any other planet and its moon in the solar system. Pluto/Charon is often thus thought of as a double planet.

401

Fig. 10-40 Models of Pluto and Charon based on results from their mutual occultations observed during 1985–89. (Keith D. Horne, Marc W. Buie, and David J. Tholen)

The best knowledge we have of Pluto's atmosphere is from a stellar occultation of a 12th-magnitude star in 1988. The atmosphere proved to be more substantial than expected.

Observing Pluto

With a sufficiently large telescope, observe Pluto as a dot in the sky, changing position among the stars from night to night. A chart that will help you find Pluto appears in the January issue of *Sky & Telescope* each year.

OBSERVING THE PLANETS

By looking for a long time through a telescope, and waiting for instants when the "seeing" is especially good (that is, when the image is constant because the air is especially steady), the human eye can often see more detail than can be recorded with a camera. Thus excellent sketches can be made. You can follow not only the planets' rotations but also seasonal and weather changes on them.

The Association of Lunar and Planetary Observers, c/o Dr. John E. Westfall, P.O. Box 16131, San Francisco, CA 94116, is an amateur society. Regional societies, such as the Amateur Astronomers Association, 1010 Park Avenue, New York, NY 10028, also may have special groups of members who are especially interested in planetary observing.

11

COMETS

A bright comet looks spectacular in the sky. Comets are bodies that orbit in our solar system, passing between the planets. Also in the spaces between the nine major planets in our solar system are minor planets known as asteroids; we discuss them in Chapter 12. In this chapter we discuss comets and how to observe them.

COMETS

Sometimes a fuzzy object becomes visible in the heavens. It may look like a smudge on the sky. If we are lucky, it will grow brighter over a period of weeks or months, and will form a tail. This tail may become so long that it extends across much of the sky (Fig. 11-1).

Fig. 11-1 Comet West, 1976. *(left)* The comet over Los Angeles. (© 1976 Ben Mayer)   *(right)* Detail in the comet's dust tail. (© 1976 Martin Grossmann)

Such bodies are *comets,* large icy snowballs in the sky. Each comet we see began as one of the hundreds of billions of small bodies in a tremendous cloud surrounding the sun, far beyond the outermost planets. Sometimes a gravitational nudge from a passing star causes one of these bodies to move closer to the sun. Solar energy heats it, and the body gives off gas and dust that form a tail. The gas is pushed away from the comet by gas flowing outward from the sun—the *solar wind.* The dust is left behind in the comet's orbit by the pressure of the sun's radiation. Thus some comets have two visible tails—a dust tail trailing gracefully behind the comet and a gas tail whose irregularities show the different puffs of the solar wind.

A dozen or more comets can be detected in the sky at a single time, but most are so faint that they can be seen only with large telescopes. Every few years, a comet can be seen with the naked eye, though most appear faint. Bright comets (1st or 2nd magnitude) might appear every decade or so. The appearance of a bright comet is usually unpredictable. Of the predictable comets, only the one known as Halley's Comet is spectacular. It returns every 76 years or so. Unfortunately, its orbit kept it too far from the earth during its 1986 return for it to appear very bright (Fig. 11-2).

Fig. 11-2 Halley's Comet (extreme right) near the Milky Way, photographed together in 1986 after Halley's perihelion. (Akira Fujii)

Fig. 11-3 Halley's Comet in 1986, showing its bluish gas tail and its yellowish dust tail. (William Liller)

We had enough warning for Halley's Comet that many nations prepared spacecraft to study it up close. The European Space Agency's Giotto spacecraft flew into the comet's head. The head is composed of a *nucleus* surrounded by a diffuse *coma*. Giotto showed that the nucleus is a potato-shaped object about 16 km long. The nucleus is an icy snowball covered with a dark crust. The crust is so dark that it reflects only about 2% of the light that hits it. Dust spews out from cracks in crust on the side that is hit by sunlight. The resulting dust jets reflect the sunlight brightly (Fig. 11-4).

Fig. 11-4 The nucleus of Halley's Comet and its dust jets. The nucleus, 16 km long by 8 km wide, is seen in silhouette. The dust jets come from the sunlighted side of the nucleus. (© 1986 Max-Planck-Institut für Aeronomie, Lindau/Harz, FRG; photographed with the Halley Multicolour Camera aboard the European Space Agency's Giotto spacecraft, courtesy of H. U. Keller)

Fig. 11-5 Halley's Comet, with its tail developed into a fan shape, passing the Centaurus A galaxy (NGC 5128) on April 15, 1986, photographed from Chile. (NOAO/CTIO)

Fig. 11-6 Comet Ikeya-Seki, observed in 1965 from Mt. Wilson overlooking Los Angeles. The photograph was a 32-second exposure on ISO 400 film at $f/1.6$. (William Liller)

A comet bright enough to be seen with the naked eye or with binoculars can be a very beautiful sight (Fig. 11-6). Comet Ikeya-Seki in 1965 and Comet West in 1975 were particularly bright; we are now awaiting another bright comet. Such a comet will be one with an orbital period so long that it will arrive unexpectedly. None of the periodic comets expected in the next century will be very bright.

If you plot a comet's position carefully against the background of stars, you will see that it changes by about 1° per day. A comet's motion, however, is not apparent to the eye. Though a comet's tail results in part from its motion through the solar system, a comet does not speed across our sky; its tail is not a result of any such apparent motion across the sky.

The time a comet takes to complete its orbit depends on the size of its orbit. Encke's Comet returns every 3.3 years, but is faint. Halley's Comet returns about every 74–79 years, and is always bright enough to be seen with the naked eye. It has been seen on at least 27 occasions since 87 B.C., though it wasn't until early in the 18th century that Edmund Halley realized that the bright comets reported by previous observers were reappearances of the same comet. However, its 1986 passage near earth was a faint one, and so will be the one in 2061. A comet loses less than 1% of its material at each passage near the sun, so it can reappear many times.

The more sensitive your observing equipment, the more comets you can find. Over a dozen comets can actually be studied in the sky at most times, if you have a sensitive electronic imager.

Fig. 11-7 A comet photographed with a camera on a tripod, a 1-second exposure at $f/1.4$ on black-and-white ISO 125 film. (Jay M. Pasachoff)

Photographing a Comet

Occasionally, a comet may be bright enough to be photographed with an ordinary camera (Fig. 11-7). No special equipment is required; a sturdy tripod and a lens that can be opened to a wide aperture (preferably about $f/1.4$, and at least $f/2$) are all that you will need. Use fast film, and be careful not to shake the camera. (Use a cable release, and raise the mirror of a reflex camera before snapping the shutter, if possible.) Both black-and-white and color film can produce pleasing results.

If you use a normal or wide-angle lens, you may be able to capture the comet at the top of the frame and the horizon or a tree on the bottom. Such a photograph gives a sense of scale, and may look more interesting than one in which the image of the comet is centered.

Take a wide range of exposures: try 1, 2, 4, 8, 15, 30, and 60 seconds. Film is cheap compared with the loss of a rare opportunity, so don't hesitate to take more pictures than you usually take at one time.

If you can place your camera piggyback on a telescope that tracks the stars, you will be able to take longer exposures. Again, take exposures over a wide range of times, with your lens wide open or almost wide open.

It can also be very interesting to draw the comet and its tail, instead of photographing it. The eye can detect very interesting detail.

If You Discover a Comet

Many new comets are discovered by amateur observers, usually with large binoculars (those with huge front lenses) or medium-sized telescopes. The main background you must have to discover a comet is a detailed knowledge of what is in the sky, so that you can tell whether an object you see is a new comet or a well-known nebula.

To search for comets, the American comet observer John Bortle recommends sweeping your field of view back and forth at a rate of no more than 1° of sky per second. He recommends starting at the horizon after sunset, and sweeping back and forth 45° on either side of the sunset point, gradually moving your binoculars or telescope upward so as to slightly overlap your preceding area of observation. Continue until you are about 45° above the horizon—halfway up to the zenith. If you are searching before sunrise, begin 45° above the horizon and sweep back and forth while moving your field of view downward.

If you think that you have found a comet, note its position in the sky (right ascension and declination) by finding its position in relation to the stars on the Atlas Charts in Chapter 7. Also note its brightness (its approximate magnitude) by comparing it with that of plotted stars and record the time. Then watch for a while to note the direction in which the comet is moving and the rate of its motion. It is helpful to plot the position of the comet in the star atlas at different times, so that its motion can be accurately charted; the presence of motion is an important sign that you have in fact found a comet. Then send that information to the Central Bureau for Astronomical Telegrams of the International Astronomical Union, which is located at the Smithsonian Astrophysical Observatory, Cambridge, MA 02138. The electronic mail addresses are "Marsden@cfa.bitnet" or "Marsden@cfa.harvard.edu." If you have access to a Telex II (TWX) machine, you can send a message to (710) 320-6842; the answerback is ASTROGRAM CAM. Or you can send a telegram (Western Union is 800 325-6000), giving this number and answerback as the address. Don't forget to include your name in the message, and to leave your address and telephone number.

The IAU Central Bureau names each comet after the first people— up to three observers, if there are near-simultaneous independent discoveries—to find it.

Articles by John Bortle in *The Sky & Telescope Guide to the Heavens* give details about searching for and observing comets.

12

ASTEROIDS

In between the major planets are thousands of minor planets ranging from one kilometer to hundreds of kilometers across; they are called *asteroids* or *minor planets*. The first asteroid, discovered on January 1, 1801, was at first thought to be a new planet; it was named Ceres. The numbers assigned to asteroids (in order of discovery) are now given along with the names, so we call this asteroid 1 Ceres. Within a few years 2 Pallas, 3 Juno, and 4 Vesta were also discovered, and scientists realized that they were dealing with several little planets instead of a few major ones.

Many asteroids only 1 km in diameter are known. Over 200 of them with diameters greater than 100 km have been discovered, and half a dozen are known to exceed 300 km in diameter. Though most asteroids are in the *asteroid belt* located between the orbits of Mars and Jupiter, many other asteroids come very close to the earth. The asteroids in one group, the Apollo asteroids (named after the first of the group to be discovered, 1862 Apollo), have orbits that cross earth's orbit. We know of about 3 dozen asteroids in this group. The orbit of an Aten asteroid (2062 Aten and those with similar orbits) not only crosses the earth's orbit but is also even smaller than the earth's orbit. The orbit of 1566 Icarus, another unusual asteroid, takes it closer to the sun than Mercury. Icarus came within 6 million

Table 18: The Brightest Asteroids

Asteroid	Brightest Visual Mag.	Diameter (in km)	Asteroid	Brightest Visual Mag.	Diameter (in km)
4 Vesta	5.1	555	15 Eunomia	7.9	261
2 Pallas	6.4	583	8 Flora	7.9	160
1 Ceres	6.7	1025	324 Bamberga	8.0	256
7 Iris	6.7	222	1036 Ganymed	8.1	40
433 Eros	6.8	20	9 Metis	8.1	168
6 Hebe	7.5	206	192 Nausikaa	8.2	99
3 Juno	7.5	249	20 Massalia	8.3	140
18 Melpomene	7.5	164			

Note: Brightness data from R. Shuort via J. U. Gunter; diameters based on Tucson Revised Index of Asteroid Data (TRIAD).

km of the earth in 1968, a near miss on an astronomical scale. Newly discovered asteroids have even come closer to the earth than the Moon, less than 400,000 km away. Such an asteroid hitting the earth some 65 million years ago may well have led to so much dust being ejected into the atmosphere that dinosaurs and many other types of animals were pushed into extinction.

Vesta can be brighter than 6th magnitude, the limit of visibility to the naked eye. With a small telescope, we can observe a number of asteroids (Table 18). Some five dozen may become brighter than 10th magnitude at some time in their orbits. The motion of these asteroids with respect to the stars can be followed from night to night.

Sometimes an asteroid goes in front of—*occults*—a star. Then, by measuring the length of time that the star is hidden, we can calculate the size of the asteroid. The stars are so far away that light rays from them are nearly parallel, so the shadow an asteroid casts on the earth is almost exactly the size of the asteroid itself. Such occultations, for example, have shown us that the size of 2 Pallas is 558 x 526 x 532 km. To observe these occultations, people had to be stationed, on the basis of last-minute observations, in the locations where the asteroid's shadow would most likely pass.

The magazine *Sky & Telescope* publishes the latest information about where asteroid occultations will take place. It also provides addresses from which special bulletins and lists are available for serious observers.

Asteroids show up as streaks on astronomical photographs made with telescopes that track the stars (Fig. 12-1). On photographs made with telescopes that track the asteroid, the stars are streaks, while the asteroid is a dot. The Galileo spacecraft, in 1991, took the first close-up photograph of an asteroid (Fig. 12-2).

Fig. 12-1 *(left)* An asteroid shows up as a trail in a photograph taken through a telescope that is tracking the stars. (Harvard College Observatory)

Fig. 12-2 *(right)* The asteroid Gaspra observed from the Galileo spacecraft. The illuminated part is 16 by 12 km (10 by 7.5 miles). Gaspra rotates on its axis in about 7 hours. (NASA)

13

METEORS AND METEOR SHOWERS

If you are outdoors and looking upward in the late evening around August 12 any year, you will probably see a "shooting star," a *meteor*, travel across the sky in less than a second (Fig. 13-1). You are actually seeing solid particles from space—larger than atoms but much smaller than asteroids (minor planets)—burn up in the earth's atmosphere. Each August 12, the earth's orbit intersects the center of a stream of particles that makes up the Perseid meteor shower, which in some years consists of meteors that are visible at rates of up to one per minute.

When in space, the bodies are called *meteoroids*. Some of the meteoroids survive their fiery passage through the earth's atmosphere. Any part of a meteoroid that reaches the earth (or, indeed, any place where we can examine it) is called a *meteorite*.

On any night with perfect observing conditions, you are likely to see a random meteor in the sky every 10 minutes or so. These are *sporadic meteors*.

Many times a year, the earth's orbit crosses a stream of particles, believed to be (in most cases) from a defunct comet. These particles make up *meteor showers* (Table 19). Some showers have more meteors per hour than others. Some, like the Perseids around August 12, the Geminids near December 14, and the Quadrantids near January 3rd, are of about the same strength each year, and we can expect to see approximately the same number of meteors at maximum. Others, like the Leonids around November 17, differ in strength from year to year. Still others, like the delta Aquarids from mid-July to late August or the Taurids in the fall, are spread out over many weeks.

The Leonid meteor shower is particularly spectacular about every 33 years. During a one-hour period of the 1966 Leonids, over 100 meteors were observed per minute, and during one 40-minute period, over 1000 meteors per minute were observed. Average magnitudes were 1.5 or 2, and some of the brighter trains lasted more than a minute. At maximum, some observers were able to see up to 40 Leonids per second! The 1998 and 1999 Leonid showers will be eagerly awaited.

The best way to observe a meteor shower is to lie back on a lawn chair or blanket on the grass and enjoy the night. A meteor shower may appear in virtually any part of the sky, so to use a telescope or even binoculars would simply limit your field of view. Instead, just look up, moving your eyes slowly around the sky. You will probably

Table 19: Major Meteor Showers

Shower	Date of Maximum	Time (E.S.T.)	Radiant (at maximum) r.a. (2000)	dec.
	1992, 1996		h m	°
Lyrids	Apr. 21	11 p.m.	18 16	+34
Eta Aquarids	May 4	2 a.m.	22 24	0
Delta Aquarids	July 28	5 a.m.	22 36	−17
Perseids	Aug. 11	8 p.m.	03 04	+58
Orionids	Oct. 21	midnight	06 20	+15
South Taurids	Nov. 3	—	03 32	+14
Leonids	Nov. 17	7 a.m.	10 08	+22
Geminids	Dec. 13	7 p.m.	07 32	+32
Ursids	Dec. 22	1 a.m.	14 28	+76
	1993, 1997			
Quadrantids	Jan. 3	3 a.m.	15 28	+50

Notes: Since the year is actually 365¼ days long, we have listed the date and time starting in March for leap years (1992, 1996, etc.); add 6 hours for each year following in the four-year sequence. Most showers are named after the constellation in which their radiant is located, or after the bright star their radiant is near. The Quadrantids were named after Quadrans Muralis (in the northern part of Boötes), a constellation suggested by J. E. Bode in 1801 that is not now accepted as a constellation.

see a meteor out of the corner of your eye. Of course, the farther you are from streetlights, the better. If the moon is up, and particularly if it is more than half full, the sky will be too bright to see the meteor shower at its best. Sometimes you can wait until the moon sets, or observe before it rises.

Try to trace the paths of meteors in a certain shower back across the sky; all the paths will seem to converge in the same part of the sky, called the *radiant* (Fig. 13-1). This is an effect of perspective, since the meteors are hitting the earth's atmosphere in parallel lines. Just as parallel railroad tracks seem to converge at a distant point on the horizon, the parallel meteor paths seem to come from a convergent point or area in the sky. During meteor showers, you can often see more meteors after midnight, because the earth is rotated then so that your side is plowing into the meteors rather than having them catch up from behind.

To tentatively identify a meteor with a certain shower, you can trace its path back to see if it came from a constellation that has a known, active radiant. On the night of a shower's maximum, most meteors will come from the shower, but on nights far from the shower's peak, determining whether a meteor came from a known radiant

Table 19: Major Meteor Showers (Continued)

Associated Object	Avg. Hourly Rate (for a single observer)*	Avg. Duration of Maximum (between days of 1/4 maximum)**
Comet 1861 I Thatcher	15	2
Comet Halley	20	3
	20	7
Comet 1862 III Swift-Tuttle	50	5
Comet Halley	25	2
Comet Encke	15	†
Comet Temple-Tuttle	15	—
Asteroid 3200 Phaethon	50	3
Comet Tuttle	15	2
	40	1

* = Number of meteors (both shower and sporadic meteors) you can expect to see under ideal observing conditions—*i.e.*, no clouds, and a clear, dark sky in which 6th-magnitude stars are visible. Shower strength fluctuates from night to night and from year to year.

** = Background rate of sporadic meteors subtracted.

— = Broad maximum; duration of shower uncertain.

† = Meteors from a large number of small radiants near the constellation Taurus are visible for several weeks in November.

is the only way to identify meteors from spread-out showers.

Occasionally a sporadic meteor is extremely bright, even brighter than Venus. Such an object is called a *fireball*; a bright fireball may be a chip of a broken-up asteroid. Sometimes a fireball will leave a *train*, a path in the sky that remains for a few seconds. You may even be able to hear a sound, in which case there is more chance that a piece of the meteoroid is falling to earth as a meteorite. One may even come through your roof, as happened in Connecticut in 1982. Fireballs are so rare that you can't plan to see one. If you should see one, you should note as much information as you can, including the time; the brightness compared to nearby stars, planets, or even the moon; and, if possible, the altitude and azimuth of the beginning and ending points of the fireball's path among the stars. This information should be reported to the Smithsonian Museum of Natural History, Washington, D.C. 20560, in the United States; to the Herzberg Institute of Astrophysics, Ottawa, Ontario K1A 0R6, in Canada; or to suitable organizations in other countries. If you hear a sound, it is particularly important to report it quickly, for a meteorite may have landed nearby and could be picked up for scientific analysis.

Fig. 13-1 The Leonid meteor shower on November 17, 1966. The meteors appear to diverge from a radiant; two meteors appear as points because they are coming straight at us. Regulus is the bright star in the lower half of the frame. About 70 Leonid trails were recorded on the negative of this 3.5-min. exposure on Tri-X film at *f*/3.5. (Dennis Milon)

Meteors ionize their paths in the earth's upper atmosphere. Both professionals and some amateur astronomers use radio astronomy to detect these paths. Radio equipment needed to do so is relatively inexpensive, and advertisements for suitable equipment can be found in many magazines for amateur radio operators and occasionally in *Sky & Telescope.*

Meteorites are particularly important to astronomers because, aside from the moon rocks brought back between 1969 and 1972 by the Apollo missions and some dust brought back by Soviet spacecraft, meteorites provide the only extraterrestrial material we have to study in a laboratory. There are two basic types of meteorites (though, of course, experts make finer divisions): nickel-iron meteorites (called *irons*) and stony meteorites (called *stones*). Most meteorites found on the ground by accident are irons; they are very dense and appear quite different from ordinary rocks. On the other hand, when someone sees a meteorite fall and then searches for it, stony meteorites are found most of the time. This indicates that most meteorites are actually "stones," but that most of them are never discovered because they resemble normal (terrestrial) stones on the ground. The largest number of meteorites have been found in recent years in Antarctica, where they have accumulated undisturbed over long periods of time.

Nobody who is interested in meteorites should miss seeing the meteorites in museums (Fig. 13-2). You can also visit the Barringer Meteor Crater in southern Arizona (Fig. 13-3). This crater is 1.2 km (almost a mile) in diameter and resulted from the most recent large meteorite to hit the earth, about 25,000 years ago. Over a dozen even larger meteorite craters are known on earth.

Fig. 13-2 The largest meteorite ever discovered and moved was the 31,000-kg (34-ton) Ahnighito meteorite, brought back by Robert Peary and Matthew Henson, the explorers who claimed to have been the first to reach the North Pole, from the Arctic in 1892. It is now on display at the American Museum of Natural History in New York City. (Jay M. Pasachoff)

To Observe Meteors

You will need a comfortable place to lie back outdoors, far from lights; an accurate watch, set to the nearest second (which formerly required receiving the station WWV on a short-wave radio but now can be done with a digital watch set from the radio or television); and perhaps a friend to take notes (which helps preserve your adaptation to darkness). When a meteor moves overhead, record the time of the event to the nearest second, the duration of the meteor (usually less than 2 seconds or so), the length of the trail, the meteor's magnitude (by comparing it to nearby stars), and the color. The data usually reported are the number of meteors seen by a single observer in an hour and changes in the average hourly rate through the night; this information shows when the peak of the shower occurred. It may even be useful to measure and plot the number of meteors during 15-minute intervals. When possible, it is good to record whether the meteor seems to be coming from the radiant, or if it is a sporadic meteor. More advanced observers often do this by recording the path of each meteor and its magnitude on a star chart, using a different chart for each hour of observation.

Your data can be reported to the American Meteor Society, Department of Physics and Astronomy, SUNY, Geneseo, NY 14454, or to the Meteor Section of the British Astronomical Association, c/o Neil Bone, 'The Harepath,' Apuldram, Chichester, West Sussex, England.

Fig. 13-3 The Barringer meteor crater near Winslow, Arizona, is 1.2 km (almost 1 mile) across and was formed about 40,000 years ago. (Meteor Crater, Northern Arizona)

14

OBSERVING THE SUN

Most of the stars are visible only at night, but one star—our sun—is visible in the daytime. The sun is much closer to us than any other star. It takes light only about 8 minutes to travel from the sun to us; the next nearest star is over 4 light-years away. As a result of the sun's closeness to earth, its disk covers $1/2°$ of the sky and we can see many details on its surface.

The Sun's Surface

The sun, like all stars, is a ball of hot gas. It has an interior and an atmosphere. The surface of the sun sends us the light and heat that provide energy for us on earth.

The solar surface is called the *photosphere*, from the Greek word *photos*, meaning "light." When we look at the sun using the protective filters and precautions described on p. 422, we can see that it is largely uniform in brightness, that it becomes slightly darker towards its edges, and that there often are a few dark areas on its surface (Fig. 14-1). The dark areas—*sunspots*—are relatively cool regions of the solar surface. (See Figs. 2-25 and 2-26 for color views.)

Fig. 14-1 The sun at solar minimum in 1983 *(left)* and at solar maximum in 1991 *(right).* On these white-light photographs, the sun is noticeably darker towards its limb; lighter areas called faculae become visible there. (William Livingston, National Solar Observatory/National Optical Astronomy Observatories)

The energy is formed deep inside the sun's interior by the process of nuclear fusion. In the sun's fusion process, groups of four hydrogen atoms are transformed into single helium atoms. Each helium atom that results has slightly less mass (0.7%) than the sum of the four hydrogens. At the turn of the century, Albert Einstein realized that mass can change into energy according to the equation $E = mc^2$. Einstein's equation tells us that the little bit of mass that disappears is transformed into a relatively large amount of energy. (Since c—the speed of light—is such a large number, the amount of energy that results adds up to a lot.) The sun is a good example of a fusion reactor, a type that we are not yet able to build on earth. The sun is a fusion reactor located 150 million kilometers (93 million miles) from us.

Each sunspot has a dark center called its *umbra* (plural, *umbrae*) and a less dark region called its *penumbra* (Fig. 14-2). Sunspots normally form in groups, and each spot can last for weeks. Since the sun rotates about once every 25 days, we can watch the sunspots form and rotate across the visible solar surface.

Sunspots are regions of the sun where the magnetic field is especially strong, perhaps 3000 times stronger than the average field of the sun, of the earth, or of a toy magnet, which are all comparable in strength. Spots tend to occur in groups. Within each group of sunspots in one of the sun's hemispheres, the sunspots that lead in the direction the sun is rotating have north magnetic poles, and the spots that trail have south magnetic poles. In the opposite hemisphere, the leading and trailing polarities are reversed.

Fig. 14-2 A sunspot, showing its dark central umbra and its surrounding penumbra. The surface of the sun itself shows a salt-and-pepper effect known as granulation. Each granule is about 500 miles (700 km) across—roughly the distance from New York to Detroit. (William C. Livingston, National Solar Observatory/National Optical Astronomy Observatories)

The number of sunspots on the sun waxes and wanes over an 11-year period (Fig. 14-3). The vertical axis plots the *sunspot number*, which is not actually a direct count; it is a compound value that makes allowance for not only individual spots but also for the presence of sunspot groups. The sunspot number $= k(10g + f)$, where k is a correction factor to account for personal decisions of each individual observer (as to what constitutes an individual spot, for example), g is the number of groups, and f is the total number of spots. (Your value for k can be assigned only by a central registry, after they compare the numbers of spots you report with the established number.) An isolated spot is considered to be a group with one spot in it, so it adds 1 to each value of g and f.

After the 11-year cycle, the polarities in opposite hemispheres of the sun (northern vs. southern) reverse; that is, in a hemisphere where the leading spots (in the sun's direction of rotation) have had north magnetic poles, those spots now have south magnetic poles. Thus it takes two cycles, or 22 years, for the leading spots in each hemisphere to regain their original polarity, so the solar activity cycle is really 22 years long.

The mid-1990s will be sunspot minimum, when few spots are visible. The next maximum of sunspots is expected in about 2001. As that time approaches, there will be more huge eruptions on the sun called *solar flares.* Flares send out particles, x-rays, and gamma rays that can hit the earth; these could cause surges in power lines, zap passengers in high-flying aircraft or astronauts on space shuttles, and contribute to creating the aurora (Fig. 2-35). The flares also excite the aurora in a way that allows it to be seen by observers at latitudes more southerly than normal. Since the earth's magnetic field guides the particles that can cause the aurora, and since the earth's magnetic field comes out of the earth at the magnetic poles, the aurora

Fig. 14-3 The sunspot cycle, with its average period of 11.2 years. (Data from World Data Center A for Solar-Terrestrial Physics)

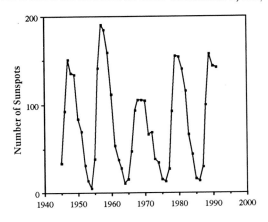

can most often be seen close to the magnetic poles. The northern magnetic pole is near Hudson Bay in Canada.

When we look at the center of the solar disk, we are looking through gas. The effect is the same as looking into the air on a foggy day; we can see only so far. When we observe near the solar *limb*—the apparent edge of the sun—we are looking diagonally through the solar atmosphere and thus through more gas that obscures our view; we cannot see as close to the sun's center before the gas appears opaque. As a result, near the sun's edge we see higher levels of the sun's atmosphere. Since these higher levels are slightly cooler than the lower atmospheric levels we can see when we look toward the center of the sun's disk, the sun's surface looks a little darker toward its limb.

When we look at the sun through the earth's atmosphere, the atmosphere bends the different colors in sunlight by varying amounts. This effect—refraction—becomes most extreme at sunrise and sunset, and leads to the beautiful, elusive phenomenon known as the *green flash.* It lasts only a second or so, and can be seen only when our view of the setting sun is completely unobstructed; usually you must be looking over water, and there must not be any haze or clouds on the horizon. (It is even harder to see the green flash at sunrise, because you don't know where to look in advance.) As the sun nears the horizon, we wind up essentially with overlapping images of the sun. The colors are in the order ROY G. BIV (red, orange, yellow, green, blue, indigo, and violet), with the red image lowest. But the blue, indigo, and violet rays are scattered so much by the atmosphere that they don't reach us. When the red image sets, we sometimes see a brief flash of green on the horizon (Fig. 2-34).

Safely Observing the Sun

Most of the time, the sun is too bright to look at safely with the naked eye. Except for certain short periods during total eclipses (see p. 425), the only time when we can safely look at the sun is when it is dimmed by haze, usually close to sunset.

The safest way to study the sun is not to look at it directly at all. You can use a telescope or binoculars with its eyepiece to project an image of the sun onto a piece of cardboard. The process is called "eyepiece projection." Stand with your back to the sun and look at the cardboard; do not look through the telescope at the sun at all. Looking at the sun through a telescope for even a second could blind you. If a finder telescope is mounted on the telescope you are using, make certain that it is securely capped.

Adjust the eyepiece of your telescope or binoculars so that it is behind its normal position. Then you can vary both the position of the eyepiece and the distance of the paper behind it to put the sun's image in focus. An image the width of your hand should show enough detail to reveal sunspots clearly. You can trace the outlines of the sunspots on a daily basis, and follow the way they change as the sun rotates and the sunspots evolve. Again, **never** look up through a telescope at the sun, not even to point or focus the telescope. (You can usually align the telescope fairly well by adjusting the shadows along the outside of the tube so that they are at a minimum.)

The sun is about one million times brighter than the full moon. So to observe the sun directly in order to see the sunspots, we need a filter that cuts out all but $1/1,000,000$th of the sun's rays. A few filters of this type are made and distributed by telescope manufacturers. The filters normally go over the front end of the telescope, so that most of the sun's light never enters the telescope tube. (Filters that cut out light near the eyepiece are no longer thought to be safe for amateur astronomers; there is always the danger that they might slip or crack.)

Once you know how to observe the sun safely, you can make your own count of the sunspot number. The AAVSO (American Association of Variable Star Observers) in Cambridge, Massachusetts, has a solar group that keeps track of sunspots.

The Chromosphere, Prominences, and Special Solar Filters

Many features of the sun's atmosphere are not visible when you look in white light (all the sun's rays together); they show up only when the light of the unique color (specific wavelength) of hydrogen is isolated from visible light. This light, represented by the hydrogen radiation and absorption known as the *H-alpha line,* falls in the red part of the spectrum. Professional solar astronomers and increasing numbers of amateurs have filters that pass only this red H-alpha line of hydrogen (see the color view in Fig. 2-28).

When we look at the sun through an H-alpha filter, we are seeing the chromosphere. The *chromosphere* (from the Greek word for color, *chromos,* since it looks colorful during eclipses) is a thin layer just above the solar photosphere. The chromosphere is not really a layer; it is actually made up of spikes of gas called *spicules* that rise and fall with a period of 15 minutes each. The spicules are usually too delicate to see except with professional equipment used at exceptional sites.

H-alpha filters often come with fittings so they can be attached to the eyepiece of a telescope; in that location, they should be used with caution. When we look through an H-alpha filter, the solar surface looks mottled, and dark lines called *filaments* snake their way across the solar surface (Fig. 14-4). When a filament is rotated so that it appears at the edge of the sun, it is then called a *prominence* (Fig. 14-5).

On any sunny day, you can see exciting things with a telescope pointed at the sun. Eyepiece projection (see p. 422) or a special light-reducing filter over the aperture (see pp. 424, 430) reveals the sunspots. An H-alpha filter shows the filaments and prominences. Since the sun's surface changes from day to day, looking at the sun provides a changing image.

Fig. 14-4 *(left)* The sun's surface photographed through an H-alpha filter that passes light in a very narrow band of spectrum. The central part of the image shows the solar disk, with dark filaments and bright active regions. Surrounding it is an image made at the same scale, but with the center of the disk occulted—hidden—by a device in the telescope. These photographs were taken by an amateur astronomer. (R. J. Poole/DayStar Filter Corp.)

Fig. 14-5 *(right)* A solar prominence. This a quiescent (long-lasting) type; others may be eruptive. (Big Bear Solar Observatory, California Institute of Technology)

Some technical notes about equipment: if you are getting filters or other apparatus to observe the sun, it is best to check the advertisements in *Sky & Telescope* to see what is currently available. As of this writing, Thousand Oaks Optical specializes in filters, and filters can also be bought from telescope manufacturers. These high-quality solar filters use reflecting metal deposited on glass to cut down the intensity of white light; they are not cheap. Roger Tuthill, Inc., supplies less expensive filters on Mylar. DayStar makes H-alpha filters. A filter that passes a band of wavelengths narrower than 1 angstrom (0.0001 micrometer) is necessary to see the filaments on the solar disk; a filter that passes as much as 3 or 4 angstroms is sufficient to see the prominences around the solar limb.

Solar Eclipses: Nature's Spectacular

The most awesome sight we can see is a solar eclipse. The moon gradually covers the sun over a period of an hour or two, and then the crescent sun abruptly gives way to night, as we showed in Figure 2-29. A few points of light on the edge of the sun—*Baily's beads*—are visible for a few seconds. A bright point of light on the edge of the moon, so bright that it glistens like a jewel and is called the *diamond-ring effect,* is the last Baily's bead; we saw it in Figure 2-32. It lasts 3 or 5 seconds and then is also covered by the moon. The pinkish chromosphere is visible for another few seconds; prominences may be visible somewhat longer.

The diamond-ring effect comes from the last bit of the solar photosphere shining through a valley on the edge of the moon. When the diamond ring is over, we see a halo of light around the sun—the *corona* (from the Latin word for "crown"). The corona is the tenuous layer of gas surrounding the sun at a temperature of 2,000,000°C. It always surrounds the sun, but is a million times fainter than the surface of the sun (the photosphere) and is normally fainter than the earth's blue sky. Normally the sky looks blue because light from the solar photosphere bounces around in it. For us to be able to see the chromosphere and the corona, the sun must be up at a time when the sky is not illuminated, and that is exactly the situation we have during a total solar eclipse (Fig. 14-6).

In the hour or two before the total phase of the eclipse, when the sun is only partially covered by the moon, even the remaining part of the sun is still too bright to look at safely. A few minutes before totality, the total amount of light from the photosphere is reduced enough that the eye-blink reflex that normally protects our eyes doesn't work. Even then, you can still hurt your eyes by looking at the remaining part of the sun without a special filter. Only when the diamond-ring effect is over—and nobody ever has trouble deciding when that is—can you take your special filter away from your eyes and stare at the sun.

The corona is irregular in shape, with *streamers* extending millions of kilometers into space (Fig. 14-7). The sun acts on the whole like a giant bar magnet, so we can sometimes see *polar tufts*—thin rays coming out of the sun's poles—as well as the streamers that

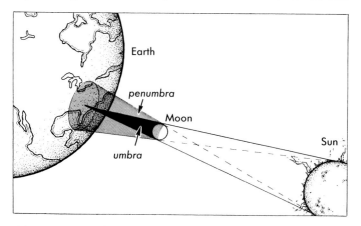

Fig. 14-6 From the inside of the umbra of the moon's shadow, we see a total eclipse of the sun. From inside the penumbra, we see a partial eclipse. In the drawing, the point of the umbra does not quite reach the earth, which means that the eclipse is annular, like the one in the United States on May 10, 1994. (Susan Eder)

Fig. 14-7 The 1991 total solar eclipse, photographed from Hawaii. The spiky solar corona silhouettes the moon, which we see as a dark circle because the sun is lighting the opposite side. The sun's diameter, barely hidden by the moon, is 1.4 million km, so we can see that the coronal streamers extend millions of kilometers into space. (Rhodes College and High Altitude Observatory)

appear at lower solar latitudes. The corona is expanding, forming the *solar wind* that extends throughout our solar system.

During the total part of the eclipse, only the corona is visible; the corona is perfectly safe to look at. It is then about the same brightness as the full moon. When the second diamond-ring effect occurs, marking the end of totality, you must again stop looking directly at the sun.

During totality, the sky is as dark as it is at night, or at least as dark as it is during evening twilight. If you look toward the horizon in any direction, you can see beyond the darkest part of the moon's shadow. You will see a pinkish glow on the horizon that looks like a sunset extending 360° around the sky.

For a minute or two before totality begins or after it ends, narrow bands of shadow seem to race across the landscape. These *shadow bands* occur when inhomogeneous regions of the earth's upper atmosphere bend the narrow crescent of light from the partially eclipsed sun. Shadow bands can be seen especially well if you spread out a white sheet on the ground, perhaps with distances measured across it to help you determine the spacing between adjacent bands and the distance a band appears to travel each second (which can be converted into velocity in kilometers or miles per hour). It is also interesting to note the direction in which the bands are travelling, which is often different before and after totality.

Solar eclipses are not especially rare; partial ones, in which the central part of the moon's shadow never touches the earth, occur about 3 times every year. Total solar eclipses occur about every 18 months (Table 20). Since the moon and the sun appear approximately the same size in the sky—the sun is actually 400 times larger than the moon but happens to be 400 times farther away—the shadow is not more than about 200 miles (300 km) wide when it hits the earth. It traces a narrow path across the earth (Fig. 14-8), thousands of miles (km) long but only tens or hundreds of miles (km) wide. Only within that narrow path can you see the corona and experience the eclipse.

More and more people are taking long trips to see total solar eclipses; once you see one, it is hard to resist going to see another (and perhaps taking a friend along). Among the observations that you can make at an eclipse are: (1) timing the *contacts*, where first contact is when the moon first begins to cover the sun, second contact is when totality begins, third contact is when totality ends, and fourth contact is when the moon's image leaves the solar disk; (2) sketching or photographing the prominences; (3) sketching or photographing the corona; and (4) observing the shadow bands. Some people like to cover one eye with an eyepatch before totality, so the eye will be dark-adapted when totality begins. Many people like to observe the corona through binoculars during totality.

Photographing an eclipse is always interesting, and it is particularly nice that the choice of exposure is not critical. Each combination of lens opening (aperture) and exposure time gives a different effect, but all are pretty. The corona falls off rapidly in brightness the farther it is from the sun, so the longer the exposure time, the more

Fig. 14-8 Total eclipses of the sun, from 1994 to 2020. The next eclipse visible from the continental United States will be in 2017. (Fred Espenak, NASA/GSFC)

Table 20: Solar Eclipses

January 4, 1992, annular. Over the Pacific Ocean, ending in southern California. Hawaii and other western states had a partial eclipse.

June 30, 1992, total. The beginning of the eclipse was visible at sunrise in Uruguay, but most of the eclipse was over the Atlantic Ocean.

May 10, 1994, annular. Crosses the United States from southwest to northeast; the end of the eclipse is visible in northwest Africa. The path of annularity reaches the U.S. in Arizona and New Mexico, crosses Texas and Oklahoma, and then continues northeast, until it passes over New York, Vermont, New Hampshire, and Maine before reaching the Canadian Maritimes. Partial phases will be visible throughout the continental U.S.

November 3, 1994, total. Crosses the middle of South America, with totality lasting 3 to 4 minutes. Totality crosses southern Peru, northern Chile, Bolivia, Paraguay, Argentina, and Brazil.

April 29, 1995, annular. The annular phase is visible from northern South America, and lasts up to 6 minutes 38 seconds. Annularity crosses southern Equador, northern Peru, southern Columbia, and northern Brazil.

October 24, 1995, total. The eclipse will be visible over south Asia, with totality lasting up to 2 minutes 10 seconds. Totality will be visible from Iran, Afghanistan, Pakistan, India, Bangladesh, Myanmar, Thailand, Cambodia, Laos, and Vietnam.

March 9, 1997, total. The path of totality crosses Mongolia, most of Siberia, and then Arctic regions. Totality lasts up to 2 minutes 50 seconds.

February 26, 1998, total. Totality will last up to 4 minutes 9 seconds, and crosses Panama, Columbia, Venezuela, and Caribbean islands (Aruba, Curaçao, Guadeloupe, Antigua, and Montserrat) for 3 minutes 20 seconds, from southwest to northeast.

August 22, 1998, annular. Annularity lasts up to 3 minutes 14 seconds, and crosses Indonesia (Sumatra and Borneo), Malaysia, and some islands of Oceania (including New Britain).

February 16, 1999, annular. Annularity crosses Australia, from near Carnavon in the west to near Cairns in the mid-north, and lasts up to 1 minute 18 seconds.

August 11, 1999, total. Totality lasts up to 2 minutes 23 seconds, and crosses Europe and southern Asia. Totality will cross England's southwestern tip, northern France, Belgium, Luxembourg, Germany, Austria, Hungary, Serbia, Romania, Bulgaria, Turkey, Iraq, Iran, Pakistan, and India.

Note: Annular eclipses are shown in italics.

corona you can see. But you also want to keep your exposure times short enough so that the moon's edge will not blur as the sun and moon move across the sky. Exposure times of up to about 1 second with a 500-mm telephoto lens, or 10 seconds with a "normal" 50-mm lens on a 35-mm camera, will do. It is important to use as steady a tripod as possible, to release the shutter carefully (preferably with a cable release), and to wait for the camera to stop vibrating after you advance the film (you may need to wait a second or two). If possible, lock up the mirror on a reflex camera to reduce vibration.

Telephotos of at least 200-mm focal length and preferably 500-mm focal length give the best images of the corona. You can use normal or wide-angle lenses to take overall views that include the corona at the top of the photo and scenery in the foreground. You will need a special solar filter to photograph the partial phases of an eclipse; remove the filter to photograph the diamond ring, prominences, or corona. Then you must put it on again at the end of the eclipse, perhaps after having taken a quick picture of the second diamond ring. Recommended exposures appear in Table 21. A difficult tradeoff must be made between faster films, which have larger grain, and slower but less grainy films; there is no "right answer" to this question. Usually slide film instead of print film should be used, because it captures a wider range of intensities; prints can be made from slides later on.

Some people see a partial eclipse and wonder why others are so awestruck by a total eclipse. But the difference is like night and day. Since the photosphere is 1 million times brighter than the corona,

Fig. 14-9 Looking over someone's shoulder through a solar filter made of fogged and exposed black-and-white photographic film. As the observer also looks through the solar filter, we see an annular eclipse. An entire circle of solar photosphere remains visible throughout. (Jay M. Pasachoff)

even a 99% partial eclipse still leaves 1% of 1 million times, or 10,000 times, more light from the photosphere than there is from the corona. And so the sky is too bright to allow the corona to be seen during a partial eclipse. It is truly worth travelling to the zone of totality each time there is an eclipse. Seeing a partial eclipse and saying that you have seen an eclipse is like standing outside an opera house and saying that you have seen the opera; in both cases, you have missed the main event.

Because the orbits of the moon around the earth and the earth around the sun are elliptical, sometimes the moon appears too small to completely cover the sun during an eclipse. Then an *annulus*—a ring—of photosphere remains visible (Fig. 14-9), and we have an *annular eclipse,* like the one that crosses the United States on May 10, 1994. (Partial phases will be visible throughout the U.S.) Since the photosphere is always visible, special filters must be used throughout an annular eclipse, both for the eye and for a camera, or pinhole cameras could be used. You should use a telephoto lens of at least 200-mm focal length to take photos through filters.

On a technical note, the same special filters that were described on p. 423–424 can also be used at eclipses. Some cheaper materials, such as aluminized Mylar, can also be used for solar filters, and are available for this purpose from Tuthill, Inc.; look for advertisements in recent issues of *Sky & Telescope* or *Astronomy* magazines. The Mylar is inexpensive, but gives a bluish cast to the sun instead of a more pleasant orange one; it is also subject to potentially dangerous pinpricks.

You can make your own solar filter for observing an eclipse if you start a few days in advance. First completely fog a roll of black-and-white film, perhaps by simply unrolling it in the sunlight. Then develop it to maximum density. Two thicknesses of this fogged and developed black-and-white film should cut down the solar intensity to a safe level; try two thicknesses first, and if they are too dense for the sun to shine through, try one thickness.

The silver in black-and-white film absorbs all sunlight across the entire spectrum, including the infrared (heat) radiation that is invisible to our eyes. Color film does not use silver, so it cannot be used to make a safe solar filter for eclipses or for any other observations of the sun. Also, gelatin photographic filters, such as Kodak's neutral-density Wratten filters, cannot be used for observing the sun with the naked eye, since they are effective only in the range for which photographic film is sensitive and pass infrared radiation that can be harmful to the eye.

No matter what filter you use, **never stare at the sun.** You will be able to see a great deal just by glancing through the filter at the sun for a few seconds. The partial phases do not change rapidly enough to make it interesting to look at the sun longer, in any case.

Table 21: Solar Eclipse Photography

Do **not** look through your viewfinder at the sun—except during totality—unless the viewfinder is covered with neutral-density filters.

Use film with the finest grain possible; for example, use Kodachrome 64 instead of any kind of Ektachrome for most purposes.

Mount your camera or telescope on as sturdy a tripod as possible. Exposure times for totality are not critical; most problems come from shaky mounts. Your camera will vibrate slightly each time you advance the film; wait a second or two to make sure the vibration has stopped before you take the next exposure. Use a cable release, and if possible, lock up the mirror on reflex cameras.

For close-ups of totality with a 35-mm camera, use a telephoto lens of at least 300 mm and preferably 500 mm.

Bracket your exposures widely—take a variety of exposures on either side of any given lens opening and shutter speed.

Make sure that you don't run out of film.

A sample eclipse sequence follows (ASA/ISO 64 film):

Partial phases: Every five minutes, take a bracketed series of exposures through a filter of neutral density 5, that is, a filter that passes only $1/100,000$ (where the density 5 means that there are 5 zeroes) of the incoming sunlight. **Note:** Do *not* look through any viewfinders unless they are also covered with a neutral-density 5 filter; Wratten photographic neutral-density filters are *not safe* for the eye. If you have made your own filter out of exposed and developed photographic film, take a wide range of exposures to make certain that you have a good one. Remember that your meter reading will probably not be accurate since it will average the light available over the entire field of view, while you are photographing a bright object surrounded by darkness. Put in a fresh roll of film five minutes before totality.

Diamond ring: Take off the neutral-density filters, and without shaking the camera, take one or two exposures at about $1/30$ second at $f/8$.

Prominences: As soon as the diamond ring disappears, take a series of exposures at $f/8$ for $1/60$, $1/30$, $1/15$, and $1/8$ second.

Corona: During totality, take a series of time exposures. If you are using an $f/8$ or $f/5.6$ lens, try $1/2$, 1, 2, and 4 seconds. If any time is left, repeat the sequence. Then get ready to take the diamond-ring effect at the end of totality. If you are using a wide-angle lens, open your lens as wide as possible (to $f/2.8$, $f/2$, of $f/1.4$, for example). Use faster film, such as ASA/ISO 200. Make certain that the eclipse is in the frame, near the top, and that some objects are visible in the foreground at the bottom of the frame. Take 1-, 2-, 4-, and 8-second exposures.

At the end of the eclipse: Photograph the second diamond ring without looking through the viewfinder, then turn your camera so it is no longer facing the sun. (Otherwise, the sunlight could burn a hole in your shutter. Add your neutral-density filters later for occasional photographs of the partial phases.

Video cameras: Maximum zoom usually gives a good image. If you can use a high shutter speed, the image is better. The effect is dramatic if you take off the filter just as the first diamond ring begins.

15

COORDINATES, TIME, AND CALENDARS

As the earth rotates on its axis, the sky overhead seems to turn in the opposite direction. The stars appear to rise in the east, move overhead in the course of the night, and set in the west. It is convenient for many purposes to think of the stars as being fixed on a *celestial sphere* that rotates every 24 hours.

Positions in the Sky: Right Ascension and Declination

On the surface of the earth, we measure the positions of cities and towns in longitude and latitude. Longitude is measured by lines that extend from north pole to south pole, usually up to 180° E and 180° W of a zero-degree (0°) line that goes through Greenwich, England.

Latitude on earth is measured by parallel lines that mark the number of degrees north or south of the equator. The north pole is +90°; the longitude scale has no meaning there, since all longitudes converge at the poles. Similarly, the south pole is –90°.

Astronomers have set up a similar set of coordinates in the sky. The celestial equator is an imaginary line around the sky, above the earth's equator. The celestial poles are the imaginary points where extensions of the earth's axis into space would meet the celestial sphere; they lie above the earth's poles.

The astronomers' coordinate that is similar to longitude is called *right ascension.* A line that extends over the sky from the celestial north pole through your zenith to the celestial south pole is your *meridian.* It crosses the celestial equator perpendicularly, and at any one moment marks a line of constant right ascension. We measure right ascension along the celestial equator. Since the sky seems to turn overhead once every 24 hours, we measure right ascension in *hours.* The celestial equator is divided into 24 hours of right ascension; since the sky turns a full circle of 360° each 24 hours, each hour of right ascension equals 15°. Each *minute* of right ascension is $^1/_{60}$ of 15°, and equals 15' (15 minutes of arc). Each *second* of right ascension is equal to $^1/_{60}$ of a minute, and so is equal to 15" (15 seconds of arc). When we speak of "minutes" or "seconds," we must be clear as to whether we mean units of arc or of time.

On the Atlas Charts in Chapter 7, right ascension is marked on the horizontal axis. As we look up when facing north, the sky seems to rotate counterclockwise around the north celestial pole, which is

Table 22: Angular Units for Coordinates in the Sky

right ascension	units of arc (degrees, minutes, or seconds)
24^h	$360°$
1^h	$15°$
4^m	$1°$
1^m	$15'$
4^s	$1'$
1^s	$15''$

marked by the North Star, Polaris. Above Polaris in the sky, we see stars rising in the east (to our right), moving overhead, and setting in the west (to our left). But some stars are *circumpolar*, that is, they always stay above the horizon. They circle under Polaris from our west (left) to our east (right). When we look at them underneath Polaris, we have a view similar to that of the Atlas Charts in Chapter 7, on which north is at the top. The hours of right ascension passing overhead increase as time goes on (1^h, 2^h, 3^h, etc.), so right ascension increases from right to left on the Atlas Charts. The vertical axis on the charts is *declination*, the number of degrees north (+) or south (–) of the celestial equator. Thus the celestial equator has declination $0°$, the north celestial pole has declination $+90°$, and the south celestial pole has declination $-90°$. The regions of right ascension and declination shown on the Atlas Charts are set out in Appendix 13 and are outlined on the endpapers of this guide.

In order to fix the scale of right ascension, we must arbitrarily assume some particular line to be zero. We choose this zero point, 0^h of right ascension, to be the *vernal equinox*. The equinoxes are the two points where the celestial equator crosses the *ecliptic*, the path the sun follows across the sky in the course of the year. The vernal equinox is one of these points the sun crosses on its way north each year; the other is the *autumnal equinox*.

Although day and night are theoretically equal in length on the days of the equinoxes, that would be true only if the sun were a point, not a disk, and if the earth's atmosphere did not bend sunlight. However, the top of the sun actually rises a few minutes before the center of the sun's disk—the point used in calculations. Also, the earth's atmosphere bends sunlight, so we can see the sun for several minutes before the time sunrise would occur and after the time sunset would occur if the earth had no atmosphere.

To find a star's celestial coordinates (Fig. 15-1), we measure the number of hours around the celestial equator to its hour circle, and the number of degrees north or south of the celestial equator to its declination. Right ascension is often abbreviated either *r.a.* or with

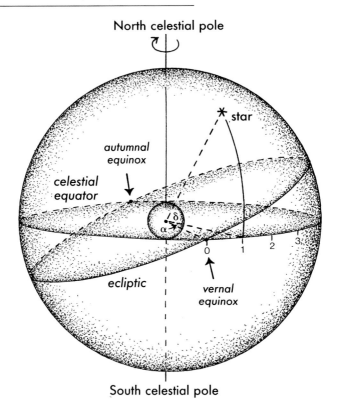

Fig. 15-1 Right ascension, noted by α (alpha), is measured in hours eastward around the celestial equator from the vernal equinox. Declination, noted by δ (delta), is measured in degrees north (+) or south (−) of the celestial equator. (Susan Eder)

the Greek letter α (alpha). Declination is often abbreviated either *dec.* or with the Greek letter δ (delta). A star's right ascension is equal to the length of time that elapses after the vernal equinox crosses your meridian until the star crosses your meridian. The interval is measured in *sidereal time;* one rotation of the sky takes 24 hours of sidereal time.

The stars are essentially fixed in the sky, and so their right ascension and declination do not change measurably over short periods of time. The sun, moon, and planets, though, wander through the sky with respect to the stars; their right ascension and declination change during the course of a year.

Precession

The axis on which the earth spins is not perpendicular to the plane of the earth's orbit. It is, rather, tipped by $23\frac{1}{2}°$. The celestial coordinate system is complicated somewhat by the fact that the earth's axis wobbles as the earth spins, just as a spinning top wobbles. For the earth, gravity from the sun and moon cause the wobbling, the same way that the earth's gravity makes a top wobble. The wobbling is called *precession*.

The earth's axis actually traces out a huge curve in the sky over a 26,000-year period. Polaris is only temporarily the North Star; in about 13,000 years, Vega will be within a few degrees of the north pole. As a result of the precession of the earth's axis, the celestial coordinates of stars "precess" slightly with time; that is, they change their values from year to year. The vernal equinox moves slowly westward along the ecliptic at about 50" per year. The effect is not large, but must be taken into account to plot the positions of astronomical objects accurately.

Stellar positions are usually given in one of a few "standard epochs," such as the year 1950 or 2000. Dates within a year are given as decimals, such as 1994.1 for February 5, 1994, or 2000.0 for the beginning of the year 2000. Changing from the epoch in which positions are given to the current date is now easily done with a pocket calculator; the computers that operate many telescopes do it automatically. Useful formulae for precession are:

new r.a. = r.a. + [3.074 = 1.336 sin (r.a) tan (dec.)] x N,
and new dec. = dec. + 20.04" cos (r.a.) x N,

where N is the number of years since a standard epoch. In this Field Guide, we join the International Astronomical Union in adopting the year 2000.0 as the standard epoch. Thus N will be negative until the year 2000. (For 1994, for example, $N = -6$.) In any case, casual sky observers do not need to worry about calculating precession.

Since the constellation boundaries fixed by the International Astronomical Union in 1930 were defined to lie along right ascension and declination lines for epoch 1875.0, the constellation boundaries no longer coincide with round numbers in epoch 2000.0 coordinates, as is clear from the Atlas Charts in Chapter 7.

A smaller effect than precession, called *nutation*, is a "nodding" of the earth's axis caused chiefly by changes in the location of the moon's orbit. The coordinates thus change in a small ellipse, with axes of only 18.5" and 13.7", over a 19-year period. No amateur telescope would have to be set to that degree of accuracy.

Another small effect, the *aberration of starlight*, is a shift of up to 20.5" resulting from the fact that the earth is moving through space. Just as you have to tilt your umbrella slightly forward to keep dry when moving rapidly through a rainstorm, since your motion makes the raindrops appear to slant toward you, aberration makes astronomers tilt their telescopes slightly forward as the earth orbits the sun.

Positions in most star catalogues, including the tables in this guide, take precession into account, but not nutation or aberration.

Time by the Stars

The stars return to the same point overhead where they were on the preceding night, but in that time, the earth has gone part (about $1/365$) of the way around the sun. So the earth has to rotate a little further for the sun to return to the same place in our sky (one *solar day*) compared to the length of time it takes the stars to return to the same place in our sky (one *sidereal day*). One day divided by 365 is about 4 minutes, so the solar day is longer than the sidereal day by about 4 minutes, actually 3^m56^s.

At about the vernal equinox each year, sidereal midnight (the beginning of a sidereal day) and solar "noon" coincide: 0 hours sidereal time = 12^h solar time. Then they drift apart by 4 minutes per day for another year. At the autumnal equinox, 12 hours sidereal time = 12^h solar time. The conversions between sidereal time and solar time are tabulated in Appendix 12.

Your sidereal time is the number of hours since the vernal equinox has crossed your meridian. Your sidereal time is also equal to the right ascension of stars now crossing your meridian. Thus if you know your sidereal time, you know which stars are most favorably placed for observing, *i.e.,* those within a few hours of the current sidereal time, if they are in the right range of declination.

The Big Dipper and the North Star actually make a convenient sidereal clock in the sky. A line from Polaris through the Pointers sweeps counterclockwise around the sky once a day. When that line is pointed straight upward, the sidereal time is 11^h, since the right ascension of the Pointers is almost exactly 11^h. When the line from Polaris through the Pointers goes due left, toward due west on the horizon, the sidereal time is 6 hours later, or 17^h. When the Pointers are below Polaris so the line from Polaris through the Pointers goes straight downward, the sidereal time is 23^h.

Calendars and Time by the Sun

One solar day for any observer is the length of time that the sun takes to return to our meridian. It takes about $365^1/4$ of those solar days to make a year. Instead of changing our clocks by $1/4$ day each year, we have three 365-day years followed by one 366-day *leap year,* a scheme worked out by the astronomer Sosigenes for Julius Caesar in 46 B.C.

But a year is 365.2422 days long, which is not exactly $365^1/4$ days. In 1582, the time had slipped substantially from the proper season because of this difference; the Gregorian calendar skipped 10 days to compensate and made some new rules about leap year: the "century years" (1900, 2000, etc.) would not be leap years unless they are evenly divisible by 4000. That is, 1800 and 1900 were not leap years, but 2000 will be a leap year.

Actual *apparent solar time* does not advance at a constant rate through the year, because the earth travels at varying speeds as it

Fig. 15-2 The analemma, the figure-8 that shows how far mean solar time is ahead of or behind true solar time for a given day of the year. (*Sky & Telescope*)

Fig. 15-3 The analemma in a single multiple-exposure photo, with an exposure of the sun taken at 8:30 a.m. E.S.T. every two weeks. The summer solstice is the highest point and the winter solstice is the lowest point; the lens was left open from dawn until shortly before the time for the standard exposure on those days and on the day of the crossover. The exposure of the foreground building was added on still another day, without the dense filter that normally allowed only the sun to be visible. (Dennis di Cicco)

traverses its elliptical orbit. As a result, it is more convenient for us to keep *mean solar time*, the average rate of solar time. Watches keep time at the same rate as mean solar time.

Your *local apparent solar time* is when the sun crosses your meridian. But your neighbors a few kilometers to the east or west have different meridians than yours. To compensate for these slight differences, we use a system of *standard time*, in which the solar time is the same in a band of earth longitudes 15° wide. The meridian of Greenwich is centered in one of these bands. The actual boundaries of the time zones often bend to follow political divisions between states, provinces, or countries.

The local apparent solar time minus the local mean solar time is called *the equation of time*. The difference can be as large as 16 minutes; we see its effect in Fig. 15-2.

The equation of time shows how far the real sun is ahead or behind the mean sun. As this value changes through the year, the sun also goes higher and lower in the sky. Thus the position of the sun at a given standard (mean) time each day appears to follow a figure-8 called the *analemma* (Figs. 15-2 and 15-3).

Astronomers keep time in *Universal Time* (U.T.), basically the time for the meridian of Greenwich, England. (The name "Greenwich mean time," G.M.T., is no longer commonly used.) Universal Time is set by the rotation of the earth, which is slightly irregular. Predictions are based on steady time unaffected by the earth's rotation, which is kept by atomic clocks. The average of predictions of steady time calculated by time services around the world is released as Coordinated Universal Time (U.T.C.). U.T.C. is kept aligned with U.T. by the occasional addition of leap seconds to U.T.C. at the end of December or June. They are publicly announced. The exact difference between the U.T. and U.T.C. can be calculated only after the fact, but is kept less than 1 second.

Time gets earlier as you move westward on earth. At a given instant, you subtract the following number of hours to go from U.T. to time zones in the U.S. and Canada.

Table 23: Time Zones

To convert from Universal Time (U.T.) to	To get standard time, subtract:	To get daylight saving time, subtract:
Atlantic Time Zone	4 hours	3 hours
Eastern Time Zone	5 hours	4 hours
Central Time Zone	6 hours	5 hours
Mountain Time Zone	7 hours	6 hours
Pacific Time Zone	8 hours	7 hours
most of Alaska	9 hours	8 hours
Hawaii Time Zone	10 hours	—

Most states employ daylight saving time, in which you add one hour to the standard time for the summer months; Arizona, Hawaii, and parts of Indiana have standard time all year. To remember to add one hour in the spring and subtract it again in the fall, think of "spring ahead, fall back," that is, move your clocks ahead one hour in the spring and move them back one hour in the fall.

Halfway around the world from Greenwich, in the middle of the Pacific, the date changes by one day at the *International Date Line*, so that the same hours on the same day don't keep endlessly circling the world. The time gets earlier by one hour each time you cross a time zone as you go from east to west; as you cross the International Date Line from east to west, one day is added.

APPENDICES

GLOSSARY

BIBLIOGRAPHY
Sky Atlases and General References

TELESCOPE INFORMATION

INDEX

Appendix 1: The Constellations

Abbre-viation	Latin Name	Pronun-ciation	Genitive	Translation
And	Andromeda	an-drom'ə-də	Andromedae	Andromeda
Ant	Antlia	ant'le-ə	Antliae	Pump
Aps	Apus	a'pəs	Apodis	Bird of Paradise, Bee
Aqr	Aquarius	ə-kwar'e-əs	Aquarii	Water Bearer
Aql	Aquila	ak'wə'lə	Aquilae	Eagle
Ara	Ara	a'rə	Arae	Altar
Ari	Aries	ar'ez, ar'e-ez'	Arietis	Ram
Aur	Auriga	o-ri'gə	Aurigae	Charioteer
Boo	Boötes	bo-o'tez	Boötis	Herdsman
Cae	Caelum	se'ləm	Caeli	Chisel
Cam	Camelopardalis	kə-mel'o-pär'-də-lis	Camelopardalis	Giraffe
Cnc	Cancer	kan'sər	Cancri	Crab
CVn	Canes Venatici	ka'nez vi-nat'ə-si	Canum Venaticorum	Hunting Dogs
CMa	Canis Major	ka'nis ma'jər	Canis Majoris	Big Dog
CMi	Canis Minor	ka'nis mi'nər	Canis Minoris	Little Dog
Cap	Capricornus	kap'ri-kor'nəs	Capricorni	Goat
Car	Carina	kə'ri'nə	Carinae	Ship's Keel
Cas	Cassiopeia	kas'e-ə-pe'ə	Cassiopeiae	Cassiopeia
Cen	Centaurus	sen-tor'əs	Centauri	Centaur
Cep	Cepheus	se'fyoos'	Cephei	Cepheus
Cet	Cetus	se'təs	Ceti	Whale
Cha	Chamaeleon	kə-mel'yən	Chamaeleonis	Chameleon
Cir	Circinus	sur'sə-nəs	Circini	Compass
Col	Columba	kə-lum'bə	Columbae	Dove
Com	Coma Berenices	ko'mə ber'ə-ni'sez	Comae Berenices	Berenice's Hair
CrA	Corona Australis	kə-ro'nə ostra'lis	Coronae Australis	Southern Crown
CrB	Corona Borealis	kə-ro'nə bor'e-al'is	Coronae Borealis	Northern Crown
Crv	Corvus	kor'vəs	Corvi	Crow
Crt	Crater	kra'tər	Crateris	Cup
Cru	Crux	kruks	Crucis	Southern Cross
Cyg	Cygnus	sig'nəs	Cygni	Swan
Del	Delphinus	del-fi'nəs	Delphini	Dolphin
Dor	Dorado	də-rä'do	Doradus	Swordfish
Dra	Draco	dra'ko	Draconis	Dragon
Equ	Equuleus	i-kwoo'le-əs	Equulei	Little Horse
Eri	Eridanus	i-rid'ən-əs	Eridani	River Eridanus
For	Fornax	for'naks'	Fornacis	Furnace
Gem	Gemini	jem'ə-ni'	Geminorum	Twins
Gru	Grus	grus	Gruis	Crane
Her	Hercules	hur'kyə-lez'	Herculis	Hercules
Hor	Horologium	hor'ə-lo'je-əm	Horologii	Clock
Hya	Hydra	hi'drə	Hydrae	Water Snake
Hyi	Hydrus	hi'drəs	Hydri	Water Snake

Abbre-viation	Latin Name	Pronun-ciation	Genitive	Translation
Ind	Indus	in'dəs	Indi	Indian
Lac	Lacerta	lə-sur'tə	Lacertae	Lizard
Leo	Leo	le'o	Leonis	Lion
LMi	Leo Minor	le'o mi'nər	Leonis Minoris	Little Lion
Lep	Lepus	le'pəs	Leporis	Hare
Lib	Libra	li'brə	Librae	Scales
Lup	Lupus	loo'pəs	Lupi	Wolf
Lyn	Lynx	lingks	Lyncis	Lynx
Lyr	Lyra	li'rə	Lyrae	Harp
Men	Mensa	men'sə	Mensae	Table
Mic	Microsco-pium	mi'krə-sko'-pe-əm	Microscopii	Microscope
Mon	Monoceros	mə-nos'ər-əs	Monocerotis	Unicorn
Mus	Musca	mus'kə	Muscae	Fly
Nor	Norma	nor'mə	Normae	Level
Oct	Octans	ok'tanz'	Octantis	Octant
Oph	Ophiuchus	of'e-yoo'kəs	Ophiuchi	Ophiuchus
Ori	Orion	o'ri'ən	Orionis	Orion
Pav	Pavo	pä'vo	Pavonis	Peacock
Peg	Pegasus	peg'ə-səs	Pegasi	Pegasus
Per	Perseus	pur'se-əs	Persei	Perseus
Phe	Phoenix	fe'niks	Phoenicis	Phoenix
Pic	Pictor	pik'tər	Pictoris	Easel
Psc	Pisces	pi'sez	Piscium	Fish
PsA	Piscis Austrinus	pi'sis os-tri'nəs	Piscis Austrini	Southern Fish
Pup	Puppis	pup'is	Puppis	Ship's Stern
Pyx	Pyxis	pik'sis	Pyxidis	Ship's Compass
Ret	Reticulum	ri-tik'yə-ləm	Reticuli	Net
Sge	Sagitta	sə-jit'ə	Sagittae	Arrow
Sgr	Sagittarius	saj'ə-tar'e-əs	Sagittarii	Archer
Sco	Scorpius	skor'pe-əs	Scorpii	Scorpion
Scl	Sculptor	skulp'tər	Sculptoris	Sculptor
Sct	Scutum	skyoo'təm	Scuti	Shield
Ser	Serpens	sur'pənz	Serpentis	Serpent
Sex	Sextans	seks'təns	Sextantis	Sextant
Tau	Taurus	tor'əs	Tauri	Bull
Tel	Telescopium	tel'ə-sko'pe-əm	Telescopii	Telescope
Tri	Triangulum	tri-ang'gyə-ləm	Trianguli	Triangle
TrA	Triangulum Australe	tri-ang'gyə-ləm o-stra'le	Trianguli Australis	Southern Triangle
Tuc	Tucana	too-ka'nə	Tucanae	Toucan
UMa	Ursa Major	ur'sə ma'jər	Ursae Majoris	Big Bear
UMi	Ursa Minor	ur'sə mi'nər	Ursae Minoris	Little Bear
Vel	Vela	ve'lə	Velorum	Ship's Sails
Vir	Virgo	vur'go	Virginis	Virgin
Vol	Volans	vo'länz	Volantis	Flying Fish
Vul	Vulpecula	vul-pek'yə-lə	Vulpeculae	Little Fox

Appendix 2: The Brightest Stars, to Magnitude 3.5

This list includes 298 stars, down to and including visual magnitude 3.5. The first column is the star's Flamsteed number, the second is the abbreviation of its Greek-letter Bayer designation and its constellation. For the few stars that have neither a Flamsteed number nor a Bayer designation, the appropriate numbers in the Smithsonian Astrophysical Observatory (SAO) catalogue are given. Positions are given for epoch 2000.0. V is the *visual magnitude*—the magnitude measured through a standard yellowish filter that simulates the range of sensitivity of the human eye. (For variable stars, the maximum brightness is given, and a small letter *v* appended.) B–V is a *color index*, the magnitude seen through a standard blue filter minus the visual magnitude; that gives the star's temperature. Then follows the star's absolute magnitude (M_v, the magnitude the star would have if it were at a distance of 10 parsecs = 32.6 light-years) and its spectral type. In the spectral type column, Roman numerals indicate the star's luminosity class: V indicates normal dwarfs like the sun; IV indicates subgiants; III, giants; II, bright giants; and I, supergiants. The notation Am means that the star (Delta Capricorni) has abnormally strong metallic lines in its spectrum. W marks Wolf-Rayet stars—stars that show broad emission lines (from gas they are ejecting) in addition to absorption lines in their spectrum; the C in WC stands for strong radiation from carbon and oxygen. Under notes, an *m* means that the star is part of a binary or multiple system or has a close optical neighbor, and an *s* means that the star is known to be a close, unresolved binary from the appearance of its spectrum. Some stars, designated *ms*, have both types of companions. Another popular name for the star, if any, appears in the last column.

Name and Catalogue Numbers	Position (2000.0) r.a. h m s	dec. ° ' "	Magnitudes V	B–V	M_v	Spectral Type	Distance (l–y)	Notes	Other Name
21 α And	0 08 23.3	+29 05 26	2.1v	−0.1	−0.6	B9 IV	120	ms	Alpheratz
11 β Cas	0 09 10.7	+59 08 59	2.3v	0.3	1.6	F2 III	46	ms	Caph
88 γ Peg	0 13 14.2	+15 11 01	2.8	−0.2	−3.3	B2 IV	580	s	Algenib
β Hyi	0 25 45.1	−77 15 15	2.8	0.6	3.7	G2 IV	21		
α Phe	0 26 17.0	−42 18 22	2.4	1.1	−0.1	K0 III	88	ms	Ankaa
31 δ And	0 39 19.7	+30 51 39	3.3	1.3	−0.4	K3 III	170	ms	
18 α Cas	0 40 30.5	+56 32 14	2.2	1.2		K0 II		m	Schedar
16 β Cet	0 43 35.4	−17 59 12	2.0	1.0	0.7	G9.5 III	62		Deneb Kaitos
24 η Cas	0 49 06.1	+57 48 56	3.5	0.6	4.6	G0 V	19	m	
27 γ Cas	0 56 42.5	+60 43 00	2.4v	−0.1		B0 IV		s	
β Phe	1 06 05.0	−46 43 07	3.3	0.9		G8 III		m	

Appendix 2: The Brightest Stars, to Magnitude 3.5

Name and Catalogue Numbers	Position (2000.0)						Magnitudes			Spectral Type	Distance (l–y)	Notes	Other Name
	r.a. h	m	s	dec. °	'	"	V	B–V	M$_v$				
31 η Cet	1	08	35.4	-10	10	56	3.5	1.2	0.1	K2 III	150	m	
43 β And	1	09	43.9	+35	37	14	2.1	1.6	0.2	M0 III	75	m	Mirach
37 δ Cas	1	25	49.0	+60	14	07	2.7	0.1	1.8	A5 V	52	s	Ruchbah
γ Phe	1	28	21.9	-43	19	06	3.4v	1.6		K5 II		s	
α Eri	1	37	42.9	-57	14	12	0.5	-0.2	-1.7	B3 V	91	m	Achernar
52 τ Cet	1	44	04.1	-15	56	15	3.5	0.7	5.7	G8 V	12	m	
2 α Tri	1	53	04.9	+29	34	44	3.4	0.5	1.9	F6 IV	65	s	
45 ε Cas	1	54	23.7	+63	40	12	3.4	-0.1		B2		m	
6 β Ari	1	54	38.4	+20	48	29	2.6	0.1	1.6	A5 V	52	s	Sheratan
α Hyi	1	58	46.2	-61	34	11	2.9	0.2	1.0	F0 III	78	m	
57 γ¹ And	2	03	54.0	+42	19	47	2.3	1.4		K3 II		s	Almach
13 α Ari	2	07	10.4	+23	27	45	2.0	1.2	0.2	K2 III	75	s	Hamal
4 β Tri	2	09	32.6	+34	59	14	3.0	0.1	0.0	A5 III	130	s	
68 o Cet	2	19	20.7	-2	58	39	3.0v	1.4		M5.5		ms	Mira
1 α UMi	2	31	48.7	+89	15	51	2.0	0.6		F7 I		ms	Polaris
86 γ Cet	2	43	18.0	+3	14	09	3.5	0.1	1.9	A3 V	68	m	
θ¹ Eri	2	58	15.7	-40	18	17	3.2	0.3		A4 III		ms	Acamar
92 α Cet	3	02	16.8	+4	05	23	2.5v	1.6	-1.1	M2 III	160		Menkar
23 γ Per	3	04	47.8	+53	30	23	2.9	0.7	0.0	G5 III	95	s	
25 ρ Per	3	05	10.6	+38	50	25	3.4v	1.7		M3 III			
26 β Per	3	08	10.1	+40	57	20	2.1v	-0.1	-0.5	B8 V	100	ms	Algol
33 α Per	3	24	19.4	+49	51	40	1.8	0.5	-4.5	F5 I	550	m	Mirfak
39 δ Per	3	42	55.5	+47	47	15	3.0v	-0.1	-2.5	B5 III	390	s	
23 δ Eri	3	43	14.9	-9	45	48	3.5	0.9	3.7	K0 IV	30		

Appendix 2: The Brightest Stars, to Magnitude 3.5

Name and Catalogue Numbers	Position (2000.0) r.a. h m s	dec. ° ' "	Magnitudes V	B–V	M_v	Spectral Type	Distance (l–y)	Notes	Other Name
γ Hyi	3 47 14.3	−74 14 20	3.2	1.6	−1.1	M2 III	220		
25 η Tau	3 47 29.1	+24 06 18	2.9	−0.1	−1.6	B7 III	400	m	Alcyone
44 ζ Per	3 54 07.9	+31 53 01	2.9	0.1	−6.5	B1 I	1,600	s	Atik
45 ε Per	3 57 51.2	+40 00 37	2.9	−0.2	−4.1	B0.5 V	680	s	
34 γ Eri	3 58 01.8	−13 30 31	3.0v	1.6	−0.7	M0.5 III	170	m	Zaurak
35 λ Tau	4 00 40.8	+12 29 25	3.5v	−0.1		B3 V		s	
α Ret	4 14 25.5	−62 28 26	3.4	0.9	0.3	G7 III	130		
74 ε Tau	4 28 37.0	+19 10 49	3.5	1.0	0.2	K0 III	150	m	
78 θ² Tau	4 28 39.6	+15 52 14	3.4v	0.2	0.2	A7 III	150	ms	
α Dor	4 33 59.8	−55 02 42	3.3v	−0.1	−0.6	A0 III	190	m	
87 α Tau	4 35 55.2	+16 30 33	0.9v	1.5	−0.7	K5 III	68	ms	Aldebaran
1 π³ Ori	4 49 50.4	+6 57 41	3.2	0.5	3.7	F6 V	26	s	
3 ι Aur	4 56 59.6	+33 09 58	2.7	1.5		K3 II			
7 ε Aur	5 01 58.1	+43 49 24	3.0v	0.5		A9 I		ms	
2 ε Lep	5 05 27.7	−22 22 16	3.2	1.5		K5 III			
10 η Aur	5 06 30.9	+41 14 04	3.2	−0.2	−1.7	B3 V	310		
67 β Eri	5 07 51.0	−5 05 11	2.8	0.1	0.9	A3 III	78	m	Cursa
5 μ Lep	5 12 55.9	−16 12 20	3.3v	−0.1	−0.4	B9	180		
19 β Ori	5 14 32.3	−8 12 06	0.1	0.0	−7.4	B8 I	1,000	ms	Rigel
13 α Aur	5 16 41.4	+45 59 53	0.1	0.8	−0.6	G5 III	46	ms	Capella
28 η Ori	5 24 28.7	−2 23 49	3.4	−0.2		B1 V		ms	
24 γ Ori	5 25 07.9	+6 20 59	1.6	−0.2	−3.6	B2 III	350	m	Bellatrix
112 β Tau	5 26 17.5	+28 36 27	1.7	−0.1	−1.6	B7 III	140	m	Elnath
9 β Lep	5 28 14.7	−20 45 34	2.8	0.8	−1.9	G5 II	290	m	Nihal

Appendix 2: The Brightest Stars, to Magnitude 3.5 (Continued)

Name and Catalogue Numbers	Position (2000.0) r.a. h m s	dec. ° ' "	Magnitudes V	B–V	M_V	Spectral Type	Distance (l–y)	Notes	Other Name
11 α Lep	5 32 43.8	−17 49 20	2.6	0.2	−4.7	F0 I	940	m	Arneb
β Dor	5 33 37.5	−62 29 23	3.4v	0.6	−8.1	F6 I	4,800	m	
39 λ Ori	5 35 08.3	+9 56 04	3.3			O8		m	Meissa
44 ι Ori	5 35 26.0	−5 54 36	2.8	−0.2	−6.3	O9 III	1,900	s	
46 ε Ori	5 36 12.8	−1 12 07	1.7v	−0.2	−6.5	B0 I	1,300	s	Alnilam
123 ζ Tau	5 37 38.7	+21 08 33	3.0v	−0.2	−2.9	B4 III	520	s	
α Col	5 39 38.9	−34 04 27	2.6	−0.1	−1.0	B7 IV	160	m	Phact
50 ζ Ori	5 40 45.5	−1 56 34	1.7	0.1		O9.5 I		ms	Alnitak
53 κ Ori	5 47 45.4	−9 40 11	2.1	−0.2		B0.5 I			Saiph
β Col	5 50 57.6	−35 46 06	3.1	1.2	0.1	K1.5 III	120		Wazn
58 α Ori	5 55 10.3	+7 24 25	0.5v	1.9	−4.5	M2 I	420	s	Betelgeuse
34 β Aur	5 59 31.7	+44 56 51	1.9	0.1	1.1	A2 V	46	ms	Menkalinan
37 θ Aur	5 59 43.4	+37 12 45	2.6v	−0.1	0.4	A0		ms	
7 η Gem	6 14 52.7	+22 30 24	3.3v	1.6	−1.4	M3 III	280	ms	Propus
1 ζ CMa	6 20 18.8	−30 03 48	3.0	−0.2	−2.4	B2.5 V	350	s	Furud
2 β CMa	6 22 42.0	−17 57 21	2.0v	−0.2	−5.0	B1 II	840	s	Mirzam
13 μ Gem	6 22 57.6	+22 30 49	2.9v	1.6		M3 III		m	
α Car	6 23 57.1	−52 41 44	−0.7	0.2	−4.7	F0 I	200		Canopus
24 γ Gem	6 37 42.7	+16 23 57	1.9	0.0	−0.3	A0 IV	85	ms	Alhena
ν Pup	6 37 45.7	−43 11 46	3.2	−0.1	−1.5	B8 III	300	s	
27 ε Gem	6 43 55.9	+25 07 52	3.0	1.4		G8 I		s	Mebsuta
9 α CMa	6 45 08.9	−16 42 58	−1.5	0.0	1.4	A1 V	9	ms	Sirius
31 ξ Gem	6 45 17.4	+12 53 44	3.4	0.4	1.9	F5 IV	65		
α Pic	6 48 11.4	−61 56 29	3.3	0.2	1.6	A7 IV	72		

Appendix 2: The Brightest Stars, to Magnitude 3.5 (Continued)

Name and Catalogue Numbers	Position (2000.0) r.a. h m s	dec. ° ′ ″	Magnitudes V	B–V	M_V	Spectral Type	Distance (l–y)	Notes	Other Name
τ Pup	6 49 56.2	−50 36 53	2.9	1.2	−0.1	K0 III	95	s	
21 ε CMa	6 58 37.5	−28 58 19	1.5	−0.2	−4.4	B2 II	480	m	Adhara
22 σ CMa	7 01 43.1	−27 56 05	3.5v	1.7	−0.2	K4 III	2,200	m	
24 o² CMa	7 03 01.5	−23 50 00	3.0	−0.1	−7.1	B3 I	2,200	s	
25 δ CMa	7 08 23.5	−26 23 36	1.8	0.7	−8.3	F8 I	2,200	s	
π Pup	7 17 08.6	−37 05 51	2.7	1.6	−0.5	K4 III	100	s	
31 η CMa	7 24 05.7	−29 18 11	2.4	0.0	−7.0	B5 I	2,200	m	Aludra
3 β CMi	7 27 09.0	+8 17 22	2.9v	−0.1	−0.7	B8 V		s	Gomeisa
σ Pup	7 29 13.8	−43 18 05	3.3	1.5	−0.7	K5 III	190	s	
66 α Gem	7 34 35.9	+31 53 18	1.6v	0.0	0.7	A1 V	49	ms	Castor
10 α CMi	7 39 18.1	+5 13 30	0.3	0.4	2.6	F5 IV	11	ms	Procyon
78 β Gem	7 45 18.9	+28 01 34	1.2	1.0	1.0	K0 III	36	m	Pollux
7 ξ Pup	7 49 17.7	−24 51 35	3.4	1.3	−4.3	G3 I	650	s	
χ Car	7 56 46.7	−52 58 56	3.5v	−0.2	−2.3	B3 IV	450	m	
ζ Pup	8 03 35.1	−40 00 12	2.2	−0.2		O5 I			
15 ρ Pup	8 07 32.6	−24 18 15	2.8	0.4				s	
γ² Vel	8 09 32.0	−47 20 12	1.8v	−0.2		WC 8		s	
ε Car	8 22 30.8	−59 30 35	1.9	1.3	−2.6	K3 III	29	s	Avior
1 o UMa	8 30 15.9	+60 43 05	3.4	0.8	−0.7	G4 II	220	m	Muscida
δ Vel	8 44 42.2	−54 42 30	2.0	0.1	0.1	A1 V	75	m	
11 ε Hya	8 46 46.6	+6 25 08	3.4	0.7		F0 V	52	ms	
16 ζ Hya	8 55 23.6	+5 56 44	3.1	1.0	1.7	G8 III	49	ms	
9 ι UMa	8 59 12.4	+48 02 30	3.1	0.2	2.2	A7 IV		ms	Talitha
λ Vel	9 07 59.8	−43 25 57	2.2v	1.7	−3.0	K4 I	300	m	

Appendix 2: The Brightest Stars, to Magnitude 3.5 (Continued)

Name and Catalogue Numbers	Position (2000.0) r.a. h m s	dec. ° ' "	Magnitudes V	B-V	M_v	Spectral Type	Distance (l-y)	Notes	Other Name
236693 Car	9 10 58.0	−58 58 01	3.4v	−0.2	−3.3	B2 IV	650	s	a Car
β Car	9 13 12.0	−69 43 02	1.7	0.0	0.6	A2 IV	55		Miaplacidus
ι Car	9 17 05.4	−59 16 31	2.2	0.2	−4.8	A8 I	750		Aspidiske
40 α Lyn	9 21 03.3	+34 23 33	3.2	1.5		M0 III			
κ Vel	9 22 06.8	−55 00 39	2.5	−0.2	−3.3	B2 IV	450	s	
30 α Hya	9 27 35.2	−8 39 31	2.0	1.4	−0.1	K3 III	65	m	Alphard
237067 Vel	9 31 13.3	−57 02 04	3.1	1.6	−0.4	K5 III	150		N Vel
25 θ UMa	9 32 51.4	+51 40 38	3.2	0.4	1.8	F6 IV	62	s	
250683 Car	9 45 14.8	−62 30 28	3.4v	0.9	−4.9	G5 I	1,500	m	l Car
17 ε Leo	9 45 51.1	+23 46 27	3.0	0.8	−2.0	G0 II	300		
υ Car	9 47 06.2	−65 04 19	3.0	0.3	−2.0	A7 II		m	
φ Vel	9 56 51.8	−54 34 04	3.5	0.0	−5.7	B5 I	2,000	m	
30 η Leo	10 07 20.0	+16 45 46	3.5	0.0	−5.2	A0 I	1,700	m	
32 α Leo	10 08 22.3	+11 58 02	1.4	−0.1	−0.9	B7 V	91	ms	Regulus
ω Car	10 13 44.2	−70 02 17	3.3	−0.1	−1.2	B8 III	240	m	
36 ζ Leo	10 16 41.4	+23 25 02	3.4	0.4	0.3	F0 III	120	s	Adhafera
250905 Car	10 17 05.0	−61 19 56	3.4v	1.5	−2.2	K3 II	350	m	q Car
33 λ UMa	10 17 05.8	+42 54 52	3.4	0.1	0.6	A2 IV	110	m	Tania Borealis
41 γ Leo	10 19 58.4	+19 50 30	2.2	1.2	−0.1	K0 III	88	ms	Algieba
34 μ UMa	10 22 19.7	+41 29 58	3.1	1.6	−1.0	M0 III	190	s	Tania Australis
251006 Car	10 32 01.4	−61 41 07	3.3v	−0.2	−1.4	B4 V	280	s	p Car
θ Car	10 42 57.4	−64 23 40	2.8	−0.2	−4.4	B0 V	480	s	
μ Vel	10 46 46.2	−49 25 12	2.7	0.9		G5 III		ms	
ν Hya	10 49 37.5	−16 11 37	3.1	1.3	0.1	K2 III	110		

Appendix 2: The Brightest Stars, to Magnitude 3.5 (Continued)

Name and Catalogue Numbers	Position (2000.0) r.a. h m s	dec. ° ' "	Magnitudes V	B–V	M_V	Spectral Type	Distance (l–y)	Notes	Other Name
48 β UMa	11 01 50.5	+56 22 57	2.4	0.0	0.5	A1 V	78	s	Merak
50 α UMa	11 03 43.7	+61 45 03	1.8	1.1	−1.0	K0 II	100	ms	Dubhe
52 ψ UMa	11 09 39.8	+44 29 55	3.0	1.2	0.1	K1 III	110		
68 δ Leo	11 14 06.5	+20 31 25	2.6	0.1	1.9	A4 V	46	m	Zosma
70 θ Leo	11 14 14.4	+15 25 46	3.3	0.0	1.4	A2 V	78	m	Chertan
54 ν UMa	11 18 28.7	+33 05 39	3.5	1.4	−0.4	K3 III	150	s	Alula Borealis
λ Cen	11 35 46.8	−63 01 11	3.1	0.0	−3.1	B9 II	550	m	
94 β Leo	11 49 03.6	+14 34 19	2.1	0.1	1.5	A3 V	42	m	Denebola
64 γ UMa	11 53 49.8	+53 41 41	2.4	0.0	0.3	A0 V	88	s	Phecda
δ Cen	12 08 21.5	−50 43 21	2.6v	−0.1	−3.0	B2 IV	390	m	
2 ε Crv	12 10 07.5	−22 37 11	3.0	1.3		K2 III			
δ Cru	12 15 08.7	−58 44 56	2.8	−0.2	−3.0	B2 IV	450		
69 δ UMa	12 15 25.6	+57 01 57	3.3	0.1	1.9	A3 V	62	m	Megrez
4 γ Crv	12 15 48.4	−17 32 31	2.6	−0.1	−1.5	B8 III	220	s	Gienah
α¹ Cru	12 26 35.9	−63 05 57	1.3	−0.2	−4.2	B0.5 IV	520	ms	Acrux
α² Cru	12 26 36.5	−63 05 57	1.7	−0.3	−3.2	B1 V	520	m	
7 δ Crv	12 29 51.9	−16 30 56	3.0	−0.1	0.2	B9 V	110	m	Algorab
γ Cru	12 31 09.9	−57 06 48	1.6	1.6	−0.9	M4 III	100	m	Gacrux
9 β Crv	12 34 23.2	−23 23 48	2.7	0.9	−1.9	G5 II	260		
α Mus	12 37 11.0	−69 08 08	2.7	−0.2	−2.7	B2 IV	390	m	
γ Cen	12 41 31.0	−48 57 35	2.2	0.0	0.0	A1 IV	98	ms	
29 γ Vir	12 41 39.6	−1 26 58	2.8	0.3	3.6	F0 V	36	ms	Porrima
β Mus	12 46 17.0	−68 06 30	3.0	−0.1	−2.1	B2.5 V	300	m	
β Cru	12 47 43.2	−59 41 19	1.2v	−0.2	−5.0	B0.5 III	480	s	Mimosa

Appendix 2: The Brightest Stars, to Magnitude 3.5 (Continued)

Name and Catalogue Numbers	Position (2000.0) r.a. (h m s)	dec. (° ′ ″)	Magnitudes V	B−V	M_v	Spectral Type	Distance (l-y)	Notes	Other Name
77 ε UMa	12 54 01.7	+55 57 35	1.8v	0.0		A0	250		Alioth
43 δ Vir	12 55 36.2	+3 23 51	3.4	1.6	−1.1	M3 III		m	
12 α² CVn	12 56 01.7	+38 19 06	2.9v	−0.1		A0		m	Cor Caroli
47 ε Vir	13 02 10.6	+10 57 33	2.8	0.9		G8 III		m	Vindemiatrix
46 γ Hya	13 18 55.3	−23 10 18	3.0	0.9		G5 III		m	
ι Cen	13 20 35.8	−36 42 44	2.7	0.1	1.0	A2 V	72		
79 ζ UMa	13 23 55.5	+54 55 31	2.1	0.0	1.1	A2 V	59	ms	Mizar
67 α Vir	13 25 11.6	−11 09 41	1.0	−0.2	−3.8	B1 V	280	s	Spica
79 ζ Vir	13 34 41.6	−0 35 45	3.4	0.1	1.7	A3 V	72		
ε Cen	13 39 53.2	−53 27 59	2.3v	−0.2	−4.4	B1 III	680		
85 η UMa	13 47 32.4	+49 18 48	1.9	−0.2		B3 V		m	Alkaid
ν Cen	13 49 30.3	−41 41 16	3.4	−0.2	−3.3	B2 IV	710	s	
μ Cen	13 49 37.0	−42 28 26	2.9v	−0.2	−3.0	B2 IV	450	s	
8 η Boo	13 54 41.1	+18 23 52	2.7	0.6	2.7	G0 IV	32	ms	Muphrid
ζ Cen	13 55 32.4	−47 17 18	2.6	−0.3	−2.9	B2.5 IV	480	s	
β Cen	14 03 49.4	−60 22 23	0.6v	−0.2	−4.7	B1 III	350	s	
49 π Hya	14 06 22.3	−26 40 57	3.3	1.1	0.1	K2 III	140		
5 θ Cen	14 06 41.0	−36 22 12	2.1	1.0	0.9	K0 III	55	m	Menkent
16 α Boo	14 15 39.7	+19 10 57	0.0	1.2	−0.3	K2 III	36		Arcturus
ι Lup	14 19 24.2	−46 03 28	3.6	−0.2	−2.6	B2.5 IV	550		
27 γ Boo	14 32 04.7	+38 18 30	3.0v	0.2		A7 III		m	Seginus
η Cen	14 35 30.4	−42 09 28	2.3v	−0.2		B1 V		s	
α² Cen	14 39 35.2	−60 50 13	1.3	0.9	6.1	K1 V	4	m	
α¹ Cen	14 39 36.5	−60 50 03	0.0	0.7	4.4	G2 V	4	ms	Rigil Kentaurus

Appendix 2: The Brightest Stars, to Magnitude 3.5 (Continued)

Name and Catalogue Numbers	Position (2000.0) r.a. h m s	dec. ° ' "	Magnitudes V	B–V	M_V	Spectral Type	Distance (l–y)	Notes	Other Name
α Lup	14 41 55.8	−47 23 18	2.3	−0.2	−4.3	B1.5 III	610	s	
α Cir	14 42 30.4	−64 58 31	3.2	0.2	1.6	A	65	m	
36 ε Boo	14 44 59.2	+27 04 27	2.7	1.0	−0.9	K0 II		m	Izar
7 β UMi	14 50 42.3	+74 09 20	2.1	1.5		K4 III		m	Kochab
9 α² Lib	14 50 52.7	−16 02 30	2.8	0.2	1.2	A3 IV	65	s	Zubenelgenubi
β Lup	14 58 31.9	−43 08 02	2.7	−0.2	−3.9	B2 III	680	s	
κ Cen	14 59 09.7	−42 06 15	3.1	−0.2	−3.3	B2 IV	580	s	
42 β Boo	15 01 56.8	+40 23 26	3.5	1.0	0.3	G8 III	130		Nekkar
20 σ Lib	15 04 04.2	−25 16 55	3.3v	1.7	2.0	M3.5 III	59		
ζ Lup	15 12 17.1	−52 05 57	3.4	0.9	0.3	G8 III	130	m	
49 δ Boo	15 15 30.2	+33 18 53	3.5	1.0	0.0	G8 III	160	s	
27 β Lib	15 17 00.4	−9 22 59	2.6	−0.1	−0.5	B8 V	140	s	Zubeneschamali
γ TrA	15 18 54.6	−68 40 46	2.9	0.0	1.2	A1 V	72	m	
13 γ UMi	15 20 43.7	+71 50 02	3.0v	0.1	−1.1	A3 II	220	m	Pherkad
δ Lup	15 21 22.3	−40 38 51	3.2v	−0.2	−3.4	B1.5 IV	680		
ε Lup	15 22 40.8	−44 41 22	3.4	−0.2	−3.0	B2 IV	610	ms	
12 ι Dra	15 24 55.8	+58 57 58	3.3	1.2	0.1	K2 III	140	s	Edasich
5 α CrB	15 34 41.3	+26 42 53	2.2v	0.0	0.4	A0 V	75	s	Alphecca
γ Lup	15 35 08.4	−41 10 01	2.8	−0.2	−3.0	B2 IV	450	m	
24 α Ser	15 44 16.1	+6 25 32	2.7	1.2	1.0	K2 III	72	m	Unukalhai
β TrA	15 55 08.5	−63 25 50	2.9	0.3	2.3	F2 III	42	m	
6 π Sco	15 58 51.1	−26 06 51	2.9	−0.2	−3.9	B1 V	650	s	
η Lup	16 00 07.3	−38 23 49	3.4	−0.2	−2.6	B2.5 IV	520	m	
7 δ Sco	16 00 20.0	−22 37 18	2.3	−0.1	−4.5	B0.5 IV	610	s	

Appendix 2: The Brightest Stars, to Magnitude 3.5 (Continued)

Name and Catalogue Numbers	Position (2000.0) r.a. h m s	dec. ° ' "	Magnitudes V	B-V	M_V	Spectral Type	Distance (l-y)	Notes	Other Name
8 β¹ Sco	16 05 26.2	-19 48 19	2.6	-0.1	-4.1	B0.5 V	520	s	Graffias
1 δ Oph	16 14 20.7	-3 41 40	2.7	1.6	-0.8	M1 III	160	m	Yed Prior
2 ε Oph	16 18 19.3	-4 41 33	3.2	1.0	0.3	G8 III	120	m	Yed Posterior
20 σ Sco	16 21 11.3	-25 35 34	2.9v	0.1	-4.9	B2 III	610	s	
14 η Dra	16 23 59.4	+61 30 51	2.7	0.9	0.9	G8 III	75		
21 α Sco	16 29 24.5	-26 25 55	1.0v	1.8		M1.5 I	110	ms	Antares
27 β Her	16 30 13.2	+21 29 23	2.8	0.9	0.0	G8 III	110	s	Kornephoros
23 τ Sco	16 35 53.0	-28 12 58	2.8	-0.3	-4.1	B0 V	750	m	
13 ζ Oph	16 37 09.5	-10 34 02	2.6v	0.0	-4.4	O9.5 V	550	m	
40 ζ Her	16 41 16.9	+31 36 10	2.8	0.7	2.9	F9 IV	32	ms	
α TrA	16 48 39.9	-69 01 40	1.9	1.4		K2 II			Atria
26 ε Sco	16 50 09.8	-34 17 36	2.3	1.2	0.7	K2 III	65		
μ¹ Sco	16 51 52.2	-38 02 51	3.0v	-0.1		B1.5 IV		s	
27 κ Oph	16 57 40.1	+9 22 30	3.2	1.2		K2 III			
ζ Ara	16 58 37.2	-55 59 25	3.1	1.6	-0.4	K5 III	140		
22 ζ Dra	17 08 47.2	+65 42 53	3.2	-0.1	-1.9	B6 III	320	m	
35 η Oph	17 10 22.7	-15 43 30	2.4	0.1	0.8	A2 V	68	ms	Sabik
η Sco	17 12 09.2	-43 14 21	3.3	0.4	2.1	F3 III	59		
64 α¹ Her	17 14 38.9	+14 23 25	3.5v	1.4		M5 II		m	Rasalgethi
65 δ Her	17 15 01.9	+24 50 21	3.1v	0.1	0.6	A3 IV	100	s	
67 π Her	17 15 02.8	+36 48 33	3.2	1.4		K3 II			
42 θ Oph	17 22 00.6	-24 59 58	3.3	-0.2	-3.3	B2 IV	680	s	
β Ara	17 25 18.0	-55 31 48	2.9	1.5	-2.9	K3 I	450		
γ Ara	17 25 23.6	-56 22 40	3.3	-0.1	-5.7	B1 I	1,700	m	

Appendix 2: The Brightest Stars, to Magnitude 3.5 (Continued)

Name and Catalogue Numbers	Position (2000.0) r.a. h m s	dec. ° ′ ″	Magnitudes V	B-V	M_v	Spectral Type	Distance (l-y)	Notes	Other Name
23 β Dra	17 30 26.0	+52 18 05	2.8	1.0	-2.0	G2 II	250	m	Rastaban
34 υ Sco	17 30 45.8	-37 17 45	2.7	-0.2	-3.3	B2 IV	550	s	Lesath
α Ara	17 31 50.5	-49 52 34	3.0	-0.2	-2.8	B2 V	450	s	
35 λ Sco	17 33 36.5	-37 06 14	1.6v	-0.2		B1.5 IV		s	Shaula
55 α Oph	17 34 56.1	+12 33 36	2.1	0.1	0.8	A5 III	59		Rasalhague
θ Sco	17 37 19.2	-42 59 52	1.9	0.4	-2.0	F1 II	180		
55 ξ Ser	17 37 35.2	-15 23 55	3.5	0.3	1.4	F0 IV	85		
κ Sco	17 42 29.3	-39 01 48	2.4v	-0.2	-4.3	B1.5 III	680	s	
60 β Oph	17 43 28.4	+04 34 02	2.8	1.2	0.1	K2 III	110	m	Cebalrai
86 μ Her	17 46 27.5	+27 43 14	3.4	0.8	3.8	G5 IV	28	m	
τ¹ Sco	17 47 35.1	-40 07 37	3.0	0.5	-8.6	F3 I	4,800	s	
209318 Sco	17 49 51.5	-37 02 36	3.2	1.2	0.1	K0 III	110	m	G Sco
33 γ Dra	17 56 36.4	+51 29 20	2.2	1.5	-0.4	K5 III	100	m	Eltanin
64 ν Oph	17 59 01.6	-09 46 25	3.3	1.0	0.2	K0 III	130		
10 γ Sgr	18 05 48.5	-30 25 27	3.0	1.0	-0.1	K0 III	130	s	Alnasl
η Sgr	18 17 37.6	-36 45 42	3.1v	1.6	-1.1	M2 III	220	m	
19 δ Sgr	18 20 59.7	-29 49 41	2.7	1.4	-0.1	K3 III	100	m	Kaus Media
58 η Ser	18 21 18.6	-02 53 56	3.3	0.9	1.9	K0 III	62	m	
20 ε Sgr	18 24 10.3	-34 23 05	1.8	0.0	-0.7	B9.5 III	95	m	Kaus Australis
α Tel	18 26 58.4	-45 58 06	3.5	-0.2	-2.3	B3 IV	450		
22 λ Sgr	18 27 58.2	-25 25 18	2.8	1.0	1.1	K0 III	72		Kaus Borealis
3 α Lyr	18 36 56.3	+38 47 01	0.0v	0.0	0.5	A0 V	26	m	Vega
27 φ Sgr	18 45 39.4	-26 59 27	3.2	-0.1	-1.3	B8.5 III	280	s	
10 β Lyr	18 50 04.8	+33 21 46	3.5	0.0	-0.3	B7 V	150	s	Sheliak

Appendix 2: The Brightest Stars, to Magnitude 3.5 (Continued)

Name and Catalogue Numbers	Position (2000.0) r.a. h m s	dec. ° ' "	Magnitudes V	B–V	M_V	Spectral Type	Distance (l-y)	Notes	Other Name
34 σ Sgr	18 55 15.9	−26 17 48	2.0	−0.2	−2.1	B2.5 V	200	m	Nunki
14 γ Lyr	18 58 56.6	+32 41 22	3.2	−0.1	−0.8	B9 III	200	m	Sulafat
38 ζ Sgr	19 02 36.7	−29 52 49	2.6	0.1	0.6	A3 IV	85	ms	Ascella
17 ζ Aql	19 05 24.6	+13 51 48	3.0	0.0	0.3	A0 V	110	s	
16 λ Aql	19 06 14.9	−4 52 57	3.4	−0.1	0.2	B9 V	140	m	
40 τ Sgr	19 06 56.4	−27 40 14	3.3	1.2	−0.2	K1 III	150	s	
41 π Sgr	19 09 45.8	−21 01 25	2.9	0.4	0.6	F3 III	95	m	
57 δ Dra	19 12 33.3	+67 39 42	3.1	1.0	0.3	G9 III	110	m	Altais
30 δ Aql	19 25 29.9	+3 06 53	3.4v	0.3	2.5	F0 IV	49	s	
6 β Cyg	19 30 43.3	+27 57 35	3.1	1.1	−2.3	K3 II	390	ms	Albireo
18 δ Cyg	19 44 58.5	+45 07 51	2.9	0.0	−1.0	B9.5 III	190	ms	
50 γ Aql	19 46 15.6	+10 36 48	2.7	1.5	−2.2	K3 II	260	m	Tarazed
53 α Aql	19 50 47.0	+8 52 06	0.8	0.2	2.2	A7 IV	17	m	Altair
12 γ Sge	19 58 45.4	+19 29 32	3.5	1.6	−0.4	K5 III	170		
65 θ Aql	20 11 18.3	−0 49 17	3.2	−0.1	−1.0	B9.5 III	240	s	
9 β¹ Cap	20 21 00.7	−14 46 53	3.1	0.8	−2.0	G5 II	320	s	Dabih
37 γ Cyg	20 22 13.7	+40 15 24	2.2	0.7	−4.3	F8 I	550	s	Sadr
α Pav	20 25 38.9	−56 44 06	1.9	−0.2	−3.3	B2 IV	350	s	Peacock
α Ind	20 37 34.0	−47 17 29	3.1	1.0	0.2	K0 III	120	m	
50 α Cyg	20 41 25.9	+45 16 49	1.3v	0.1	−7.5	A2 I	1,600	m	Deneb
β Pav	20 44 57.5	−66 12 11	3.4	0.2	1.2	A5 IV	88		
3 η Cep	20 45 17.4	+61 50 20	3.4	0.9	2.7	K0 IV	46	m	
53 ε Cyg	20 46 12.7	+33 58 13	2.5	1.0	0.7	K0 III	75	s	
64 ζ Cyg	21 12 56.2	+30 13 37	3.2	1.0	−0.4	G8 III	150	s	

Appendix 2: The Brightest Stars, to Magnitude 3.5 (Continued)

Name and Catalogue Numbers	Position (2000.0) r.a. h m s	dec. ° ' "	Magnitudes V	B-V	M_v	Spectral Type	Distance (l-y)	Notes	Other Name
5 α Cep	21 18 34.8	+62 35 08	2.4	0.2	1.4	A7 IV	52	m	Alderamin
8 β Cep	21 28 39.6	+70 33 39	3.2v	-0.2	-3.9	B2 III	810	ms	Alfirk
22 β Aqr	21 31 33.5	-5 34 16	2.9	0.8	-4.1	G0 I	680	m	Sadalsuud
8 ε Peg	21 44 11.2	+9 52 30	2.4v	1.5		K2 I		m	Enif
49 δ Cap	21 47 02.4	-16 07 38	2.9	0.3	1.9	Am	49	s	Deneb Algedi
γ Gru	21 53 55.7	-37 21 54	3.0	-0.1	-1.2	B8 III	220		
34 α Aqr	22 05 47.0	-0 19 11	2.9	1.0	-4.0	G2 I	550	m	Sadalmelik
α Gru	22 08 14.0	-46 57 40	1.7	-0.1	0.2	B7 IV	65	m	Al Na'ir
26 θ Peg	22 10 12.0	+6 11 52	3.5	0.1	1.6	A2 V	78	s	Biham
21 ζ Cep	22 10 51.3	+58 12 04	3.4v	1.6	-3.9	K1 I	710	s	
α Tuc	22 18 30.1	-60 15 35	2.9	1.4	-0.4	K3 III	120	s	
27 δ Cep	22 29 10.3	+58 24 55	3.5v	0.4		G2 I		s	
42 ζ Peg	22 41 27.7	+10 49 53	3.4	-0.1	0.0	B8.5 V	150	m	Homam
β Gru	22 42 40.1	-46 53 05	2.1v	1.6	-0.7	M5 III	110		
44 η Peg	22 43 00.1	+30 13 17	3.0	0.8	-1.9	G8 II	310	s	Matar
ε Gru	22 48 33.3	-51 19 01	3.5	0.1	1.7	A3 V	75		
48 μ Peg	22 50 00.2	+24 36 06	3.5	0.9	0.3	G8 III	140		Sadalbari
76 δ Aqr	22 54 39.0	-15 49 15	3.3	0.1	1.7	A3 V	68	m	Skat
24 α PsA	22 57 39.1	-29 37 20	1.2	0.1	2.0	A3 V	22		Fomalhaut
53 β Peg	23 03 46.5	+28 04 58	2.4v	1.7		M2 II		m	Scheat
54 α Peg	23 04 45.7	+15 12 19	2.5	0.0	-1.0	B9.5 III	160	s	Markab
35 γ Cep	23 39 20.8	+77 37 57	3.2	1.0	2.2	K1 IV	52		Errai

The information in this table was kindly extracted for us from *Sky Catalogue 2000.0*, Vol. 1, by Alan Hirshfeld, Roger W. Sinnott, and François Ochsenbein (© 1991 by Sky Publishing Corp.), and is reprinted with permission.

Appendix 3: Properties of the Principal Spectral Types

Spectral Type	Apparent Color	Color Index (B–V)	Surface Temperature (K)	Primary Absorption Lines in Spectrum	Examples
O	blue	less than −0.2	25,000–40,000	Strong lines of ionized helium and highly ionized metals; hydrogen lines weak	ζ Orionis (O9.5)
B	blue	−0.2–0.0	11,000–25,000	Lines of neutral helium prominent; hydrogen lines stronger than in type O	Spica (B1) Rigel (B8)
A	blue to white	0.0–0.3	7,500–11,000	Strong lines of hydrogen, ionized calcium, and other ionized metals; weak helium lines	Vega (A0) Sirius (A1) Deneb (A2)
F	white	0.3–0.6	6,000–7,500	Hydrogen lines weaker than in type A; ionized calcium strong; lines of neutral metals becoming prominent	Canopus (F0) Procyon (F5) Polaris (F8)
G	white to yellow	0.6–1.1	5,000–6,000	Numerous strong lines of ionized calcium and other ionized and neutral metals; hydrogen lines weaker than in type F	Sun (G2) Capella (G8)
K	orange to red	1.1–1.5	3,500–5,000	Numerous strong lines of neutral metals	Arcturus (K2) Aldebaran (K5)
M	red	greater than 1.5	3,000–3,500	Numerous strong lines of neutral metals; strong molecular bands (primarily titanium oxide)	Antares (M1) Betelgeuse (M2)

Note: The number after the letter in each spectral type (see last column, above) indicates a further subdivision within each type. For example, Sirius (type A1) is hotter than Deneb (type A2).

From *Sky Catalogue 2000.0* by Alan Hirshfeld and Roger W. Sinnott, courtesy of Sky Publishing Corp.

Appendix 4: The Nearest Stars

No. (Rank)	Name	Position (2000.0) r.a. h m	dec. ° '	Distance (light-years)	Spectral Type	Magnitude V	M_v	Luminosity (L_{sun} = 1)
1	Sun				G2 V	−26.72	4.85	1.0
2	Proxima Cen	14 30	−62 40	4.24	M5.5 V	11.12	15.49	0.00006
	α (alpha) Cen A	14 40	−60 50	4.37	G2 V	−0.01	4.37	1.6
	α (alpha) Cen B				K1 V	1.34	5.71	0.45
3	Barnard's star	17 58	+04 41	5.97	M3.8 V	9.56	13.22	0.00045
4	Wolf 359 (CN Leo)	10 57	+07 00	7.80	M5.8 V	13.45	16.65	0.00002
5	BD +36°2147	11 03	+35 58	8.22	M2.1 V	7.48	10.50	0.0055
	(Lalande 21185)							
6	L 726-8 = A	01 39	−17 57	8.55	M5.6 V	12.56	15.46	0.00006
	UV Cet = B				M5.6 V	12.96	15.96	0.00004
7	Sirius A	06 45	−16 43	8.58	A1 V	−1.43	1.42	23.5
	Sirius B				DA	8.44	11.2	0.003
8	Ross 154 (V 1216 Sgr)	18 50	−23 49	9.56	M3.6 V	10.45	13.14	0.00048
9	Ross 248 (HH And)	23 42	+44 10	10.3	M4.9 V	12.29	14.78	0.00011
10	ε (epsilon) Eri	03 33	−09 28	10.6	K2 V	3.73	6.14	0.30
11	Ross 128 (FI Vir)	11 48	+00 48	10.8	M4.1 V	11.12	13.47	0.00036
12	L 789-6	22 38	−15 18	11.1	M5.5 V	12.30	14.49	0.00014
13	BD +43° 44 A (GX And)	00 18	+44 00	11.3	M1.3 V	8.08	10.39	0.0061
	+43° 44 B (GQ And)				M3.8 V	11.06	13.37	0.00039
	(Groombridge 34 AB)							
14	ε (epsilon) Ind	22 03	−56 47	11.3	K3 V	4.69	7.00	0.14
15	61 Cyg A	21 07	+38 45	11.3	K3.5 V	5.21	7.56	0.082
	61 Cyg B				K4.7 V	6.03	8.37	0.039

Notes: V = visual magnitude; M_v = absolute magnitude. Under Spectral Type, V = normal dwarfs like the sun and DA is a class of white dwarfs. Distances derived from the *Yale Trigonometric Parallax Catalogue* (1990), courtesy of John T. Lee and William Van Altena and of Wilhelm Gliese. Other information courtesy W. Gliese (1989, 1990), with spectral types on a consistent scale by Robert F. Wing and Charles A. Dean (1983), and additional comments from Dorrit Hoffleit (1983).

Appendix 5: Selected Bright Planetary Nebulae

Planetary Nebula	Name and Constellation	Position (2000.0) r.a. h m	dec. ° '	Magnitude (visual)	Diameter (arc sec)
NGC 7293	Helix in Aquarius	22 30	−20 48	6.5	>770
NGC 6853	Dumbbell in Vulpecula, M27	19 60	+22 43	7.6	350/910
NGC 246	in Cetus	00 47	−11 53	8.0	225
NGC 3132	Eight-burst in Vela	10 08	−40 26	8.2	>47
NGC 7009	Saturn in Aquarius	21 04	−11 23	8.3	25/100
NGC 3242	Ghost of Jupiter in Hydra	10 25	−18 38	8.6	16/1250
NGC 6543	Cat's Eye in Draco	17 59	+66 38	8.8	18/350
NGC 6572	in Ophiuchus	18 12	+06 51	9.0	8
NGC 7662	in Andromeda	23 26	+42 33	9.2	20/130
NGC 6210	in Hercules	16 45	+23 49	9.3	>14
NGC 1535	in Eridanus	04 14	−12 44	9.6	18/44
NGC 6720	Ring Nebula in Lyra, M57	18 54	+33 02	9.7	70/150
NGC 6826	Blinking Planetary in Cygnus	19 45	+50 32	9.8	30/140
NGC 6818	Little Gem in Sagittarius	19 44	−14 09	9.9	>17
NGC 2392	Eskimo in Gemini	07 29	+20 55	9.9	13/44

Notes: Under diameter, two values separated by a slash indicates a bright inner core surrounded by a faint, extended halo; the symbol ">" indicates that, while only the size of the core is listed, a larger halo exists.

Courtesy of Yervant Terzian, Cornell University, with data from *Sky Catalogue 2000.0*, Vol. 2.

Appendix 6: Double Stars

ADS	Star	Position (2000.0) r.a. h m	dec. ° "	Magnitudes	1995 PA °	Sep. "	2000 PA °	Sep. "	Period (years)
558	55 Psc	00 39.9	+21 26	5.5, 8.7	193	6.6	193	6.6	–
561	α Cas	00 40.5	+56 32	2.2, 8.9	282	69.5	282	69.8	–
671	η Cas	00 49.1	+57 49	3.5, 7.5	315	12.7	317	12.8	480
940	42 φ And	01 09.5	+47 15	4.6, 5.5	130	0.5	127	0.5	372
996	ζ Psc	01 13.7	+07 35	5.6, 6.6	62	22.8	62	22.8	–
1129	ψ Cas	01 25.9	+68 08	4.7, 9.6	122	20.8	122	20.5	–
1507	γ Ari	01 53.5	+19 18	4.6, 4.7	0	7.6	0	7.6	–
1563	λ Ari	01 57.9	+23 36	4.8, 7.3	47	37.5	47	37.5	–
1615	α Psc	02 02.1	+02 46	4.2, 5.2	275	1.9	272	1.8	933
1630	γ¹ And	02 03.9	+42 20	2.2, 5.1	63	9.7	63	9.7	–
1630	γ² And	02 03.9	+42 20	5.5, 6.3	105	0.5	103	0.4	61
1697	ι Tri	02 12.4	+30 18	5.3, 6.9	69	3.9	69	3.9	–
1860	ι Cas	02 29.1	+67 24	4.6, 6.9	235	2.5	235	2.5	–
1477	α UMi	02 31.8	+89 16	2.0, 8.9	222	18.3	222	18.3	–
2080	γ Cet	02 43.3	+03 14	3.6, 6.2	297	2.8	297	2.8	–
2157	η Per	02 50.7	+55 54	3.8, 8.5	301	28.4	301	28.4	–
–	θ¹,²Eri	02 58.3	–40 18	3.2, 4.3	90	8.2	90	8.2	–
2850	32 Eri	03 54.3	–02 57	4.7, 6.2	347	6.8	347	6.8	–
2888	ε Per	03 57.9	+40 01	2.9, 8.0	9	9.0	9	9.0	–
3137	φ Tau	04 20.4	+27 21	5.1, 8.7	256	49.3	256	49.1	–
3321	α Tau	04 35.9	+16 31	0.9, 10.7	31	132.6	31	133.3	–
3823	β Ori	05 14.5	–08 12	0.2, 6.7	202	9.4	202	9.4	–
4179	λ Ori	05 35.1	+09 56	3.6, 5.5	44	4.3	44	4.3	–
4186	θ¹ Ori	05 35.3	–05 23	5.1, 6.7	31	8.8	31	8.8	–
4241	σ Ori	05 38.8	+02 36	3.8, 6.6	85	12.8	85	12.8	–
4566	θ Aur	05 59.7	+37 13	2.6, 7.1	307	3.8	305	3.9	–
5107	β Mon	06 28.8	–07 02	4.6, 5.1	132	7.2	132	7.2	–
5400	12 Lyn	06 46.2	+59 27	5.4, 6.0	71	1.7	69	1.7	699
5423	α CMa	06 45.2	–16 43	–1.5, 8.5	231	3.1	150	4.6	50
5654	ε CMa	06 58.6	–28 58	1.5, 7.8	161	7.5	161	7.5	–
5983	δ Gem	07 20.1	+21 59	3.6, 8.2	224	5.9	225	5.8	1200
6175	α Gem	07 34.6	+31 53	1.9, 2.9	72	3.5	67	4.0	511
6321	κ Gem	07 44.5	+24 24	3.6, 9.4	241	7.3	241	7.3	–
6988	ι¹ Cnc	08 46.7	+28 46	4.0, 6.6	307	30.4	307	30.4	–
7203	σ² UMa	09 10.4	+67 08	4.9, 8.2	356	3.6	354	3.8	1141
7402	23 UMa	09 31.5	+63 04	3.7, 9.2	268	22.7	268	22.7	–
7724	γ Leo	10 20.0	+19 51	2.2, 3.5	125	4.4	125	4.4	619
7979	54 Leo	10 55.6	+24 45	4.5, 6.4	110	6.5	110	6.5	–
8119	ξ UMa	11 18.2	+31 32	4.3, 4.8	317	1.1	273	1.8	60
8148	ι Leo	11 23.9	+10 32	4.0, 6.7	117	1.6	110	1.7	183
8489	2 CVn	12 16.1	+40 40	5.9, 9.0	260	11.5	260	11.5	–
8531	17 Vir	12 22.5	+05 18	6.5, 8.6	337	20.8	337	20.8	–
–	α Cru	12 26.6	–63 06	1.6, 2.1	113	4.0	113	4.0	–
8630	γ Vir	12 41.7	–01 27	3.5, 3.5	277	2.2	259	1.5	169
8706	α CVn	12 56.0	+38 19	2.9, 5.5	228	19.3	228	19.3	–

458

Appendix 6: Double Stars (Continued)

ADS	Star	Position (2000.0) r.a. h m	dec. ° "	Magnitudes	1995 PA °	Sep. "	2000 PA °	Sep. "	Period (years)
8891	ζ UMa	13 23.9	+54 56	2.3, 4.0	152	14.4	152	14.4	–
–	α Cen	14 39.6	–60 50	0.0, 1.2	218	17.2	222	14.1	80
9338	π Boo	14 40.7	+16 25	4.9, 5.8	109	5.5	109	5.5	–
9343	ζ Boo	14 41.2	+13 44	4.5, 4.6	301	0.9	300	0.8	123
9372	ε Boo	14 45.0	+27 05	2.5, 5.0	340	2.8	341	2.8	–
9375	54 Hya	14 46.0	–25 27	5.2, 7.2	123	8.4	123	8.4	–
9413	ξ Boo	14 51.4	+19 06	4.7, 6.9	322	6.9	318	6.6	152
9494	44 Boo	15 03.8	+47 39	5.3, 6.0	51	2.0	53	2.2	225
9617	η CrB	15 23.2	+30 17	5.6, 5.9	42	1.0	64	0.8	42
9701	δ Ser	15 34.8	+10 32	4.1, 5.2	175	4.1	174	4.1	–
9737	ζ CrB	15 39.4	+36 38	5.1, 6.0	305	6.3	305	6.3	–
9909	ξ Sco AB	16 04.4	–11 22	4.9, 4.9	95	0.3	308	0.4	46
9913	β Sco	16 05.4	–19 48	2.7, 4.9	20	13.6	20	13.6	–
10074	α Sco	16 29.4	–26 26	0.9v, 5.5	276	2.9	276	2.9	–
10087	λ Oph	16 30.9	+01 59	4.2, 5.2	26	1.5	30	1.5	130
10157	ζ Her	16 41.3	+31 36	2.9, 5.5	61	1.5	13	0.7	34
10345	μ Dra AB	17 05.3	+54 28	5.7, 5.7	22	2.0	15	2.0	472
10417	36 Oph	17 15.4	–26 36	5.1, 5.1	149	4.8	147	4.9	549
10418	α Her	17 14.7	+14 23	3.2, 5.4	105	4.6	105	4.6	3600
10424	δ Her	17 15.0	+24 50	3.1, 8.7	276	10.3	281	10.8	–
10526	ρ Her	17 23.7	+37 09	4.6,5.5	314	4.0	314	4.0	–
10993	95 Her	18 01.5	+21 36	5.1, 5.2	257	6.3	257	6.3	–
11005	τ Oph	18 03.1	–08 11	5.2, 5.9	282	1.7	284	1.7	280
11046	70 Oph	18 05.5	+02 30	4.2, 6.0	170	2.4	149	3.8	88
11336	39 Dra	18 24.0	+58 48	5.1, 7.8	349	3.7	349	3.7	–
11635	ε¹ Lyr	18 44.3	+39 40	5.0, 6.1	352	2.6	350	2.6	1165
11635	ε² Lyr	18 44.4	+39 37	5.2, 5.5	85	2.3	82	2.3	724
12540	β Cyg	19 30.7	+27 58	3.2, 5.4	54	34.2	54	34.2	–
12880	δ Cyg	19 45.0	+45 08	2.9, 6.3	225	2.5	222	2.5	828
13007	ε Dra	19 48.2	+70 16	3.9, 7.0	13	3.1	13	3.1	–
13632	α¹ Cap	20 17.6	–12 31	4.3, 9.0	222	45.5	222	45.5	–
13645	α² Cap	20 18.1	–12 33	3.6, 10.0	181	6.6	182	6.6	–
14279	γ Del	20 46.7	+16 08	4.3, 5.2	266	9.4	266	9.3	–
14296	λ Cyg	20 47.4	+36 30	4.9, 6.1	9	0.9	6	0.9	391
14636	61 Cyg	21 06.9	+38 45	5.2, 6.0	149	30.2	150	30.6	722
15032	β Cep	21 28.6	+70 34	3.2, 7.8	249	13.3	249	13.3	–
15270	μ Cyg	21 44.1	+28 45	4.8, 6.1	304	1.9	307	1.8	713
15971	ζ Aqr	22 28.8	–00 01	4.3, 4.5	194	1.8	186	1.9	760
17140	σ Cas	23 59.0	+55 45	5.0, 7.2	326	3.1	326	3.1	–

Notes: Compiled by Robert W. Argyle, Royal Greenwich Observatory. The first column (ADS) is the number in R. G. Aitken's *New General Catalogue of Double Stars* (1932). The position angle and separation are given for each star at two different epochs; v = variable.

Appendix 7A: Long-period Variable Stars

Name	Type	Position (2000.0) r.a. h m	dec ° '	Magnitude (Range)	Period (Days)
T Cas	M	0 23.2	+55 48	[6.9–13.0]	445
o Cet	M	2 19.3	–2 59	[2.0–10.1]	332
R Tri	M	2 37.0	+34 16	[5.4–12.6]	266
R Hor	M	2 53.9	–49 53	[4.7–14.3]	404
X Cam	M	4 45.7	+75 06	[7.4–14.2]	144
R Pic	SR	4 46.2	–49 15	6.7–10.0	164
L² Pup	SR	7 13.5	–44 39	2.6–6.2	140
S CMi	M	7 32.7	+8 19	[6.6–13.2]	333
U Gem	UG	7 55.1	+22 00	8.2–14.9	103
R Car	M	9 32.2	–62 47	[3.9–10.5]	309
ZZ Car	C	9 45.2	–62 30	3.3–4.2	36
R Leo	M	9 47.6	+11 26	[4.4–11.3]	312
S Car	M	10 09.4	–61 33	[4.5–9.9]	150
R UMa	M	10 44.6	+68 47	[6.7–13.4]	302
T UMa	M	12 36.4	+59 29	[6.6–13.4]	257
S UMa	M	12 43.9	+61 06	[7.0–12.4]	226
T Cen	SR	13 41.8	–33 36	5.5–9.0	90
R CVn	M	13 49.0	+39 33	[6.5–12.9]	329
R Cen	M	14 16.6	–59 55	5.3–11.8	546
S Boo	M	14 22.9	+53 49	[7.8–13.8]	271
V Boo	SR	14 29.8	+38 52	7.0–12.0	258
R CrB	RCB	15 48.6	+28 09	5.7–14.8	†
R Ser	M	15 50.7	+15 08	[5.2–14.4]	356
U Her	M	16 25.8	+18 54	[6.5–13.4]	406
R Dra	M	16 32.7	+66 45	[6.7–13.0]	245
R Oph	M	17 07.8	–16 06	[7.0–13.8]	303
T Her	M	18 09.1	+31 01	[6.8–13.9]	165
R Sct	RV	18 47.5	–5 42	4.5–8.2	†
R Cyg	M	19 36.8	+50 12	[6.1–14.2]	426
R Vul	M	21 04.4	+23 49	[7.0–14.3]	136
T Cep	M	21 09.5	+68 29	[5.2–11.3]	388
SS Cyg	UG	21 42.7	+43 35	8.2–12.4	50
R Peg	M	23 06.6	+10 33	[6.9–13.8]	378
V Cas	M	23 11.7	+59 42	6.9–13.4	229

Notes: C = Cepheid variable; M = Mira variable; RCB = R Coronae Borealis variable; RV = RV Tauri variable; SR = semiregular variable; UG = U Geminorum variable. Brackets indicate an average range of magnitude; † = irregular, no period.

Drawn from *Sky Catalogue 2000.0*, vol. 2, by Alan Hirshfeld and Roger W. Sinnott, 1985

Appendix 7B: Other Variable Stars of Long Period

Name	Type	Position (2000.0) r.a. h m	dec ° '	Magnitude (Range)	Period (Days)
U Gem	UG	7 55.1	+22 00	8.2–14.9	103
R CrB	RCB	15 48.6	+28 09	5.7–14.8	†
R Sct	RV	18 47.5	−5 42	4.5–8.2	†
SS Cyg	UG	21 42.7	+43 35	8.2–12.4	50

Notes: C = Cepheid variable; M = Mira variable; RCB = R Coronae Borealis variable; RV = RV Tauri variable; SR = semiregular variable; UG = U Geminorum variable. Brackets indicate an average range of magnitude; † = irregular, no period.

Drawn from *Sky Catalogue 2000.0*, vol. 2, by Alan Hirshfeld and Roger W. Sinnott, 1985

Appendix 8: Short-period Variable Stars

Name	Type	Position (2000.0) r.a. h m	dec ° '	Magnitude (Range)	Period (Days)
Algol (β Persei)	E	3 08.2	+40 57.0	2.1–3.4	2.9
λ Tauri	E	4 00.7	+12 29.4	3.4–3.9	3.95
RT Aurigae	C	6 28.6	+30 29.6	5.1–5.8	3.73
ζ Geminorum	C	7 04.1	+20 34.0	3.7–4.2	10.2
δ Librae	E	15 01.0	−8 31.1	4.9–5.9	2.32
u Herculis	E	17 17.3	+33 06.0	4.8–5.4	2.05
W Sagittarii	C	18 05.0	−29 34.8	4.3–5.1	7.59
β Lyrae	E	18 50.1	+33 22.0	3.3–4.3	12.9
RR Lyrae	RR	19 25.5	+42 47.0	7.0–8.1	0.6
η Aquilae	C	19 52.5	+1 00.3	3.5–4.5	7.18
δ Cephei	C	22 29.2	+58 25.0	3.5–4.4	5.4

Notes: C = Cepheid variable; E = eclipsing binary; RR = RR Lyrae variable (cluster variable). Finding charts for beta Lyrae and beta Persei (Algol) appear at the end of Chapter 6.

Appendix 9: Properties of the Planets

Intrinsic and Rotational Properties of the Planets

Name	Equatorial Radius [km]	Equatorial Radius ÷ Earth's	Mass ÷ Earth's	Mean Density (g/cm³)	Oblate-ness	Surface Gravity (Earth=1)	Sidereal Rotation Period	Inclination of Equator to Orbit (degrees)	Apparent Magnitude During 1991–1992	Apparent Equatorial Diameter (arc sec)
Mercury	2,439	0.3824	0.0553	5.43	0.0553	0.378	58.646^d	0.0	2.3 to +5.6	4–12
Venus	6,052	0.9489	0.8150	5.42	0	0.894	243.01^dR	177.3	−4.6 to −3.9	9–58
Earth	6,378.140	1	1	5.515	0.0034	1	$23^h56^m04.1^s$	23.45	—	—
Mars	3,393.4	0.5326	0.1074	3.94	0.005	0.379	$24^h37^m22.662^s$	25.19	−1.4 to +1.8	3–25
Jupiter	71,398	11.194	317.89	1.33	0.064	2.54	9^h50^m to $>9^h55^m$	3.12	−2.6 to −1.7	31–49
Saturn	60,000	9.41	95.17	0.70	0.108	1.07	$10^h39.9^m$	26.73	+0.1 to +0.7	15–19
Uranus	26,071	4.1	14.56	1.30	0.03	0.8	17^h14^m	97.86	+5.6 to +5.8	3.4–3.9
Neptune	24,764	3.9	17.15	1.64	0.017	1.2	16^h3^m	29.56	+7.9 to +8.0	2.1–2.3
Pluto	1,150	0.2	0.002	2.03	?	0.01	$6^d9^h17^m$	120	+13.7 to +13.8	0.1

R = retrograde; d = days; h = hours; m = minutes; s = seconds.

Orbital Properties of the Planets

Name	Semimajor Axis (A.U.)	Semimajor Axis (10^6 km)	Sidereal Period (years)	Sidereal Period (days)	Synodic Period (days)	Eccentricity of Orbit	Inclination to Ecliptic
Mercury	0.3871	57.9	0.24080	87.96	115.9	0.2056	7°00'26"
Venus	0.7233	108.2	0.61515	224.68	584.0	0.0068	3°23'40"
Earth	1	149.6	1.00004	365.26	—	0.0167	0°00'14"
Mars	1.5237	227.9	1.8808	686.95	779.9	0.0934	1°51'09"
Jupiter	5.2028	778.3	11.862	4337	398.9	0.0483	1°18'29"
Saturn	9.5388	1427.0	29.456	10,760	378.1	0.0560	2°29'17"
Uranus	19.1914	2871.0	84.07	30,700	369.7	0.0461	0°48'26"
Neptune	30.0611	4497.1	164.81	60,200	367.5	0.0100	1°46'27"
Pluto	39.5294	5913.5	248.53	90,780	366.7	0.2484	17°09'03"

Appendix 10: Planetary Satellites

Satellite	Semimajor Axis of Orbit (km)	Sidereal Revolution Period (d h m)	Orbital Eccentricity	Orbital Inclination (°)	Radius (km)	Visual Magnitude
Satellite of the Earth						
The Moon	384,400	27 07 43	0.055	18–29	1738	−12.7
Satellites of Mars						
1 Phobos	9,378	0 07 39	0.015	1.1	14 × 11 × 9	11.8
2 Deimos	23,459	1 06 18	0.0005	0.9–2.7	8 × 6 × 6	12.9
Satellites of Jupiter						
XV Adrastea	127,000	0 07 04			13 × 10 × 8	19.1
XVI Metis	129,000	0 07 06			20	17.5
V Amalthea	180,000	0 11 57	0.003	0.4	135 × 83 × 75	14.1
XIV Thebe	222,000	0 16 11	0.015	0.8	55 × 45	15.6
I Io	422,000	1 18 28	0.004	0.0	1815	5.0
II Europa	671,000	3 13 14	0.009	0.5	1569	5.3
III Ganymede	1,070,000	7 03 43	0.002	0.2	2631	4.6
IV Callisto	1,883,000	16 16 32	0.007	0.5	2400	5.6
XIII Leda	11,094,000	240	0.148	26.1	8	20
VI Himalia	11,480,000	251	0.158	27.6	90	14.7
X Lysithea	11,720,000	260	0.107	29.0	20	14.8
VII Elara	11,740,000	260	0.207	24.8	40	14.8
XII Ananke	21,200,000	671R	0.169	147	15	18.9
XI Carme	22,600,000	692R	0.207	164	20	18.0

Appendix 10: Planetary Satellites (Continued)

Satellite	Semimajor Axis of Orbit (km)	Sidereal Revolution Period (d h m)	Orbital Eccentricity	Orbital Inclination (°)	Radius (km)	Visual Magnitude
VIII Pasiphae	23,500,000	735R	0.378	145	20	17.0
IX Sinope	23,700,000	758R	0.275	153	20	18.3
—						20
Satellites of Saturn						
18 Pan	133,583				10	
15 Atlas	137,670	13 48			20 × 10	17
16 Prometheus	139,353	14 27	0.000	0.3	70 × 50 × 40	16
17 Pandora	141,700	14 43	0.003	0.0	55 × 45 × 35	16
11 Epimetheus	151,400	15 05	0.004	0.0	70 × 60 × 50	14
10 Janus	151,500	16 40	0.009	0.3	110 × 100 × 80	15
1 Mimas	185,500	16 40	0.007	0.1	195	12.9
2 Enceladus	238,000	22 37	0.020	1.5	250	11.7
3 Tethys	294,700	1 08 32	0.005	0.0	530	10.2
13 Telesto	294,700	1 22 15	0.000	1.9	17 × 14 × 13	19
14 Calypso	294,700	1 22 15			17 × 11 × 11	19
4 Dione	377,400	1 22 15	0.002	0.0	560	10.4
12 Helene	377,400	2 17 36	0.005	0.0	18 × 16 × 15	19
5 Rhea	527,000	2 17 45	0.001	0.4	765	9.7
6 Titan	1,221,800	4 12 16	0.029	0.3	2575	8.3
7 Hyperion	1,481,000	15 21 51	0.104	0.4	205 × 130 × 110	14.2

Appendix 10: Planetary Satellites (Continued)

Satellite	Semimajor Axis of Orbit (km)	Sidereal Revolution Period (d h m)	Orbital Eccentricity	Orbital Inclination (°)	Radius (km)	Visual Magnitude
8 Iapetus	3,561,300	79 03 43	0.028	14.7	730	11.1
9 Phoebe	12,952,000	549 03 33	0.163	177	110	16.5
Satellites of Uranus						
6 Cordelia	49,771	08 02	<0.001	0.3	13	24.1
7 Ophelia	53,796	09 02	0.01	<0.5	15	23.8
8 Bianca	59,173	10 25	<0.001	0.2	21	23.0
9 Cressida	61,777	11 07	<0.0001	0.2	31	22.2
10 Desdemona	62,676	11 22	<0.0001	0.2	27	22.5
11 Juliet	64,352	11 50	0.001	<0.2	42	21.5
12 Portia	66,085	12 19	<0.001	<0.2	54	21.0
13 Rosalind	69,942	11 54	<0.0005	0.4	27	22.5
14 Belinda	75,258	14 57	<0.003	0.1	33	22.1
15 Puck	86,000	18 17	<0.0003	0.3	77	20.2
5 Miranda	129,783	1 09 56	0.003	3.4	240	16.3
1 Ariel	191,239	2 12 29	0.003	4.2	579	14.2
2 Umbriel	265,969	4 03 27	0.005	0.4	586	14.8
3 Titania	435,844	8 16 56	0.002	0.1	790	13.7
4 Oberon	582,596	13 11 07	0.001	0.1	762	14.0
Satellites of Neptune						
N6 Naiad	48,230	07 04	<0.001	4.74	~25	24.7

465

Appendix 10: Planetary Satellites (Continued)

Satellite	Semimajor Axis of Orbit (km)	Sidereal Revolution Period (d h m)	Orbital Eccentricity	Orbital Inclination (°)	Radius (km)	Visual Magnitude
N5 Thalassa	50,070	7 29	<0.001	0.21	~ 40	23.8
N3 Despina	52,530	8 02	<0.001	0.07	~ 75	22.6
N4 Galatea	61,950	10 17	<0.001	0.05	~ 80	22.3
N2 Larissa	73,550	13 19	<0.0014	0.20	104×89	22.0
N1 Proteus	117,640	1 02 56	<0.001	0.55	$218 \times 208 \times 201$	20.3
I Triton	354,800	5 21 03R	0.03	160.0	1350	13.5
II Nereid	5,513,400	360 5	0.76	27.4	170	18.7
Rings and ring arcs of Neptune						
Galle	41,900					
Leverrier	53,200					
Adams	62,900					
Liberté	62,900					
Egalité	62,900					
Fraternité	62,900					
Satellite of Pluto						
I Charon	19,000	6 9 17	0?	94	590	17

Notes: R=Retrograde; visual magnitudes are given for the mean opposition distance.

Appendix 11: Planetary Longitudes

Year	Date	Julian Day 2440000+	Sun	Mercury	Venus	Mars	Jupiter	Saturn
1993	Jan 2	8990	282	270	328	109	193	316
1993	Jan 12	9000	292	285	338	105	194	317
1993	Jan 22	9010	303	302	350	101	195	318
1993	Feb 1	9020	313	319	359	99	144	319
1993	Feb 11	9030	323	337	8	98	194	321
1993	Feb 21	9040	333	351	15	98	194	322
1993	Mar 3	9050	343	354	19	100	193	323
1993	Mar 13	9060	353	345	21	102	192	324
1993	Mar 23	9070	3	340	17	106	191	325
1993	Apr 2	9080	13	345	11	109	189	326
1993	Apr 12	9090	22	356	5	113	188	327
1993	Apr 22	9100	32	10	2	118	187	328
1993	May 2	9110	42	27	5	123	186	329
1993	May 12	9120	52	47	9	127	185	329
1993	May 22	9130	61	69	16	132	184	330
1993	Jun 1	9140	71	89	25	138	185	330
1993	Jun 11	9150	80	104	34	143	185	330
1993	Jun 21	9160	90	115	44	149	185	330
1993	Jul 1	9170	99	118	54	155	186	330
1993	Jul 11	9180	109	115	65	161	187	330
1993	Jul 21	9190	118	109	76	166	188	329
1993	Jul 31	9200	128	109	87	173	190	328
1993	Aug 10	9210	138	120	99	179	191	327
1993	Aug 20	9220	147	138	111	185	192	326
1993	Aug 30	9230	157	158	123	192	194	324
1993	Sep 9	9240	167	176	135	193	196	325
1993	Sep 19	9250	176	193	147	205	198	324
1993	Sep 29	9260	186	208	159	211	201	323
1993	Oct 9	9270	196	221	171	218	203	323
1993	Oct 19	9280	206	230	184	225	205	323
1993	Oct 29	9290	216	232	196	232	207	323
1993	Nov 8	9300	226	221	209	239	210	323
1993	Nov 18	9310	236	217	222	246	212	324
1993	Nov 28	9320	246	227	234	254	213	324
1993	Dec 8	9330	256	242	247	261	215	325
1993	Dec 18	9340	267	257	259	269	217	326
1993	Dec 28	9350	277	273	272	276	219	326
1994	Jan 7	9360	287	289	285	284	220	327
1994	Jan 17	9370	297	306	297	292	222	328
1994	Jan 27	9380	307	323	309	299	223	325
1994	Feb 6	9390	317	336	322	307	224	330
1994	Feb 16	9400	327	336	324	315	224	331
1994	Feb 26	9410	338	326	347	323	225	333
1994	Mar 8	9420	348	323	0	330	224	334
1994	Mar 18	9430	358	330	12	338	224	335
1994	Mar 28	9440	7	341	25	346	223	334
1994	Apr 7	9450	17	356	37	354	223	337
1994	Apr 17	9460	27	13	50	2	222	338

Appendix 11: Planetary Longitudes (Continued)

Year	Date	Julian Day 2440000+	Sun	Mercury	Venus	Mars	Jupiter	Saturn
1994	Apr 27	9470	37	33	62	10	220	339
1994	May 7	9480	44	55	74	17	219	340
1994	May 17	9490	56	75	86	25	218	341
1994	May 27	9500	66	89	98	32	217	341
1994	Jun 6	9510	75	97	110	40	216	342
1994	Jun 16	9520	85	97	122	47	215	342
1994	Jun 26	9530	94	91	134	55	214	342
1994	Jul 6	9540	104	89	145	62	214	342
1994	Jul 16	9550	113	93	156	69	215	342
1994	Jul 26	9560	123	105	167	76	215	342
1994	Aug 5	9570	133	124	178	82	216	341
1994	Aug 15	9580	142	145	188	89	217	340
1994	Aug 25	9590	152	164	198	96	219	339
1994	Sep 4	9600	161	180	207	102	220	338
1994	Sep 14	9610	171	195	216	108	222	337
1994	Sep 24	9620	181	207	223	114	223	336
1994	Oct 4	9630	191	215	227	120	225	336
1994	Oct 14	9640	201	215	229	125	227	335
1994	Oct 24	9650	211	204	226	130	229	335
1994	Nov 3	9660	221	202	221	135	231	335
1994	Nov 13	9670	231	213	216	140	234	335
1994	Nov 23	9680	241	229	213	144	236	335
1994	Dec 3	9690	251	245	215	147	238	336
1994	Dec 13	9700	261	261	220	150	241	336
1994	Dec 23	9710	271	276	227	152	243	337
1995	Jan 2	9720	282	293	235	153	245	338
1995	Jan 12	9730	292	309	245	151	247	339
1995	Jan 22	9740	302	320	255	149	248	340
1995	Feb 1	9750	312	319	266	147	250	340
1995	Feb 11	9760	322	307	277	142	252	342
1995	Feb 21	9770	332	307	289	138	253	343
1995	Mar 3	9780	342	315	300	136	254	344
1995	Mar 13	9790	352	328	312	134	255	345
1995	Mar 23	9800	2	342	324	132	255	347
1995	Apr 2	9810	12	0	336	133	256	348
1995	Apr 12	9820	22	19	348	135	255	350
1995	Apr 22	9830	32	41	0	138	255	350
1995	May 2	9840	41	60	12	141	254	350
1995	May 12	9850	51	73	24	144	253	351
1995	May 22	9860	61	78	36	149	252	352
1995	Jun 1	9870	70	76	48	154	251	353
1995	Jun 11	9880	80	70	60	158	249	353
1995	Jun 21	9890	89	70	73	163	248	354
1995	Jul 1	9900	99	77	85	169	247	354
1995	Jul 11	9910	108	91	97	174	246	354
1995	Jul 21	9920	118	110	110	180	245	354

Appendix 11: Planetary Longitudes (Continued)

Year	Date	Julian Day 2440000+	Sun	Mercury	Venus	Mars	Jupiter	Saturn
1995	Jul 31	9930	128	131	122	186	245	354
1995	Aug 10	9940	137	151	134	192	245	354
1995	Aug 20	9950	147	168	147	198	246	353
1995	Aug 30	9960	156	182	159	205	247	352
1995	Sep 9	9970	166	193	172	211	247	351
1995	Sep 19	9980	176	200	184	218	249	350
1995	Sep 29	9990	186	198	196	225	250	349
1995	Oct 9	10000	196	187	209	232	252	348
1995	Oct 19	10010	205	187	221	239	253	348
1995	Oct 29	10020	215	200	234	246	255	347
1995	Nov 8	10030	226	216	246	253	257	347
1995	Nov 18	10040	236	233	259	261	259	347
1995	Nov 28	10050	246	249	271	268	261	347
1995	Dec 8	10060	256	264	284	276	264	348
1995	Dec 18	10070	266	280	296	284	266	348
1995	Dec 28	10080	276	295	308	291	269	349
1996	Jan 7	10090	284	305	320	299	271	349
1996	Jan 17	10100	297	301	333	307	273	350
1996	Jan 27	10110	307	290	345	315	275	351
1996	Feb 6	10120	317	292	357	323	277	352
1996	Feb 16	10130	327	301	9	331	279	353
1996	Feb 26	10140	337	314	20	339	281	354
1996	Mar 7	10150	347	329	32	346	283	356
1996	Mar 17	10160	357	347	43	354	284	357
1996	Mar 27	10170	7	6	53	2	286	358
1996	Apr 6	10180	17	27	63	10	287	0
1996	Apr 16	10190	27	45	72	18	287	1
1996	Apr 26	10200	36	57	80	25	288	2
1996	May 6	10210	46	58	85	33	288	3
1996	May 16	10220	56	53	88	40	288	4
1996	May 26	10230	65	49	87	47	288	4
1996	Jun 5	10240	75	51	82	55	287	5
1996	Jun 15	10250	84	61	76	62	286	6
1996	Jun 25	10260	94	76	71	69	285	6
1996	Jul 5	10270	103	96	70	76	283	7
1996	Jul 15	10280	113	118	73	83	282	7
1996	Jul 25	10290	122	137	79	90	280	7
1996	Aug 4	10300	132	154	87	96	279	7
1996	Aug 14	10310	142	168	95	103	278	7
1996	Aug 24	10320	151	179	105	110	278	6
1996	Sep 3	10330	161	184	115	116	278	5
1996	Sep 13	10340	171	179	126	123	278	5
1996	Sep 23	10350	181	170	137	129	279	4
1996	Oct 3	10360	190	172	149	135	279	3
1996	Oct 13	10370	200	186	160	140	280	3
1996	Oct 23	10380	210	203	172	146	281	2

Appendix 11: Planetary Longitudes (Continued)

Year	Date		Julian Day 2440000+	Sun	Mercury	Venus	Mars	Jupiter	Saturn
1996	Nov	2	0390	220	220	184	152	282	0
1996	Nov	12	0400	230	236	196	157	284	0
1996	Nov	22	0410	240	252	209	162	286	0
1996	Dec	2	0420	251	267	221	166	288	0
1996	Dec	12	0430	261	281	233	171	290	0
1996	Dec	22	0440	271	290	246	175	292	0
1997	Jan	1	0450	281	283	259	179	295	1
1997	Jan	11	0460	291	273	271	182	297	2
1997	Jan	21	0470	302	277	284	185	300	2
1997	Jan	31	0480	312	288	296	186	307	3
1997	Feb	10	0490	322	301	309	184	305	4
1997	Feb	20	0500	332	317	322	184	307	5
1997	Mar	2	0510	342	334	334	182	309	6
1997	Mar	12	0520	352	352	346	179	312	7
1997	Mar	22	0530	2	13	359	174	313	9
1997	Apr	1	0540	12	30	11	171	315	10
1997	Apr	11	0550	21	40	24	168	317	11
1997	Apr	21	0560	31	38	36	167	319	13
1997	May	1	0570	41	31	48	166	320	14
1997	May	11	0580	51	29	61	167	321	15
1997	May	21	0590	60	34	73	170	322	16
1997	May	31	0600	70	46	86	173	322	17
1997	Jun	10	0610	79	62	98	177	322	18
1997	Jun	20	0620	89	82	110	181	323	19
1997	Jun	30	0630	98	104	123	186	322	19
1997	Jul	10	0640	108	124	135	191	321	20
1997	Jul	20	0650	118	141	147	196	320	20
1997	Jul	30	0660	127	154	159	202	319	20
1997	Aug	9	0670	137	163	171	207	317	20
1997	Aug	19	0680	146	166	183	213	316	20
1997	Aug	29	0690	156	160	194	220	315	20
1997	Sep	8	0700	166	153	206	226	313	19
1997	Sep	18	0710	175	157	218	233	312	18
1997	Sep	28	0720	185	173	229	240	312	17
1997	Oct	8	0730	195	191	240	247	312	16
1997	Oct	18	0740	205	208	251	254	312	15
1997	Oct	28	0750	215	224	262	261	313	14
1997	Nov	7	0760	225	240	272	269	313	14
1997	Nov	17	0770	235	254	282	276	314	13
1997	Nov	27	0780	245	267	290	284	316	13
1997	Dec	7	0790	255	274	298	292	317	13
1997	Dec	17	0800	266	266	303	300	319	13
1997	Dec	27	0810	276	257	305	307	321	13
1998	Jan	6	0820	286	263	303	315	323	13
1998	Jan	16	0830	296	275	298	323	325	14
1998	Jan	26	0840	306	289	292	331	328	15

Appendix 12 : Local Sidereal Time at 00:00 Local Standard Time
(computed for the year 1993)

Date	Jan	Feb	Mar	Apr	May	Jun	Jul	Aug	Sep	Oct	Nov	Dec
1	6:42	8:45	10:35	12:37	14:35	16:38	18:36	20:38	22:40	0:39	2:41	4:39
2	6:46	8:49	10:39	12:41	14:39	16:42	18:40	20:42	22:44	0:43	2:45	4:43
3	6:50	8:52	10:43	12:45	14:43	16:46	18:44	20:46	22:48	0:47	2:49	4:47
4	6:54	8:56	10:47	12:49	14:47	16:50	18:48	20:50	22:52	0:51	2:53	4:51
5	6:58	9:00	10:51	12:53	14:51	16:53	18:52	20:54	22:56	0:54	2:57	4:55
6	7:02	9:04	10:55	12:57	14:55	16:57	18:56	20:58	23:00	0:58	3:01	4:59
7	7:06	9:08	10:59	13:01	14:59	17:01	19:00	21:02	23:04	1:02	3:05	5:03
8	7:10	9:12	11:03	13:05	15:03	17:05	19:04	21:06	23:08	1:06	3:09	5:07
9	7:14	9:16	11:07	13:09	15:07	17:09	19:08	21:10	23:12	1:10	3:12	5:11
10	7:18	9:20	11:10	13:13	15:11	17:13	19:11	21:14	23:16	1:14	3:16	5:15
11	7:22	9:24	11:14	13:17	15:15	17:17	19:15	21:18	23:20	1:18	3:20	5:19
12	7:26	9:28	11:18	13:21	15:19	17:21	19:19	21:22	23:24	1:22	3:24	5:23
13	7:30	9:32	11:22	13:25	15:23	17:25	19:23	21:26	23:28	1:26	3:28	5:27
14	7:34	9:36	11:26	13:28	15:27	17:29	19:27	21:29	23:32	1:30	3:32	5:30
15	7:38	9:40	11:30	13:32	15:31	17:33	19:31	21:33	23:36	1:34	3:36	5:34
16	7:42	9:44	11:34	13:36	15:35	17:37	19:35	21:37	23:40	1:38	3:40	5:38
17	7:45	9:48	11:38	13:40	15:39	17:41	19:39	21:41	23:43	1:42	3:44	5:42
18	7:49	9:52	11:42	13:44	15:43	17:45	19:43	21:45	23:47	1:46	3:48	5:46
19	7:53	9:56	11:46	13:48	15:46	17:49	19:47	21:49	23:51	1:50	3:52	5:50
20	7:57	9:59	11:50	13:52	15:50	17:53	19:51	21:53	23:55	1:54	3:56	5:54
21	8:01	10:03	11:54	13:56	15:54	17:57	19:55	21:57	23:59	1:58	4:00	5:58

Appendix 12 (Continued): Local Sidereal Time at 00:00 Local Standard Time
(computed for the year 1993)

Date	Jan	Feb	Mar	Apr	May	Jun	Jul	Aug	Sep	Oct	Nov	Dec
22	8:05	10:07	11:58	14:00	15:58	18:00	19:59	22:01	0:03	2:01	4:04	6:02
23	8:09	10:11	12:02	14:04	16:02	18:04	20:03	22:05	0:07	2:05	4:08	6:06
24	8:13	10:15	12:06	14:08	16:06	18:08	20:07	22:09	0:11	2:09	4:12	6:10
25	8:17	10:19	12:10	14:12	16:10	18:12	20:11	22:13	0:15	2:13	4:16	6:14
26	8:21	10:23	12:14	14:16	16:14	18:16	20:15	22:17	0:19	2:17	4:19	6:18
27	8:25	10:27	12:17	14:20	16:18	18:20	20:18	22:21	0:23	2:21	4:23	6:22
28	8:29	10:31	12:21	14:24	16:22	18:24	20:22	22:25	0:27	2:25	4:27	6:26
29	8:33		12:25	14:28	16:26	18:28	20:26	22:29	0:31	2:29	4:31	6:30
30	8:37		12:29	14:32	16:30	18:32	20:30	22:33	0:35	2:33	4:35	6:34
31	8:41		12:33		16:34		20:34	22:36		2:37		6:37

Compared with the sidereal time for dates in 1993:
From February 29, 1992, through December 31, 1992, add 1 minute.
From January 1, 1994, through December 31, 1994, subtract 1 minute.
From January 1, 1995, through December 31, 1995, subtract 2 mintues.
From January 1, 1996, through February 28, 1996, subtract 3 minutes.
From February 29, 1996, through December 31, 1996, add 1 minute.
1997: Same as 1993; see table.
1998: Same as 1994.

Appendix 13: Regions Covered by the Atlas Charts

Each chart covers roughly the area between the coordinates given below. The right ascension column in the middle can be used with either the left-hand or the right-hand columns of declination.

Constellation for + declination zone	Atlas Chart for declination +50° to +90°	right ascension	Atlas Chart for declination −50° to −90°
Cas, Cep	1	$22^1/_2{}^h - 1^1/_2{}^h$	45
Cam, Cas, Cep, Per	2	$1^1/_2{}^h - 4^1/_2{}^h$	46
Cam, Lyn	3	$4^1/_2{}^h - 7^1/_2{}^h$	47
Cam, Dra, UMa	4	$7^1/_2{}^h - 10^1/_2{}^h$	48
Dra, UMa, UMi	5	$10^1/_2{}^h - 13^1/_2{}^h$	49
Dra, UMa, UMi	6	$13^1/_2{}^h - 16^1/_2{}^h$	50
Dra, UMi	7	$16^1/_2{}^h - 19^1/_2{}^h$	51
Cep, Cyg, Dra, Lac	8	$19^1/_2{}^h - 22^1/_2{}^h$	52
	for declination +20° to +50°		for declination −20° to −50°
And, Psc, Tri	9	$0^h - 2^h$	33
And, Air, Per, Tau, Tri	10	$2^h - 4^h$	34
Aur, Per, Tau	11	$4^h - 6^h$	35
Aur, Gem, Lyn, Tau	12	$6^h - 8^h$	36
Can, LMi, Lyn, UMa	13	$8^h - 10^h$	37
Leo, LMi, UMa	14	$10^h - 12^h$	38
Com, CVn	15	$12^h - 14^h$	39
Boo, CrB	16	$14^h - 16^h$	40
Her	17	$16^h - 18^h$	41
Cyg, Lyr, Vul	18	$18^h - 20^h$	42
Cyg, Vul	19	$20^h - 22^h$	43
And, Lac, Peg	20	$22^h - 24^h$	44
			for declination −20° to +20°
Aqr, Cet, Peg, Psc		$23^h - 1^h$	21
Ari, Cet, Psc		$1^h - 3^h$	22
Eri, Tau		$3^h - 5^h$	23
CMa, Lep, Mon, Ori		$5^h - 7^h$	24
CMi, Cnc, Hya, Mon, Pup		$7^h - 9^h$	25
Leo, Hya, Sex		$9^h - 11^h$	26
Com, Crt, Crv, Leo, Vir		$11^h - 13^h$	27
Boo, Lib, Vir		$13^h - 15^h$	28
Her, Lib, Oph, Sco, Ser		$15^h - 17^h$	29
Her, Oph, Sct, Ser, Sgr		$17^h - 19^h$	30
Aql, Cap, Del, Sge, Sgr		$19^h - 21^h$	31
Aqr, Cap, Equ, Peg		$21^h - 23^h$	32

Note: Constellation abbreviations are shown in Appendix 1. The Atlas Charts where each constellation is found are also listed in Chapter 4.

Appendix 14: Days of the Year

Date	Day (Regular Year)	Day (Leap Year)
January 1	1	1
January 10	10	10
January 20	20	20
February 1	32	32
February 10	41	41
February 20	51	51
March 1	60	61
March 10	69	70
March 20	79	80
April 1	91	92
April 10	100	101
April 20	110	111
May 1	121	122
May 10	130	131
May 20	140	141
June 1	152	153
June 10	161	162
June 20	171	172
July 1	182	183
July 10	191	192
July 20	201	202
August 1	213	214
August 10	222	223
August 20	232	233
September 1	244	245
September 10	253	254
September 20	263	264
October 1	274	275
October 10	283	284
October 20	293	294
November 1	305	306
November 10	314	315
November 20	324	325
December 1	335	336
December 10	344	345
December 20	354	355
December 31	365	366

Note: 1996 and 2000 are leap years.

GLOSSARY

Aberration of starlight: The tiny apparent displacement of stars resulting from the motion of the earth through space.

Absolute magnitude (M): The magnitude a celestial object would appear to have if it were at a distance of 10 parsecs.

Absolute visual magnitude (M_V): The absolute magnitude of an object measured through a special yellowish filter that approximates the visual range of the human eye.

Absorption nebula: A nebula seen in silhouette as it absorbs light from behind; also called a dark nebula.

Altitude: Angular distance (usually measured in degrees) above the horizon.

Analemma: The figure-8 representing the equation of time and the variation of the sun's altitude in the sky during the course of a year.

Angstrom: A unit of wavelength or distance, equivalent to $1/10,000$ micrometer or $1/10,000,000,000$ meter.

Annular eclipse: A solar eclipse in which a ring—an annulus—of solar photosphere remains visible.

Aphelion: The farthest point from the sun in an object's orbit around it.

Apparent magnitude (m): Magnitude as seen by an observer.

Apparent solar time: Time determined by the actual position of the sun in the sky; corresponds to time on most sundials.

Asterism: A noticeable pattern of stars that makes up part of one or more constellations; not a constellation itself.

Asteroid: A minor planet, smaller than any major planet in our solar system; not one of the satellites (moons) of a major planet such as the earth or Jupiter.

Astronomical unit (A.U.): The average distance from the earth to the sun, which equals 149,598,770 kilometers.

Autumnal equinox: The intersection of the ecliptic and the celestial equator that the sun passes each year on its way to southern (negative) declinations.

Baily's beads: A chain of several bright "beads" of white light, visible just before or after totality at a solar eclipse. The effect occurs when bits of photosphere shine through valleys at the moon's edge. See also **diamond-ring effect.**

Bayer designations: The Greek letters assigned to the stars in a constellation, usually in order of brightness, by Johann Bayer in his sky atlas (1603).

Belts: Dark bands in the clouds on giant planets such as Jupiter; compare with **zones.**

Binary star: A double star; a system containing two or more stars. In an *eclipsing binary,* one star goes behind the other periodically, changing the total amount of light we see.

Black hole: A region of space in which mass is packed so densely that (according to Einstein's general theory of relativity) nothing, not even light, can escape.

Cassini's division: The major division in Saturn's rings, which separates the A-ring from the B-ring.

Celestial equator: The imaginary great circle that lies above the earth's equator on the celestial sphere.

Celestial longitude: Longitude measured (in degrees) along the ecliptic to the east from the vernal equinox.

Celestial poles: The points in the sky where the earth's axis, extended into space, intersects with the celestial sphere.

Celestial sphere: The imaginary sphere surrounding the earth, with the stars and other astronomical objects attached to it.

Cepheid variable: A star that varies in the manner of delta Cephei. The absolute magnitudes of these variable stars can be calculated from their periods of variation; by comparing the absolute and apparent magnitudes, the distances to these stars and the galaxies they are in can be determined.

Chromosphere: A layer in the sun and many other stars just above the photosphere. During eclipses, the solar chromosphere glows reddish from hydrogen emission.

Circumpolar: Refers to a star, asterism, or constellation that is close enough to the celestial pole that, from the latitude at which you are observing, it never appears to set.

Comet: A body, probably resembling a "dirty snowball," between 0.1 and 100 miles across that travels through the solar system in an elliptical orbit of random inclination to the ecliptic. A comet grows a tail if it comes close enough to the sun.

Conjunction: The alignment of two celestial bodies that occurs when they reach the same celestial longitude. The bodies then appear approximately closest to each other in the sky. See also **inferior conjunction, superior conjunction.**

Constellation: One of the 88 parts into which the sky is divided; also refers to the historical, mythological, or other figures that represented earlier divisions of the sky.

Contact(s):   The stage(s) of an eclipse, occultation, or transit when the edges of the apparent disks of astronomical bodies seem to touch. At a solar eclipse, first contact is when the advancing edge of the sun first touches the moon; second contact is when the advancing edge of the sun touches the other side of the moon, beginning totality; the third contact is when the trailing edge of the sun touches the trailing edge of the moon, ending totality; and fourth contact marks the end of the eclipse.

Corona: The outermost layer of the sun and many other stars; a faint halo of extremely hot (million-degree) gas.

Crepe ring: Saturn's inner ring, also known as the C-ring, which extends inward to the planet from the brightest ring (the B-ring).

Crescent: One of the phases of the moon or the inner planets (Venus and Mercury) as seen from earth, caused by the relative angles of sunlight and the observer's viewpoint. From spacecraft, crescent phases of the earth, Mars, Jupiter, Saturn, Uranus, and Neptune have also been seen.

Declination: The celestial coordinate analogous to latitude, usually measured in degrees, minutes, and seconds of arc north (+) or south (–) of the celestial equator.

Diamond-ring effect: An effect created as the total phase of a solar eclipse is about to begin, when the last Baily's bead—a remaining bit of photosphere—glows so intensely by contrast with the sun's faint corona that it looks like the jewel on a ring. Also refers to the equivalent phase at the end of totality.

Double star: A system containing two or more stars. In a true double, the stars are physically close to each other; in an *optical double*, they lie in approximately the same direction from the earth and appear close to each other, but are actually far apart. See also **binary star.**

Earthshine: Sunlight reflected off the earth, which dimly lights the side of the moon that does not receive direct sunlight.

Eclipse, lunar: The passage of the moon into the earth's shadow.

Eclipse, solar: The passage of the moon's shadow across the earth. See also **annular eclipse, contact(s), penumbra, umbra.**

Ecliptic: The apparent path the sun follows across the sky during the year; the same path is also followed approximately by the moon and planets.

Ejecta blanket: Chunks of rock, usually extending from one side of a crater, that were ejected during the crater's formation.

Elongation: Angular distance in celestial longitude from the sun in the sky.

Emission lines: Extra radiation at certain specific wavelengths in a spectrum, compared with neighboring wavelengths (colors).

Emission nebula: A gas cloud that receives energy from a hot star, allowing it to give off radiation in emission lines such as those of hydrogen. The characteristic reddish radiation of many emission nebulae is mostly from the hydrogen-alpha line.

Encke's division: A thin division in the A-ring of Saturn.

Equation of time: The variation of local apparent solar time minus local mean solar time over the year.

Equinox: One of the two intersections of the ecliptic and the celestial equator: see **autumnal equinox, vernal equinox.**

Filament: A dark region snaking across the sun; a prominence seen in projection against the solar disk.

Fireball: An extremely bright meteor, usually with an apparent magnitude brighter than –5; some fireballs are as bright as magnitude –20.

Flamsteed number: The number assigned to a star in a given constellation, in order of right ascension, in the 1725 catalogue of John Flamsteed.

Galactic: Pertaining to our galaxy, the Milky Way Galaxy.

Galactic cluster: An irregular grouping of stars of a common and possibly recent origin. Also called an **open cluster.**

Galactic equator, galactic poles: The equator and poles in a coordinate system in which the equator is placed along the plane of our galaxy, the Milky Way Galaxy.

Galaxy: A giant collection of stars, gas, and dust. Our galaxy, the Milky Way Galaxy, contains 1 trillion times the mass of our sun.

Giant: A star brighter and larger than most stars of its color and temperature. Stars become giants (normally **red giants**) when they use up all the hydrogen in their cores and leave the "main sequence" part of their life cycle. See also **supergiant.**

Gibbous: A phase of a moon or a planet in which more than half of the side we see is illuminated. Remember: it "gibb us" ("gives us") more light.

Globular cluster: A spherical grouping of stars of a common origin; globular clusters and the stars in them are very old.

Graben: On the surface of the earth, the moon, or other planets or moons, a long and narrow region between two faults that has subsided.

Half moon: The first-quarter or third-quarter phase, when half the visible side of the moon is illuminated.

Hour angle: The sidereal time elapsed since an object was on the meridian, or, if the hour angle is negative, before the object reaches the meridian. (The hour angle equals the difference between the right ascension of an object and of your meridian.)

Hour circle: A line along which right ascension is constant, lying on a great circle that passes through the celestial poles and the object.

Hubble's Law: The relationship between the velocity and distance of galaxies and other distant objects; it shows that the universe is expanding.

Hydrogen-alpha line: The strongest spectral line of hydrogen in the visible part of the spectrum. It falls in the red, so that an emission hydrogen-alpha line is red; an absorption hydrogen-alpha line is the absence of that wavelength of red.

IC: The prefix used before numbers assigned to nonstellar objects in the *Index Catalogues* published as supplements to the *New General Catalogue* of J. L. E. Dryer.

Inferior conjunction: The conjunction in which a planet whose orbit is inside that of the earth passes between the earth and the sun.

Intrinsic brightness: The amount of energy (usually light) an object gives off; its true brightness, independent of the effects of distance or dimming by intervening material.

Ionized hydrogen: Hydrogen that has lost its electron; ionized hydrogen gas, commonly found in stars and nebulae, has free protons and free electrons.

Julian day: The number of days since noon on 1 January 4713 B.C. Variable star observers and other astronomers commonly calculate the interval between dates of events by subtracting Julian days, eliminating the necessity to keep track of leap years and other calendar details.

Libration: The turning of the visible face of the moon, which allows us to see different amounts of the lunar surface around the limb (edge).

Light-year: The distance that light travels in a year, which equals 9,460,000,000,000 km or 63,240 A.U. (astronomical units).

Limb: The edge of the apparent disk of an astronomical body, such as the sun, moon, or a planet.

Magnitude: A logarithmic scale of brightness, in which each change of five magnitudes is equivalent to a change by a factor of 100. Adding one magnitude corresponds to a decrease in brightness by a factor of 2.512.... See also **absolute magnitude, apparent magnitude.**

Main-sequence star: A star in the prime of its life, when hydrogen inside it is undergoing nuclear fusion; such stars form a band—the main sequence—across a graph of stellar temperatures vs. stellar brightness.

Maxima: The times when a variable star reaches its maximum brightness.

Mean solar time: Time as kept by a fictitious "mean" sun that travels at a steady rate across the sky throughout the year.

Meridian: The great circle passing through the celestial poles and your zenith.

Messier Catalogue: The list of 103 nonstellar, deep-sky objects compiled by Charles Messier in the 1770s, and subsequently expanded to 109 or 110 objects.

Meteor: A meteoroid streaking across the sky; a shooting star.

Meteorite: The part of a meteoroid that survives its passage through the earth's atmosphere.

Meteor shower: The appearance of many meteors during a short period of time, as the earth passes through a comet's orbit.

Minima: The times of a variable star's minimum brightness.

Mira variable: A long-period variable star, like the star omicron Ceti (called "Mira").

Nebula: A region of gas or dust in a galaxy that can be observed optically. See also **emission nebula, absorption nebula,** and **reflection nebula.**

NGC: The prefix used before numbers assigned to nonstellar objects in the *New General Catalogue,* published by J. L. E. Dryer in 1888.

Neutron star: A small (20-km diameter), dense (a billion tons per cubic cm) star, resulting from the collapse of a dying star to the point where only the fact that its neutrons resist being pushed still closer together prevents further collapse.

Nova: A newly visible star, or one that suddenly increases dramatically in brightness.

Nutation: A small nodding motion of the earth's axis of rotation with a period of 19 years; this motion is superimposed on precession.

Oblate: A nonspherical shape formed by rotating an ellipse around its narrower axis; the equatorial diameter of an oblate body (such as Jupiter) is greater than its polar diameter.

Occultation: The hiding of one celestial body by another.

Open cluster: An irregular grouping of stars of a common and possibly recent origin. Also called a **galactic cluster.**

Opposition: The point in a planet's orbit at which its celestial longitude is 180° from that of the sun. A planet at opposition is visible all night long.

Parsec: The distance from which 1 A.U. appears to subtend (cover) 1 second of arc; 1 parsec equals 3.261633… light-years.

Penumbra: At an eclipse, the part of the earth or moon's shadow from which part of the solar disk is visible. Also refers to the outer, less dark portion of a sunspot.

Perihelion: The nearest point to the sun in an object's orbit around it.

Photosphere: The visible surface of the sun or of another star.

Planetary nebula: A shell of gas ejected by a dying star that contains about as much mass as the sun.

Polar tufts: Small spikes visible in the solar corona near the sun's poles, formed by gas following the sun's magnetic field.

Position angle: The angle, centered at the brighter component of a double star, that an observer follows counterclockwise from north around to the fainter component.

Precession: The slow drifting of the orientation of the earth's axis over a period of 26,000 years. Also refers to its effect on the location of the equinoxes, and thus on the coordinate system of right ascension and declination used to plot positions of stars and other objects.

Prominence: Gas suspended above the solar photosphere by the sun's magnetic field; ordinarily visible at the solar limb (edge). A prominence glows reddish during eclipses because of its characteristic hydrogen-alpha radiation.

Proper motion: Apparent angular motion across the sky, shown as a change in an object's position with respect to the background stars.

Pulsar: A rotating neutron star that gives off sharp pulses of radio waves with a period ranging from about 0.001 to 4 seconds.

Quasar: a "quasi-stellar object" with an extremely large redshift: presumably a powerful event going on in the central region of a galaxy. Using Hubble's Law tells us that quasars must be among the most distant objects in the universe.

Radiant: The location on the celestial sphere from which meteors in a given shower appear to radiate, because of perspective.

Red giant: A swollen star; a stage occurring at the end of a star's main-sequence period of life. See also **giant.**

Reflecting telescope: A telescope that uses a mirror in the principal stage of forming an image.

Reflection nebula: A dust cloud that reflects a star's light to us.

Refracting telescope: A telescope that uses a lens in the principal stage of forming an image.

Retrograde motion: The apparent backward (westward) loop in a planet's motion across the sky over a lengthy period of time. Copernicus explained it as the projection effect when the earth overtakes another planet as they both orbit the sun.

Revolution: The orbiting of a planet or other object around the sun or another central body. (Compare with **rotation.**)

Right ascension: The angle of an object around the celestial equator, measured in hours, minutes, and seconds eastward from the vernal equinox.

Rotation: The spinning of a planet or other object on its axis. (Compare with **revolution.**)

Separation: The angular distance (measured in degrees, minutes, and seconds of arc) between components of a double star.

Shadow bands: Light and dark bands that appear to sweep across the ground in the minutes before and after totality at a solar eclipse; caused by irregularities in the earth's upper atmosphere.

Sidereal time: Time by the stars; technically, the hour angle of the vernal equinox, which is equal to the right ascension of objects on your meridian.

Solar flare: An explosive eruption on the sun reaching temperatures of millions of degrees. Note: a flare is not a prominence.

Solstice(s): The positions of the sun when it reaches its northernmost declination (in northern-hemisphere summer) or southernmost declination (in northern-hemisphere winter).

Spectral line: A wavelength of the spectrum at which the intensity is greater than (an *emission line*) or less than (an *absorption line*) neighboring values.

Spectrum (plural **spectra**): The radiation from an object, spread out into its component colors, wavelengths, or frequencies.

Star cloud: One of several regions of the Milky Way where great numbers of stars appear.

Streamers: Large-scale structures in the sun's corona, usually near the solar equator, shaped by the sun's magnetic field.

Sunspots: Relatively dark regions on the solar photosphere, corresponding to areas with exceptionally high magnetic fields.

Supergiant: A star brighter and larger than even giants of the same color and temperature. Only the most massive stars become supergiants, after passing through the giant stage.

Superior conjunction: The conjunction in which a planet whose orbit is inside that of the earth passes on the far side of the sun with respect to the earth.

Supernova: The explosion and devastation of a very massive star.

Supernova remnant: Gas left over from a supernova that can be seen in the sky or detected from its radio or x-ray emission. (The Crab Nebula, for example, can be detected all three ways.)

Surface brightness: The brightness of a unit area of an object's surface. For spread-out objects such as nebulae, the surface brightness determines the amount of contrast the object has against the background sky, and whether the object's surface is bright enough to make an image on your retina. Even though the object's total brightness may be high, it still may be hard to see if it is spread out enough so that its surface brightness is low.

Synodic: Related to the alignment of three bodies, often the earth, the sun, and a third body, such as the moon or a planet.

Terminator: The edge of the lighted region of a moon or planet; the line between day and night.

Train: A path left in the sky by a meteor.

Transient Lunar Phenomena (TLP's): Changes, such as emissions of gas, observed on the moon.

Transit: The passage of an inner planet (Mercury or Venus) across the sun's disk as seen from earth, or of a moon (such as one of Jupiter's Galilean satellites) across its planet's disk. Also, the passage of an object across an observer's meridian.

Umbra: At an eclipse, the part of the moon or earth's shadow from which the solar disk is entirely hidden. Also refers to the inner, darker portion of a sunspot. See also **penumbra.**

Universal Time (U.T.): Solar time based on time at the meridian of Greenwich, England.

Variable star: A star whose apparent brightness changes over time.

Vernal equinox: The intersection of the ecliptic and the celestial equator that the sun passes on its way to northern (positive) declinations.

Zenith: The point directly overhead (wherever an observer is), 90° above the horizon.

Zodiac: Traditionally, a set of 12 constellations through which the sun, moon, and planets pass in the course of a year. Actually, that band of sky contains many more parts of constellations, and because of precession, the sun is no longer in the constellations associated with its "traditional" dates at those times.

Zones: Bright bands in the cloud layers of the giant planets (Jupiter, Saturn, Uranus, and Neptune).

BIBLIOGRAPHY

Sky Atlases and General References

Audouze, Jean, and Guy Israël. 1988. *Cambridge Atlas of Astronomy.* 2nd ed. New York: Cambridge University Press.

Hirshfeld, Alan, and Roger W. Sinnott. 1982 (vol.1), 1985 (vol. 2). *Sky Catalogue 2000.0.* Cambridge, MA: Sky Publishing Corp. Volume 1 is a list of stars; volume 2 provides lists of double stars, variable stars, galaxies, clusters, nebulae, and other objects. All positions are precessed to epoch 2000.0.

Maran, Stephen P., ed. 1992. *The Astronomy and Astrophysics Encyclopedia.* New York: Van Nostrand. Long entries on all aspects of astronomy.

Meeus, Jean. 1983. *Astronomical Tables of the Sun, Moon, and Planets.* Richmond, VA: Willmann-Bell. Lists of astronomical phenomena, including planetary oppositions and conjunctions, eclipses, transits, etc.

Mitton, Jacqueline. 1991. *A Concise Dictionary of Astronomy.* New York, Oxford, Tokyo: Oxford University Press. Short entries on all aspects of astronomy.

Pasachoff, Jay M. 1990. *Contemporary Astronomy.* 4th ed. Philadelphia: Saunders College Publishing. A nonmathematical, well-illustrated survey.

———. 1993. *Astronomy: From the Earth to the Universe.* 1993 ed. Philadelphia: Saunders College Publishing. An all-color college text by the author of this Field Guide.

———. 1992. *Journey Through the Universe.* Philadelphia: Saunders College Publishing. An all-color, short text.

Ridpath, Ian, ed. 1989. *Norton's 2000.0.* 18th ed. New York: John Wiley & Sons, Inc. The old standard, updated.

Scovil, Charles E., ed. 1990. *AAVSO Variable Star Atlas.* 2nd ed. Cambridge, MA: American Association of Variable Star Observers. Includes over 2000 variable stars brighter than magnitude 9.5, along with comparison stars and many deep-sky objects.

Sinott, Roger W., ed. 1988. *NGC 2000.0: the complete new general catalogue and index catalogues of nebulae and star clusters.* Cambridge, MA: Sky Publishing Corp. and New York: Cambridge University Press. A centennial reissue of Dreyer's work with updated data.

Tirion, Wil. 1982. *Sky Atlas 2000.0.* Cambridge, MA: Sky Publishing

Corp. and New York: Cambridge University Press. Twenty-six larger-scale versions of the Atlas Charts used in Chapter 7 of this Field Guide, with stars that are one-half magnitude fainter. The Atlas comes in three versions: white stars on black background for use outside, black stars on white background for use indoors, and colors on white background (deluxe).

———. 1991. *Cambridge star atlas 2000.0.* Large-book-size color star maps.

Tirion, Wil, Barry Rappaport, and George Lovi. 1987. *Uranometria 2000.0.* 2 vols. Richmond, VA: Willmann-Bell. A star atlas complete to magnitude 9.5. Vol. 1, for example, which goes from the north celestial pole to declination –6°, contains over 332,000 stars.

Vehrenberg, Hans. 1983. *Atlas of Deep Sky Splendors.* 4th ed. Cambridge, MA: Sky Publishing Corp. and New York: Cambridge University Press. Color and black-and-white photographs, at a uniform scale, of the most interesting parts of the sky. Includes close-ups of Messier and other objects.

Observing Handbooks

Bishop, Roy L., ed. *Observer's Handbook* (published annually). Toronto: Royal Astronomical Society of Canada. A popular guide to sky objects and events, available from the society at 124 Merton St., Toronto, Ontario, Canada M4S 2Z2.

Burnham, Robert, Jr. 1978. *Burnham's Celestial Handbook.* 3 vols. New York: Dover. Detailed constellation-by-constellation discussions, with photographs of a wide variety of objects.

Chartrand, Mark R., III. 1982. *Skyguide.* New York: Western Publishing Co., Golden Press. Observing hints and constellation maps, with beautiful illustrations by Helmut K. Wimmer.

Clark, Roger N. 1990. *Visual Astronomy of the Deep Sky.* New York: Cambridge University Press. How and what to observe.

Dickinson, Terence, and Alan Dyer. 1991. *The Backyard Astronomer's Guide.* Camden House Publishing (distributed by Firefly Books, 250 Sparks Ave., Willowdale, ON, Canada M2H 2S4). A guide to equipment and observing.

Gallant, Roy A. 1980. *Our Universe.* Washington, D.C.: National Geographic Society. A picture atlas of astronomy for children; includes an observation kit.

Harrington, Philip S. 1990. *Touring the Universe Through Binoculars.* New York: John Wiley & Sons.

Jones, Kenneth Glyn. 1991. *Messier's Nebulae and Star Clusters,* 2nd ed. New York: Cambridge University Press. Messier's catalogue, discussed object by object.

Kirby-Smith, H. T. 1976. *U.S. Observatories: A Directory and Travel Guide.* New York: Van Nostrand Reinhold.

Levy, David H. 1991. *The Sky: A User's Guide.* New York: Cambridge University Press. An introduction to observing.

Mallas, John H., and Evered Kreimer. 1978. *The Messier Album.* Cambridge, MA: Sky Publishing Corp. Discussions of each Messier object, with black-and-white photographs. Includes historical background and observing notes by Owen Gingerich.

Newton, Jack, and Philip Teece. 1989. *Guide to Amateur Astronomy.* New York: Cambridge University Press. A guide to observing.

Pasachoff, Jay M. 1988. *Peterson First Guide to Astronomy.* Boston: Houghton Mifflin. A short, simple introduction to astronomy, illustrated entirely in color. Includes simplified monthly sky maps and drawings of mythological constellation figures.

———. 1990. *Peterson First Guide to the Solar System.* Boston: Houghton Mifflin. A short, simple introduction to the planets, the sun, comets, and other objects in the solar system, in color.

Rey, H. A., updated by Jay M. Pasachoff, 1989. *The Stars: A New Way to See Them.* Boston: Houghton Mifflin. Nontraditional constellation outlines, drawn to resemble actual objects more than the usual ways that stars are connected.

Webb Society Deep-Sky Observer's Handbook, Hillside, NJ 07205: Enslow Publishers (Box 777), vol. 1: Double Stars, 2nd ed., 1986; vol. 2: Planetary and Gaseous Nebulae, 1979; vol. 3: Open and Globular Clusters, 1980; vol. 4: Galaxies, 1981; vol. 5: Clusters of Galaxies, 1982; vol. 6: Anonymous Galaxies, 1987; vol. 7: The Southern Sky, 1987; vol. 8: Variable Stars, 1990.

Whitney, Charles A. 1989. *Whitney's Star Finder.* 5th ed., New York: Alfred A. Knopf.

Most of these publications are available from Sky Publishing Corp., 49 Bay State Rd., Cambridge, MA 02138, (617) 864-7360 ext. 176; Wilmann-Bell, Inc., P.O. Box 35025, Richmond, VA 23235, (804) 320-7016; and Astronomy Sky Mart, 21027 Crossroads Circle, P.O. Box 1612, Waukesha, WI 53181, (800) 533-6644 or (414) 796-8776.

Sky Bulletins

Astronomical Calendar (yearly). The changing sky and astronomical events such as eclipses. Available from Guy Ottewell, Astronomical Workshop, Furman University, Greenville, SC 29613. Also available: *The Astronomical Companion,* a companion volume that serves as a general reference, and *The View from the Earth,* a children's version of the *Astronomical Calendar.*

Graphic Timetable of the Heavens (yearly). A more detailed version of the Graphic Timetables in this field guide, available as a full-color poster from Scientia, Inc., 1815 Landrake Rd., Baltimore, MD 21204.

Sky Calendar (monthly). Easy-to-use diagrams of the moon's phases and its daily changes in position against the starry background, plus diagrams of planetary conjunctions with bright stars, with the moon, and with other planets. Available by subscription from Abrams Planetarium, Michigan State University, East Lansing, MI 48824.

Skywatcher's Almanac (yearly). Computer-generated information on the visibility of the sun, moon, and other objects, tailored for the individual observer at a given longitude and latitude. Available from the Astronomical Data Service, 3922 Leisure Lane, Colorado Springs, CO 80917.

Magazines

Astronomy (monthly). Monthly sky features and articles summarizing different fields of astronomy in lay terms. 21027 Crossroads Circle, P.O. Box 1612, Waukesha, WI 53181. (800) 446-5489.

Sky & Telescope (monthly). The standard journal for amateur observers; includes popular articles on astronomical topics and sky events, in addition to regular monthly features. For subscription information, write to 49 Bay State Rd., Cambridge, MA 02138. (617) 864-7360.

Mercury (bimonthly). Published by the Astronomical Society of the Pacific, 390 Ashton Ave., San Francisco, CA 94112. (415) 661-8660.

Odyssey (10 times a year). For children. Published by Cobblestone Publishing, Inc., 30 Grove St., Peterborough, NH 03458.

For Calculators and Computers

Duffett-Smith, Peter. 1989. *Practical Astronomy With Your Calculator.* 3rd ed. New York: Cambridge University Press.

———. 1990. *Astronomy With Your Personal Computer.* 2nd ed. New York: Cambridge University Press.

Meeus, Jean. 1991. *Astronomical Algorithms.* Willmann-Bell, P.O. Box 35025, Richmond, VA 23235. Routines for equinoxes and solstices, conjunctions and oppositions, rising and setting of sun and moon, Jupiter's Galilean satellites, and so on. A disk of programs for IBM-compatible computers is available.

———. 1988. *Astronomical Formulae for Calculators.* 4th ed. Richmond: Willmann-Bell. Using older formulae but simpler to use and thinner than *Astronomical Algorithms.*

Lawrence, Jackie. 1989. *Introduction to BASIC Astronomy with a PC.* Richmond: Willmann-Bell. A lower-level introduction, including a disk.

Electronic Detectors

Berry, Richard. 1991. *Introduction to Astronomical Image Processing.* Richmond: Willmann-Bell. About CCD's.

Buil, C. 1991. *CCD Astronomy.* Richmond: Willmann-Bell.

Amateur Societies

Sky & Telescope publishes lists of planetariums, observatories, clubs, and societies in its September issues.

International Amateur-Professional Photoelectric Photometry Assoc., c/o Douglas Hall, Dyer Observatory, Vanderbilt University, Nashville, TN 37235.

American Association of Variable Star Observers (AAVSO), 25 Birch St., Cambridge, MA 02138.

American Meteor Society, Dept. of Physics and Astronomy, SUNY, Geneseo, NY 14454.

Association of Lunar and Planetary Observers (ALPO), c/o Harry D. Jamieson, P.O. Box 143, Heber Springs, AR 72543.

The Astronomical League, the umbrella group of amateur societies. For their newsletter, *The Reflector*, write The Astronomical League, Executive Secretary, c/o Science Service Building, 1719 N Street NW, Washington, D.C. 20030.

The Astronomical Society of the Pacific, 390 Ashton Ave., San Francisco, CA 94112.

British Astronomical Association, Burlington House, Piccadilly, London W1V 0NL, England.

Royal Astronomical Society of Canada, 124 Merton St., Toronto, Ontario, Canada M4S 2Z2.

Western Amateur Astronomers, 13617 E. Baily, c/o Margaret Matlack, Whittier, CA 90601.

Planetary Society, 65 N. Catalina Ave., Pasadena, CA 91106.

Professional Society

American Astronomical Society, 2000 Florida Ave, NW, Suite 300, Washington, D.C. 20009. For a booklet on "A Career in Astronomy," write to Mary K. Hemenway, Education Officer, AAS, Univ. of Texas, Dept. of Astronomy, Austin, TX 78712.

Translations

Donald H. Menzel and Jay M. Pasachoff. 1986. Spanish edition of *Field Guide to the Stars and Planets. Guía de Campo de las Estrellas y los Planetas*, Ediciones Omega S.A., Plató, 26, 08006 Barcelona, Spain.

Donald H. Menzel and Jay M. Pasachoff. 1989. French edition of *Field Guide to the Stars and Planets. Guide des Etoiles et Planetes*, Delachaux et Niestle, 79 route d'Oron, CH-1000 Lausanne 21, Switzerland.

Donald H. Menzel and Jay M. Pasachoff. 1990. Italian edition of *Field Guide to the Stars and Planets. Stelle e Pianeti*, Zanichelli Editore S.p.A., via Irnerio, 34 - 40126 Bologna.

Jay M. Pasachoff. 1990. French edition of *First Guide to Astronomy. Astronomie*, Les petits guides Peterson, Editions Broquet, Inc., C.P. 310, LaPrairie, QC, Canada, J5R 3Y3.

TELESCOPE INFORMATION

The human eye collects light very efficiently, but all the light it collects must pass through its tiny pupil. A telescope gathers much more light in a given time and so allows you to see fainter objects. Further, the larger the lens or mirror the telescope has, the finer the detail that you can see. Telescopes can also magnify, but this is usually less important than their light-gathering power or resolution. It is not useful to magnify a faint or blurry image.

Anyone who is planning to buy a telescope should pay special attention to the sturdiness of the mount, for a telescope on a flimsy mount is useless. A mount not only supports the telescope but also may track astronomical objects across the sky as the earth rotates. With a mount that isn't tracking, an object drifts out of sight from the center of a 1° field of view in only two minutes. The effect of the earth's motion shows up in photographs of stars taken without a tracking mount. When the shutter is left open for several minutes to capture the images of fainter stars, the stars' images show up as curved trails rather than as points of light.

Many telescopes come on *equatorial mounts*, in which one axis — the polar axis — points up at an angle so that it is directed at a celestial pole. Another, perpendicular, axis allows the telescope to point anywhere in the sky. A single motor on the polar axis allows the telescope

(Below) Tripod-mounted photographs taken with a standard 35-mm camera and a 50-mm lens at $f/2$. A 30-second exposure *(left)* shows the constellation Orion, including the nebula in its belt. A 2-minute exposure *(right)* shows more stars, though they are more obviously trailed. The bright star Sirius is visible at lower left. Its distorted shape shows the effect of being at the edge of the field of view. (Jay M. Pasachoff)

to track stars, planets, or galaxies so they won't drift out of view.

The alternative—an *altazimuth mount*—has one axis that points straight up, around which rotation around the compass (azimuth) takes place, and another axis that points from side to side, around which up-and-down rotation (altitude) takes place. Astronomical objects move across the sky at a slant, so varying motions on both axes are necessary for an altazimuth mount.

Types of Telescopes

A *reflecting telescope* uses a mirror to collect and focus light, while a *refracting telescope* uses a lens. The larger the telescope, the better the resolution it can provide, so the more magnification images can tolerate. Large telescopes allow you to see fainter objects and more detail, but you can enjoy studying the planets and other objects with a small telescope. After all, Galileo discovered the phases of Venus and the moons of Jupiter with a refracting telescope only about $1\frac{1}{2}$ inches (4 cm) across. You can increase the magnification of a small telescope by using an eyepiece with a shorter focal length.

The traditional Newtonian telescope is still very popular and typically uses a mirror 4 to 8 inches across and a tube 48 inches long, although it is available in other sizes as well. Other telescopes that are now popular with amateurs are neither pure reflectors nor refractors; in these *compound telescopes*, the light passes through a lens and is then focused by mirrors inside the telescope's tube. Since the light bounces back and forth between the mirrors, the tube can be short and therefore more portable. Most telescopes of this type are Schmidt-Cassegrains: Schmidt telescopes have wide fields; Cassegrain telescopes are those in which the image is directed through a hole in the main mirror to your pupil. Most of these telescopes come on equatorial mounts.

SECONDARY MIRROR

PRIMARY MIRROR

(Above) A reflecting telescope of the Newtonian type. Isaac Newton invented the method of using a small diagonal flat mirror to reflect the focused light out to the side, where it can be viewed without blocking the incoming light. *(Telescope drawings by Robin Brickman)*

(Below) A refracting telescope, in which the light is focused by a lens.

LENS

A compound telescope of the Schmidt-Cassegrain type can show a wide field in good focus because of the combination of lens and mirrors used.

Dobsonian telescopes use thin mirrors, wooden cases with plastic bearings, and altazimuth mounts to obtain large apertures (mirror sizes) relatively inexpensively. These reflectors are designed for visual observation rather than for photography, since they do not track the stars.

Anyone evaluating telescopes should look at advertisements in recent issues of *Sky & Telescope* and *Astronomy* magazines to see what types and models are currently available. An article on selecting your first telescope is available from the Astronomical Society of the Pacific, 390 Ashton Ave., San Francisco, CA 94112.

The following manufacturers make telescopes, mounts, and filters that are popular with amateurs:

Celestron International, 2835 Columbia St., Torrance, CA 90503. (310) 328-9560, (800) 421-1526. Binoculars and telescopes, including Schmidt-Cassegrain and Schmidt telescopes, a wide-field Schmidt-Newtonian telescope, and refractors.

Coulter Optical, Inc., P.O. Box K, Idyllwild, CA 92349-1107. (714) 659-4621. Dobsonian telescopes.

DayStar Filter Corp., P.O. Box 1290, Pomona, CA 91769. (714) 591-4673. Solar hydrogen-alpha filters.

Edmund Scientific, 101 East Gloucester Pike, Barrington, NJ 08007. (609) 573-6250, FAX (609) 573-6295. Newtonian telescopes, refractors, and the inexpensive wide-field *Astroscan 2001* telescope, plus miscellaneous.

Meade Instruments, 1675 Toronto Way, Costa Mesa, CA 92626. (714) 556-2292, (800) 854-7485, FAX (714) 556-4604. Schmidt-Cassegrain telescopes and mounts; Newtonian telescopes, refractors.

Parks Optical, 270 Easy Street, Simi Valley, CA 93065. (805) 522-6722, (800) 44-PARKS. Newtonians and other types.

Questar Corp., P.O. Box 59, New Hope, PA 18938. (215) 862-5277, (800) 247-9607, FAX (215) 862-0512. Expensive but high-quality 3.5-in. compact, Maksutov-type folded telescopes.

Tele Vue Optics, 20 Dexter Plaza, Pearl River, NY 10965. (914) 735-4044. Eyepieces.

Thousand Oaks Optical, Box 248098, Farmington, MI 48332-8098. (313) 353-6825, FAX (313) 350-3111. Solar filters.

Roger W. Tuthill, Inc., Box 1086, Mountainside, NJ 07092. (800) 223-1063, FAX (908) 232-3804. Telescopes, accessories.

INDEX

The index provides references to objects, definitions, and general discussions of topics in astronomy. The most commonly observed individual objects are indexed, but not all objects on the Atlas Charts or their descriptions are included. The index should be used in conjunction with the tables and the glossary, the contents of which are not indexed. References to figures are in *italics.* References to tables showing which Sky Maps include given constellations are <u>underlined</u>. References to Atlas Charts and the descriptions facing them are **boldfaced**. References to tables are followed by "t." References to Graphic Timetables are followed by "*gt.*" Appendices are referred to by number following an "A." Data in appendices are referred to by Appendix number: A5, for example.

To find a constellation in the sky, use the <u>underlined</u> reference to get a list of Sky Maps on which the constellation appears. To look at the Atlas Chart showing a given constellation, use the **boldfaced** reference.